ARENA OF AMBITION

A History of the
Cambridge Union

Stephen Parkinson

ICON BOOKS

Published in the UK in 2009 by
Icon Books Ltd, Omnibus Business Centre,
39–41 North Road, London N7 9DP
email: info@iconbooks.co.uk
www.iconbooks.co.uk

Sold in the UK, Europe, South Africa and Asia
by Faber & Faber Ltd, Bloomsbury House,
74–77 Great Russell Street, London WC1B 3DA

Distributed in the UK, Europe, South Africa and Asia
by TBS Ltd, TBS Distribution Centre, Colchester Road,
Frating Green, Colchester CO7 7DW

This edition published in Australia in 2009
by Allen & Unwin Pty Ltd,
PO Box 8500, 83 Alexander Street,
Crows Nest, NSW 2065

Distributed in Canada by
Penguin Books Canada,
90 Eglinton Avenue East, Suite 700,
Toronto, Ontario M4P 2YE

ISBN: 978-184831-061-2

Typeset in Garamond by Hands Fotoset

Printed and bound in the UK by CPI Mackays, Chatham ME5 8TD

It is in such societies as this that you will learn the value of political forms ... You will learn that, while there is here an open field for your interests, for the exhibition of all your powers, the great gain that you acquire is not in the expression of your own opinion, nor in the hearing the opinion of others; it is in the fair conflicts of intellects; it is in the meeting of man and man, of mind and mind. Go on then as worthy as you have done. Make this noble room a worthy arena of your young ambitions, teaching you to respect your brother and to respect yourself, teaching you to tolerate even the intolerable; place this edifice under the protection of good manners and good sense, and no one will ever find fault within the Cambridge Union Society.

Richard Monckton Milnes, Lord Houghton,
at the opening of the new Union building,
October 1866

I have suitably distant memories of the Cambridge Union from my time as an undergraduate at Trinity College; memories that are suffused with anxiety at the thought of speaking in such a forum. It was in fact during the Easter term of 1970 that I was persuaded to make my maiden speech in a Union debate, which was entitled 'This House believes that technological advance threatens the individuality of man and is becoming his master'. Perhaps my contribution was not as bad as I feared because I was actually invited back to the Union to deliver the Hugh Anderson Memorial Lecture in November 1978.

The Union, I am glad to say, has a notable association with my family. My Grandfather, King George VI, and his brother Henry, Duke of Gloucester, both joined and attended its debates during their own time at Trinity. My Great-Uncle, Lord Mountbatten, was elected to the Standing Committee when he was at Christ's College; and the Union made my Father, The Duke of Edinburgh, an honorary member in 1952 – many years before he became Chancellor of the University.

Even against the backdrop of an ancient and respected University, the Cambridge Union stands out as a distinguished forum for the free and rigorous exchange of ideas. For nearly two hundred years, undergraduates have come through its doors to consider questions old and new, to test their opinions and hone their skills of debate, and to speak as equals with their opponents – be they students or statesmen. The lessons it provides – in self-confidence; in clear-thinking; in challenging others' beliefs while always respecting them – are valuable ones indeed.

I am delighted that this account of the Union's remarkable history has been written, and I wish the Union well for many more years ahead.

CONTENTS

PREFACE

The rich history of the Cambridge Union is perhaps the Society's greatest asset. It is proudly trotted out to encourage new members to join; it is what attracts world-class statesmen, academics and celebrities to visit on a regular basis; it is the standard to which newly-elected Presidents aspire; it hits you when you walk into its debating chamber for the very first time. Given this, there have been surprisingly few attempts to bring this history together in a single place. Two ex-Presidents have set it down on the page: Ged Martin's *The Cambridge Union and Ireland, 1815–1914* contains much on the early history of the Society besides its debates on the Irish Question; Percy Cradock's older volume, *Recollections of the Cambridge Union, 1815–1939*, beautifully evokes the character of the Union in the nineteenth century, and invites a gallery of renowned ex-Presidents – including the politician Rab Butler, the Archbishop of Canterbury Michael Ramsey and the jurists Arnold McNair and Norman Birkett – to recall their days at the Union in the early decades of the twentieth.

It is Cradock's book which provided the inspiration and the lodestar for this one. While Martin wrote his study after a distinguished career as a professor of history, Cradock wrote his as a recent ex-President (before an equally distinguished career as a diplomat). He had the good sense to end his account a suitable distance before his own time, as the closing words of his postscript explained:

As for the post-war generation, there is no doubt that it has produced characters and friendships, and has heard speeches, as rare and worthy of account as any in the past. But the period is too close to us and must be left to form a chapter in some later book.

More than 50 years have passed since those words were written. Those which follow might, I hope, be considered to form that account. Like Sir Percy, I have asked a number of notable ex-Presidents (and one ex-Secretary) to give their recollections of their own time at the Union: I am deeply grateful to them for doing so, particularly as many of the requests came out of the blue and before I had found a publisher. I have also followed Sir Percy's sound practice and suspended my enquiries before reaching the present day, using the Society's 175th anniversary in 1990 as a suitable juncture at which to end this account. I could undoubtedly have continued beyond, but – with one or two exceptions (such as the BBC's Clare Balding) – the officers of the last eighteen years have not yet reached the heights for which history suggests they are destined.

The conspicuous achievements of those who do fall within the scope of the book have made it an easier one to write. No small number of them are in *Who's Who*, making that a useful first port of call. As a breed, the former Union President needs little persuasion to talk about his days of undergraduate glory. I could happily have spent much longer tracking down and enjoying these stories, and my book would have been a richer one for it – but it would have been a much longer one, and would have taken even longer to write. It is not intended as a comprehensive chronicle: the stories and events it contains have been included because they capture the mood of the day, sum up some fundamental characteristic of the Union – or simply because they are amusing.

I have not dredged up every detail of the procedural rows, constitutional wrangling and electoral disputes which accompany many Union terms – these would seem petty and arcane even to devotees of Union scandal – and have tried not to distract the reader with too much technical information. It will suffice to outline the Society's structure very briefly. The Cambridge academic year is split into three terms: Michaelmas, Lent and Easter. For each of these, the Union elected three principal officers: these were a President, a Treasurer and a Secretary until 1852, when the office of Treasurer was put on a more permanent footing and held by a senior member of the University. The termly triumvirate thenceforth became a President, Vice-President and Secretary – a system which prevailed until 1995. Union hopefuls would serve a term or two as elected members of the governing standing committee, then vie to become Secretary – generally the most hotly contested position. Election as Secretary would often (but not always) guarantee smooth transition to the presidency two terms later. The Society's laws could only be changed at a 'Private Business Meeting' (PBM) of all members, held at regular intervals each term. These were renamed 'Members' Business Meetings' in 1968, a change reflected in this text; in most other instances I have stuck with consistent terminology. Two exceptions relate to Cambridge itself, which was a town until 1951 and a city thereafter, and to the legions of new undergraduates who arrived in it each year: I have used the archaic 'freshmen' which had wider currency in the early years of our narrative than it does now, and the gender-neutral 'freshers' from the point at which women were admitted to the Union.

———•———

I have amassed a large debt of gratitude over the past four years. HRH The Prince of Wales has done me – and the Union – a great honour in writing a foreword to this volume. I am deeply grateful to him and to all the other contributors, especially Lord Lamont, who has provided help and encouragement for this project since its inception. I was sorry that ill health prevented Sir Percy Cradock from contributing as well, but his kind correspondence ensured that I was able to make some amends for the authorial modesty he exercised in his own history of the Union.

Peter Elwood and Liz Newman generously lent me the memoir their father, Sydney Elwood, wrote about his years in the Union's employment; it was an invaluable resource, covering more than four decades, and displaying his evident love for the Society on every page. I also spent a very enjoyable evening talking with them, and Liz's husband John, about their own memories of growing up in and around the Union. Martin Tod introduced me to Derick Mirfin, who very kindly shared with me his detailed notes on the Union in the 1950s, as well as excerpts from his undergraduate diaries and letters home. Martin and Derick both gave generously of their time on a number of occasions during my research.

I am grateful to all those who allowed me to interview them about their Union experiences: Sir James Bottomley KCMG, His Honour Judge Burford QC, Kevin Carey, the Rt. Hon. Charles Clarke MP, Tam Dalyell, Denzil Freeth MBE, the Rt. Hon. John Gummer MP, the Revd David Johnson, Andrew Mitchell MP, Barry Thoday, and Lord Thomas of Swynnerton. I had a most enjoyable lunch with Peter Fullerton, who provided advice and recollections both then and subsequently. Others kindly answered my questions or were graciously interrogated at little notice: the Hon. Mr Justice Binnie, Dr Vince Cable MP, Professor Paul Crossley, Professor Christie Davies, Professor Rajeev Dhavan, Professor John Dunn, Lance Forman, David Grace, Charles Lysaght, Peter Pagnamenta, Nick Stadlen QC, and Cllr Adrian Vinson. Andrew Lownie shared not only his recollections as an ex-President but also his professional advice as a literary agent. Dinah Hutchinson gave me valuable information about the Women's Union Society; and Fr Rob Mackley and Cllr Henry Pipe helped me fill in the blanks for the list of officers of the mid-1990s. The Revd Paul Hamlet's own historical enquiries – which were passed to me via the Union – allowed me to restore the 'missing' President and Treasurer for Easter Term 1817.

I am grateful for the understanding of the Presidents and officers whose terms covered the period of my research, particularly Livvy Potts, in whose term it was finally completed, and Dr Nick Hartman and Tristan Pedelty, who provided great assistance while they were still in Cambridge. Pat Aske, the Union's dedicated and much-loved Senior Librarian, allowed me free rein in the Union's archives at the University Library; Godfrey Waller, Louise Clarke and their colleagues in the Manuscripts Reading Room were helpful throughout. I am grateful also to Dr Patrick Zutshi, the Keeper of Manuscripts and University Archives, for permission to make copies of certain material; and to Sue Slack at Cambridgeshire County Council Central Library. Tim Milner, a former Steward of the Union, provided generous introductions to others within the University – such as Peter Agar at the University Development Office.

The whole team at Icon Books have made the publication of my first book an unfalteringly enjoyable experience: Peter Pugh and Simon Flynn showed great kindness and enthusiasm from the outset, as have Najma Finlay, Andrew Furlow, Sarah Higgins and Nick Sidwell.

Finally, my thanks go to my parents and sister for not batting an eyelid on the many weekends when I came home to colonise the dining table with my laptop and folders of notes; and to my grandma, who furnished me with regular cups of tea while I revised the text. Any errors or infelicities which remain in it are, of course, my own.

1815–1939:
An Introduction

The origins of the Cambridge Union Society lie, perhaps fittingly, in a factional dispute among the members of two or three pre-existing societies. One of these was the Speculative, a discussion group of about twenty, of which Lord Palmerston was a member. Another was 'nicknamed the Anticarnalist, in consequence of one of its members having been expelled on account of some flagrant act of immorality'.[1] There is some confusion over the identity of the third. Two accounts – one from an early detractor of the Union and another from a future MP for the borough about to begin lecturing at the University – recall just two societies.[2] But the Union's own statement of its establishment, written just two years after the event, states clearly that it was 'formed by the combination of the three other Societies which had previously existed in the University'.[3]

In 1814, Edward Gambier, an Old Etonian at Trinity, tried to join one of these, and was blackballed for membership. Martin wonders whether it was the Anticarnalist, as this would explain 'the furious response ... to the implied slur of his rejection'.[4] Whatever the reason, Gambier's friends rallied to his defence, and the old societies were merged into one. A letter to the editor of *The Times* some years later from one of the founding members tells us that the new society 'was placed provisionally under the direction of two noted Whigs, both godsons of the statesman whose name they bore' – Charles Fox Townshend and Charles Fox Maitland.[5] Proper officers

1

were soon introduced, and Gambier was elected the Union's first President.

The inaugural meeting was held on 13 February 1815, and the first motion – 'Was the conduct of the Opposition in refusing Places in 1812 justifiable?' – debated a week later (the Noes won, by 35 votes to 33). The Society met every week in a small room at the back of the Red Lion inn in Petty Cury, now long since demolished. It had some 200 members elected by ballot – but blackballing was rare. The weekly motions for debate were selected by the whole membership a week in advance, with serious political or historical subjects preferred, and theological topics avoided. In addition, a small library of periodicals was kept.

The Union's remarkable line of eminent alumni starts right at the very beginning: Gambier became Chief Justice of Madras; the second President, Viscount Normanby, was later Home Secretary, Irish Viceroy, and Ambassador in Paris at the time of Louis Napoleon's *coup d'état*. His term as President was rather less successful, however: no debates were held, as an open drain in Jesus Lane caused an outbreak of fever and everyone at the University was sent home.

Although 1815 is recent history by the University of Cambridge's standards, the Union's foundation in that year does make it older than fourteen colleges and such Cambridge institutions as the Boat Race (first held in 1829) and Trinity May Ball (1891). It was, however, an inauspicious time for a debating society to take its first steps, for Europe was on the eve of the Hundred Days which ended the Napoleonic Wars. Even after the war, when students came up to Cambridge in greater numbers again, and the remnants of the huge feast held on Parker's Piece to celebrate victory at Waterloo had been cleared away, an atmosphere of alarm and suspicion persisted. In 1817, following what appeared to be an attempt on the life of the Prince Regent, the Tory government was determined to take swift action. It cracked down on blasphemous and seditious writings, introduced extreme restrictions with the Seditious Meetings Act, and passed the Habeas Corpus Suspension Act in a single sitting of the House of Lords. A number of harmless bodies suffered: the proceedings of the Literary Society of Manchester were suspended, and a licence was refused to the Academical Society of Oxford.

In Cambridge, it was no different. James Wood, Master of St John's and Vice-Chancellor of the University, was an obstinate and reactionary figure.[6] In such a climate, the Union was bound to attract his attention: the name alone suggested a cell of radicalism, like the 'union societies' or Hampden Clubs which had recently been founded by the well-known agitator Major John Cartwright. Moreover, some of the Union's recent motions had been uncomfortably topical – members had debated the question of public meetings, and even voted against the suspension of *habeas corpus*.

There was further provocation in the form of a letter sent to Wood by a bitter ex-member of the Union. Whatever the cause for his anger towards the Union, J.M.F. Wright of Trinity was clearly resentful of his friends' 'flattering themselves into a hope of one day … reaching the lofty eminence' of the Union presidency, and wrote to the Vice-Chancellor with 'a concise statement of my views of the mischiefs inseparable from the Society' – namely, that it involved 'the almost total abandonment' of study.[7]

Dr Wood hesitated no longer. On the night of 24 March 1817, when the Union was discussing the question 'Is the increased attention which has been paid to our army likely to have a good effect on society?', the proctors burst into the meeting with a message from the Vice-Chancellor demanding its dissolution and forbidding any resumption of debates. By one of the twists of fate which adorn the Union's history, the President that term was William Whewell who, as a future Master of Trinity, would follow in Wood's footsteps as Vice-Chancellor of the University – in 1842 and 1855. (He is also the only ex-President of the Union to have been accorded the peculiar distinction of having a lunar crater named after him.) On that evening, he rose from his chair and replied with masterful, if precocious, dignity to the University authorities: 'Strangers will please to withdraw, and the House will take the message into consideration.'

The intruders gone, the meeting appointed a committee to watch over its interests. It then voted that a remonstrance should be presented to the Vice-Chancellor, and, in the event of that proving unsuccessful, a petition to the Chancellor. The Society then adjourned. Thus empowered, Whewell immediately led a deputation of three to see Wood, who seems to have been in the Red Lion in person.[8] Whether or not Whewell maintained his cool demeanour during the meeting, it had evaporated entirely by early the next morning, when he wrote a letter to Hugh James Rose, the Treasurer that term, who was not in Cambridge at the time:

> My dear Rose,
> Did you ever curse the university? Did you ever curse the v. chancellor? Then now curse the university ten times and the vice-chancellor a hundred times: for the university is a vile university and the vice-chancellor is a damned vice-chancellor.[9]

Wright's denunciation of the Union was clearly a factor in Wood's harsh action: Whewell explained that the Vice-Chancellor informed the delegation he had received a letter from a former member 'who says that his prospects have been ruined and that the prospects of several of his friends have been ruined by the time and attention he has bestowed on the Society'. The Union appealed directly against this in the remonstrance which they drew up and presented to the Vice-Chancellor on 1 April, emphasising:

> That their Meetings for Debate occur but on One Evening of the week.
> That they are on average of not more than Two Hours' duration.
> That they have in general only commenced after the Division of each Term.
> That they are usually attended by only about Half the Resident Members.[10]

Moreover, it pointed out, the Union had on its list of members 'three University Scholars, seven Chancellor's Medallists, twelve Browne's

Medallists, and many more names which ranked high on the Tripos'. Even so, the remonstrance expressed the Union's willingness to submit to reasonable restrictions in the light of the national mood, noting in italics: 'That the Members are willing to exclude political subjects from their debates, and to submit to any regulation which may not be utterly incompatible with their wish to practise themselves in speaking' – a study, they suggested, 'which they humbly conceive not to be utterly useless.' The authors of the remonstrance further submitted that the Society's existence 'has materially tended to diminish the attendance on weekly Clubs or Meetings, whose conduct is likely to be less orderly, as their amusements are less intellectual than those of the Union'. Finally, they begged that their Society not be shut down at a time 'when the universal suppression of Societies bearing accidentally the same name, may lead those unacquainted with the real state of the University to suppose, that this Club has been put down from political motives, and that it has been guilty of seditious Meetings or treasonable language.'

But the Vice-Chancellor was unmoved by any of these arguments, and his reply was curt:

> I do not think it necessary, nor perhaps proper, to return any answer to this statement. I had considered the subject fully in my own mind.

The members continued to fight valiantly. A 'Statement' including the remonstrance and Dr Wood's reply was prepared and printed. The Masters of Arts petitioned the Chancellor of the University, the Duke of Gloucester, and news of their protest was carried in *The Times*.* News of the Union's suppression was even mentioned in the House of Commons.[11] But these efforts were unsuccessful, and, as Cradock notes, the Union 'fell into silence, and remained merely as a Reading Club for the next four years'.[12]

---

* Although they carefully billed the Union as 'The University Debating Club' to avoid confusion with the radical cells (*The Times*, 14 April 1817).

In fact, the picture may not have been quite as bleak as Cradock paints. In the list of officers at the end of his volume, he suggests that no officers were elected for the Easter Term 1817. But Hugh James Rose's personal copy of the Statement includes manuscript additions listing Connop Thirlwall (Secretary at the time of interrupted debate, and later Bishop of St Davids) as President, and Charles Brinsley Sheridan (son of the playwright) as Treasurer. It seems that elections may have continued to take place uninterrupted. Certainly, members found ingenious ways of continuing to debate. Fortunately for the Union, the more extreme parts of the Seditious Meetings Bill had not made it onto the statute book, so it was still legal to operate as a reading club. Private business meetings concerning which newspapers the Union should subscribe to became fronts for clandestine debates. Thus a motion to cancel the *Morning Chronicle* allowed a debate on the merits of that organ's Whig opinions; another to subscribe to a newspaper from Athens digressed to consider the rights of the Greeks to resist Turkish rule.[13]

Perhaps aware of this, Wood's successor as Vice-Chancellor, Dr Wordsworth of Trinity, allowed debates to be resumed in March 1821 on the condition that no political subject from the last twenty years be discussed. Martin wonders whether this restitution was partly thanks to the efforts of Whewell, Gambier and Thirlwall, who were all by now Fellows of Trinity. Once again, however, the restrictions were easily evaded by Union members – this time by the simple device of adding 'before 1800' or 'twenty years ago' to the wording of contentious motions. Alternatively, ostensibly innocuous motions were chosen to provide cover for more topical debates, such as one on Adam and Eve to allow a debate on women's suffrage. All constraints on political motions were finally set aside in 1830 – albeit at the objection of the proctors – and, although this was to be the subject of much debate and redefinition in the Society's private business meetings over the next ten years, the Union was in effect free once more to debate all topics except those that were strictly theological.

———

The Union's passage through the rest of the nineteenth century was considerably smoother. The decade after the resumption of debates included a number of notable figures. These early alumni were true polymaths: Thomas Babington Macaulay, Secretary in Easter 1820 and Treasurer in Lent 1823, won several prizes for his poetry at Cambridge. By 1830 he had begun the parliamentary career which saw him serve as Secretary at War and Paymaster General, and finally raised to the peerage as Lord Macaulay. But it is as a historian that he is best remembered: although his *magnum opus*, *The History of England*, was unfinished at the time of his death, it is the quintessential Whig interpretation of history. Another poet-turned-politician was Winthrop Mackworth Praed, Secretary in Easter 1823 and Treasurer the following term. His career at Trinity was a brilliant one: he gained the Browne Medal for Greek verse four times, and the Chancellor's Medal for English verse twice. He won a fellowship at his college in 1827, before embarking on a political career like Macaulay. He entered the Commons in the same year, although as a Tory, having moved away from the Whiggism towards which he had inclined in the Union. Both Praed and Macaulay had been called to the Bar between Cambridge and the Commons: a common progression even today. Spencer Horatio Walpole (President, Michaelmas 1827) was a successful silk before entering Parliament, where he served thrice as Home Secretary. Charles Pelham Villiers (President, Easter 1822) also moved from the Bar to Westminster and remained there for 63 years, making him the longest-serving MP ever. Alexander Cockburn (President in Easter 1824), however, stayed in the law, and rose to become Lord Chief Justice.

Two Presidents combined literary and ecclesiastical success: Benjamin Hall Kennedy (President, Easter 1825) was both Regius Professor of Greek and Canon of Ely, and is all too familiar to generations of schoolchildren for his *Latin Primer*, still in use today. Richard Chevenix Trench (President, Easter 1828) was later Archbishop of Dublin, as well as one of the driving forces behind the *Oxford English Dictionary*.

There was, indeed, a strong literary element to the Union in the nineteenth century. The rhetoric of Union speeches was laced with epigrams and classical allusions – frequently, even, with poems or couplets. Alfred Tennyson, Edward Bulwer Lytton and William Makepeace Thackeray were among the literary figures up at this time and, though Bulwer Lytton – who coined the phrases 'the great unwashed' and 'the pen is mightier than the sword' – was the only one of the three to hold Union office (as Treasurer in Michaelmas 1824), they all participated in its debates, which were often on literary themes. In November 1828 a debate on the question 'Is Wordsworth or Lord Byron the greater poet?' was dissolved by the President 'in consequence of the turbulent state of the society'.[14]

It was on a poetic motion – this time pitting Byron against Shelley – that a Cambridge delegation made the first visit to the Oxford Union on 26 November 1829. A debating society, modelled on the Union at Cambridge, had been established there in 1823 and was re-founded as the Oxford Union Society two years later. The two Unions' interest in one another – usually veiled in rivalry and feigned disinterest – has continued down the centuries, and their members have enjoyed reciprocal rights since 1825 (it would have been earlier had Cambridge formally notified its sister society of its own generous decision, taken some months earlier).[15] On the occasion of this first visit – held the same year as the first university Boat Race – the Cambridge speakers were Thomas Sunderland (Treasurer, Easter 1827), Arthur Hallam (subject of Tennyson's *In Memoriam*) and Richard Monckton Milnes, later Lord Houghton. Among the Oxford speakers was Henry Manning, the future Cardinal. But the man who most struck Milnes was a young Mr Gladstone from Liverpool. Nowadays, the 'Varsity debate' has become a regular fixture, but the logistics of this first trip did not bode well. The journey was by coach and took ten hours through the snow. There had also been some uncertainty about obtaining permission to leave Cambridge in term-time, and Dr Wordsworth, Master of Trinity, appeared to be under the impression that it was another poet – namely his brother – that the Cambridge debaters were going to defend.

The debate was deemed a success – although the two Unions evidently had differing oratorical styles, as Cardinal Manning later recalled:

> We Oxford men were precise, orderly, and morbidly afraid of excess in word, or manner. The Cambridge oratory came in like a flood into a mill-pond. Both Monckton-Milnes and Arthur Hallam took us aback by the boldness and freedom of their manner. But I remember the effect of Sunderland's declamation and action to this day. It had never been seen, or heard before among us; we cowered like birds, and ran like sheep. I acknowledge that we were utterly routed.[16]

The Union's renown was extending farther afield than Oxford, however; and it continued to grow as figures such as Macaulay and Praed made their names in London and beyond. John Stuart Mill, who did not attend university (probably on account of his family's objection to the religious tests imposed on university entrants), was part of the extended circle of Union figures at this time, keeping in touch with his friends at the Society and describing it in his *Autobiography* as 'an arena where what were then thought extreme opinions, in politics and philosophy, were weekly asserted, face to face with their opposites, before audiences consisting of the *élite* of the Cambridge youth'.[17] In particular, he was influenced by Charles Austin (President, Lent 1822), during whose term he visited the Union. 'The effect he produced on his Cambridge contemporaries deserves to be accounted an historical event', Mill suggests, for he was 'the really influential mind among these intellectual gladiators'.[18] Impressed by what he saw at Cambridge, Mill established the London Union Debating Society along the same lines in 1825. 'There seems to have been a close connection between the two societies,' notes Karl Britton: 'Mill evidently drew in ex-Presidents and others as they came down from Cambridge to live in London.'[19]

By the 1830s, the Society was sufficiently large and well established to seek new premises, and in 1832 it moved from the Red

Lion into new rooms built for it at the back of the Hoop Inn in Bridge Street – part of the land where the Union building stands today. The rest of that decade is marked by the emergence of the 'Young England' group – in many ways a Cambridge counterpart of the Oxford Movement, but with its focus the Tory party rather than the Church. Foremost among its members were Lord John Manners and George Sydney Smythe, who did not hold elected office in the Union; there were also Alexander Baillie-Cochrane (President, Lent 1837) and Alexander Beresford Hope, who served as President in Lent 1839 – until he was forced to resign in a row provoked by Smythe. The group all entered Parliament almost immediately after going down from Cambridge, and by 1842 the 'Young England Party' in the Commons had been launched, with Benjamin Disraeli at its head. Although the group, both collectively and individually, did not live up to its early promise and foundered after 1845, its sense of youthful hope and purpose – and its figures themselves – were immortalised in the characters of Disraeli's books *Coningsby* and *Sybil*. Another ex-President fared better under Disraeli once the great man had bounced back and climbed the greasy pole: President in Michaelmas 1845, Richard Assheton Cross was Home Secretary in Disraeli's second administration.

In Easter Term 1964 the retiring President, Charles Lysaght, held a ceremony to celebrate the centenary of the death of William Smith O'Brien, believed to have been President in Lent 1831. A portrait of the Irish rebel leader, who was sentenced to be hanged, drawn and quartered for high treason in 1848, was presented to the Union by his great-grandson and hung in the chamber. But Lysaght has since come to doubt whether it was this O'Brien who was President. That was the view taken by Cradock and by Martin, based on the monumental *Alumni Cantabrigienses*, a directory of all known members of the University up to 1900.[20] But there is much evidence to suggest that it was another O'Brien who served as President: Smith O'Brien was up in Cambridge 1821–5, and does not appear to have spoken at the Union during these years; by Lent 1831 he had been a graduate of six years' standing, and was already the Member of Parliament for Ennis. It is more likely that it was another O'Brien who was the President. There were two undergraduates by this name at Trinity in 1831: one was Smith O'Brien's younger brother, while the other was Augustus Stafford O'Brien, who later stood against him in County Limerick (and dropped his last name to avoid confusion between them). There is no record that one of these O'Briens spoke at the Union either, but Augustus Stafford had proposed the presidential candidate in the previous term, so was clearly active in the Society at this time. He was also, as both Cradock and Martin note, associated with the Young England group. It seems, then, that he is the more likely President of 1831. After failing to unseat his namesake in Limerick, he sat as the Conservative MP for Northamptonshire North, serving as Secretary to the Admiralty in 1852. (Smith O'Brien's end was rather happier too: his sentence was later commuted to transportation, and he was eventually granted an unconditional pardon.)

The great speakers of the late 1840s were William Vernon Harcourt (President, Easter 1849) and James Fitzjames Stephen, who often clashed in debates. Harcourt, after a spell at the Bar, and as Whewell Professor of International Law at Cambridge (named after the ex-President), entered Parliament as a Liberal. He became one of the great parliamentary figures of the Gladstonian period, serving as Home Secretary and twice as Chancellor of the Exchequer. Stephen did not hold office in the Union, but was a compelling debater. Like Harcourt he went to the Bar after Cambridge, but stayed in the law – with great success. He was a Professor of Common Law at the Inns of Court, and a High Court judge. As a member of the Colonial Council, he was responsible for drafting significant pieces of Indian legislation in the 1870s, which made him an ardent supporter of codification in England, and his *History of the Criminal Law of England* remains an important jurisprudential work. His brother, the Revd Leslie Stephen (fellow of Trinity Hall, father of Virginia Woolf, and the first editor of the *Dictionary of National*

Biography), served as one of the first trustees of the Union Society from 1857; and his son, J.K. Stephen, was President in Michaelmas 1880.

The Hon. Arthur Hamilton Gordon, President in Lent 1849, also worked in the colonies. The youngest son of the 4th Earl of Aberdeen, he found easy employment after Cambridge when his father became Prime Minister in 1852. He worked as his father's assistant private secretary and entered the House of Commons himself in 1854, but lost his seat three years later. Thereafter, he spent nearly 30 years as a colonial administrator – successively Governor of Trinidad, Mauritius, Fiji, New Zealand, and Ceylon.

In Lent 1850, Alfred Louis became the first Jewish President of the Union – six years before Jews were allowed to take their degrees from the University.[21] A second Jewish President – the future Liberal MP, Arthur Cohen, in Easter 1853 – became the first professing Jew to graduate from Cambridge. With the debates over the removal of religious tests raging throughout the 1850s and '60s, it is perhaps little surprise that these decades produced a number of notable academics and educationalists among those attaining the office of President. Henry Montagu Butler, later headmaster of Harrow and Master of Trinity, was President in Michaelmas 1855. His successor the following Michaelmas, Edward Bowen, also taught at Harrow. Henry Sidgwick, President in Lent 1861, was later a professor of moral philosophy, a leader in the movement for the higher education of women and a founder of the British Academy. A number of buildings in Newnham College – the women's college which he founded and ran with his wife, its second Principal – as well as the Sidgwick site opposite, where most of the University's arts faculties are now located, are named in his honour.

By far the most colourful of the pedagogues from this period was Oscar Browning, President in Easter 1859. He was an assistant master at Eton until his dismissal in 1875, after allegations of impropriety with the young George Curzon which were to haunt both men for the rest of their lives. After leaving Eton, he returned to King's, where he was a Fellow of legendary reputation. Countless anecdotes collected around this regular fixture of Cambridge society, universally known as 'O.B.', who Cradock acknowledges 'has an unassailable right to inclusion in any account of the Society'. As Cradock records, 'he knew everything and everyone ... He was a permanent official in the undergraduate clubs. He was also a standing joke in the undergraduate magazines.' Browning returned to the Union and served as Treasurer for an impressive 21 years (1881–1902). Indeed, he would have served even longer had he not been eased out by the undergraduate officers. Cradock tells us that Browning was 'unseated as he felt by the unspeakable malice of Edwin Montagu', President that Michaelmas.[22] Another ex-President thinks it might have been Montagu's predecessor Percy Haigh who precipitated Browning's retirement with the more diplomatic tactic of presenting a portrait of the Treasurer as a token of the Society's appreciation for his long years of service – which were doubtless soon to come to a much lamented end.[23] The portrait, painted by the father of Goldsworthy Lowes Dickinson, currently hangs in the lobby outside the chamber.

The two first Michaelmas Presidents of the 1860s were the nephews of Praed and Macaulay – Sir George Young (who had already inherited the baronetcy by the time he was at Cambridge) and George Otto Trevelyan. Like his uncle, Trevelyan became known for both his literary and political endeavours, publishing *The Life and Letters* of his famous forebear while sitting as a Liberal MP in the Commons. He later became Chancellor of the Duchy of Lancaster and Secretary for Scotland, before returning to historical writing with his three-volume *History of the American Revolution*. The family's dual interests were continued in the careers of his sons, C.P. Trevelyan, who followed him as a Liberal MP, and G.M. Trevelyan, who continued in the family line of historians and became Master of Trinity.

In 1850, the Union had moved from the Hoop Inn to a former Wesleyan chapel in Green Street. But this ill-ventilated space was not suited to the Society's now well-established status, and there was a desire for the Union to have premises of its own. In 1857, spurred

A DEBATE at the UNION.

'A debate at the Union', c. 1859. At this time, the Society met in a former Wesleyan chapel in Green Street – but its debates were already laid out in the familiar British parliamentary style. (*A Cambridge Scrapbook*)

by the Oxford Union's construction of its own site that year, the Society established a building fund from its operating profits and a proportion of members' subscriptions. Progress was slow, but eventually a piece of land behind the Church of the Holy Sepulchre – or, as it is better known in Cambridge, the Round Church – was purchased from St John's College. Much of the credit for the building which the Union inhabits to this day should go to Sir Charles Dilke of Trinity Hall, President in Michaelmas 1864 (and later a Liberal MP, his career cut short by a notorious adultery scandal). The need to supervise the building plans was one of the reasons Dilke stayed up in Cambridge for a fourth year and took office as President for a second time in Lent 1866 – the fourth and final person to do so, the Society's rules having subsequently been amended to prohibit this. In keeping with the nature of the Society, the architect for the commission was chosen by a ballot of all members. There was a shortlist of three: George Gilbert Scott, whose chapel at St John's was then in construction; Digby Wyatt, who designed the new buildings of Addenbrooke's Hospital (nowadays the Judge Business School); and Alfred Waterhouse, perhaps the least known at this time, who won. Waterhouse had made his name as a champion of the Gothic revival with his own practice in Manchester, and the Union was the first of a number of his works in Cambridge – which include Girton College, the Hall at Pembroke, and Tree Court in Gonville and Caius. His later commissions – for the Natural History Museum and the National Liberal Club – earned him considerable acclaim. He was also commissioned to design a new debating chamber for the Oxford Union, opened in 1879.[24]

The cost of the project was £11,000 – partly funded by an appeal to 4,000 life members. The foundation stone was laid 'with much state and pomp' on 4 June 1884 – along with a metal box containing a copy of the Union rules, a list of officers and committee members, and some recent coins and newspapers.[25] The new building was completed two years later; it was formally opened on 30 October 1866, with tickets issued for 800 people. The Lord High Steward of the University, the Earl of Powis, opened the proceedings, and among the speakers was Monckton Milnes, who had now become Lord Houghton. The President overseeing the celebrations was Lord Edmond Fitzmaurice, who would succeed Dilke as Under-Secretary of State for Foreign Affairs under Gladstone. The Union's new home won a favourable reception, and is today a Grade II listed building – although some of its period features, not least the early Victorian gentlemen's conveniences and the many gathering places for the carcasses of dead pigeons in its gables, are not so lavishly praised by modern-day staff and officers.

With its own premises – not only a large parliamentary chamber for its debates, but also the full features of a fine clubhouse, including a library boasting over 15,000 volumes – the Union flourished. Such was its success that a new wing had to be added within twenty years. This, again, was designed by Waterhouse, who was invited to become

'The new building of the Cambridge Union Society' – seen before the addition of a new wing in 1886.　(*Illustrated London News*, 17 November 1866)

the first honorary member of the Society as a result. He was also invited to the banquet for 180 diners which marked its opening on 24 February 1886, with Prince Albert Victor of Wales, a life member of the Society, as the guest of honour.

Soon after the enlargement of the building came another, more significant development. Hitherto, debates had almost exclusively been between student members and, although visitors had spoken before, they had always been old members or visitors from Oxford. In 1887, however, it was resolved:

> That when questions of great interest are under debate, it is desirable that strangers distinguished as orators and politicians who are entitled to speak with authority on such questions should be invited to take part in debate, provided that the necessary arrangements are submitted to the House for approval.

The big political topic of the day was Ireland – from the Fenian bombing campaigns to the Liberal split over Home Rule – and the vexed nature of the issue was one of the prime reasons for the introduction of guest speakers. Martin says that it was 'a direct by-product of the Home Rule crisis' and 'an appropriate way of shoring up the perennially under-represented Catholic and Nationalist viewpoint in Union debates'.[26] Although outside speakers only came once or twice a term, their advent changed the nature of Union debates: they became less closed, and attracted more attention from the outside world, particularly as those eminent figures who came up to Cambridge to speak in them spread the word to their colleagues on their return. These visiting dignitaries eased the passage from the Union to Westminster or to other echelons of the Establishment for those young men who dined with them, sat alongside them in the chamber, or challenged them in debate with carefully prepared speeches. Indeed, as the frequency of guest speakers has grown over the ensuing generations (today it is common for there to be only two student speakers in a typical debate), some have regretted the impact this has had on the nature of Union debating. There have been several attempts to limit the number of guest speakers or to reinstitute student-only debates in order to reclaim what their supporters believe to be a less theatrical, less partisan and more intellectual style of debate.

Whatever the long-term impact of the resolution, its effect was not immediate, for it came in the midst of one of the most celebrated Union careers, that of J.K. Stephen. The son of Fitzjames Stephen, he attended Eton and King's as a King's Scholar, a hero of the wall game and a prize-winning historian. He was President of the Union in Michaelmas 1880, constantly returned to Cambridge during that decade, when he was a Fellow of King's and tutored Prince Albert Victor, and settled there again in 1891. To Cradock, 'he dominates the whole period' and as a speaker was 'pre-eminent'.[27] But his brilliance was cut short at the end of 1891: he suffered an acute brain fever, probably as the result of an accident five years earlier when he had struck his head on the vane of a small windmill. He was committed to hospital suffering from mental illness, where, after refusing all nourishment, he died in February 1892.

Other ex-Presidents of the period were more fortunate in their later lives: T.E. Scrutton (President, Lent 1880) became a Lord Justice of Appeal, and Frederic Maugham (President, Lent 1889) was the first ex-President of the Union to become Lord Chancellor. Though he wrote that 'the Union claims most of my time', Sir Austen Chamberlain never held its highest office, serving as Vice-President in Lent 1885 and losing the presidency to Edward Goulding, the future Lord Wargrave.[28] Twice Chancellor of the Exchequer, Chamberlain's work as Foreign Secretary in securing the Locarno Treaties led to his investiture as a Knight of the Garter. It also made him the first of two Union alumni to win the Nobel Peace Prize. (The other, Philip Noel-Baker, President in Easter 1912, can also boast a silver Olympic medal, won for the 1,500 metres at the 1920 Games.)

The first non-white President of the Union was Sir James Peiris, who won a scholarship from Ceylon to study at St John's. There he took a double first and was elected President of the Union for Michaelmas 1882 – fifty years before another black or Asian President was elected at either Cambridge or Oxford. He was called to the Bar of Lincoln's Inn and returned to practise in Ceylon. He was elected to the island's legislative council and served as its Vice-President from 1924 until his death in 1930.

It is a favourite boast of the Oxford Union's members that it has nursed six prime ministers, while the Cambridge Union has produced none. Apart from those who have been contenders – notably Austen Chamberlain, W.V. Harcourt, Rab Butler, Douglas Hurd and Michael Howard – the only head of government the Society can boast to date is Gerald Strickland, President in Michaelmas 1887. The heir of a Westmorland landowner, he also inherited at the age of fifteen – through his mother and after a protracted legal battle – the Maltese title of the Count della Catena. Active in both British and Maltese politics, he was successively

Governor of the Leeward Isles, Tasmania, Western Australia and New South Wales. Then, while still sitting as a Conservative MP in Westminster, he became Prime Minister of Malta, serving from 1927 to 1932 and leaving the Commons in 1928 when he was raised to the peerage as Baron Strickland.

Three Masterman brothers were President in the 1890s, the most notable of whom was Charles Masterman (Lent 1896). As a Liberal MP, he had a successful career as a junior minister and a champion of the working classes, publishing his most well-known book, *The Condition of England*, in 1909. However, his promotion to the Cabinet in 1914 effectively finished his career. It was then the law that MPs promoted to ministerial office had to re-contest their seats in a by-election: Masterman lost this election, and another held for him subsequently. By the time he re-entered the Commons in 1923, the Liberal party was in decline, and he lost again in the rout of 1924.

Frederick Lawrence, who was President two terms after Masterman, had a more successful parliamentary career – despite a rather unconventional beginning. After Cambridge, he married Emmeline Pethick, an active socialist and women's suffragist (converting to socialism and adding her surname to his on their marriage). Their home became the offices of the Women's Social and Political Union, and its militant window-smashing campaign led to their imprisonment in 1912. An anti-war campaigner, Pethick-Lawrence escaped a second custodial sentence when he refused to be conscripted in 1917. But these scrapes with the law did not hold back his political career: he was elected to Parliament in 1923 as the Labour member for Leicester West, beating Winston Churchill. The seat has continued to have strong links to the Cambridge Union: it was later held by Greville Janner (President, Lent 1952) and is currently represented by Patricia Hewitt, who served on the Union's standing committee in the late 1960s. Pethick-Lawrence also set another Union precedent when he became the first ex-President to serve as Leader of the Opposition – he was one of several senior

Labour figures who nominally held this post during the Second World War, and was followed in 2003–6 by Michael Howard (President, Easter 1962). Ennobled in 1945, Pethick-Lawrence finished his career as Secretary of State for India, overseeing the negotiations which led to Indian independence in 1947.

The Union elected its first American President, William Everett, in Michaelmas 1862. This was in the middle of the American civil war – and Everett, from Massachusetts, was snubbed when a debate held in his term divided heavily in favour of the Confederate states. Indeed, Everett does not seem to have kept particularly fond memories of his time at the Union: on his return to the USA, he gave a series of lectures about his years in Cambridge to young men at Harvard. In these, he complained that although the Union's members made full use of its building, they were 'to a vast extent wholly careless of who controls it, or what it does as a society … When a contested election does arise, it is generally on some point like college rivalry, wholly apart from the real business.'[29] He was even more scathing about the debates, which he thought 'beneath contempt':

> In general, they are death itself. There comes every now and then a season when a few active souls stir the Union into life. But even then the animation cannot create the habit of good speaking, to which the whole genius of the place is opposed; and the most intelligent audiences of Cambridge young men, always professing the most thorough contempt for rhetoric, are habitually carried off their feet by the most worn-out claptrap.[30]

Everett had a strong political pedigree from which to make these criticisms: his father had been the unsuccessful Constitutional Union candidate for the vice-presidency of the USA in the divisive 1860 election – as well as a Congressman, Senator, Governor, Ambassador in London and Secretary of State. William Everett followed in his father's footsteps when he was elected as a Congressman, but was unsuccessful when he tried to follow him by running for Governor of Massachusetts on the Democratic ticket in 1897. A later American President of the Union also entered Democratic politics when he returned to the USA. Lewis Stuyvesant Chanler (Michaelmas 1895) was Lieutenant Governor of New York and the Democrats' nominee for Governor in 1908, but was powerfully opposed by his former running mate, the press magnate William Randolph Hearst.

John Ellis McTaggart (President, Michaelmas 1890) became noteworthy without leaving Cambridge. Part of an aesthetic group which included Goldsworthy Lowes Dickinson and was in many ways a precursor of the Bloomsbury Set, McTaggart was elected to a prize fellowship at Trinity on the basis of a dissertation on Hegel's *Logic*. He stayed there until his retirement in 1923, becoming the leading Hegelian scholar in England and a renowned philosopher. His long residence in Cambridge allowed him to stay closely involved with the Union – as Librarian in 1894–5 and 1902, as Treasurer from 1915 to 1920, and as a trustee from 1914.

———

The first President of the twentieth century was Arthur Cecil Pigou, professor of political economy at Cambridge for 35 years. Personifying Cambridge's neoclassical orthodoxy, Pigou was a great influence on colleagues and students in the nascent economics faculty – including his fellow Kingsman John Maynard Keynes, who was President of the Union in Lent 1905. Although they came to disagree robustly on economic theory, the two men retained a warm personal regard for one another.

Keynes was signed up to the Union by his father, a don, in his first term at Cambridge. He made his maiden speech that same term, telling his father it was 'the bravest thing I ever did'.[31] It made a favourable impression on both *Granta*, the undergraduate newspaper, which thought it 'quite excellent', and on the President, Edwin Montagu, who invited him to speak 'on the paper' a fortnight later.[32] Keynes spoke regularly throughout the rest of his first year, and was elected to standing committee – on his second attempt – at the end of Easter Term. His contributions to the debates of his second year did not live up to his early promise: his biographer notes that his delivery 'was not impressive' and showed a 'lack of passion'. One speech, in defence of free trade in Michaelmas 1903, received such a poor review in *Granta* that his father considered procuring speaking lessons for him.[33] Keynes evidently took his Union speeches seriously, preparing careful notes and drafts which can still be found among his papers; at the end of his second year he was elected Secretary – again, at his second attempt. By a stroke of fate, he proceeded to the presidency more swiftly than expected: H.G. Wood, the Quaker theologian, had been elected to serve as President in Lent 1905 but was unable to remain in Cambridge beyond the first few debates, so Keynes moved up from the vice-presidency a term early, 'and his Tripos term was thus clear of official duties at the Union'.[34] It was perhaps just as well, for he was also president of the Liberal Club that year. By the time of his retirement debate, his speaking style was assured: on that occasion, *Granta* thought it 'cool, logical, yet full of regard primarily ... for the highest and best moral principles of statesmanship ... We look forward to a great career for him in other circles.'[35] Keynes showed a 'characteristic touch' of that future career when he established a committee to consider the employment hours of the Union's staff. Determined to ensure that his successors adhered to its recommendations, he passed a standing order obliging all future Vice-Presidents to make a report on staff conditions.[36]

Keynes was succeeded by the man he had beaten to the secretaryship, J.K. Mozley of Pembroke – later Canon of St Paul's Cathedral. His predecessor was his fellow King's member, John Tressider Sheppard, 'one of Cambridge's "characters",' who would later become Provost of the college.[37]

Edwin Montagu, the President who had advanced Keynes's early Union career, was later Secretary of State for India, and a bronze copy of the statue erected of him in Calcutta is still to be found in the Union chamber.* Montagu was evidently a forceful character: as well as his altercation with Oscar Browning, he adopted the practice of flying a flag above the Union to show that he was in residence. Perhaps most surprisingly, shortly after his presidency, the future architect of the Montagu-Chelmsford reforms became embroiled in a controversy surrounding the defeat of C.R. Reddy, who was unsuccessful in his bid to become the Union's first Indian President. Reddy had been leading in the early hours of polling, but in those days the ballot boxes were empted periodically throughout the day, and any ex-President could watch the progress of the count. One ex-President from Trinity, the same college as Reddy's opponent, did just that. Seeing the state of the poll, he rushed back to whip up more Trinitarians and swung the vote for his candidate. In the private business meetings which followed, when the rules governing the count were altered, Montagu was eloquent among those senior figures 'defending a result in which colour prejudice had undoubtedly played a part'.[38] Ramalinga Reddy returned to India, where he entered politics, founded Andhra University, and was Vice-Chancellor both there and at the University of Mysore. He was knighted in 1942, but relinquished the title after Indian independence.

The Reddy episode has been recorded by H. Wilson Harris, President that term and later editor of the *Spectator*. He was also, in 1945, one of the last pair of MPs elected for Cambridge University, standing as an Independent and narrowly beating J.B. Priestley on the fourth count.[†]

Two renowned jurists were President at the end of this decade: Arnold McNair (Easter 1909) and Norman Birkett (Michaelmas

---

* The choice of sculptress, Kathleen Scott, was very appropriate: her husband, Edward Hilton Young – later Minister of Health and Lord Kennet – had been President of the Union in Michaelmas 1900, exactly 40 years after his father, Sir George.

† Created by Royal Charter in 1603, the University constituency returned two members – or Burgesses – until its abolition at the general election of 1950. From 1918, it used the single transferable vote system of election.

1910). McNair was professor of international law and later of comparative law at Cambridge, and turned down the mastership of Caius to become a judge at the International Court of Justice in The Hague, becoming its President in 1952–55. Afterwards, as Lord McNair, he was the first President of the European Court of Human Rights at Strasbourg. His years lecturing in Cambridge allowed him to serve the Union again – first as Treasurer and then as a trustee. Norman Birkett, as Vice-President of the Union, had proposed honorary membership for Theodore Roosevelt when he visited in Easter 1910. He achieved rare success as both a barrister and a judge, winning accolades as 'one of the foremost advocates of his time' as well as 'an excellent judge of first instance'.[39] He was also active in politics but, as a Liberal at an inauspicious time for his party, sat only briefly in the Commons, in 1923–24 and 1929–31. His role overseeing the internment of detainees under the notorious Defence Regulation 18B during the Second World War led to his appointment as one of the British judges to the international military tribunal at Nuremburg. He joined McNair in the House of Lords in 1958. Another Emmanuel lawyer, Sir Barclay Nihill (President in Michaelmas 1914) became Chief Justice of Kenya and President of the Court of Appeal for Eastern Africa.

The outbreak of the First World War in 1914 meant that plans to celebrate the Union's centenary the following year were abandoned: a celebratory dinner was not held until November 1921. Soon, the war put a halt to the Union's regular activities too. Although debates continued initially, it was resolved at a private business meeting on 8 May 1916 not to hold any further elections for the duration of the war, and the functions of the standing committee were entrusted to a committee of *ex officio* members, chaired by Mozley. Debates and elections were not resumed until February 1919, though the Union stayed open, offering basic amenities to officers and cadets stationed at Cambridge. More than 2,000 members of the University were killed in the First World War, among them three ex-Presidents: A.C.O. Morgan (Easter 1906), F.D. Livingstone (Easter 1907) and J.H. Allen (Easter 1911).

A record number of new members joined the Union as Cambridge swelled with renewed activity after the war. Among the new members were Prince Albert (the future King George VI) and Prince Henry, both at Trinity, and their second cousin, Sub-Lieutenant Lord Louis Mountbatten of Christ's. The Princes were merely observers of the Union's debates, sitting on the crossbenches, but Mountbatten spoke on a number of occasions and was elected to the standing committee in his first year – a rare achievement for a freshman. His most notable speech came when he was invited to lead for Cambridge in the Varsity debate in Lent 1920, opposing a motion that the time was now ripe for a Labour government. Sir Geoffrey Shakespeare, President that term – and, as a National Liberal, someone who would later prop up a Labour Prime Minister in a National government – recalls that the Union 'was packed to suffocation with over a thousand members. Several late-comers climbing in through the windows were passed from shoulder to shoulder till they could find room for their feet.'[40] Mountbatten had enlisted Churchill, then Secretary of State for War, to help his side (he spoke for over an hour), and together they soundly defeated the motion by 651 votes to 265. The young naval officer drew warm praise from Churchill that evening, but opinions on his oratorical skills were generally divided. A previous speech had been described as 'full of beans and enthusiasm and though he certainly did talk to some extent through his hat, still, never mind. It was a great effort'; and his upper-class idiom, infused with naval slang, gave the student periodical *New Cambridge* plenty of scope for parody: 'I'm frightfully bucked to have a chance of blowing the gaff for half a jiff.'[41]

Packed though the Varsity debate of Lent 1920 was, it did not surpass the record division figures set by a debate the previous term, and never since beaten. This was a debate between the Duke of Northumberland and Lord Robert Cecil on the motion 'That this House considers the League of Nations to be worthless as a guarantee of international peace and to be a radically unsound and dangerous project'. To a generation of students for whom the horrors of total war were a recent and vivid memory, this was an electrifying debate, and more than 1,000 members voted – with many more packing the chamber, sitting on the floor between the speakers and under the Secretary's table. It was Cecil who carried the majority of the House, appealing to their youthful idealism and determination never again to have such a war. When the record vote had been counted, the motion was defeated by 723 to 280 – a total vote of 1,003.*

The President in Easter 1924 was R.A. Butler who, being narrowly passed over for the premiership in 1957 and 1963 and holding every other major office of state in the meantime, is probably the Union's most successful political alumnus. Rab already had a strong family connection to the Union by the time he came up to Cambridge: seven of his forebears had held office in the Society.[42] As well as his great-uncle Henry Montagu Butler, the Master of Trinity, there was his grandfather, Spencer Percival Butler (Secretary, Michaelmas 1850 and Treasurer, 1852–53); his father, Montagu Sherrard Dawes Butler (President, Easter 1895), later Master of Rab's undergraduate college, Pembroke; and his uncle, Arthur Francis Butler (President, Lent 1897).

Two of Rab's relatives were President consecutively in the Lent and Easter terms of 1910. Sir James Ramsay Montagu Butler followed in the footsteps of his father, H.M. Butler, as a Fellow, Senior Tutor, and Vice-Master of Trinity. He was Regius Professor of Modern History, and was elected MP for the University as an Independent Liberal in 1922, losing his seat the following year to his cousin, Sir Geoffrey Butler, who had been his successor at the Union. Sir Geoffrey was a Fellow of Corpus Christi, and was a driving force behind the nascent Cambridge University Conservative Association (CUCA) in the early 1920s, enlisting Rab in his efforts. He was an enormous influence on his young nephew and a generation of Cambridge Conservatives, not least through his lectures on 'The Tory Tradition', published in 1914. Sir James's younger brother,

---

* The lowest division recorded was in 1839, when the question 'Does the philosophy of Locke deserve the approbation of posterity?' was defeated by five votes to nil.

Gordon Kerr Montagu Butler, was President in Easter 1914. Both brothers served with the Scottish Horse Brigade in Gallipoli and Egypt, where Gordon died after contracting an illness in 1916.

With such an array of Union antecedents – and another great-uncle, Arthur Gray Butler, President of the Oxford Union in 1853 – Rab was naturally drawn to the Union, which he described as 'a wonderful training ground' which 'simply should not be missed by those at the University aiming at public life'.[43] But his younger brother, Jock, failed to follow in the family tradition when, choosing to run with Labour backing, he was beaten to the presidency in Easter 1935 by Cub Alport, later a Conservative minister for Commonwealth relations. After Jock was killed in the Second World War, Rab and Alport became close friends, and Butler gave him one of his first jobs in politics as director of the Conservative Political Centre. Alport was not the only ex-President to whom Rab showed preferment: he also appointed his contemporary Reggie Northam (Easter 1923) principal of Swinton Conservative College, made Selwyn Lloyd (Michaelmas 1927) his parliamentary private secretary, and recruited Peter Goldman (Michaelmas 1944) into the Conservative Research Department – his advancement only halted by his defeat in the ill-timed Orpington by-election in 1962.

Rab had a very successful term as President: on his first night in the chair, he boldly used his casting vote against Stanley Baldwin to uphold the motion 'That this House has the highest regard for rhetoric'. He also led the first Union debating tour of America with two other Presidents: the barrister A.P. Marshall (Michaelmas 1924) and Rab's future biographer Gerald Sparrow (Easter 1925). While the tours continue to this day, another of Butler's ventures was less enduring. Against 'considerable opposition', he persuaded the Union to affiliate to the National Union of Students – an association which was soon reversed.[44]

Butler's contemporaries form a prestigious Union generation: his close friend Geoffrey Lloyd (President, Lent 1925) became a ministerial colleague; Michael Ramsey (Lent 1926) rose to become Archbishop of Canterbury; and Patrick Devlin (Michaelmas 1926) was the youngest judge appointed that century. He became the youngest law lord in 1961, before resigning unexpectedly and turning to writing; he was also High Steward of the University for 25 years. Alan King-Hamilton (Easter 1927) was another successful judge at the Old Bailey and celebrated his 104th birthday in December 2008; while Selwyn Lloyd, although president of the Liberal Club while at Cambridge, became a Conservative Foreign Secretary and Chancellor of the Exchequer, and the second ex-President to become Speaker of the House of Commons (after W.C. Gully, President in Easter 1855). Lloyd's successor at the Liberal Club, Hugh Foot, was also President of the Union. As with Butler, this was almost a familial duty: his three brothers, Dingle, John and Michael (the Labour party leader), were all President of the Oxford Union – as was his own son Paul in 1961. Foot chose not to follow his father and brothers into politics, but to go into the diplomatic service, becoming Governor of Jamaica and of Cyprus, and, as Lord Caradon, the UK's representative at the United Nations.

Two left-wing Presidents of the '20s remained involved in the Union for many years. As President in Michaelmas 1925 – the first Labour man to hold the office – David Hardman headed the list of signatories to a letter avowing that 'all disputes between nations are capable of settlement either by diplomatic negotiation or by some form of international arbitration', and solemnly declaring 'that we shall refuse to support or render war service to any government which resorts to arms'.[45] He served the Union again as Treasurer during the difficult years of 1938–46 until his appointment as a junior minister forced him to step down, having been elected MP for Darlington in 1945. Another signatory to Hardman's 1925 letter was Lionel Elvin, President in Lent 1928. A Fabian and pacifist from a trade union background, Elvin became a prominent member of the English faculty and a professor of education, after taking firsts in both history and English (and gaining a Blue for athletics). He served alongside Hardman as the Union's Librarian from 1936 to 1939, but was unsuccessful in his attempt to become a Labour MP for the University in the 1935 general election.

Plenty of other ex-Presidents of this period found success beyond the narrow world of politics. Two Leathem brothers – John (Lent 1929) and Terry (Lent 1933) – were President in quick succession, and became headmasters of Taunton and Ludlow schools respectively. The nascent BBC was a source of employment for many others: Lionel Gamlin (Michaelmas 1930) was an announcer and broadcaster for the corporation before returning to the stage; his successor as President, J.D.F. Green, was controller of talks. Kenneth Adam (Lent 1930) held a number of posts in the BBC before becoming director of BBC television in the 1960s. Leonard Miall (Michaelmas 1936), having inaugurated the BBC's talks broadcasts to Europe in 1939, went to the USA as part of the British Political Warfare Mission. Returning to the corporation after the war, he was its chief correspondent in America, head of television talks and, as a special assistant to Adam in 1962, helped to plan the start of BBC2.

Union alumni infiltrated other parts of the show-business world. Miall's successor as President, Gerald Croasdell, became general secretary of Equity, though not an actor himself. Robert Stevenson, President in Easter 1928, went to Hollywood, where he directed more than two dozen movies – including *Mary Poppins* (for which he was nominated for an Oscar), *Bedknobs and Broomsticks* and two of the 'Herbie' films.

President the term after Stevenson was Geoffrey (later Lord) Crowther, editor of the *Economist* and the first Chancellor of the Open University. But none of these diverse career paths deflected some Presidents from success in the old staples of law and politics. Sir Samuel Cooke (Lent 1934) was a High Court judge; Sir Geoffrey de Freitas, his immediate successor, was a Labour MP, High Commissioner in Ghana and Kenya, and Vice-President of the European Parliament. Albert Holdsworth (Easter 1932) was tempted by journalism and politics, but finally settled on the law, becoming a silk and a circuit judge. Sir Charles Fletcher-Cooke (Lent 1936) first stood for Parliament as a Labour candidate, but entered the Commons as a Conservative in Darwen – after another ex-President, Vyvyan Adams (Lent 1924), who had beaten him to the nomination, was drowned on holiday in Cornwall. Adams, a barrister whose father was vicar of the Round Church, had previously sat as an MP in Leeds and lost his seat in the Labour landslide of 1945.

Young men of differing backgrounds found success in the Union in the early '30s – Elwyn Jones, the future Lord Chancellor, was undeterred by President Lord Pentland's comment on one of his early speeches that 'Elwyn Jones made a charming speech, but his Welsh accent amounted to an impediment in it'.[46] He was President in Michaelmas 1931. A year later, Shanti Swaroop Dhavan of Emmanuel became the first Indian President. Later a judge in the Allahabad High Court, a popular Indian High Commissioner in London and Governor of West Bengal, his son Rajeev followed him in the President's chair in 1970.

———

Two final changes bring us to the Union as it existed on the eve of the Second World War. By the 1930s, the Victorian clubhouse of Waterhouse's design was 'losing its attraction', according to Sydney Elwood, who began his long career at the Union as a junior clerk in 1923. Certainly, the building as he describes it at the time of his arrival sounds elegant to the modern reader:

> The entrance hall and ground floor corridor were paved with coloured and patterned tiles and York stone. The main staircase, wide and constructed of similar stone, was heavily carpeted in red, and under the watchful eye of Demosthenes portrayed in the stained glass window which lit that side of the entrance hall. The wrought iron balustrade of the staircase, with clustered columns and corniced mouldings, supported one side of the large landing above.

But, as Elwood also explains, this all seemed outdated to the modernist tastes of that time, 'and serious thought was being given to its effect on the Society.'[47]

Serious thought was needed indeed, for the effects of the financial depression of the late 1920s were also being felt by the Union.

Undergraduates of the period, before the days of student grants or loans, were more dependent on their families' incomes, and the number of new members joining fell from 908 in 1929–30 to 767 and 639 over the next two years. Happily, the high levels of membership in the rest of the inter-war period had allowed the Society not only to repay the overdraft it had accumulated during the war, but to amass a reserve fund of some £15,000. In Easter 1933, members approved plans to spend £11,500 of this on a scheme of renovation. The library, which had previously occupied most of the ground floor with access via an entrance hall opposite the main office, was moved upstairs to the old smoking and drawing rooms, where teas had previously been served. The old dining room was the room immediately above the main office, served by kitchens housed in the roof space above the chamber via a hand-operated lift. The new dining room took the place of the main library stacks in the large ground-floor room abutting Round Church Street, where a spiral iron staircase had previously led down to the shelves of magazines and journals in the basement below. A new window, running almost the whole length of the room, made this new dining room a bright and airy space. Next to it was a new bar lounge and a smoking room, furnished with black glass and chromium tables and red canvas chairs on springy metal frames. The bar jutting out into the room was a later addition; initially, this was hidden behind a retractable panel in the wall.

The new library, with its barrel-vaulted ceiling, was a handsome example of the new modernist style, as were the two new squash courts added to the back of the Union. Elsewhere in the building, old was replaced with new: arches with mouldings in the corridors were replaced with square lintels, and the stone and tiled floors covered with rubber. The ornate iron columns on the staircase were encased to form square plastered pillars, and joined by a simple black handrail. The renovations had the desired effect: aided by a smart booklet circulated to all new undergraduates with glossy photographs of the new rooms, membership levels increased considerably. It was prudently decided, however, that the photograph of the new lounge should be shown with the bar shut, lest revealing such an amenity would dissuade anxious parents from contributing to their offspring's subscription fees.

The second significant change of this period was a procedural one. In Lent 1939, the President, the Hon. P.T.T. Butler, later the 28th Lord Dunboyne, keen to allow more maiden speakers to participate in debates, allowed members to speak from their places in the 'floor debate' which followed the main speeches. He also extended to the whole House the prerogative of interruption, hitherto limited to the President. This innovation, which allowed members to offer interruptions to main speakers with questions or points of information, ushered in 'an era of licensed interjection' which has not been reversed, and was felt to 'add greatly to the speed and liveliness of debate'.[48]

So from the merger of three small debating societies in 1815, meeting in a dingy room at the back of a public house, the Union had become by 1939 a place where ordinary undergraduates could challenge great statesmen and other eminent figures in open debate, in the fine surroundings of their own debating chamber and clubhouse. But they would not have much chance to do so in the years which immediately followed: for an interruption much less welcome than those introduced by Lord Dunboyne was just around the corner.

'A debate at the Union club', *c.* 1887. Guests and speakers no longer wear gowns, but the format of debates has barely changed otherwise since the nineteenth century.   (*The Graphic*, 8 October 1887)

1939–45:

THE SECOND WORLD WAR

In common with the rest of the country, Union members returned from the horrors of the First World War determined never to allow such a conflict to arise again. For most, it was a simple desire to avoid a repetition of such terrible carnage; for others, this pacifism took a more ideological form. For many of them, another seismic event of that decade – the Russian revolutions of 1917 – was also an influence, and there was a notable communist movement in Cambridge between the wars.

Chief among them was Maurice Dobb, educated at Charterhouse and Pembroke. He joined the Communist Party of Great Britain on its foundation in 1920, and was elected to the Union's standing committee at the end of that year. T.E.B. Howarth, a Fellow of Magdalene who wrote a history of inter-war Cambridge, says that Dobb became 'Cambridge's leading polemicist' and was 'adept at presenting radical views in a relaxed and unalarming manner'.[1] He spoke frequently and effectively for the communist cause in the Union: in May 1932, for instance, he persuaded the House that it should have more hope in Moscow than in Detroit.

At the start of the 1930s, there was only a small communist group at Cambridge, concentrated around Trinity and King's. In 1932, it had just two dozen members – far fewer than the more moderate Cambridge University Socialist Society, which provided the forum for most left-wing undergraduates. One of the early members of the

33

communist cell was Kim Philby, who was introduced to the Communist International by Dobb, his tutor, and became the most successful member of the infamous Cambridge spy ring. Philby was a member of the Union, but not an active one. Anthony Blunt, the 'fourth man' of the ring, did not join the Union – but one of his lovers, Julian Bell (son of the Bloomsburyites Clive and Vanessa, who was later killed driving an ambulance during the Spanish civil war), made passionate socialist speeches in debates of the late 1920s.[2]

Blunt was up at Cambridge for the longest period of any of the spy ring – he came up to Trinity as an undergraduate in 1926 and remained there until 1937. During these years, he saw the politics of Cambridge change dramatically. According to Blunt, 'Marxism hit Cambridge' in Michaelmas 1933 – he came back from a sabbatical that term to find that 'almost all my younger friends had become Marxists and joined the Communist Party'.[3] Blunt's biographer Miranda Carter highlights the national and international backdrop to this shift in undergraduate opinion. The effects of the Great Depression were being keenly felt, and the newspapers were full of the sufferings of the poor. (They were brought even closer to home when the Hunger Marchers reached Cambridge in February 1934, and a reception was held for them in the town.) Unemployment hit a peak of three million in January 1933. That same month, Hitler was elected German Chancellor. But while these external events undoubtedly played a role, Carter explains that the real catalyst in Cambridge was the takeover of the small communist group by 'two determined and persuasive young men from Trinity', James Klugmann and John Cornford.[4] Klugmann and Cornford systematically targeted sympathetic non-party members, devoting hours to all-night political discussions with them. Under their auspices, the communists took over the Socialist Society and its members were engaged in clandestine tasks for the benefit of the party. Some were entrusted with cultivating foreign students; others were told to work hard in order to get into the BBC or the Foreign Office. One young American who had joined the Socialist Society was given the task of infiltrating the Union.

Michael Straight was born in New York, the youngest son of Willard Straight, an investment banker, and Dorothy Payne Whitney, an heiress and social reformer. After his father died, Straight's mother married a British educationalist and moved the family from New York to Devon, where they ran an experimental school. Straight was educated there, and at the LSE, before going up to Trinity in 1934 to read economics. He quickly became known as one of the most glamorous figures of Cambridge society. His elder brother Whitney was a racing driver, and Straight drove alongside him in the first South African Grand Prix in December 1935. Both finished on the podium: Whitney in first place, Michael in third.

Straight fell under the spell of Klugmann and Cornford, for whom he later wrote he 'would have done anything'. So when they decided 'to make an open assault on the Union', Straight went along willingly – though it was a prospect which 'filled me with apprehension'.[5] One Cambridge contemporary, Gavin Ewart, remembered Straight as someone with a taste for cloak-and-dagger activity: 'He was very melodramatic. You felt he was in a deep conspiracy all the time. He wanted to be.'[6] Both Cornford and Straight spoke regularly during Michaelmas 1935, and were elected to the standing committee at the end of that term. By the following Michaelmas, Straight had built up a sufficient profile in the Union to run for Secretary. He stood against John Churchill, 'a supercilious, well-established Conservative' in what was 'an all-out contest between the Left and the Right.'[7] Straight won narrowly, being informed of his victory by Gerald Croasdell, the President that term and a communist sympathiser.[8] His victory put him on track to become Vice-President the following term, and President in Michaelmas 1937. But a dramatic start to the new year meant that Straight would achieve only the first of these higher offices.

John Cornford had left Cambridge in the summer of 1936 to fight in the Spanish civil war. His romantic departure as the first British volunteer increased his heroic standing among left-wing undergraduates. That December, shortly before his 21st birthday, he was killed in a skirmish near Córdoba. Straight learnt of his death through party associates in mid-January – before even Cornford's father, to whom Straight broke the news. He also took it upon himself to find a job for Cornford's girlfriend and a home for their infant son. A memorial meeting was held in the Union, and Cornford's picture adorned the mantelpieces of many student rooms for years to come.

Amid this mourning, Straight received a message from Anthony Blunt, asking him to come to his rooms in Nevile's Court, in Trinity. In his memoirs, Straight says he believed that Blunt had been deliberately cultivating him for some time, insinuating his way into his life and making him emotionally dependent on him. When Straight had run into trouble in Trinity in his second year as the suspected organiser of a petition demanding higher wages for college servants (his was the first signature on the list), Blunt had helped to calm the waters. Blunt also advised Straight on his love life, helping him to woo his future wife by acting as a go-between via her sister.[9] By the time of this meeting shortly after Cornford's death, Blunt had become a 'wise and valued counsellor' to Straight.[10] He asked him what plans he had for the future: Straight replied that he would probably become a British subject like his brother had done, then run for Parliament as a Labour candidate. Blunt listened attentively. 'Some of your friends,' he told him, 'have other ideas for you.'[11]

These 'friends' – figures in the Communist International – wanted Straight to go to America to work on Wall Street, as his father had done, and to provide them with appraisals of the American economy. He was instructed to cut all ties with his communist friends in the UK, using Cornford's death as an excuse to feign a nervous breakdown or crisis of belief. He would also have to leave Cambridge, abandoning both his degree and his anticipated presidency of the Union. Straight pleaded against these instructions: he had lived in Britain since he was nine, and barely remembered the United States. Blunt agreed to carry his appeal back to his superiors, assuring him that it would 'be considered in the highest circles in the Kremlin'.[12] But it was rejected. So Straight began to make his break with his friends in Cambridge. He started rows with friends in the

Socialist Society, and 'upset the Communist caucus in the Union by instructing them to vote for a Conservative':

> I said that I might not return to Cambridge in the autumn to serve out my term as President ... I voiced my disgust at the adolescent nature of its debates.[13]

At his mother's insistence, and with the agreement of Blunt and his 'friends', Straight stayed on to sit his final Tripos exams. He had taken firsts in both his first and second years, but had neglected his studies in his third year as he both feigned a nervous breakdown, and tried to cope with the very real turmoil of Cornford's death and the party's plans for him. With only a few weeks to go, the only option was to cram. But Straight showed admirable ingenuity in this regard: plotting a graph of the questions which had been asked in the economics Tripos over the past ten years, he drew a probability curve from them and revised the top 10 per cent, which he guessed would recur. When he achieved another first, the economics faculty met and revised the examinations system.

Straight had salvaged his degree, but was unable to do the same with his hopes of staying on to become President of the Union. He did, however, manage to secure an admirable swan-song during his vice-presidential term. Haile Selassie, the Emperor of Ethiopia, had been driven out of Addis Ababa by Mussolini and gone into exile in Bath. For some, his presence in Britain was an embarrassment, and there were suggestions in the right-wing press that he might be happier elsewhere. Ronald Gibson, a Liberal who was President in Easter 1937, decided to invite him to the Union and offer him an honorary membership as a gesture of solidarity. It was a highly political act, and one which provoked heated controversy in both the Union and the national press. Straight was instrumental in marshalling left-wing support in the Society for the invitation.

The imperial visit was a grand occasion. As Vice-President, Straight delivered the welcome speech – translated into French for him by Anthony Blunt. That evening, Victor Rothschild threw a lavish farewell party for Straight and his friends at Merton Hall, the Rothschilds' house opposite St John's. The party was already in full swing as the ceremony at the Union took place. As His Imperial Majesty accepted his honorary membership, 'fireworks lit up the debating chamber with unpredictable flashes'.[14] After the meeting, Straight jumped into his sports car with Leonard Miall, an ex-President of the Union, and roared over Magdalene bridge towards Merton Hall. What a scene awaited them: 'Entering the Rothschilds' house that night was like entering the Athenian Wood in *A Midsummer Night's Dream*,' wrote Straight. To Miall, 'it was straight out of Evelyn Waugh … It was a lovely, balmy night, there was a supper of caviar and vodka on the terrace.'[15] A Hungarian band filled the floodlit garden with music, while Victor Rothschild played duets with the jazz pianist Cab Calloway. Unsurprisingly, Miall recalls many hangovers around the table in the Union the next morning, at the breakfast given for its new honorary member.[16] Blunt did not attend this breakfast, but had been at the party at Merton Hall, and had followed the events at the Union that term. In his weekly column in the *Spectator* the following week, he applauded the Society's recent rejection of rearmament, condemnation of British imperialism, and election of Haile Selassie as an honorary member. 'All of which,' he concluded, 'shows that its heart is in the right place and rather solidly fixed there.'[17]

As planned, Michael Straight embarked for America at the end of term. He worked not on Wall Street, but for the US government as an unpaid economic adviser at the State Department. There, and at the Interior Department, he passed on reports to a Soviet handler he called 'Michael Green' – though he always insisted that he never divulged any restricted material. Like many, he made a break with the Communist party during the Second World War. He became editor of the *New Republic*, the magazine his parents had founded, and was a staunch critic of McCarthyism, a brave stance in light of his own chequered past. In 1963, he was offered a position in the Kennedy administration. Aware that he would be vetted, he revealed all to the FBI. His confession unmasked Blunt, and was passed on to

MI5. By now surveyor of the Queen's pictures and a knight of the realm, Blunt was offered immunity from prosecution in return for a full confession of his own. He was finally named publicly by Margaret Thatcher and stripped of his knighthood in 1979.

———•———

Of course, not all left-wing undergraduates went on to betray their country. Charles Fletcher-Cooke, a future President of the Union, accompanied Michael Straight, Anthony Blunt and his brother Wilfrid, and others on a trip to the Soviet Union in 1935 organised by Intourist, the Soviet state travel agency. But Fletcher-Cooke was not impressed with what he saw. He 'revised his views on Russia and socialism as a result of the trip' so firmly that he later became a Conservative MP.[18]

Two of the last Presidents before the war were prominent communists overseas. Mohan Kumaramangalam (Michaelmas 1938) was an Old Etonian who became a prominent theorist and organiser for the Communist Party of India, and was imprisoned by the British for a year following his return to India in the early 1940s.[19] After years of service, however, he drifted from the party when it split in the mid-1960s. Attracted by Indira Gandhi's more moderate politics, he became one of her closest advisers and joined her Cabinet as minister of steel and mines in 1971. But his new political career was cut short: he was killed two years later in a plane crash in New Delhi. For his retiring debate at the Union he had proposed 'That the continued existence of the British Empire is a danger to world peace' – and won, by 204 votes to 184. The President the following Michaelmas was Pieter Keuneman, the scion of a bourgeois family in Ceylon who had attended Bertrand and Dora Russell's experimental school. Also editor of *Granta*, he visited Spain during the civil war and made a six-week visit to the Soviet Union in 1937, returning via Poland and Nazi Germany. He drew on his first-hand experiences of these countries in his Union speeches, telling members in Michaelmas 1937 that there was freedom of conscience, press and assembly in the Soviet Union.[20] He later returned to his native

Ceylon, where he became general secretary of the Communist Party of Sri Lanka and a government minister.

The Marxist historian Eric Hobsbawm recalls both men in his memoirs: Kumaramangalam was an 'elegant charmer' and Keuneman, with whom Hobsbawm rented a house in Round Church Street, was 'dashing, witty and handsome': a 'debonair socialite' and 'a great figure in university society'. He was also 'the lucky partner of the ravishing Hedi Simon' with whom Hobsbawm 'vainly fell in love'.[21] The daughter of a rich Jewish banker, Simon came to Newnham from Austria to escape the Nazis in 1936, and became a leading member of the Communist party in Cambridge. She and Keuneman married on the eve of war in 1939 and she returned with him to Ceylon. They divorced in 1952 and she married the concert pianist and music critic Peter Stadlen. With him, she had two sons – one of whom, Nick, came up to Cambridge and was President of the Union in 1970. Brilliantly clever, she had gained the only first in moral sciences in her year but, as a woman, was barred from graduating. She finally took her degree in 2002, accompanied by her son and grandson, who collected their MA and BA degrees respectively on the same day.[22]

If some undergraduates were drawn to the far left, others were attracted to the far right. There was a small fascist organisation at Cambridge, presided over in 1933 by F.H. Lawton of Corpus, a future Lord Justice of Appeal. That February, the two ends of the political spectrum clashed in a Union debate: 'This House prefers Fascism to Socialism'. Speaking for the proposition was Sir Oswald Mosley, who had formed his British Union of Fascists the previous year; Aneurin Bevan had been due to oppose but was ill, so was replaced at the last minute by a young Labour MP, Major C.R. Attlee. The *Cambridge Daily News* reported that 'the House was packed, members even sitting on the President's platform, and when Sir Oswald entered, boos mingled with the cheers'.[23] Sir Oswald 'gave a scintillating performance' and, though he was continually interrupted and the President had to call several members to order, 'his magnificent oratory carried an enthusiastic House off its feet'.[24]

The first opposition speaker, Samuel Cooke – the future chairman of the Law Commission – banged his fist down on the despatch box so hard that a glass of water was overturned. Attlee, however, was calmer and more effective, and soundly overturned the motion despite a substantial fascist vote: the result was 335 to 218 in favour of socialism.*

This probably reflects the general mood of Union members in the early 1930s well: although only a few were out-and-out communists (and while others did not yet know enough about fascism to deplore it in greater numbers), on the whole they leaned more to the left than the right. In part, this may have been down to the changing social base of the University – by the early 1930s, nearly half of its undergraduates were in receipt of financial assistance.[25] But it was also part of the broader belief that socialism was a way of building a better, more peaceful world. Thus most Union members sided with the Republicans in the Spanish civil war. A motion deploring the government's policy of non-intervention in Spain was carried by 208 votes to 166 in Lent 1936. In Michaelmas 1938, the Union decided that the defeat of the Republican government 'would be a defeat for progress and civilisation' by 246 to just 44.

The Union had more complicated views on war in general. In 1928 it decided it was not in favour of 'peace at any price' by 304 to 222, G.K. Chesterton prevailing over Beverley Nichols. And if 200 members had preferred fascism to socialism in February 1933, members were much clearer two months later that 'this House hates Hitlerism' – doing so by 148 to 62. But these declamations did not yet translate into support for rearmament. The House supported the abolition of military training in schools in October 1930, voted by huge majorities in favour of disarmament in October 1932 and November 1933, and preferred arms talks to armed forces in March

---

* Mosley was due to speak in a near rerun of the debate three years later, with 'Socialism' replaced by 'Communism' in the motion. Michael Straight was to have been one of the student speakers, and 'cast aside all my studies to work on my speech' (Straight, p. 91). But King George V died on the eve of the debate, and it was cancelled.

1934. At the 1932 debate, Leo Amery felt it significant not only that he was outvoted by nearly four to one, 'but that a passionately excited body of undergraduates found it difficult even to give me a hearing'.[26] Members voted comfortably against rearmament again the following month, but by April 1937 were less certain, supporting a more strident motion on the 'refusal to bear arms' and 'complete national disarmament' by only four votes in a House of 180.

The Union's views towards His Majesty's government were similarly mixed. It condemned its foreign policy in 1934 and 1936 when that policy signified rearmament, but viewed it 'with grave concern' and 'condemned' it in March and October 1938 respectively when it meant appeasement. These debates attracted great attention. The first was held shortly after Anthony Eden's resignation as Foreign Secretary. His Cabinet colleague Walter Elliot came to defend the government, but 'made only a brief reference to the resignation'.[27] The attack was led by the retiring President, John Simonds of Magdalene. The son of a future Lord Chancellor, Simonds had been one of the most robust Conservative speakers in the Union – and joked of setting up 'The Cambridge Society for the Prevention of Cruelty to Conservatives' – until he met Michael Straight. Simonds was strongly influenced by his politics, as a letter he wrote to Straight during the war recalled:

> I was curious about you. You represented a point of view that I'd never attempted to understand. There seemed to be something big and important about it all.

John Cornford's death, and Straight's grief at that loss, also affected Simonds profoundly:

> I remember very vividly the night we spoke about him in the Union … I felt that something young and precious had come and gone and I had had none of it.[28]

Their deepening friendship sealed Simonds's political conversion. Frank Singleton, President in Michaelmas 1937, recalls how his

Vice-President literally crossed the floor of the House in the first debate of term, being received 'in a wide embrace of welcome' by the left-wing Aubrey Eban of Queens' – later Abba Eban and Deputy Prime Minister of Israel.[29]

By the time of his retirement debate, Simonds's speeches against the government had become extremely powerful, and he won a rare ovation that night. Robert Boothby MP, who spoke opposite him, said it was 'one of the most brilliant speeches he had ever listened to', while the *Cambridge Review* thought it 'by far the best that the House had heard during the past few years'.[30] It won the debate by 316 votes to 174. Eighteen months later, when the war came, Simonds enlisted in the army. He was killed at Arnhem in 1944.

The October debate condemning the government's policy of appeasement also drew in a packed House, coming less than three weeks after the Munich Agreement. The motion was proposed by Pieter Keuneman, who said that Czechoslovakia had been 'stabbed in the back'. It was opposed by Peter Hague of Emmanuel, Norman Birkett's nephew, who invited his uncle to speak in his last debate when he followed in his footsteps as President in Easter 1939. Another gifted speaker and a loyal Conservative, he was a staunch defender of the government's policy in Union debates, telling the House that 'the only justifiable grounds upon which one could ask a population to fight was in the defence of its vital interests'.[31] When the time came he took up that fight, rising to the rank of lieutenant in the Royal Naval Volunteer Reserve (RNVR). He was killed, aged 25, in 1942, while leading people to shelter during an air raid in Malta.

Hague failed to persuade the Society to support the government's position in October 1938, and the motion was carried by 471 to 282. A series of heavy defeats followed. By February 1939 the *Cambridge Daily News* reported such results with little surprise: 'The Government "got it" again at the Cambridge Union Society's debate last night', it wrote after one such trouncing.[32] Even in Michaelmas 1939, after war had been declared, the Union was still anti-government, affirming – albeit by a single vote – that 'this House would welcome a change of His Majesty's Government'. Members did, however, carry a motion that the war 'must go on until the objects for which we entered upon it are secured' later that term, and in February 1940 threw one out suggesting 'That the successful prosecution of the war is beyond the powers of the present Government'.

Of course, the most famous debate of the 1930s was held not at Cambridge but at the Oxford Union, which decided in February 1933 'That this House will in no circumstances fight for its King and Country'. A great deal has been written about this debate, which Churchill denounced as an 'abject, squalid, shameless avowal' by the 'callow, ill-tutored youths' of Oxford.[33] In an excellent article in the *Historical Journal*, Martin Ceadel has unpicked some of the more hysterical claims which have attached themselves to the debate – not least the wild suggestion that it encouraged Hitler and Mussolini to believe that Britain's young would not stand in their way.[34] The Oxford resolution attracted a great deal of press attention – but not immediately. Most of the furore was the effect of a letter planted in the *Daily Telegraph* by one of its leader writers, and the heavy-handed attempt by Randolph Churchill to have the motion expunged. Nonetheless, Ceadel concludes, there was some significance to the debate. The controversy reflected the way in which the Unions were widely regarded at this time as a training ground for future leaders. Such a vote suggested that their members were starting to behave like continental students rather than deferential British undergraduates. And the wording of the motion – particularly the phrase 'King and Country' – had a strong emotional impact on an older generation who had fought for precisely that.

By and large, the Cambridge Union was bemused by the attention the Oxford debate received – not least because its own similar resolutions had passed largely unnoticed. A historian of the Oxford Union, Christopher Hollis, notes that in 1927 Cambridge 'had passed by 213 votes to 138 a motion almost identical with that of the Oxford Union, "That lasting peace can only be secured by the people of England adopting an uncompromising attitude of pacifism," and no breath of notice was taken.'[35] The term after the 'King and Country' motion, the Cambridge President, Michael Barkway, spoke at a debate in London with the President-elect from Oxford, Anthony Greenwood. To cries of 'abominable' from the back of the room, Barkway called the Oxford result 'probably one of the most intelligent motions passed by a debating society for a great many years,' adding: 'I sincerely hope that if that motion is going to be debated in Cambridge it will be carried.'[36] But the Cambridge Union did not pass judgment on its younger sister's decision. The nearest it came was when one wag suggested it debate the merits of fighting for 'King & Harper', a garage which neighboured the Union.

The Oxford controversy did have the effect of heightening outside interest in the two Unions' debates in the rest of the decade. When the Union debated conscription in April 1939, pictures of the debate were wired to London and appeared in the following day's *Daily Express*. At that debate, Captain Basil Liddell Hart 'expressed the view that the Union was a more appropriate place to debate this subject than the Houses of Lords or Commons'.[37] His argument – that the fate of youth was being decided by politicians who were mostly too old to have fought in the last war – was a popular one with Union members, who supported him and voted against conscription by 204 to 144. The result so angered Churchill that he came to Cambridge to address a meeting in the Corn Exchange the following month 'specifically to counter the Union vote against conscription'.[38] The debate had been held at the same time that the Military Training Bill was going through Parliament. Cambridge rejected the motion on the Tuesday, the day before the debate in Parliament; on the Thursday, the night of the vote in the Commons, the same topic was debated at Oxford, where it was approved, much to Cambridge's amusement. It also amused Leo Amery, who had lost the Cambridge debate: when Liddell Hart reprised his speech at Oxford two days later, one of the undergraduates who beat him was Amery's son, Julian.[39]

When war broke out shortly before the beginning of Michaelmas Term 1939, the Union was much better prepared than it had been at the outbreak of the First World War. At a standing committee meeting on 11 October chaired by the Vice-President, E.H. Ades, it was decided to suspend the usual election of officers. Most undergraduates had been put on the reserve by the Joint Recruiting Bureau, and told to wait at the University and join the Officers' Training Corps until they were sent for. With so many thinking that they would be called up imminently, it was felt that it would be disruptive to keep changing officers during the term. So a committee of management was appointed to carry on the activities of the Society as far as possible during the period of the war. It was decided that this should include the senior members – the Treasurer, Librarian and Steward – and that the other half of its members should be elected from those undergraduates in residence. This was approved at a private business meeting five days later.

The committee immediately set about preparing the Society for the days ahead. Anticipating the arrival of large numbers of outsiders in Cambridge, it decided to offer temporary membership to members of other universities while they were resident in the town (as 2,000 from the LSE were) and to officers and cadets stationed nearby as had been the case during the last war. The Union building was made ready too. Sydney Elwood was given the task of organising the blacking-out of the windows. Dark paper was pasted over the glass panes in the debating chamber, and large sheets of corrugated cardboard were used to screen the large windows on the staircase, at the front of the building and in the bar.

Yet this was the period of the phoney war, and the Society's affairs soon returned largely to normal. Debates were resumed by 24 October and the dining room was reopened, serving *à la carte* meals in the evening. It had been agreed that a sub-committee be constituted to arrange and carry on debates each term, and that it appoint a chairman and secretary each term to preside over them. Thus Robert Pittam, paying tribute to the way in which Pieter Keuneman had conducted the business of the House over the trying recent weeks, took the chair at the debate on 14 November as chairman of the debates sub-committee. One of the early secretaries was J.F. Donaldson of Trinity, later Lord Donaldson, Master of the Rolls.

These first wartime debates were not unlike regular meetings of the Society. Over 350 members voted at the No Confidence debate at the start of Michaelmas, and again at a debate at the start of the Lent Term condemning the Soviet Union for its invasion of Finland. Well-known guest speakers still came up, such as the Postmaster General Major G.C. Tryon, Sir William Beveridge and Kingsley Martin. Yet despite these efforts to continue as normal, 'it somehow lacked the lustre' of a regular term – and things were about to take a turn for the worse.[40]

The beguiling comfort of the phoney war came to an abrupt end in the spring of 1940. Norway and Denmark were invaded, followed by Luxembourg, Holland and Belgium. At the end of June, France fell. In Cambridge, attendance at debates was dropping. Although most of the normal summer term frivolities were put on hold, the usual competition of fine weather and looming examinations diverted people away from the Union, and the number of members in residence was substantially lower than during peacetime. It became almost impossible to attract guest speakers up from London because of the growing drama of the war. Such was the background against which the chairman of debates for the Easter Term 1940, James Bottomley, put forward the motion for 21 May: 'This House would welcome the imminent overthrow of Western Civilisation'. The debate attracted a great deal of unfavourable attention. Sydney Elwood thought it was 'an unfortunate choice, but there was no doubt it was intended to be treated in a light-hearted manner'.[41] One of the people put down on the paper was Jimmy Edwards of St John's, a regular humorous speaker who became a household name as a comedian after the war, and the origins of two of the proposers – D.V.A.S. Amarasekara of Queens' and K.C. Lim of Jesus – suggest that it was intended as a jocular nod to the Society's members from Eastern civilisations. But this was the immediate run-up to Dunkirk (the evacuation began six days after the debate was to be held) and there was a nervous atmosphere.

It was also the middle of the exam period, and Bottomley had two three-hour Tripos papers the day before the debate. He came

CAMBRIDGE UNION SOCIETY

EASTER TERM, 1940

FIFTH DEBATE
On TUESDAY, 21st MAY, 1940
At 8.15 p.m.

" That this House welcomes the imminent overthrow of Western Civilisation."

Proposed by Mr. D. V. A. S. AMARASEKARA, Queens' College.

Opposed by Mr. E. G. GOLDREIN, Pembroke College.

Mr. K. C. LIM, Jesus College, will speak third.

Mr. J. K. O'N. EDWARDS, St. John's College, will speak fourth.

Mr. H. J. S. HENDERSON, Downing College, will speak fifth.

Mr. W. H. BEALE, Trinity College, will speak sixth.

For the AYES :	TELLERS	For the NOES :
Mr. F. E. R. Peach,		Mr. J. Singh,
Emmanuel College.		Trinity College.

Trinity College,	J. R. A. BOTTOMLEY,
15th May, 1940.	Chairman of Debates.

48

back to his rooms for a brief lunch between them to find notes waiting for him from the Vice-Chancellor, the senior proctor and his tutor, all demanding his presence at eleven o'clock that morning. He went hurriedly to see his tutor, who told him that some dons had decided that the debate 'was a pro-German thing … and were organising various rugger clubs, I suppose, to bust the place up'.[42] His tutor said that he would speak to the Vice-Chancellor and arrange a meeting for Bottomley with the senior proctor for after his afternoon paper. On his way to the examination, Bottomley called in at the Union and told Stanley Brown, the chief clerk, to announce that the debate had been cancelled. He did not want the proctors to impose pre-censorship for all Union debates, and 'it seemed to me that we needed a breathing space to decide how to handle all this'. The tactic worked: at his meeting with the proctors later that afternoon he was able to pull 'a bit of a rug from under their feet' by saying that the debate had already been cancelled. But the proctors were not appeased: one of the pro-proctors at the meeting started suggesting that the Union's activities sounded rather seditious. Bottomley, outnumbered at this meeting by at least four proctors and pro-proctors, said 'that it seemed to me that the whole thing was perfectly ridiculous and that much the best thing was for us to suspend debates until people's nerves were not quite so much on edge as they were at this moment'. Bottomley had not had a chance to consult with the rest of the debates sub-committee, but was keen not to surrender any of the ground that had been established in the Union's disputes with the University in the past. He left the meeting without any rule being imposed upon the Society: having said that debating would be suspended for the rest of the time for which he was responsible, he left it open for 'other people to decide later how to proceed' – and guaranteed 'that they would proceed from the existing position of freedom'.

The rest of the sub-committee, however, did not view this outcome with the same sense of triumph. Its membership, which had a strong left-wing element, 'thought that we ought to fight for freedom and immolate ourselves – or, anyhow, me as chairman – on the altar of free speech'. It was only with the backing of the management committee's senior members that Bottomley was able to win backing for his approach. Thus after its meeting on 27 May a notice was posted on the Society's boards, signed by Pittam, who was now chairman of the management committee, and Bottomley, as chairman of debates:

> In view of the difficulties of the present situation no further debates shall be held this term.

Looking back, Sir James Bottomley sees two things that he thought important at the time.

> The first thing was the immediate business of sorting the thing out when I was just about to join the army and might well go off and get killed … why the hell should I worry about this bloody nonsense here in Cambridge? … But the other thing was, I think, a genuine feeling that I was against accepting or provoking pre-censorship – that was a thing we ought to aim to preserve.

Certainly, a letter he received from the senior proctor once the matter was over contained the strong implication that the Union maintained the upper hand. The senior proctor wrote 'that it would be very helpful on the part of the Union Society' if they would inform his successor 'when they propose to begin debates again', and that 'he would appreciate the courtesy' of being informed of the subject of the debate in advance.[43]

As promised, no debates were held for the rest of that term. Despite the interruption on the day of his Tripos exams, Bottomley got a first in classics. He was called up in July 1940, so did not return to Cambridge for a third year. He was shot through the lungs and had most of his lower jaw blown off in Normandy in August 1944, but survived. After the war he joined the diplomatic service, rising to become Ambassador to South Africa, 1973–6.

By the beginning of the new academic year, the management committee was keen to resume debating. The number of undergraduates in residence was 2,000 lower than it had been two years earlier and the committee wanted to revive interest in the Society. It therefore resolved, at its meeting on 15 October 1940, to hold debates on Sunday afternoons, starting with a motion 'That this House believes the Ministry of Information'. As entreated by the old senior proctor, Stanley Brown wrote to his successor, C.T. Seltman of Queens', informing him of this decision. The Union was not seeking proctorial approval, but said that it 'would be glad to know the views of the University authorities on this experiment'.[44] Seltman replied immediately. The suggested motion, he said, clearly verged on the political 'and therefore leads the debaters into danger from the Law'. The proctors had understood from Mr Bottomley that debates would be suspended for the duration of the war, and they would regard it 'as good sense and good taste on the part of the Union Society' if this were the case. He did not deny the freedom of the Union to hold a debate anyway – but said that it would have to be a closed debate with no press representation in order to avoid prosecutions.[45] On this advice, the committee dropped its plans to resume debates at a meeting the following week.

A number of members were unhappy with this decision, and a petition of 152 signatures was handed in calling for it to be reversed (although the committee noted that 79 of the names were found to be non-members, two were duplicates, three were 'posted' members, one had resigned and ten had not paid their subscriptions). But there was growing pressure from within the management committee, particularly from two left-wing members who were appointed to it at the end of November 1940. One of these was John Maynard Smith, who had joined the Communist party after he left Eton. In defiance of the party's line he had volunteered for war service, but was rejected because of poor eyesight and told to finish his degree in engineering; he then helped the war effort in military aircraft design from 1942. After the war he switched to biology, becoming a devoted follower of his fellow Old Etonian and communist J.B.S. Haldane;

he went on to become one of the leading evolutionary biologists of the twentieth century. The other was the 'unquenchable and highly visible' Raymond Williams, who came up to Trinity on a state scholarship from Abergavenny Grammar School.[46] Like Maynard Smith, Williams joined the Communist party at Trinity, where he read English. He kept his Marxist views throughout his long academic career as a literary critic and cultural theorist, returning to Cambridge as a Fellow of Jesus in 1961, and becoming a professor of drama.

Because of this disgruntlement, the Librarian, Lionel Elvin, and the Steward, Dr E.M. Wilson, approached the senior proctor to discuss the situation. After their meeting with him on 23 November, the management committee proposed new arrangements for the resumption of debates. The motions would be non-political, and made known in advance to the senior proctor and the regional commissioner (these were wartime administrators delegated wide powers from the Crown in the event of enemy invasion – in East Anglia's case Sir Will Spens, the Master of Corpus). Non-members and guests would not be admitted. Now that an arrangement which met with the approval of both the Union and the University authorities had been found, the way was cleared for debates to continue from the start of Lent 1941. Five debates were held that term, with Maynard Smith in the chair, but attendance was disappointing: only 98 members voted in total.[47]

Maynard Smith and Williams maintained that part of the reason for this poor attendance was the lack of political motions, so proposed to the management committee on 12 February that political topics be included among those sent to the senior proctor. The vote was split evenly between the senior and junior members on the committee, so Dr Wilson suggested that Maynard Smith approach the senior proctor about it. This he did, but the proctors could not see their way to approving any change in the Union's policy.[48] So debates ceased once again.

Here the picture becomes less clear. Elwood says that no debates were held in the Easter or Michaelmas terms of 1941 – but he was not in Cambridge at this time, having been called up to the RAF.[49]

Percy Cradock's list of officers says that debates were suspended – but Raymond Williams, writing in the late 1970s, stated clearly that he was elected chairman of debates in Easter 1941.[50] It is possible that they are all right – that Williams was elected chairman of the debates sub-committee in order to continue the struggle to resume debates, but that none were held – or that some debates were held secretly so as to escape the notice of the proctors.

Whatever happened in the Easter Term, there was a 'strong desire for the resumption of debates' by Michaelmas 1941.[51] By now there was another new senior proctor, J. Stevenson of St John's. The management committee wrote to him at the end of November to see if he had any objection to the resumption of debates on Tuesday evenings from the beginning of the new year. They suggested a programme of eight debates for Union members only. The new proctors saw 'no objection' to the resumption of debates: indeed, Stevenson wrote, 'I should rather say that we are glad that the Management Committee considers that it is now possible to consider restarting this activity'. He said that the list of proposed motions need only be 'reported', not 'submitted' to him in advance. His only proviso was that 'the choice of subject should not leave any loophole for the press or for enemy agents to make capital out of the fact that a certain subject has been proposed for debate'.[52]

So eight debates were held in Lent and Easter 1942, with H.B. Dunkerley of King's in the chair. With more interesting motions – for instance 'That Britain has yet to face full implications of total war' – they were much better attended. So Bottomley's hope, 'that people would eventually recover their nerve and common sense could prevail and things go ambling along as they always had done', seemed to have been fulfilled.[53]

———

While the rows went on regarding debates, the Union was far from empty. Its building was commandeered for use early on in the war. The no. 2 Initial Training Wing of the RAF had been established in Cambridge, with its headquarters in Jesus College. The

Union was called upon to provide classrooms for the teaching of navigation. Soon the Society's use of its premises became largely confined to the smoking room, dining room and shared use of the chamber. The bar lounge became a NAAFI, although a small bar for members was set up at one end of the room. The basement under what was then the dining room was converted into a public air raid shelter, its easy access from Round Church Street making it very suitable for this purpose.

Towards the end of 1940, a local committee was established to provide entertainment for the forces stationed in and around Cambridge. The Union readily agreed to provide facilities for tea, dancing and cocktails, and became the regular host to the Officers' Sunday Club.

If members thought that the building's direct connection to the war would be limited to such frivolous matters, then they were abruptly disabused of the notion. Cambridge was largely spared the depredations of aerial bombardment – supposedly because of a *quid pro quo* arrangement with Heidelberg, another historic university city – but shortly after three o'clock in the morning of 28 July 1942 a German aircraft, flying in from the south-east at a height of under 100 feet, dropped eight high explosive and three incendiary bombs on the town. A further three high explosives failed to detonate, but the damage was considerable: ten buildings were demolished or ruined, and over 100 properties were damaged to a lesser extent.[54] One bomb flung a 2 lb cobblestone nearly half a mile and lifted a steel girder some distance, embedding it in a wall. One of the main casualties was the Union – the only building connected to the University which received a direct hit during the war. One of the high explosives and several firebombs hit the library, smashing an enormous hole in the roof and starting a huge blaze. The weight of falling masonry ripped a hole in the floor, exposing the reference room below. Some of the valuable Erskine Allon and Fairfax Rhodes bequests were lost, but the steel stacks protected the Union's 50,000 volumes from most of the damage. The fire service eventually brought the flames under control, but so much water was pumped into the upper storeys that it was still trickling down to the ground floor the next morning.[55] Many of the windows at that end of the building were blown out. Nearby buildings were luckier and escaped largely unscathed: the Round Church suffered only a broken window, and the outer wall of Whewell's Court in Trinity was peppered by shrapnel scars which can still be seen today.

Initially, wartime censorship meant that the damage to the Union went unreported. The only mention of the raid that month was a reference to 'the dining room and library of a well-known assembly place' in an 'East Anglian town'.[56] But reports were carried in the national press at the end of August. Eleven people had been injured in the raid and three killed – including an active member of the Union, Ephraim 'Ram' Nahum, a first-class natural sciences graduate who was 'by general consent, the ablest of all communist student leaders' of Hobsbawm's generation.[57] Within seven months, it claimed another victim. Stanley Brown was in the cellar on the night of the air raid. Aged 67, he had recently completed 39 years' service as chief clerk, having joined the Society as a junior clerk in 1892. He was one of the first on the scene, helping wardens and fire-watchers to tackle the blaze while still wearing his slippers. He had been suffering from asthma for some years and it was clear that the shock of the bomb and the damage to the building upset him more than he cared to admit. His asthma attacks became more frequent, and he was confined to his bed periodically over the winter of 1942–3. He was in the Union office on 11 February and seemed in good health during the rest of that week. But on St Valentine's Day, a Sunday, he suffered a severe attack and fell into a state of unconsciousness from which he did not recover. He died on the morning of 16 February 1943. It was a huge loss to the Society, particularly coming at one of its lowest ebbs. For four decades, Brown had *been* the Union: running its staff and building, keeping its records, and making sure the undergraduate officers stayed on the straight and narrow. He was a permanent fixture of the Society to almost every living member. The House stood in silence to express its deep regret before the next debate. An annuity was purchased for Brown's widow; his successor as chief clerk was Fred Curzon, his assistant of almost 46 years.

A year after Stanley Brown's death, in March 1944, the 30th Army Corps took complete possession of the Union building for a week. All the staff were sent away on a week's leave apart from Curzon, who was confined to his office and allowed no communication with the rest of the building.[58] A section of soldiers came, all doors to the basement were securely fastened, and sentries with Bren guns were posted round the building. Two anti-aircraft guns were installed on Midsummer Common a short distance away.[59] This was Operation 'Conqueror' – the planning exercise for another operation, 'Overlord', which was shortly to be launched. It began ten weeks later, and is better known today as the D-Day landings.

Because of the great secrecy of the operation, the exact details are still unclear. But it seems that the Union was one of a handful of buildings in the University used to plan the landings on large-scale models of the Normandy beaches. One of the other locations was St John's College, and one of the best attempts to uncover the details of the operation was made in an article for the college magazine by the Master, the Revd J.S. Boys Smith.[60] As part of the research for that article, 'extensive inquiries' were made by Harry Hinsley, but even he – a former Bletchley Park codebreaker who later wrote the official history of wartime intelligence – yielded little. The best information he could elicit was a note from General G.C. Bucknall, who commanded the 30th Corps, dated September 1967. According to Bucknall, the main study room was based in St John's, but 'there were also a number of study rooms for all formations'. Boys Smith adds in a footnote that 'Professor C.D. Broad and Mr A.S.F. Gow [both longstanding Fellows of Trinity] tell me that the Trinity College Lecture Rooms and the Union Society were used'.[61]

The operation lasted four days from 28 to 31 March, after which the men and material used were taken away with the same secrecy, and no trace of their work was left behind. We should be sceptical about some of the more dramatic details of the operation which emerged in post-war articles in the national press, through which the

Union was seeking publicity for its fundraising appeal.[62] Not least among these details was the suggestion that Generals Montgomery and Eisenhower visited the models in person. This was reported in *The Times* and elsewhere after the war, but was 'denied officially some years later'.[63] Wilfred Stuart, the chief reporter of the *Cambridge Daily News* during the war, wrote in 1948 that he had 'good reason to believe that in fact other duties prevented their personal participation'.*

It is difficult to know for certain whether Montgomery and Eisenhower were in attendance – but we should not let this overshadow the certain fact that the Union made a significant contribution to the preparations for the D-Day landings. It was just one of many contributions that the Society and its members made to the national effort. Some were involved in other intelligence work – such as Terry Leathem (President, Lent 1933), who was an intelligence officer in the BEF in Norway, then worked at Bletchley Park, or Charles Fletcher-Cooke (President, Lent 1936) who served in naval intelligence. Many others served in the armed forces and, once again, the Union shared in the bloodshed. A number of former officers in addition to Hague and Simonds lost their lives. Eddie Ades, the Vice-President who had proposed the suspension of officerships in 1939, was killed in action as a Desert Rat in Libya. Anthony Blackwell, President in Michaelmas 1933, became a second lieutenant but was killed by a premature explosion in his gun while still in England. Gervase Stewart, chairman of debates in Lent 1940, was killed in a mid-air explosion over the Caribbean in 1941.

---

* *Cambridge Daily News*, Diamond Jubilee Supplement, May 1948. The *Sunday Times* of 9 December 1945 makes the more credible suggestion that Montgomery and Eisenhower visited the model rooms but 'did not stay in Cambridge'. Eisenhower's wartime papers reveal that he was in London throughout the period, making an 'inspection trip' on 28 March and holding meetings in his Bushy Park headquarters throughout the rest of the period in question. The only possibilities are the afternoons of 30 and 31 March, when he was 'out of the office during the afternoon', but no further details are given (see A.D. Chandler (ed.), *The Papers of Dwight David Eisenhower: The War Years, vol. V* (Baltimore/London: The Johns Hopkins Press, 1970), pp. 148–9).

The Normandy landings to which the Union had made its small contribution marked a turning point in the war, and prospects for the future began to look much brighter. Debates had already regained some of their vitality – 'one of the best attended and most exhilarating debates' of the war was one on the role of public schools held under the chairmanship of Neville Sandelson, later a Labour MP and long-standing rebel until his defection to the SDP.[64] At the end of Lent 1943 the proctors decided, in answer to an application by Sandelson's predecessor R.S. Taylor, to remove all existing restrictions on debates. The senior proctor told the student press he had 'no desire to interfere with the freedom of the Society' and would impose 'only those conditions incumbent on the community in general'.[65] In May 1944, the committee of management felt able to recommend a return to the normal election of officers from the following term. Thus Cyril Salmon of Trinity Hall, as the last chairman of debates, was heavily responsible for the transition from the emergency to the normal constitution – perhaps putting into use some of the legal skills he would later display as a circuit judge.

The first elections for more than five years were held on 26 October 1944, three days after the first debate of term. Peter Goldman, later the protégé of Rab Butler, was elected as the first post-war President. He assumed office on 30 October. The following day, the RAF ended their occupation of the building. Things were returning to normal. But with annual recruitment down by three quarters, a four-figure overdraft and roofing felt barely covering the damage to the library and rooms below, the new officers had good reason not to feel too jubilant.

1945–50:
Post-war Regeneration

The second President after the return to the peacetime constitution was Stanley Clement Davies in Lent 1945 – whose father, 'an occasional speaker' before the war, would become leader of the Liberal party later that year.[1] Stanley was the only surviving of four children, as his two brothers and sister had died within the space of three years after the outbreak of the war – one as a result of natural causes related to his epilepsy, the others in separate accidents while on active service. Each of them was just 24 years old at the time of their death. Friends of the family remember Stanley telling them of the sigh of relief he breathed when he reached the age of 25.[2]

As the first Vice-President to write a termly report since 1939, Clement Davies was able to record the revival of some of the Union's social functions. 'The smoking-room', he noted, had 'been re-opened for the benefit of members' – while the dining room, though not yet serving meals again, 'is being used for the purpose of enabling members to bring their friends to play ping-pong on week-days and their partners to dance and have tea on Thursday afternoons.' By VE Day, which was declared during Easter Term 1945, the blackout boards were removed and, 'after almost six years of stygian gloom', the Vice-President for that term was pleased to report that 'the light of day once more flows into the Debating Hall'.

But the Union had some serious challenges to address. Its resident membership was some 2,000 fewer in 1944 than it had been in

1938, and very few new members had signed up during the war. During the whole of the academic year 1940–41, only 61 new members had been enrolled. This had a profound impact on the Society's finances. In June 1939, the Union had had a bank balance of £555 and investments which were valued at £2,155; by June 1945, with a daunting list of repair work to carry out, the Society faced an overdraft of £8,379 and had been forced to cash in all its investments. There was little option but to restore the subscription fees to their peacetime rate immediately. Fortunately, the great increase in the number of undergraduates in Michaelmas 1945 – some 3,110 were back in residence – resulted in 'a gratifying intake of new members'. The President for that term, Martin Frankel of Peterhouse, organised a full programme of seven debates – six of them on political motions, perhaps making up for the wartime proctorial restrictions.

The Union was able to claim £438 16s 6d from the War Damage Commission for repairs and a similar amount from the RAF for the dilapidation caused by its use of the Society's buildings. But neither this nor the increase in new memberships was enough to cover its debts and fund the rebuilding work which had to be undertaken. It was therefore decided at a meeting of the standing committee and the trustees in October 1945 that a restoration appeal should be launched. An admirably phrased letter was composed and dispatched to all life members, and the services of distinguished alumni were called in. Rab Butler wrote a long article highlighting the appeal in the *Sunday Times*. The results were touching: over £3,000 was raised by the end of the academic year. There was further improvement at the start of the next one when more than 1,000 new members were recruited in Michaelmas 1946. The lucky thousandth was warmly welcomed with a drink on the House.

By the end of 1946, then, the Union's financial position had improved considerably. The overdraft of £8,000 was transformed into a healthier balance of about £1,000. This was particularly welcome news to David Hardman, the Union's hard-working Treasurer. Already a councillor and justice of the peace in Cambridge, he had been elected MP for Darlington in the 1945 election, but continued to serve the Society until it was back in the black. At the end of this term he felt able to step down to devote himself to his new role as parliamentary secretary in the Ministry of Education. His successor as Treasurer was the senior tutor of Clare, N.G.L. Hammond. A Greek scholar, Hammond had been sent to Greece during the war as a member of the Special Operations Executive. Escaping after the German invasion in 1941, he was parachuted back into Thessaly in 1943 to encourage the Greek resistance forces. He reached the rank of lieutenant colonel, was mentioned twice in dispatches and was awarded the DSO.

Though the Union's deficit had been largely remedied, Hammond was cautious about the state of its finances as he took them over. The restoration fund was meant for repairs, not repaying the overdraft – and those repairs were still needed. The roof, damaged in the air raid in 1942, was finally retiled at the end of 1945, and plenty of other things were restored even more slowly. Staff shortages meant that the dining room could not be reopened until October 1946 and, despite the celebratory lunch held to mark its return, food was still rationed and monthly reports of the number of meals and hot drinks it served had to be made to the local Food Office. The dilapidation to the squash courts and bar caused by RAF occupation could not be made good until Lent 1947 because of a lack of materials. One of the courts was reopened that term and the 'President's Racquet' tournament was brought back to herald its return. At the suggestion of Sydney Elwood, back in the Union's employment after five years in the RAF (where he had become a flight lieutenant and radar operator), the bar was enlarged when the repair works were carried out. He shrewdly pointed out that the old alcove bar would prove too small to satisfy the requirements of a new generation of undergraduates who had been accustomed to standing around the mess bar while serving in the armed forces.

Most delayed of all were the repairs to the library. Though it had been in general use since the debris from the air raid had been cleared, none of the much-needed structural repairs could be made until the Union had been granted a permit by the Ministry of Works. The new Librarian, Sydney Smith of St Catharine's, reported that the appearance of the library put many members off using it, as 'only the most bold appear to risk a passage across the undulating floor'. The licence to carry out the most significant repairs to the Union was not granted until Easter 1949. The work was done over the long vacation and completed in time for the start of the new academic year. *Varsity*, covering the first debate of Michaelmas 1949, was pleased to report: 'All was new and shiny at the Union on Tuesday night. The brown stains and cracks and watermarks which had disfigured the ceiling were gone. The walls had lost their sere and yellow look. Even the ponderous brown lamp-shades had airy white successors.'[3] Ten years after the war had disrupted the smooth running of the Society, things could finally be said to have returned to something resembling normality.

A more pleasant post-war task was the bestowal of honorary membership on prominent leaders of the armed forces, as the Union had done after the First World War. This was done at a special private business meeting on 31 January 1946. But one was singled out for special honouring – a former member of the Union's standing committee, Admiral the Viscount Mountbatten of Burma. Officers had called upon him when he came to Cambridge to receive an honorary doctorate, and he agreed to accept his honorary membership of the Union in person. The occasion was a youth vs. age debate – 'That this House would like to go back to Methuselah' – on 19 November 1946. The turnout was the largest the Union had seen since the last time Mountbatten had spoken – as an undergraduate in February 1920. This had evidently been anticipated as, for the first time, microphones were installed in the chamber and the speeches were relayed by loudspeaker to the clubroom and bar, both of which were filled. The experiment was a successful one, and has been repeated many times since. Those listening in, however, were not allowed to vote, hence the lower division figures (Mountbatten won soundly, defeating the motion 488 to 230).

As Viscount Mountbatten entered the chamber wearing the gown of a Doctor of Literature over his naval uniform, he was greeted with loud applause. There was a piece of stage-managed constitutional wrangling when, before the debate commenced, the President, Granger Boston, called upon the Vice-President, Bill Richmond, to propose Mountbatten's election as an honorary member. Richmond, on a point of order, pointed out that the noble lord was already a life member. The President, unperturbed, said this was clearly a case where he could exercise his powers of summary expulsion and proceeded to do so, leaving Mountbatten free to be readmitted to the Society as an honorary member. Expressing his thanks, Lord Mountbatten presented the Society with a ceremonial samurai sword. To great cheers, he told the House: 'When I was here there was a tendency for hon. members to speak rather too long, so I have brought here a Japanese sword for you, Mr President, to cut their speeches shorter.'[4]

———•———

For all the apparent return to normality, the Cambridge of the late 1940s was a different place to the Cambridge which had existed before the war. Although some old faces came back up to resume their interrupted studies, the undergraduate body looked markedly different. In 1946, 90 per cent of places were filled by ex-servicemen.[5] For one thing, this meant a wide variation in age between those returning from service and those coming up straight from school. For instance, Bill Richmond, President in Lent 1947, was 28 – ten years older than the freshmen of that year – and George Pattison, a former trooper who was President in Lent 1949, was 30. Known as Pat, he was also married and lived not in Cambridge, but in a small village outside the town. The new undergraduate body was also drawn from a slightly wider social base as some ex-servicemen seized the opportunity of a university place. Leonard Miall, a socialist President before the war, had said during a debate in January 1939 – 'That Cambridge is not what it was' – that 'there will come a time when Cambridge will be peopled by people for whom a University education will be a privilege, and not a happy waste of time'.[6] Now, his prediction seemed to have come true. Covering the No Confidence debate of Michaelmas 1947, the *Varsity* reviewer thought that:

> Unquestionably the most impressive speech of the evening was made by G. Probert, St Catharine's, who comes from Grimethorpe, and said that he was the only member of his family not working in the pits. Probert held the attention of an absorbed House whilst he described the conditions under which the miners worked, and spoke bitterly of those who from a comfortable distance urged a higher output.[7]

But despite the presence of such undergraduates as Probert, and despite the Labour landslide in the general election of 1945, Union members leaned strongly towards the Conservatives in the immediate post-war years. In one of the earliest political debates after the war on 4 June 1945, Peter Goldman moved a motion welcoming the return to power of Churchill's caretaker government at the coming general election. He spoke with Walter Elliot MP against J.B. Priestley, who was standing as an Independent Progressive candidate for Cambridge University, and Union members proved themselves out of touch with the tide of public opinion by narrowly passing the motion by 69 votes to 63. In fact, the Union voted against the Attlee government at each of the seven No Confidence debates held during its existence. At the first such debate, on 12 November 1945 – just four months in to the new administration – the anti-government majority was 72. On three occasions – in 1947, 1949 and 1951 – it was over 300.

The government's defeats were not for want of prominent advocates. Over 900 members came to see Herbert Morrison, as Lord President of the Council, debate on 15 October 1946. The doors to the Union had to be shut a quarter of an hour before the debate because of the great number wanting to enter: 'At one time there was something resembling a scrum in the doorway of the chamber, as a crowd outside tried to get in,' reported the *Cambridge Daily News*. 'Mr Morrison himself had to push his way through to get to his seat, and found himself stepping over those seated over the floor.'[8] The motion Morrison had come to oppose – 'That this House deprecates the increasing tendency of the State to interfere in economic affairs' – took the place of the traditional No Confidence debate as the first debate of term, and had been agreed with him in advance. This had obviously not been made known to everyone on his side of the House, as the *Daily Mail* mirthfully reported. The Vice-President, Bill Richmond, had proposed the motion, and J. Murray Hunter of Clare had risen to reply:

> 'This motion seems to me to have been drafted by an elderly and dyspeptic civil servant,' began Mr Hunter.
>
> The President sharply rang his bell and, rising to his feet, said: 'I should like to point out that this motion was drafted by Mr Morrison himself.'
>
> Immediately the sedate debate was interrupted by peals of laughter, which continued for several minutes.[9]

But even though Morrison had helped to pick the motion he hoped to overturn, it was carried by 475 votes to 448.

The following year, 1947, was a year of further defeats for the left. In January, a motion deploring 'the growing tyranny of the trade unions' was passed by 256 votes to 75 – a result which was seized upon by the *Daily Express* and the *Daily Mail*, the latter announcing that 'Cambridge slapped the trade unions last night, and it was a firm, well-planted slap'.[10] In February, the House decided that it 'would not have voted for the Transport Bill [which proposed the nationalisation of the railways and other forms of transport] on its second reading' and in May was of the opinion that 'the pace of nationalisation is ruining Parliament as a legislature'.

There were two No Confidence debates that year: the first was held on 11 March. It was proposed by the retiring President, Bill Richmond, a firm Conservative. Richmond had come up to Trinity in 1938 and joined the RNVR as a midshipman during the war – appropriately, as his father was Admiral Sir Herbert Richmond, Master of Downing. Richmond had risen to the rank of lieutenant before returning to his studies at Cambridge. He was also active in the University Conservative Association and had been elected a town councillor in Cambridge – the first undergraduate, it seems, to have done so. He was joined for his retirement debate by Lord Tweedsmuir – or John Buchan, an ex-President of the Oxford Union. His opponents included the current Treasurer of the Oxford Union, Tony Benn, and Lord Pakenham, the Under-Secretary of State for War, who turned up in full tails. The President explained this attire to the House: 'Lord Pakenham caught a late train after attending a Territorial review. He hoped to change coming down – but was unable to do so, owing to the presence of a great many ladies in the carriage.'[11]

Richmond carried his motion by 266 to 217. There was a much larger vote of no confidence in Michaelmas Term. In a three-and-a-half hour debate, the food minister, John Strachey, tried to defend the government to a packed House. The Secretary, David Price, a former guardsman and intelligence officer known as 'Mufti' for his activities in the Middle East – and later a long-serving Conservative MP for Eastleigh – opened for the proposition, roundly condemning the government as 'the worst in the history of this country'. He was opposed by Peter Shore of King's, the future Labour Cabinet minister. It was a lively debate, as *Varsity* reported: 'accusation and counter accusation were hurled backwards and forwards across the House with bitterness and venom … At one moment, when Mr Strachey had alleged that the second world war was the fruit of Conservative policy, the din of boos, hisses and counter-cheers grew so loud and prolonged that the President had to intervene to restore order'.[12] What a change this was from the series of defeats inflicted by Union members on the Chamberlain government before the war.

The motion was carried by a massive 624 to 242 – 'almost inconceivable to those who knew the undergraduates of the inter-war years,' exclaimed the *Economist*.[13]

There was brief respite for the government in June 1947, when the attendance of the Chancellor of the Exchequer, Hugh Dalton, persuaded the House to break from its anti-government trend. Dalton had been a 'dominating figure' at the Union in his undergraduate days, although his political views and 'gift for making people hostile to him' denied him election beyond the standing committee: he was defeated three times for the secretaryship.[14] But the man whom *Granta* had dubbed 'Comrade Hugh' knew how to win a Union debate: 'If this House has "no confidence in the economic and financial policy of the present Government", I am quite sure the country at large will have no confidence in the judgment of this House,' he said.[15] His tactics resulted in a rare eight-vote majority for the government. But the year ended with further anti-government votes. In Michaelmas, the Union did not approve of the proposed reform of the House of Lords in what was to become the 1949 Parliament Act, nor the imperial policy of His Majesty's government.

In Lent 1948, the Union decided that 'Socialism today provides insufficient incentive to work' by a majority of 99. Percy Cradock, reviewing the debate, spotted young talent in the form of the parliamentary secretary to the Ministry of Transport, Mr L.J. Callaghan MP. 'Evidently one on whom the cares of office sit lightly, he was disposed at the outset to be jovial,' Cradock wrote of the future Prime Minister. His contribution to the debate was well received: 'The speech was a high example of debating skill, and he was wildly acclaimed as he sat down.'[16]

The Secretary that term was Clyde Hewlett, a lieutenant in the Royal Marines during the war. His father had been a Tory MP in Manchester, but had lost his seat in the 1945 landslide. Although he did not follow his father into Parliament, Hewlett was a staunch Conservative himself – as CUCA chairman, a member of Manchester City Council, and eventually President of the National Union of the

Conservative party. But he would become better known as an industrialist, specifically as managing director and chairman of Anchor Chemical Company. Also active in many charities, he was knighted in 1964 and raised to the peerage in 1972. His name is still well known in the Union for the Lord Hewlett debating competition, held annually to determine the best debater in the Union. Lord Hewlett first presented his debating trophy in Lent 1973, and the competition continues to this day. His early route to Union office was largely by chance: in a by-election for a vacant place on the standing committee, he was tied with Peter Shore and, instead of holding another election, the men agreed to decide the result by a toss-up. Hewlett won, but Shore had his revenge the following term when he was elected to the standing committee and Hewlett failed to win re-election. The two both ran for Secretary the following term, with three other candidates. Shore was ahead on the first ballot by 124 to 116, but the transfer of the other candidates' votes increased Hewlett's tally to 182 and Shore's to just 172. Thus elected, Hewlett's transition to Vice-President and President in the following two terms was relatively smooth, while Shore never became an officer. Hewlett perhaps had extra reason to be thankful for his continued involvement in the Union. He proposed to his wife in the gallery of the chamber, where she sat frequently as a visitor at debates.

For his final debate as President, Hewlett chose to oppose a motion considering 'that the return of a Labour Government in 1950 will assure the prosperity of Great Britain'. Two ex-Presidents spoke for and against the government – Philip Noel-Baker and Selwyn Lloyd. *Varsity* was not surprised at the choice of debate: 'Anti-socialist motions are taken for granted in post-war Cambridge,' it said.[17] Nor was the result a surprise, although the margin was perhaps a little less expected: the motion was defeated by 436 to 173.

If anything, the Union hardened in its opinion in 1949, deciding in Lent that 'The Labour Party has betrayed the British electorate' and in Easter that it would welcome the return to power of the

Conservative party at the next general election. In Michaelmas, it even devoted two debates to discussing the titles of the parties' pre-election manifestos. In November, it threw out 'This House believes in *Labour Believes in Britain*' by 257 to 175; in December it affirmed that 'The Conservative way is *The Right Road for Britain*' by 299 to 206.

By the No Confidence debate of Michaelmas 1950 (won by 355 to 208), the *Cambridge Review* was growing weary of these predictable results:

> Following our long-established tradition, the motion was carried. One wonders what would happen were the Conservative Party to get into power on a small majority in Parliament. Would all those in the Union who now clamour for a Conservative government change sides and support the 'No Confidence' motion, or would they defeat it? Would it be tradition or Conservatism that won the day? A difficult question indeed.[18]

In fact, it was not a difficult question at all, and was soon answered. In 1951, Churchill did scrape home with a narrow victory, and the Union rallied to the new government immediately, defeating the No Confidence motions by majorities of well over 200 for the duration of his premiership.

It is perhaps surprising that the foregone conclusion of most political debate of this period did not put people off from attending. Indeed, party loyalty seems to have encouraged members to turn up in exceptionally large numbers: attendance at such debates rarely dipped below 500, and was regularly well above this. But there were plenty of people who criticised the partisan climate. Ian Lloyd, as Vice-President in Lent 1947, bemoaned 'the predominance of speakers at the present time who attempt to crowd all conceivable motions on to a party platform instead of at least attempting to treat each motion freely on its merits. It is both amusing and regrettable that before a recent debate one party is supposed to have debated for two hours what its "line" should be, thereby exhausting arguments which should have been heard inside rather than outside the House'. Lloyd, President the following term, was later a Conservative MP himself – but was never the most partisan of politicians. He was a somewhat distant figure and had to fight a reselection battle when his Portsmouth seat was redrawn as Havant in 1971–72. Nonetheless, he held his seat from 1964 to 1992, and was knighted in 1986. Having grown up in South Africa and served as a Spitfire pilot in the South African Air Force during the war, he was known as a staunch supporter of the South African government despite his opposition to apartheid.

It is not surprising that such a Tory-dominated period at the Union produced a number of Conservative MPs. In addition to Lloyd, Humphry Berkeley, David Price and Denzil Freeth passed from the President's chair to the Conservative benches in the House of Commons. Freeth, who had served with the RAF and was also CUCA chairman, sat as the MP for Basingstoke from 1955 to 1964. But in a sign that the two-party stranglehold on the Union was not as strong as it might at first seem, he became the first sitting Vice-President since 1905 not to win election directly to the presidency when he was beaten by Paul Curtis-Bennett of Christ's, a Liberal who had never made a paper speech, by almost 100 votes. Freeth had missed two weeks at the beginning of term while on the American debating tour, and Curtis-Bennett had stolen a march on him, managing to build a strange coalition of Liberals, socialists and 'the hunting-shooting-fishing brigade'. When the election came, recalls Freeth, 'all the extreme right wing of the University voted for him. And the socialists said, "hooray, we can beat the Tories", so they voted for him. And I was defeated.' But Freeth was not entirely vanquished: he decided 'straight away' to stay for a third year and fight back. But first, he says, 'I went round to two people I knew who had been unfaithful to me, and thanked them for all their efforts on my behalf ... They blushed slightly, but didn't refuse it.' He duly ran the following term, beating the new Vice-President, Percy Cradock, and becoming President for 'the very much better winter term' in Michaelmas 1949.[19]

Two other Presidents from the late 1940s made their names in other political spheres. Godfrey Carter had come up to study law at Magdalene before the war, but his studies were interrupted when he was called up to serve in the Rifle Brigade. He reached the rank of captain but was mercifully discharged after a severe leg wound, which led to many years of suffering and eventually ended in the amputation of the affected leg. President in Lent 1946, he went to the Bar before becoming a highly successful parliamentary counsel. He was the draftsman of what was then the longest Act ever passed in Parliament, the Companies Act 1985, for which he was appointed CBE. His successor as President, Jack Coventon, became a teacher. Active in the Labour party, he moved into local government administration and sat on the executive of the National Union of Teachers. As Vice-President, he successfully changed the laws of the Union to allow ladies 'of distinction' to be invited to speak on no more than one occasion a term. He therefore had the distinction of welcoming the first female speakers to the Union at his presidential debate on 11 June 1946.

Granger Boston, who took over from Coventon at that debate, served in the army early in the war, but a motorcycle accident led to his discharge. An athletic man, he was captain of squash, played Eton fives for the University and was secretary of the cricket club, for which he obtained his Blue. Like Coventon, he was also a parliamentary candidate, standing unsuccessfully for the Conservatives in 1950 and 1955. He was also a history teacher – at Oundle, Sandhurst and Clifton – and held business directorships. But a protracted period of ill health forced him to retire from his work. In February 1958, his stepson found him dead in his Harley Street flat with a shotgun beside him.[20]

Robert (later Sir Robin) Mackworth-Young was President in Michaelmas 1947. He served in the RAF, going to Normandy two days after D-Day to help plan tactical air cover. After a spell in the Foreign Office, he became a royal courtier as librarian of Windsor Castle and assistant keeper of the Queen's archives. During his term as President came another novelty for the Union: the debate on

Armistice Day 1947 – 'That this House considers that the Conservative Party makes a poor Opposition and would, if returned to office, make an even poorer Government' – was broadcast live on the BBC Third Programme. It was the first time a university debate had been broadcast, and Oxford showed their frustration at being beaten to it by Cambridge in a light-hearted exchange of telegrams before the debate. They wrote:

> The President and Committee of the Oxford Union Society send to the President and members of the Cambridge Union Society their cordial good wishes, and deem it proper that the second University finds its level in the Third Programme.

Cambridge replied magnanimously:

> The officers and members of the Cambridge Union Society thank the President and Committee of the Oxford Union Society for their kind message and look forward to hearing the Dark Blues in the Light Programme.

Unsurprisingly, the debate drew an enormous crowd, and every seat in the chamber was taken a full hour before the meeting began. The student speakers were R.G.M. Brown of Trinity in proposition and Humphry Berkeley of Pembroke in opposition. The two men were often pitted against one another in this era of Conservative-Socialist debates, and both ran for President at the end of term, Berkeley securing the victory. *Varsity* felt that 'it must have been a considerable ordeal for both of them' to speak not just to a packed House but also to a live radio audience, but reported that both rose to the occasion. Brown's speech, it said, 'for sheer oratorical skill has not been equalled this term' – and Berkeley's reply was 'a sparkling debating speech'. The student newspaper was less impressed with the invited guest statesmen, however: the Labour minister Lewis Silkin was evidently 'uncomfortable in the atmosphere of the Chamber' and Leo Amery's speech, which was considered good by those in the

House, 'was much less effective on air, simply because his voice, when detached from his person, sounds incredibly affected with its heavy Oxford drawl'. But 'the high spot' of the evening was Peter Shore's floor speech. It was a 'master move' to fade in the second part of the broadcast 'in the middle of a hullabaloo of cheers and jeers, out of which Shore's voice rose in a vigorous, provocative and exciting speech. It was the best piece of pure radio of the evening'.[21] To ensure accuracy in the division and to save time while on air, eight tellers were appointed: four in the gallery and four in the main lobby. They recorded another strong Conservative victory – the motion was defeated by 503 to 267.

Everyone was pleased with the way the debate had gone. George Barnes, head of the BBC Third Programme, wrote to Mackworth-Young to say: 'From our point of view it was very successful indeed, and I congratulate you on the way in which it was managed ... I am greatly encouraged by the success of this experiment, and I am certain that anyone who heard the broadcast will have enjoyed it.'[22]

The debate was also covered by the *Illustrated London News*, which photographed Union debates over the Michaelmas and Lent terms. As such, they followed Berkeley's passage to the presidency and his handover to David Price at the end of term, when a number of members voiced their discomfort at the flashing bulbs and intrusive cameras. But Berkeley probably liked the attention. Exempted from military service because of his asthma, he had come straight up to Cambridge from school, so was considerably younger than many of his Union peers. Having stayed beyond graduation in order to become President, he reinstated the tradition of having a photograph taken before the Change of Officers debate. While at Cambridge, he was also exposed as the author of a series of hoax letters to the great and the good purporting to come from 'H. Rochester Sneath', the headmaster of a fictional public school. When the hoax was revealed in the *News Review*, the pompous schoolmasters who had fallen for his prank were far from amused and M.S.D. Butler, Master of Pembroke, barred him from entering the college for two years. But his son, Rab Butler, took pity on Berkeley and arranged a job for him at Conservative Central Office. He also advised him to keep the letters and their replies safely: they were published a quarter of a century later in a compendium, *The Life and Death of Rochester Sneath*.

Although the son of a Liberal MP, Berkeley was a Conservative. He also served as chairman of CUCA and was elected Conservative MP for Lancaster in 1959. He was not to stay in the House of Commons for long, but his impact there was well noted. In his second term, he introduced a Private Member's Bill to decriminalise homosexual acts between consenting adults. The Bill won a second reading, but fell when Parliament was dissolved for the general election in 1966. Berkeley lost his seat at that election, and had 'no doubt' that it was on account of his Bill – the swing against him was twice the national average.[23] Berkeley stood out for his progressive views on a variety of issues – a year earlier he had seconded another private member's bill which suspended the death penalty for murder, and was at odds with the Tory party over Rhodesia, the sale of arms to South Africa, and the Vietnam war. In 1968 he left the party over its opposition to the Race Relations Bill. He joined again the following year, before breaking finally with it in 1970. He tried twice to re-enter the Commons, for Labour in 1974 and for the SDP in 1987, but did not succeed.

At the end of Easter Term 1948 Fred Curzon, the chief clerk, retired after 51 years' loyal service. He had started working for the Union in 1897 as a young man, when two of his brothers were up at the University. So young did he look when he began that the standing committee asked him to grow a moustache in the hope that it would make him look more mature.[24] He served in the army during the First World War, but suffered a severe foot wound which involved a long spell in hospital and his eventual discharge. He returned to the Union's service and had expected to retire in 1944, but had stepped into the breach when Stanley Brown died the previous year. Some three-quarters of an hour were taken up with tributes to Curzon at the final debate of that term, and he was presented with a silver tankard. Saying a few words in reply, the

Varsity reporter said he made 'the most charming, unaffected speech of the evening'.[25] Curzon was succeeded as chief clerk by Sydney Elwood, on a salary of £500 per annum, with Roland Thompson, a former outfitter at Ryder & Amies on King's Parade who had for some time been a junior clerk, as the new assistant clerk. Born in Cambridge, Elwood had gone straight into the Society's employment after leaving school at the age of fifteen. The Union coursed through his veins. He lived on site, in the chief clerk's house at the back of the building, and the Union was constantly under his watchful and affectionate eye. Also a keen rowing coach, his meticulously drawn charts showing the results of the college 'bumps' races still hang in the Union corridors.

The role of the chief clerk, as Tam Dalyell noted in an obituary of Elwood published in the *Independent* after his death in October 2001, is 'somewhat elastic':

> In theory, he is answerable to the student President and Committee. In practice, since Presidents are ephemeral creatures, lasting about seventeen weeks from election to the end of term when they pass the baton to a successor, the Chief Clerk keeps the Union on the rails. He does the accounts, organises the catering, places contracts for maintenance, and a host of other matters, besides dealing with day-to-day business. He is also a source of advice and experience.[26]

It is clear from the warm recollections of those whose Union careers he spanned that Sydney Elwood excelled himself in all this and more. Ken Clarke is full of admiration for the diplomatic support he offered: 'He remained calm, quiet, smiling, and reassuring in the face of the over-excited and hyperactive activities of the student debaters and politicians all around him.' Charles Lysaght states it quite simply: 'Mr Elwood saved us from our own follies.' He recalls Thompson fondly too: 'They reminded me of experienced barristers' clerks with callow young barristers, guiding them firmly but in tones of deference.'[27]

Unfortunately for both men, Thompson was stricken by pneumonia a couple of weeks into the new academic year, so Elwood's first term as chief clerk was a tough one. But he rose to the challenge admirably, even helping bring about the most notable debate of term. Éamon de Valera, the former Irish Taoiseach, was on a speaking tour of the UK to call for an end to partition, and Elwood spotted a letter in the *Daily Telegraph* suggesting that he be invited to debate the subject at Oxford or Cambridge. The new chief clerk lost no time in calling this to the attention of the President, Clyde Hewlett; he issued an invitation, which de Valera warmly accepted. Hewlett also invited Sir Basil Brooke, the Northern Irish Prime Minister, but he declined. The issue, he wrote back, had been established by Act of Parliament in 1920, and was not a matter for debate – at the Cambridge Union or elsewhere. But Conolly Gage, the MP for South Belfast and a graduate of Sidney Sussex, agreed to defend the Unionist cause instead. In the days before the debate, which was held on 16 November, Cambridge was flooded with leaflets by those opposing reunification. *Varsity* said the debate 'aroused more high feeling than any other for years'.[28] Many interruptions had been expected, but when the evening came, the packed House listened 'in a silence that was electric in its intensity'.[29]

It is difficult to recreate in print the atmosphere at any Union debate, let alone such occasions as de Valera's visit. Fortunately, in the gallery that evening was one of *Varsity*'s most talented reviewers. Percy Cradock had not yet become President, but he had marked himself out through his well-received speeches and regular reviews for the student press. As even the opening paragraph shows, his report of the de Valera debate was a masterful piece, exhibiting the linguistic flair and evident affection for the Union which characterised his student articles, his speeches in debate, and his own volume on the Society's history:

> The Irish debate; the Union in full regalia and extraordinary numbers, rather obviously proud of arousing questions in the N. Ireland Parliament, and of acquiring Mr de Valera; a little

conscious of its ignorance in matters purely Irish, but resolved
to pronounce on them as confidently as on the American elections or the Palestine issue or any other matters local or cosmic;
the flash bulbs; the crowds swaying in the lobby doors; the odd
unabashed photographer trespassing on consecrated grounds
and expelled amid execrations; the committee members
convivial with the conviviality that does credit to the Society's
wines and to their own powers of dissimulation; the House now
more ready to laugh at its own jokes than those of the speaker;
the unexpected silences and circumstance of the big Union
occasion.[30]

The debate attracted much attention outside Cambridge. It dominated the front page of the next morning's *Irish Press*, which was not
put off by the fact that the results of the division were not available at
the time of going to print: 'it was obvious that the motion would be
defeated by the mechanical two-to-one Tory majority', it said.[31] In
fact, de Valera's defeat was even heavier: on the motion 'That this
House would welcome the re-unification of Ireland', the Ayes won
236 votes; the Noes 542.

1950–55:

Golden Austerity

The decade after the Second World War appears to have been something of a golden age for the Union. The University was much larger – and not just compared to the lean wartime years. There was now a record number of undergraduates in Cambridge. In 1938–39, almost 5,400 had been in residence; by 1954–55, there were over 7,000.[1] The consequences of this expansion were clearly felt: every college has constructed new buildings since the war.[2] Moreover, the striking disparity in the ages of the undergraduates raised concerns about competition between ex-servicemen and more youthful freshmen, and fears that they would not rub along together. But Denzil Freeth recalls little tension: 'I think the answer was we were all so pleased to be in civilian life again and back at Cambridge – you were accepted for what you were. You weren't treated because you were older with any degree of deference'.[3]

In the Union, this new influx of members spawned an era of unusual competition – both in debates and in elections. The early 1950s produced some highly celebrated orators, and hard-fought elections which often divided along party lines.

One of the most feted Union figures of this period is Percy Cradock, who made his first speech on the paper in Michaelmas 1947. *Varsity* thought it 'of a particularly high order' even though he was 'faced with a difficult task' of speaking second in favour of the motion 'That falsehood and deception are essential to good

79

government'.[4] He continued to make a good impression in his regular speeches in ensuing terms. Douglas Hurd remembers him as 'a sparkling performer ... with outstanding panache and wit'.[5] To fellow Labour undergraduates like Greville Janner, Cradock was a 'brilliant mentor'. 'A master speaker,' Janner recalls, 'he drew his black gown up above his shoulders, like a hawk about to swoop. A warm and humorous friend but a skilful, artful and dangerous opponent.'[6] Of course, Cradock's rhetoric did not always work: his attempt to win over the House in support of the proposed abolition of University representation in Parliament in May 1948 was dismissed by his opponent as 'linguistic exuberance'. But reviews of his debating are remarkably generous. 'Like Lady Astor and the University Library,' the *Varsity* reviewer wrote in Easter 1949, 'Mr P. Cradock is in a class of his own. He is the one man whom your Scribe can consistently eulogise without laying himself open to charges of bribery and corruption ... The House expects him to make it laugh, though from the brain rather than the belly, and he does not disappoint it.'[7]

Despite such reviews, Cradock's path to the presidency was disrupted by Denzil Freeth's electoral setback in Lent 1949. Freeth chose to stand again the following term, opposing Cradock, who was by then Vice-President. It was a straight Tory vs. Socialist fight, as Freeth was the incoming CUCA chairman and Cradock the junior treasurer of the University Labour Club (CULC). The party battle was mirrored in the election for the vice-presidency: Norman St John-Stevas, the junior treasurer of CUCA, was fighting David Reece, a member of the CULC committee. Turnout was over 450, and the results were narrow: Freeth won by just seven votes and St John-Stevas by four, after trailing Reece in the first round.

Cradock ran again the following term, this time preventing St John-Stevas's smooth transition to the presidency, beating him by a majority of 109 – one of the largest for some time. Consequently, he inherited the first motion of term from Stevas, 'who had arranged it, as Vice-President, as a rousing introduction to his presidential term'.[8] It was not an easy inheritance, for its controversial subject was birth control, and Cradock was summoned before the Vice-Chancellor 'to give assurances that good order would be maintained'. It was, and a packed House decided that the wider application of birth control was 'in the best interests of morality and social welfare' by 342 to 260. Cradock was able to select his own motions for later in the term, choosing as his retirement debate the very fitting motion: 'This House despairs at the decline in the art of public speaking'. A 'galaxy of talent' spoke from the paper: the ex-Presidents Norman Birkett and Patrick Devlin, the Marquess of Reading, and Dingle Foot. 'It was undoubtedly one of the memorable debates of the post-war period,' Elwood recalls – although many who were present thought that Cradock's 'outstanding speech may have sabotaged the motion'.[9]

The 1950 general election fell in the middle of Cradock's term, and he held a debate on polling day 'praying for the return of a Labour government'. Arrangements were made to announce those constituency results which were received during the course of the debate. Union members showed themselves out of step with the mood of the country, dismissing the motion by a majority of over 100 while the Attlee government crept back with a much smaller one – although Cambridge borough was one of the seats to change hands that night, the Conservatives regaining it from Labour.

Cradock was called to the Bar and briefly became a law don. But, bored by the prospect of an endless series of dry undergraduate essays, he joined the Foreign Office and forged a distinguished diplomatic career. In 1977–78 he led the UK delegation to the comprehensive test ban discussions at Geneva while still serving as Ambassador to East Germany. But Sir Percy (as he became in 1980) became best known as a sinologist – as a counsellor, *chargé d'affaires* and later Ambassador in Beijing, leading the negotiations on the future of Hong Kong. He was foreign policy adviser to two Prime Ministers – Thatcher and Major – and was chairman of the Joint Intelligence Committee during the final years of the cold war. He was awarded the GCMG in 1983, and appointed to the Privy Council in 1993.

Cradock's successor as President was Norman St John-Stevas. He had undoubtedly set his eyes on the presidency early on, for he had entered his name in the book of members wishing to speak within his first few days at Cambridge. Sydney Elwood remembers 'saying to Roland Thompson at the time that there was undoubtedly a young man we would hear a lot of in the next three years'.[10] And they did. The keen young freshman spoke from the floor in his first debate at Cambridge and – an unusual distinction – was asked by the President, Robert Mackworth-Young, to propose the second debate of term from the paper. Elwood says it was hinted that Mackworth-Young was having trouble finding a proposer for what was thought to be a difficult motion to support – 'That there is insufficient justification for setting up an independent Jewish State in Palestine' – and *Varsity* found the debate 'dull and colourless'.[11] But the motion was carried by 230 to 203, and Stevas soon became a renowned speaker. By the following Michaelmas *Varsity* was reporting that he 'has a rare gift; whatever the subject, whatever his attitude towards it, and whatever the temper of the House, he always holds his audience from the moment he begins to speak.'[12]

One of the reasons he held the House's attention was his strange habit of referring to his aunts in his speeches – and indeed bringing them along to watch him debate. At the No Confidence debate in October 1949, for instance, 'the Stevas family were once more on parade, the regiment of aunts being commanded this time by his grandmother'.[13] At the debate on birth control in January 1950, *Varsity* wondered how he would bring his aunts into the debate 'without offending the six or so who were bound to be sitting in the gallery'.[14] But these materteral references were more than a rhetorical device, as Stevas himself has explained. He credits his aunts for his initiation into public speaking. From the age of twelve he was taken to speak at Hyde Park Corner, 'where I used to be a regular attender at the Catholic Evidence Guild, supported by my Aunt Beryl'.[15]

Stevas's Catholicism was undoubtedly of great importance to him. He was expelled from the chamber in a debate on 8 February 1949 for not withdrawing a question to the President – George

Pattison of St John's – asking whether it would be in order to introduce a motion of sympathy for the persecuted Christians of eastern Europe. This was a seemingly innocuous question in light of the show trial of Cardinal Mindszenty in Hungary, but it was the culmination of a heated row between the President and the second-year standing committee member. Earlier that month, Stevas had asked Pattison to hold a debate on the issue and had been turned down. He wrote a long and detailed letter to the President to complain about his refusal, and to inform him: 'I shall raise this motion on a point of order at the debate next Tuesday as I feel it is my duty to do so.' He closed his letter with a barbed assurance of his 'continued co-operation in all matters where a matter of conscience and morality are not involved'.

Pattison reiterated his position, pointing out that the chamber could be hired to hold an open protest meeting, and that he was willing to call an emergency meeting to consider this. Nonetheless, Stevas raised his point of order at the following debate and, after some bandying of words between them, was ordered to leave the chamber. This, however, was not to be the end of the matter. A few days later, a requisition signed by 78 members and calling for the House to meet as a judicial committee to censure the President was handed in. 'Its announcement,' recalls Elwood, 'was something of a sensation. One estimate was that it was the first for 50 years'.[16] Curzon, who had just retired as chief clerk, was 'appalled' and encouraged his successor to get one of the trustees to intervene. Dennis Robertson, an ex-President who was then a professor of political economy, did speak to both parties just before the judicial meeting. But no acceptable solution could be found, 'and they moved into the crowded hall unreconciled'.[17] The meeting was held on 14 February and was packed out on both sides by members who obviously had no more enticing plans for St Valentine's Day. Paul Curtis-Bennett was chosen to chair the meeting – most likely because he was a Liberal, and therefore not 'whipped' by the supporters of either Stevas on the right or Pattison on the left. The obvious choice of chairman would have been Denzil Freeth, as Vice-President, but he was a CUCA member. His displacement that evening was perhaps another factor in his defeat at the end of term: Elwood says it was considered that Curtis-Bennett had chaired the meeting very well, 'and he certainly looked the part. If he had at that time thought of standing for office in the election at the end of term, then that night's experience must have strengthened his resolve.'[18]

Many people spoke during the meeting, including Pattison and Stevas, and the House did not adjourn until 11.55 pm. When a vote was finally taken, the motion of censure was defeated by 213 to 111. Nonetheless, says Stevas, 'I felt vindicated, since later in the term I was elected Secretary'.[19]

Stevas was still just nineteen when he became Secretary in Lent 1949 – making him the youngest to be elected for some years, especially with the large number of older ex-servicemen in residence. His opponents were David Hirst of CUCA (later a Lord Justice of Appeal) and David Reece of the Labour Club; he beat the latter to the vice-presidency the following term. After losing to Percy Cradock on his first attempt, he finally became President for the Easter Term 1950. Even in the chair, Stevas's debates were just as flamboyant. The first debate of his term was noted for its long and tendentious motion: 'This House maintains that no loyal Englishman should associate with British Communists and that no self-respecting government should contain ministers who have been intimate with them in the past and have not since disavowed their faith in Communism.' Unsurprisingly, speakers in the debate appealed to him about its meaning – but 'the President's ruling was remarkably felicitous. He denied that the motion contained any innuendo and added, "It means what it says, whatever that may mean".' An attempt by the second speaker to define the motion was rather disastrous, if the *Varsity* account is anything to go by: 'He began with "loyalty" and managed that fairly well, but when he got to "intimate" the House was amused, though embarrassed. After that it seemed determined to misinterpret him.'[20]

After Cambridge, Stevas went as a postgraduate to Oxford – and came closer than anyone before or since to becoming President of both the Cambridge and Oxford Unions. As an ex-President from Cambridge, Stevas was invited to speak from the moment of his arrival in Oxford, and he was regularly given paper speeches, describing himself spicily as a Cambridge virgin on the brink of an Oxford union.[21] He was elected Secretary of the Oxford Union for the Hilary (i.e. Lent) Term 1952, and made little secret of his plans to run for the presidency.

Stevas faced a four-cornered fight. His opponents included Oleg Kerensky, grandson of the inter-revolutionary Russian Prime Minister, and Pat Hutber, chairman of Oxford University Labour Club. But the candidate who won was an American ex-Librarian of the Union, Howard E. Shuman, later a long-serving legislative assistant in the US Senate. In Shuman's view, 'I won because I was most people's second choice.'[22] Hutber had led on the first ballot and Kerensky, coming fourth, had been knocked out. Shuman got most of his redistributed votes and won on the second ballot by twelve votes. Stevas's hopes of becoming the first President of both Unions had been dashed. But if he was disappointed, he was not nearly so angry as Hutber, whom Shuman met later in the private offices of the Oxford Union: 'He was so angry about being defeated … that he took most of the glass and china and threw it into the fireplace, broke it into pieces. He threw a fit.'[23]

At Oxford, unlike at Cambridge, candidates for the presidency traditionally vie with each other in the last debate before the election. For this debate, Shuman decided to take Stevas on directly by working something out with Jeremy Thorpe, an ex-President, to provoke an interruption from him. Throughout his speech Shuman referred to him not as 'Sinjun', but as Mr '*Saint John* Stev-as'.[24] Stevas had been called that before, of course, so had an answer: 'Well,' he said, playing also on his Roman Catholicism, 'the Pope may canonize me, but the ex-Librarian, never.' This delighted the Oxford crowd, but Shuman had his own riposte: 'He objects to the way I pronounced his name, but at Cambridge he was called Norman Saint John Stev-as, and after all, that's where he made his name.' It may have been 'absolutely contrived', Shuman admitted, but it won him a cheer.[25]

Stevas was also thwarted in his Oxford presidential bid by the man who had been his immediate counterpart when he was President of the Union at Cambridge, the future newscaster Robin Day. Day, by then in his final year, 'lived and breathed the Oxford Union for almost his entire university career,' according to a historian of that society.[26] He was opposed to his Cantabrigian counterpart following in his own footsteps not just because he thought it was 'pot-hunting', but also because it seemed unjust: a Cambridge graduate with three years' debating experience and the cachet of an ex-President 'would have an unfair advantage over the undergraduates of Oxford,' he felt. So Day mounted 'a Stop Stevas campaign ... openly conducted by ridicule and interruption'.[27] In an early instance, he made an elaborately satirical introduction of the new arrival, as the Oxford Union historian, David Walter, records:

'One has only to visit his elegant rooms in Christ Church,' he said, 'to see that there is a man of taste, of refinement, a man of society. There on the mantelshelf are 100 invitation cards: some accepted, some rejected, many of them quite genuine. Here on a table are carelessly strewn cultured periodicals and books – books about art ... And there on the sideboard are the bottles, the bottles of a man of discernment: Chateaubriand '32, Chablis '27, and Chanel Number 5.'[28]

Later, Day changed his tactics to feigning complete boredom during Stevas's speeches. Unnerved after previous onslaughts, Stevas remarked that Day was being unusually quiet. Day describes his response in his memoirs:

With a show of reluctance, I lumbered, amid loud cheers, to the despatch box: 'I am willing to go to any lengths in order to make the speech of the honourable gentleman memorable'.[29]

Day was, of course, also the bane of another Cambridge President, John Nott, who stormed out of an interview in which Sir Robin dubbed him a 'here today, gone tomorrow' politician as Defence

Secretary in 1982. But despite these run-ins, Day had a particularly happy association with the Cambridge Union. As a young graduate, he shared a flat with another ex-President, Ronald Waterhouse, and it was he who drew his attention to an ITN advertisement for a 'newscaster' in 1955.[30] His first job in television owed much to three other ex-Presidents of the Cambridge Union: Leonard Miall (Michaelmas 1936), the head of television talks at the BBC, gave him tips on getting into broadcasting; his first temporary contract came because Jack Ashley (Lent 1951) was away for a year on a university fellowship in the USA; and, filling in for Ashley, he worked with the chief assistant of talks, John Green (Lent 1931). To cap it all, Sir Robin was made an honorary member of the Cambridge Union in Michaelmas 1980 – notwithstanding his run-ins with two of its alumni.

But Day was contrite about his campaign against Stevas at Oxford: 'I regretted, in a way, having to put a spoke in his wheel'. When they had been opposite numbers, he later recalled, 'our relations were cordial'.[31] Indeed, they were more than cordial – for during that term Day and Stevas had organised a 'Boat Race' between their two Unions. It took place on the river Cam in May Week 1950, and was filmed by the BBC. The two Presidents coxed their respective boats. But the race was not altogether serious: Stevas and Day arrived in a Rolls Royce, emerging in full evening dress and top hats. Stevas wore a silk-lined opera cloak; Day, who weighed in at over seventeen stone, an enormous pink carnation and gold-handled cane.[32] The oarsmen were more informally attired in dinner jackets. The Oxford boat included a future Conservative MP, Peter Emery, as stroke; the future Liberal leader Jeremy Thorpe at number seven; and the writer Godfrey Smith at number six. Stanley Booth-Clibborn, then Secretary of the Oxford Union, later Steward of the Cambridge Union and Bishop of Manchester, was number four. Numbers three and two were the journalist Keith Kyle and Dick Taverne, the Social Democrat.

The race, Day records, 'was conducted with dignity, except when May Week crowds on the bridge bombed us with tins and apples as we passed underneath'.[33] Halfway down the course, staff from the

Cambridge Union came out in a boat to serve the crews sherry. Whether by design or by equal incompetence, the two boats crossed the finishing line together. Norman St John-Stevas was ceremonially ducked, but Robin Day 'begged to be excused this honour for fear of damaging my tail-coat'.[34]

———

Such colourful characters, well-attended debates and memorable antics would lead one to assume that these years were viewed with a golden hue by those who lived through them, especially against the contrast of the bleak war years. But they were not. Indeed, there was a mood of gloomy introspection among many in the Union at this time. Percy Cradock wrote an article in *Varsity* in February 1948 entitled 'Union Jokes Deadly Dull'. In it, he noted a lack of strong debaters: 'The prattlers are legion, but the speakers of the Union would scarcely fill a front bench'. His was not the only such article in this period. Douglas Hurd, the future Home Secretary and Foreign Secretary who was President in Easter 1952, echoes that pessimistic tone in his contribution to this volume, bemoaning the deficiencies of contrived, adversarial debates. If Lord Hurd's views have been shaped by his long, distinguished years in both Houses of Parliament, there are indications of them in his undergraduate speeches. In a debate on South Africa in Lent 1950, Hurd 'likened the Union to the Assembly of the United Nations in its ignorance and unrepresentative nature'.[35] But it was not only the format of its debates which caused him distress, as he admitted in his *Memoirs*:

> There was a great deal of time-consuming intrigue and domestic jockeying in the Union, together with worry about its finances. I did not particularly relish hours spent in the dark red Union building behind the Round Church, designed by Waterhouse in a gloomy mood. But a rather narrow ambition drove me on.[36]

There was indeed a great deal of worry about the Union's finances. This was a time of general austerity, with wartime debts to pay, and food and many basic commodities still rationed. Union officers had to pool their coupons in order to give guest speakers a generous breakfast the morning after debates. By Easter 1951, the financial state of the Union so perturbed the standing committee that a financial sub-committee was established to find ways of making economies and raising the Society's revenue. At the end of that year, the retiring Treasurer, Nigel Hammond, reported a 'grave deterioration in the finances of the Society ... due to the decline in membership coinciding with the rise in costs and in wages'. With the monies from the War Damages Commission and the post-war restoration fund appeal soon to be exhausted, the cost of repairs and maintenance would once again fall upon the Society's reserves.

The sub-committee – which included Hurd, then on the standing committee – identified a novel range of economies. They suggested typing rather than printing agendas for PBMs and the Society's annual reports, and using paper rather than card for menus. They also recommended charging for the use of the squash courts and for tickets to the gallery for non-members, and only making writing paper available on request from the porter. Most of their recommendations were accepted immediately – but not all instances of profligacy were eliminated. The political columnist Alan Watkins remembers a row about whether or not the bar should be decorated with Pugin wallpaper. Christopher Norwood, a future MP from the Labour Club, calculated that it would be cheaper to paper the area with ten-shilling notes. 'The issue became politicised: the left against the right, with the left maintaining that the money could be better expended on other causes, such as cheaper beer.'[37] But these dissenting voices were defeated, and the wallpaper was duly purchased and pasted. It was removed ten years later when the bar was decorated again.

The most controversial response to the Union's financial woes was the proposal to raise the membership fee, which had stood at its present level since 1886. The standing committee agreed to this, but a thinly attended business meeting in May Week did not produce a majority for the proposal. When, at a later attempt in Lent 1956, the

89

fee was raised, the news made *The Times*.[38] The change was not revolutionary – the annual subscription was raised from three to four guineas, life membership rose from seven-and-a-half guineas to ten, and an entrance fee of one guinea remained the same – but it meant additional revenue of some £2,000 a year for the Society. And it did not deter new members: the recruitment figures that Michaelmas were higher than the previous year's.

In the meantime, a membership drive was undertaken and brought healthier bank balances. The new Treasurer, Kenneth Scott, was able to record an increase of almost 30 per cent in annual recruitment in 1951–52. In Easter 1953 the Vice-President, Hugh Thomas, proudly reported another year of increased recruitment, which meant that 'the Society now possesses the largest membership it has ever recorded'. The new economies also showed quick successes: new tariffs for room hire brought in an additional £74 per year, and charges for the squash courts a further £15. Even the extravagant purchase of a billiards table – Douglas Hurd had to use his discretionary powers as President and deem it an item of furniture in order to authorise its purchase as 'ordinary expenditure' – proved lucrative: it paid half its cost within the first year, and had turned a profit by Easter 1954.

So even if those who lived through it did not think of it as such, there are a number of signs that this was a particularly successful period for the Union. For one, the Society enjoyed a certain status, both in Cambridge and beyond. High-ranking politicians came up to its debates, bringing with them the attention of the national media and taking back accounts of high-quality debates to their colleagues in public life. Undergraduates were energised by the finely balanced nature of contemporary politics, and took an active interest in the nation's affairs.* They found themselves, as a generation, more welcome to do so: young men and women who had fought for their

---

* Labour had won a narrow majority of five in the 1950 general election; the following year, the Conservatives scraped back into power with the support of the National Liberals – and a minority of the national vote.

country during the war, or participated in national service since, earned a respect not accorded to their forebears. This was the age of Angry Young Men and the Beat Generation. Their representatives in the debating societies of the leading universities made eloquent – and probably more palatable – spokesmen for their generation.

Indeed, when the cessation of national service was debated, there was considerable interest in the debate from outside Cambridge, and it was broadcast on the Third Programme. Thirty-two members spoke from the floor that night, and almost 700 voted, deciding narrowly – by 354 to 337 – to preserve it.

When Queen Juliana of the Netherlands came to London and asked to meet 'British youth', the two men chosen to represent their generation were the Presidents of the Oxford and Cambridge Unions: Godfrey Smith and Ronald Waterhouse. Looking back, Smith noted wryly: 'We were about as convincing in the role as Laurel and Hardy, whom we faintly resembled.'[39] But it was a reflection of the Unions' status – and one of a number of examples from this time. In 1950, the Union was approached by Bowes & Bowes Ltd., a small publishing firm in Cambridge, who offered to publish a history of the Society. The President that term was Norman St John-Stevas, who eagerly volunteered to write it. But this noble gesture was politely rejected by a committee established to consider the offers, who hoped 'to discover an author with all the necessary qualities and the time at his disposal'. Sydney Castle Roberts, a former Librarian and Steward, and now Vice-Chancellor of the University, was approached but was unwilling. By January 1951, the favoured author was Percy Cradock – but it was not until May that he agreed to accept the commission. He was awarded the princely sum of £50 for expenses that month; another £50 was granted in 1953 towards the cost of a party to mark the book's publication. It was held at Brown's Hotel on 24 April 1953, and attended by many ex-Presidents and 'no end of fashionable literati'.[40]

As well as Cradock's history, the Union collected some other trappings of a well-established society. A Union tie was discussed in Easter 1950, and a sample design of Cambridge shields on a light blue background was commissioned. But this perturbed the Vice-Chancellor who, despite his previous involvement with the Union, was 'unhappy' about the proposed design. The use of the University coat of arms, he wrote to the President, was not appropriate, and even the choice of Cambridge blue was 'awkward': 'It would imme-diately suggest that the wearer was "a blue" of some sort and might give rise to much criticism and confusion.'[41] A new design was there-fore proposed in the Michaelmas Term: a dark blue background, with golden 'U's and red lions arranged in alternating diagonal lines. It has remained the Union tie ever since, with a separate tie for officers being adopted later.

The Union 'brand' was further developed with the introduction of membership cards by Neil Crichton-Miller, President in Michaelmas 1955. (The integrity of members and non-members had previously been taken at face value – or checked against the list in the office.) His successor, Martin Rosenhead, even procured some Union-branded cigarettes.

There was continued interest in the Union's debates from beyond Cambridge, which, along with those of the Oxford Union, were frequently broadcast on the radio. In Easter 1950, Cambridge became the first to have a debate televised – albeit from London rather than Cambridge. The BBC transported the President's chair, Secretary's desk and a number of benches to Alexandra Palace, and even built a replica of a section of the visitors' gallery. As President, Norman St John-Stevas chaired the proceedings. When another televised debate was proposed for the following term, however – this time between Cambridge and Oxford – there was a row as to who should preside over it. Again, Cambridge were providing the furni-ture, but the Oxford Union committee had decided that their President should take the chair and a deadlock had been reached. The Cambridge standing committee agreed that it would not be proper for the Oxford President to sit on the Cambridge chair, but was prepared to let the BBC choose if Oxford did not withdraw their demand. In the end, a neutral figure was chosen and the debate held at Lincoln's Inn, presided over by Graeme Finlay, a member of neither University. A graduate of UCL, he was nonetheless well qualified as President of the Hardwicke Society, the debating club for aspiring lawyers; he later became an MP and a circuit judge.

The following term, the Union took its first steps into new territory by agreeing to host dances for members and their guests. This was the first time the Union had branched out from debating into purely social events, and it came about largely through pressure from Brian Abel-Smith, the senior committee member.* He was allowed to form a dance sub-committee – which included an unlikely party-planner in the form of a young Geoffrey Howe – and proposed that weekly dances be held on Saturdays in the smoking room. The first two were duly held the following Michaelmas Term, and were a great success. Seventy people attended the first, and over 100 came the following week, making a handsome profit. Dances were soon bringing in over £80 a year – not to mention a large number of young ladies, who were nevertheless still ineligible for membership. When Abel-Smith stood down from the standing committee at the end of that term, it was unanimously decided that he 'had earned the lasting gratitude of the Society'. His legacy was certainly an enduring one: his committee became the dance and entertainments sub-committee in Easter 1952, signalling the advent of Union 'Ents'.

Another reflection of the Union's stature came in Michaelmas 1952 when the Duke of Edinburgh agreed to visit and accept honorary membership of the Society – long before he was made Chancellor of the University. The evening of the presentation, 13 November, was a gilded one. It was decided, in view of the large numbers anticipated, to reserve the front two rows on each side of the chamber for members who had spoken from the paper that term and the college secretaries; all other seats were allocated by ballot. Everyone attending wore evening dress, which made for quite a spectacle. Percy Cradock, as ex-President, took the chair while the President, Alistair Sampson, invited His Royal Highness to accept

---

* i.e. the candidate who had topped the poll for the standing committee.

his membership and presented him with a special membership card and silken Union tie. Sampson then took the chair for the debate, a humorous motion proposed by Derick Mirfin of Magdalene: 'This House does not find it surprising that it needs analysing'. The Duke did not take part in the debate itself, but made a short speech beforehand. 'The navy isn't a good school for learning how to argue,' he explained. 'You either give orders or take them.'[42] There had been some disgruntlement at the way the University had muscled in on the event once they heard the Duke was coming to Cambridge. 'The University behaved with rank discourtesy to the Union, which had been the prime mover of the royal visit,' complained Mirfin. There had to be 'quite a tart exchange of letters between the President and those in Authority' before the Union's officers were allowed to join the guests at high table for the dinner laid on at Trinity. But the Union had the last laugh at the post-debate reception, when the Duke 'paid little attention to the dons and their appalling wives ... He stationed himself within arm's length of the bar, and pitched into a succession of anecdotes, jests and reminiscences that delighted all of us ... He got brighter and more happy as the evening went on.' When his valet came at 10.40 pm to suggest his leaving, the Duke replied: 'No, no. Let the car wait. We'll stay another half hour.' When he finally departed, close to midnight, he was cheered by a large crowd which had collected in Bridge Street.[43]

The evening was a great coup for Alistair Sampson. Known as 'one of the strongest wits in the University', he joked that the Duke's visit was a 'great fillip' to the Society.[44] The first President from Selwyn, Sampson also wrote lyrics and music for the Footlights, and his contributions to Union debates were often in the form of hilarious rhyming speeches. The author of a profile of him in *Varsity* during his term felt that 'few Presidents have seemed so eminently Presidential, so well fitted for the post' and noted that 'a smile is the mark of punctuation to most of his sentences'.[45] He continued to delight and amuse until his death from cancer in January 2006, when his *Times* obituary called him 'a man of immense charm and humour, great knowledge, and several careers'.[46] A barrister on the western circuit until his 40th birthday, he enacted a long-pondered career change and became an antiques dealer, opening shops on the Brompton Road and in Mayfair. He was an SDP/Liberal Alliance candidate in Devon in 1983 and was a prolific writer and humorist, appearing on the *Tonight* programme and *Call My Bluff* in the 1950s and '60s. He wrote a weekly column for *Punch*, and numerous collections of humorous poems, limericks and short stories.

Another witty speaker at this time was one of the Union's senior members, Dr Glyn Daniel. A brilliant archaeology student and research fellow at St John's in the 1930s, Daniel returned to Cambridge after wartime service as an intelligence officer, and eventually became Disney Professor of Archaeology. But he was well known beyond the cloistered world of academia, particularly as chairman of the popular panel show *Animal, Vegetable, Mineral?*, which made him a household name and brought him the accolade of 'television personality of the year' in 1955. He was also a founding director of Anglia Television, and was 'widely known and recognized' as a 'brilliant and entertaining speaker'.[47] He served as the Union's Steward between 1950 and 1955, and was later a trustee.

———•———

The mood of the Union was still predominantly Tory in these years. Douglas Hurd recalls CUCA as 'a formidable force, with more than a thousand undergraduate members', and describes the general mood of Union debates as 'one of boisterous contempt for what felt like a failed and exhausted Labour Government.'[48] Unsurprisingly, this generation produced a number of strong Tories – including Hurd's future Cabinet colleague Geoffrey Howe. Howe was elected to standing committee but never made Union office, winning mixed reviews for his speeches – such as the following by Norman St John-Stevas:

> R.E.G. Howe, Trinity Hall, was quiet and effective, though at intervals he appeared to be blowing at an invisible musical instrument as he talked.[49]

Another Conservative who did make Union office was Julian Williams, of Eton and Trinity, President in Michaelmas 1951. Also CUCA chairman, he contested a Birmingham constituency in the 1955 general election, but forsook national politics when he inherited his family estate, Caerhays Castle, in that same year. Instead, he devoted himself to local life – as chairman of Cornwall County Council, 1980–89, and president of Cornwall Cricket Club for 22 years. Very suitably, his presidential debate was on the motion that Cornish civilisation was a beacon to the world. He was one of the few Vice-Presidents of the 1950s to accede to the presidency unopposed – 'undoubtedly a measure of his popularity', says Elwood.[50]

But if the left were generally beaten in the Union's debates, they fared better in its termly elections, and a number of Labour figures stand out from this period too. Ronald Waterhouse was a Liberal as President in Michaelmas 1950, but joined the Labour party after Cambridge and was a parliamentary candidate for them in his native Flintshire in 1959. But he stayed at the Bar and became a High Court judge, earning a knighthood in 1978 and the GBE in 2002.

His successor as President was Jack Ashley – a former trade unionist and councillor who, as the first working-class President of the Union, was Labour through and through. Though his decision not to wear evening dress at debates caused quite a stir, he was a very popular figure. 'There is a straightforward integrity about Mr Ashley which makes him one of the most popular figures in the Union,' said *Varsity*, while the *Cambridge Review* noted that there were 'few so universally regarded with affection and respect as Jack Ashley'.[51] Even so, his term was not without political squabbles: Geoffrey Howe remembers leading a rebellious group demanding that Ashley call a private business meeting:

> As I handed him the petition, he reacted with the utmost ferocity: 'I'm never going to speak to another bloody Tory again – never as long as I live'.

In fact, Howe records, he ended up marrying one – his future wife, Pauline Crispin, was 'one of our best Conservative college representatives'.[52]

Ashley's selection to participate in the American debating tour compelled him to resign before the end of his presidential term, and his farewell debate – 'This House pledges itself to democratic socialism' with Hugh Dalton, the ex-Chancellor of the Exchequer – was held on 2 March. Rather than being succeeded by his Vice-President Donald Macmillan, who had been elected to serve the following term, a by-election was held and Gautam Mathur, later president of the Indian Economic Association and Vice-Chancellor of Osmania University, became President for the four-day period until the Change of Officers debate.

Another Labour President who was 'an opponent impossible to dislike' was Greville Janner, President in Lent 1952.[53] Janner's early Union career was aided by a fortunate alliance in Trinity Hall: he shared his rooms with Edward Greenfield, the Union commentator for the *Cambridge Review*, who admitted that he 'finds it almost impossible to criticise him'. Not that there was much call for criticism: 'For the student of Union technique, there is much to learn from Mr Janner's spectacle manipulation,' Greenfield continued: 'Most effective.'[54] Janner later compiled other, non-ocular tips in *Janner's Complete Speechmaker* (1989). Some of these must have rubbed off on his son Daniel, who also became President of the Union in Michaelmas 1978.

If Greenfield was a boon to Janner in the Union, he was an adversary in the Labour Club, beating him for the chairmanship when Janner precociously ran at the end of his first year. He was successful at a later attempt, and was also president of Trinity Hall Athletics Club. He was opposed when he ran for President of the Union, and there was an anti-Jewish element to the campaign, but he won. He knew, after all, how to bend the rules. Though canvassing was not permitted, 'nothing could prevent me from dropping in to see my friends,' he wrote:

'How are you?' they would ask. 'Worried,' I would reply.
'Why?'
'Well, it's the Union elections today.'
'Oh, I'd better get along to vote, hadn't I?'
'That would be very kind of you – but I haven't asked you to
   do it!'[55]

An innovation of Janner's term was inviting members of the Society's staff to speak in a debate. Sydney Elwood and his assistant, Roland Thompson, took opposing sides for the motion 'That this seat of learning needs darning'. Another future chief clerk, Barry Thoday, then a junior clerk, spoke from the floor, as did Fred Hitchings who had just celebrated 60 years in the Union's service, finishing as head waiter. The evening was deemed a great success. A similar debate was held in Easter 1955, with the contribution of Percy Aldhous, the popular barman, relayed to the chamber from the bar.[56]

———

From the distance of half a century, then, the early 1950s seem a particularly lustrous chapter in the Union's history. To Sydney Elwood, who had a far greater frame of reference than anyone else, they 'were years of progress, expansion and success'.[57] Whether, as an age, it was golden or austere is an assessment best left to those who experienced it – and to their recollections which follow.

RECOLLECTION: THE RT. HON. THE LORD ASHLEY OF STOKE CH

(Mr J. Ashley, Gonville & Caius College)
President, Lent Term 1951

Jack Ashley was born in Widnes, a chemical town near Liverpool, in 1922. He left school at the age of fourteen, becoming a labourer and then an active trade unionist and local councillor. In 1946, he won a scholarship to Ruskin College, Oxford and, after two years' study there, a further scholarship to Gonville and Caius College, Cambridge, where he became the first working-class President of the Union.

After Cambridge, he spent fifteen years as a BBC radio and television producer before being elected as the Member of Parliament for Stoke-on-Trent South in 1966. Two years into his parliamentary career, he lost his hearing completely as the result of a routine ear operation. He remained, however, in Parliament, successfully leading campaigns on behalf of thalidomide children, victims of domestic violence, vaccine-damaged children, and the disabled. He has served as president of the Royal National Institute for the Deaf since 1987.

He was made a Companion of Honour in 1975 and, on retiring from the House of Commons in 1992, was raised to the peerage as Lord Ashley of Stoke and Widnes. This recollection has been adapted from his two volumes of autobiography: Journey Into Silence *(The Bodley Head, 1973) and* Acts of Defiance *(Penguin, 1994).*

On my first day at Cambridge, I felt a sense of exhilaration which lasted throughout my stay. Although I had been happy at Ruskin,

I never loved Oxford; its atmosphere, which many students found heady or inspiring, did not affect me deeply. Yet I was captivated by Cambridge, where few things ever quenched my exuberant spirits – and never any of them for long. I did not feel the same jolting sense of sudden shunting from factory to college as at Oxford; now I was a full member of the University, acclimatised to an academic atmosphere.

I played an active part in the University Labour Club and, just before the end of my first year, I was elected chairman. The leaders of the University Conservative Association, our main opponents, included some interesting characters, later to make their way, and their names, in Parliament. The most flamboyant, and one of the wittiest, was Norman St John-Stevas. His dress, manner, and speech all seemed calculated to provoke, but when attacked he was usually ready with a sparkling riposte. If on occasion he appeared foppish, with a yellow waistcoat and cravat, he proved in debate that appearances were deceptive: he was one of the most able men in the University.

My direct counterpart was Geoffrey Howe, chairman of the Conservative Association. After one explosive first meeting, I grew to like him, and our friendship has endured over the years. There was an interesting contrast between him and the leader of the Labour Club who preceded me as chairman, Percy Cradock. Howe was amiable, diligent and astute, and although he never became President of the Union, he was an able debater. Cradock was dry, sparkling and satirical. He was the most scintillating debater I heard. Although he gave the impression of not working, he, too, must have been diligent because he got two double firsts, in English and Law.

I joined the Union Society at the suggestion of the administrator of my scholarship who believed I would get much interest and pleasure from the debates. Before handing over my membership fee I attended the opening debate of my first term as a visitor. It was a sparkling occasion, the chamber crowded with eager students for a motion of no confidence in the Labour government. Precisely on time, the President and officers, all in evening dress, escorted the guest speakers to their seats. At a single ping from the President's bell the students fell silent and listened to the terms of the motion – then battle commenced. The opening speech by a Conservative student, quite impressive in both content and delivery, was enthusiastically received and I did not envy the following speaker. But it was Cradock, then unknown to me, who rose, swirling his long graduate gown and smiling at the opposition. Within moments he had the audience laughing at his barbed mockery, the prelude to a brilliant speech. I resolved that night to join the Union Society, a decision that gave me pleasure throughout my years at Cambridge.

Shortly afterwards I made my first speech in a debate on Ireland, initiated by de Valera. I didn't know a great deal about the intricacies of the Irish question but this did not deter me. My speech was fairly well received but I knew that I could do better with more familiar subjects. A few weeks later Percy Cradock told me that I would shortly receive an invitation from the President to be one of the two main speakers in a forthcoming debate. I hoped for a political subject but Cradock said the motion was to be 'The scientist and the artist must accept responsibility for the social consequences of their work'. He looked at me wryly when I asked him who my opponent was to be, and admitted, with a smile, that he was.

I had never thought about the subject; when I did, the question of an artist's responsibility baffled me. Obviously this was an abstruse problem deserving careful study so I headed for the University Library where I was offered a pile of books which might be relevant, although the library assistant was doubtful. The doubt was justified; I left with an empty notebook after studying for hours. In the debate I devoted a little of my time to jocular criticism of the President for his choice of motion and for saddling me with the responsibility of dealing with it. This was received better than any erudite passage about artistic responsibility, but the debate was notable for yet another eloquent contribution from Cradock.

I attended the Union Society regularly throughout my first year and spoke as often as I could, although never as frequently as I wished. There were always more people trying to speak than the time allowed. Yet I could not complain, because I had many opportunities, especially when I became chairman of the Labour Club. In my second year I was elected to the Union committee and a few terms later, I headed the poll and became the senior member.

The next stage was to stand for the secretaryship. My opponent was Tony Bullock, an intelligent and able Conservative and, although I just managed to beat him, my term as Secretary aroused some controversy. Just before the election, *Varsity*, the undergraduate newspaper, published a profile of me which my opponents claimed influenced the result. To make matters worse, I wore my lounge suit at debates, even when sitting in a prominent position at the Secretary's desk, despite the long-standing tradition that evening dress should be worn by the officers of the Society. My action should have been no surprise to anyone, as I had made my intention quite clear before the election. I was not standing on any great principle – I simply couldn't afford an evening suit and I had no intention of hiring one. I was incredulous that there should be such concern over my clothes but they became an important issue when I stood for the vice-presidency.

Shortly before the election a pointed personal attack on me was printed in the Oxford *Isis*. The anonymous critic wrote: 'No one would object to an officer appearing at debates in a lounge suit through financial necessity, but to do so (as no other officers who were Socialists have done) on account of perverted political principle seems to many to amount to a gratuitous insult to the dignity of his office.'* The article, timely for my opponents, was given much publicity in Cambridge. My natural reaction was to fire off a strong rejoinder, but I was dissuaded by two of my colleagues, Percy Cradock and a Jewish mathematician, Ivor Robinson, who were generally regarded as the elder statesmen of the Labour Club. They were to be the diplomatists and professors of a decade later, and they displayed their talents with the advice they offered. Instead of an

---

* The author of the letter signed off as 'Cantab.'; *Varsity* (3 June 1950) reported that it was Peter Jenkin-Jones, a former CUCA chairman.

angry retort, I made a restrained reply saying that I was sorry that so violent a personal attack should have been launched upon me in an election which I had hoped would have been conducted along very different lines. I never knew whether my reply was effective or if the original had backfired. Perhaps it was regarded as irrelevant by members of the Union; in any case I won the vice-presidency and with a comfortable majority of over 90. The following term I was returned unopposed as the first working-class President of the Cambridge Union Society – still wearing a lounge suit.

Despite my years in the slums and factories of Widnes I felt completely at ease in the Union and enjoyed my term of office. The Society at that time was predominantly middle-class with a sprinkling of aristocrats. Their experience and values were different from mine – not better or worse, but different. Yet I moved as easily and comfortably among them as with my friends at home. I didn't change them, and looking back I can see that they never changed me.

There were many new experiences, though. The dinners which preceded the weekly debates were the first official dinners of my life and I found them interesting affairs; the food and service were excellent, but two things surprised me: the formal atmosphere soon became convivial and the port and brandy moved around the table with impressively casual precision.

My guests included such contrasting characters as Selwyn Lloyd, Gilbert Harding, Hugh Dalton, Godfrey Winn, Donald Soper and Jeremy Thorpe – although, of course, some care was exercised in pitting one against another. Inviting a politician with a comedian, no matter how attractive a proposition, would have insulted the one and discomfited the other. Two people I thought would make good opponents in a debate on world peace were my friend Bob Edwards of the Chemical Workers' Union and Randolph Churchill.

Although Edwards was a fine conference orator, the Union Society was not the place for his particular talents and he did not really adapt his style. His speech, which would have electrified a political conference, was received with some banter by unimpressed though friendly students. When he was speaking of the horrors of war, Churchill baited him by waving his handkerchief as the white flag of surrender; in fact Edwards was no pacifist, having fought bravely in the Spanish civil war. But the scene is etched in my mind as an example of misplaced oratory on the one hand and the caricature of it by Churchill on the other.

Near the end of my presidential term I was invited to make a debating tour of universities in the USA, along with Ronald Waterhouse, my predecessor – later Sir Ronald, a High Court judge. He was a tall, well-groomed Liberal lawyer who came from a middle-class home. Although our backgrounds were different we were friends who greatly enjoyed each other's company. We lightly agreed to speak on any of six motions which were sent to twenty American universities – each choosing the one it preferred. The two most provocative motions were that we 'deplored the banning of Communist parties in free, democratic states' and that we 'regretted the American way of life'. These were the two most popular subjects although one of the others – 'that Democratic Socialism is the most effective barrier against Communism' – was chosen by a few universities. We combined on the first two issues and opposed each other on the last one.

I was to be away for six weeks and my final examinations were due within a month of my return from America, so I took a case full of books on the journey. The tour was so hectic that the case was never opened; I had simply given myself an added burden to carry around the States. Because of the pressure of time, neither Waterhouse nor I had prepared speeches on any of the six subjects when we embarked on the *Queen Elizabeth* but we intended to work on them during the voyage. It was a silly idea; the entertainments on that magnificent ship, together with the excitement of our first trip to the United States, induced us to a frivolous and relaxed voyage. Originally we had been allocated berths deep in the ship, but Waterhouse had a well-connected friend in the Cunard Line. As a result we were promoted to a top-deck cabin, and enjoyed all the entertainments that entailed. When the ship berthed in New York we took stock of the situation – a tour of twenty universities begin-

ning the next day, a journey from the Atlantic to the Pacific, and no
speeches prepared.

Our first debate was at St Joseph's College, Philadelphia; I
expected it to take a similar form to our own in Cambridge though
perhaps in a more modern building. We were accustomed to speaking in a small debating chamber, with our audience around us, inter-
jecting at will in the debate. At Philadelphia there was no audience
participation in this sense, although they listened intently. Instead
we were perched, with our opponents, on a stage in a vast stadium –
the Union Jack draped behind us, the Stars and Stripes behind them
– and facing us were 3,000 people. The event had been advertised as
an international debate, adjudicated by a distinguished panel of
judges which included a Federal Court judge, a Congressman, a
professor and the president of an insurance company; the British
consul turned out to give us moral support which, in the circumstances, we appreciated.

Doubtless the organisers intended it to be a serious occasion, but
Cambridge debates were often liberally spiced with humour and we
decided not to change our style. The audience readily responded,
although I suspect they were laughing at our accents more than our
wit. The American team were more solemn, adopting a formal
pattern we were to recognise throughout the tour – introduction,
facts, interpretation of facts, conclusion and peroration. This rigidity
made our opponents predictable targets, and we took full advantage.

The Americans treated us like visiting celebrities. After the debate,
a crowd of teenagers would ask us for autographs before we left for
late-night parties. Exhausted, we were rushed on to the next university. It was a rigorous schedule which was to take us to the Pacific
coast and back. During the next few weeks we accepted warm
American hospitality while maintaining in debates that we deplored
their way of life. But they were tolerant and generous hosts.

After our intensive debating across the USA, we hoped to resume
studying for our exams on the return voyage. I achieved very little,
arriving back in Cambridge to find most students revising material
I had not even heard of. With exams in less than a month, a friend

helpfully brought his notes to my room. We were interrupted by an undergraduate who was working on *Varsity* – a lovely young woman with dark brown hair and blue eyes. She wanted to ask me about the debating tour, but I was too busy cramming, and asked her to return the following day. Unable to do so, she said that she would ask the editor to send someone else. I told her that since this was the first time that *Varsity* had ever sent me a pretty reporter, if she would not interview me no one else could; she accepted the compliment and came back the next day. This was near the end of April 1951; we were married in the December. In many ways, I suppose, I have the Union to thank for our meeting.

RECOLLECTION: LORD JANNER OF BRAUNSTONE QC

(Mr G.E. Janner, Trinity Hall)
President, Lent Term 1952

Greville Janner came up to Trinity Hall after national service in 1952. As well as being elected President of the Union, he was chairman of the University Labour Club and president of Trinity Hall Athletic Club. After Cambridge, he won a scholarship to Harvard Law School, became a barrister, and was appointed Queen's Counsel in 1971.

In 1970, he succeeded his father, Sir Barnett Janner, as Labour MP for Leicester North West (later Leicester West). He stood down in 1997, and was raised to the peerage as Lord Janner of Braunstone. He was president of the Board of Deputies of British Jews from 1979 to 1985, and is chairman of the Holocaust Educational Trust. He speaks nine languages, has written more than 60 books, and is a member of the Magic Circle. His son, Daniel, was also President of the Union in Michaelmas 1978.

Election as President of the Cambridge Union was and remains one of the great moments of my life. Since then, I have often returned, and have always enjoyed a unique mixture of nostalgia and delight, revival of memories of elections, debates, and friendships, and especial delight that the Society has managed to change so much in its composition whilst retaining the basic procedure and thrust of its argumentative and humorous battles.

I first arrived in the Union in 1950. Like most of its members, I had returned from two years' national service, stretching our spirits in relaxed freedom. I soon found that to speak in the Union was a stressful experience, especially if you hoped for office. One day, a Labour Club colleague called John Nevin approached me. 'Your content is excellent, Greville,' he said. 'But you talk like an express train. Your mind is faster than your speech and your speech is incomprehensible to the audience.'

'Oh dear,' I replied. 'What can I do about that?'
'Don't be so arrogant,' John replied. 'Get yourself some training in slowing down. Then you'll be great.'

I found a speech trainer in Notting Hill. His recording machine was an ancient gramophone, but it did the trick. He ... slowed ... me ... down ... and he taught me the key to public speaking. You must ask yourself four questions: Who? What? Why? and How?

Who? means who are your audience? The Union was entirely male. Yes, we had women guest speakers. But no lady members. First job, then: to battle for the admission of women. Our campaign was led by Jack (now Lord) Ashley, famous because he did not wear black tie. He refused to do so while his family's lives were difficult.

What? What do they want? What does your audience want to hear from you? In Union terms, that meant clear speech, reaching the back of the debating chamber – and argument, laced with wit.

Why? Why are you making the speech? What do you want to put across? That means preparing your case and deciding what the key points are, especially those that will win victory for your side.

Finally: How? That means technique. Talking to your audience and not ranting at them ... not reading your speech ... putting notes on the despatch box and consulting them, but not being tied to a script ... above all, always watching the House and reacting to it, including responding to questions from the floor.

I did my best to follow all of these rules and to learn from our outstanding speakers. My hero was Percy Cradock. He was a brilliantly witty speaker. We all had to wear our gowns for our speeches and he lifted his up with both elbows, like a hawk about to pounce.

The competition for office was fierce but once you worked your way up to Secretary, you were rarely challenged for the presidency. I was, by a man called John Silberrad, who raised the banner of anti-tradition, happily to little effect.

Next stage: planning your programme. I wrote to many great leaders inviting them to join us. One was the great American general, Dwight D. Eisenhower, and I have a letter from him in which he refused, 'with real regret ... I have had to make it a matter of policy to confine my engagements strictly to those connected with NATO or my command.' But the eventual list was remarkable.

What a fabulous thrill it was to take the chair for the first time as President. I could scarcely believe my good fortune as I looked around at my colleagues, political friend and foe alike, generously applauding.

Then for the programme. Our first debate was on 22 January 1952: 'This House will deplore the restoration of university representation', proposed by the Labour leader, Hugh Gaitskell. Then: '*Si vis pacem para bellum*' – if you want peace, prepare for war. The key pacifist speaker was the Revd Dr Donald Soper.

The next debate and the first presidential ball were both cancelled, following the death of King George VI, but we still managed a Victorian musical evening. We argued 'that the English Channel should be abolished' – opposers included Douglas (now Lord) Hurd, then Vice-President. And I organised the first staff debate.

The sixth debate: 'This House would eat, drink and be merry, for tomorrow we die', including the then famous comedians Jimmy Edwards and Richard Goolden. Seventh debate: 'The English moral code is out of date' – a battle between free livers and religious traditionalists.

On 10 March 1952, Douglas Hurd was elected as President, unopposed. As retiring President, I proposed the motion: 'This House deplores the cynicism of our age' – opposed by the famous writer Stephen Potter and the first woman MP, Lady Astor.

My favourite excursion was to Dublin, together with Douglas Hurd, to debate in Trinity College. The argument itself was not memorable, but the basement booze-up that followed it was remarkable. We were required to fill our mugs with beer and to raise them in salute, singing out a greeting to their bosses: 'Hey ho – bugger the Board!'

I have often been invited back as a guest speaker. Recently, I argued for a maximum 90-day detention period for suspected terrorists, and was happily surprised to lose by only half a dozen votes. As I sat listening to the speeches, I thought about the remarkable changes over the half century. The most obvious: the President and the officers to each side of her were all women. What a waste of talent and beauty was female absence; in my day we kept losing the battle for women to be members.

Strangely, everything else is remarkably unchanged. First, the dress of the male officers and speakers. White tie and tails for the mighty men and black tie for the paper speakers ... and evening dress for the very handsome lady officers. True, most of the audience are much more relaxed in their clothing, which makes the contrast even more notable.

Next: the formalities remain. Paper speakers still rest their papers on the despatch boxes and most read too much and pretend to be speaking informally, which still gives an advantage to people like myself who prefer to chat to the members, both those before you and not forgetting those behind, who are mostly your supporters.

Procedures remain much the same – including the right to try to interrupt, but also the speaker's privilege of deciding whether or not to accept questions from the floor.

The overall and happy result for ancient officers of the Union like myself is that we feel at home there. I am still apprehensive before I speak, with fear dropping away once the first words emerge – an art which I learned in the Union and have practised since, both within Parliament and outside it. As in the House of Commons, disagree-

110

ment is vocal and expected. But while you do battle in public, when the debate is over so is your aggression.

For me, then, Union experience proved crucial to my later public and parliamentary work. As a fellow ex-President once said to me: 'If you can hold your nerves with a Union audience, you can cope with anything.' Well, most things, anyway. And for that I am and will remain grateful to the Cambridge Union.

Recollection: The Rt. Hon. the Lord Hurd of Westwell CH CBE

(Mr D.R. Hurd, Trinity)
President, Easter Term 1952

A scholar at Eton and Trinity, Douglas Hurd was chairman of Cambridge University Conservative Association in Michaelmas 1951 and President of the Union in Easter 1952. After Cambridge, he spent fourteen years in HM Diplomatic Service before joining the Conservative Research Department in 1966. He was private secretary to Edward Heath as Leader of the Opposition, and his political secretary as Prime Minister.

Elected to Parliament in February 1974, Hurd served as Secretary of State for Northern Ireland (1984–5), Home Secretary (1985–9) and Foreign Secretary (1989–95). He was created a Companion of Honour in 1996, and raised to the peerage the following year. He has written a number of history books, nine novels and a collection of short stories.

It all seems a very long time ago. The turning point in my under-graduate career at the Cambridge Union came on 3 June 1951 when I won the secretaryship by one vote, beating the better known Labour candidate, Brian Abel-Smith. My diary for the next twelve months, my last year at Cambridge, is full of references, often in a complaining tone, about the Union. I moved smoothly enough up what was then a normal ladder, serving as Vice-President under Greville Janner in 1952 and becoming President for the summer term that year.

Perhaps more revealing than the laconic diary entries are two dreams which still occasionally revisit me. The first is that I am about to sit the Cambridge Tripos having done no work on the subjects examined. The second is that I have organised, as President, a Union debate but all the proposed speakers have pulled out at the last minute. No other dreams come back to me as regularly as those two.

The Union in those days was highly politicised. This reflected a real sense of political excitement which, I suspect, ran deeper in the University then than at any time since. These were the dying days of the Attlee Labour government. This government has received a verdict from history better than it deserved, and certainly much better than most of us felt justified at the time. The Union, for example, held a vote of no confidence in the Labour government during the general election campaign of 1951. I was not satisfied with my own speech proposing the motion, but we beat the government by 513 votes to 204. Those weeks many of us were out night after night in the villages of Cambridgeshire and Norfolk, heckling the Labour candidate or holding the fort at village meetings until our own candidate appeared.

In February 1952, the BBC broadcast a Union debate and my diary records: 'I speak against the abolition of the English Channel – a flop, very similar to last time because I concentrated too much on the jokes which were laboured and too little on the serious stuff which could have worked into something reasonable. The best speaker was Peter Blaker, President of the Oxford Union, together with a visiting American, but on the whole I thought we put up a feeble performance for the BBC.'

The summer presidential term of 1952 went reasonably well, though behind the scenes I was often frantic because speakers pulled out or failed to answer letters. The Union was approaching financial difficulty but efforts to raise the subscription fee failed. Sometimes, as happens, a small group of undergraduate members were particularly fond of the sound of their own voices in committee meetings. They complicated the life of the President and of the admirable Mr Elwood, who steered the ship quietly from the chief clerk's office while the rest of us were arguing on the bridge. My final presidential debate on 3 June 1952 attracted a distinguished bunch of speakers – A.L. Rowse, Harold Nicolson and Enoch Powell – debating the motion taken from Pope, 'For forms of government let fools contest, whate'er is best administered is best'. Once again I thought my own speech was undistinguished but the evening as a whole went without mishap.

All this sounds rather negative. I suspect that most contributors to this volume will be genuinely recording the lively enjoyment which they felt at the Union. The fault lies with me rather than the Union. The time which I spent in politics at Cambridge, including the Union, was at the expense of other things which I neglected. I am not thinking of work, for I worked hard and did reasonably well. But there are many gaps in my education – music, painting, philosophy, European literature – which I could have started to fill at Cambridge had I not spent so much time at the Union and the Conservative Association.

In recent years, Presidents of the Union have been generous in their invitations. Each time I have gone I have enjoyed myself and the events have been pleasantly organised. Increasingly, however, I turn down invitations to the classic adversarial debates. Here, again, this is no criticism of the Union. It simply reflects my growing conviction that there are rarely only two sides to a debate. To force a topic into the straitjacket of a two-sided debate is to narrow that debate and make it, to some extent, artificial. I am not sure whether this is a quirky prejudice of old age on my part, or whether it reflects the general dissatisfaction in this country with the style of politics elaborated in the House of Commons and copied in the Cambridge Union. I am sure that the Union is right to experiment with new ways of organising discussion, not just of politics but of all other subjects which should ripen through debate in any university, outside lecture rooms and examinations.

1955–59: Scandals,
Squabbles and Suez

If the early years of the 1950s were a golden age, the latter half of the decade was one of greater turbulence and controversy. Though political scandals and disputes have been essential characteristics of the Union from its inception, they emerge from the records of this period with particular frequency. In their way, perhaps, they are a sign of a new decadence: the absence of external pressures – no war, no debts, no clash of radical ideologies – allowing student intrigues to come to the fore. Only major international crises, in Hungary and in Suez, would turn undergraduate attention back to the world beyond Cambridge.

A perennial ingredient of Union controversies has been the Society's relationship with the student press. Before the Second World War, the main publications were the *Cambridge Review* and *Granta*, more nineteenth-century literary magazines than newspapers. Both carried reviews of Union debates which, although they gently mocked the speakers, were essentially reverential to the institution. After the war, a new publication was added in the shape of *Varsity*. Founded by a Californian and some of his friends who decided that Cambridge needed an American-style campus newspaper, the first issue appeared on 19 April 1947. Although the editorial line of the paper has changed frequently, each new editor recasting it on an almost termly basis, the existence of *Varsity* in Cambridge has meant greater coverage of the Union's affairs – and often greater criticism. Aspirant officers have vied to get their names in print believing that this would boost their electoral prospects; rejected candidates have turned to it as a medium for retribution; most of all, those who simply thought the Union to be a waste of time and money have used its pages to say so. But the relationship has been a symbiotic one: fragile Union egos have enjoyed the attention as much as frantic *Varsity* editors have been grateful for juicy stories to fill their pages. As one former editor who has trawled its archives extensively asks: 'What would there be to report on if nobody took the Union seriously?'[1]

The minutes and reports of the 1950s record the Union's fraught relations with *Varsity*, and hint at many squabbles long since forgotten. In Lent 1953, for instance, Peter Mansfield – himself later a distinguished journalist and Middle East correspondent for the *Sunday Times* – presided over a debate on the motion 'That *Varsity* is no credit to this University'. Sydney Elwood could recall 'no special significance' for the debate, in which the paper's honour was successfully defended by Tam Dalyell – though he might later have had cause to reassess his opinion.[2] A Vice-President's report the following year recorded 'the straining of the Society's relationship with the less responsible of the undergraduate weeklies' and hoped 'that a change of shepherd might bring the flock back into the fold next year'.[3] It was, of course, a vain hope. Another row erupted in Lent 1955, when Ken Post of St John's was elected Secretary. Post, a 22-stone working-class boy, had been the subject of an article entitled 'Popular Prole' in the previous week's edition of *Varsity*, which his defeated opponent, the CUCA chairman Robin O'Neill, claimed had affected the outcome of the election. A select committee found insufficient evidence to suggest his connivance with the article, but fined the editor of *Varsity* – one Michael Winner of Downing – five guineas. Post, who was well-liked as a humorous speaker, went on to become President in Michaelmas 1956, and died young. There was further controversy in the No Confidence debate during his term, when two coloured smoke bombs were thrown through the window of the chamber just after the speech of Sir Geoffrey de Freitas, an ex-

President and Labour MP. The debate was adjourned and the House of more than 600 had to be evacuated, 'blinded by clouds of billowing red and blue smoke'. The proceedings were resumed twenty minutes later, after Post had encouraged members to help clear the fumes by 'flapping their gowns'.[4]

A heated private business meeting in Easter 1953 ended with the expulsion of a member from the Society – 'an event unparalleled within living memory'.[5] Michael Moss of Trinity was ordered to leave the chamber after a heated exchange with the President, Ian McIntyre, who would later become the presenter of the BBC's *Analysis* programme and the controller of Radio 4 and Radio 3. Moss, a regular contributor to Union debates and former presidential candidate (finishing bottom of the poll with thirteen votes), had been involved in a similar incident the previous term, for which he had been fined. He obeyed McIntyre's order to leave, but returned at the end of the meeting to vote in the division. Ordered to leave again, he refused and was fined two guineas. Still he stayed in his place, commencing a lengthy defence of his conduct. When he ignored a final order to leave, McIntyre announced that, under the laws of the Society, he was expelled as a member. The situation was only defused when a surprised Elwood was asked to come into the chamber, and quietly suggested Moss step outside. Over the next few days, Moss took to sitting on the low wall at the entrance to the Union, but made no attempt to enter the premises. Interviewed by *Varsity*, he declined to make any comment, other than to say: 'Of course, I should like to be readmitted if it is possible'.[6] Five days later, when tempers had cooled, another private business meeting was called to consider the incident. McIntyre read a letter of apology from Moss, which he accepted, and the laws were suspended to allow his readmission.

Later that term Mark Boxer, the editor of *Granta*, was rusticated for publishing a poem which the proctors considered blasphemous. The Union rallied to the defence of free speech. A private debate was held in which a motion deploring the action of the proctors and the suppression of the magazine was passed by 104 to 46. On 24 May, a 'mock funeral' was held for Boxer, with a procession from King's College chapel to the railway station. A magnificent Victorian hearse was borrowed for the occasion and Hugh Thomas, newly elected as President of the Union, was asked to delivered the eulogy. He had been lunching in Trumpington, and had only the short walk back to gather his thoughts:

> I imagined there'd be about ten people there, but when it came to the point, I went out through the King's porters' lodge [and] suddenly found the street was absolutely packed. People were hanging out the windows and standing on the scaffolding everywhere. It was my most challenging hour.[7]

Although Thomas's speech went well, the protest did not overturn the proctors' ruling and Boxer was unable to come back up at the end of term to take his degree. Not that it held him back, recalls Lord Thomas: 'It made him a name in London. He immediately got a job offer, and he went from strength to strength.'[8] One further consequence of the *Granta* row was the Union's decision to lift its ancient and self-imposed ban on debating theological motions the following Easter.

Thomas's role as the dissidents' orator did not land him in trouble personally. He graduated at the end of that term, staying on at Queens' for a tenth term to preside over the Union before going to the Sorbonne. After three years in the Foreign Office he became a lecturer at Sandhurst, and then professor of history at Reading. His numerous works include acclaimed histories of the Spanish civil war, the Suez affair, and Cuba. He was chairman of the Centre for Policy Studies, the free-market think-tank established by Margaret Thatcher and Sir Keith Joseph, from 1979 to 1990. He entered the House of Lords as a Conservative in 1981, but now sits as a crossbencher.

Free speech was once more an issue in Easter 1954, when the President, Nicholas Tomalin, invited Sir Oswald Mosley to speak in a debate. Tomalin, who was also editor of *Granta* during his time at

Trinity Hall, later became a celebrated journalist. From humble beginnings as a gossip column editor, he developed a well-rounded career. He was literary editor of the *New Statesman*, wrote a history of the National Theatre, and sent despatches from Vietnam for the *Sunday Times*. He was killed in the Middle East while reporting on the Arab-Israeli war in 1973. His obituary in *The Times* was subtitled: 'One of the finest reporters of his generation'; the paper's editor, William Rees-Mogg, said he was 'a great loss to English reporting'.[9] His widow was the author and biographer Claire Tomalin, who later married another Cantabrigian writer, Michael Frayn.

The debate to which Mosley had been invited was one 'welcom[ing] the attempt by the Union Movement of Great Britain to advocate by legal means a complete change in the system of government'. Two motions were brought to a private business meeting at the start of term. One, asking Tomalin to cancel the debate, was lost by 19 votes to 15; another regretting his action was lost even more heavily by 22 to 13. Though it drew only a small House, the minute book mentions 'a scuffle during the meeting'.

So the debate went ahead as planned on 11 May. It was preceded by a motion proposed by the Vice-President, Giles Shaw, 'thanking the President for his arrangement and conduct of the debate'. It was seconded by the ex-President Derick Mirfin of Magdalene, who was speaking opposite Sir Oswald, and was overwhelmingly carried by a chamber filled almost to capacity. A large crowd had assembled on the pathway and the lawn outside, where 'scores of people were hammering to get in'.[10] Some were protesters against the debate; others were plucky members who climbed the fire escapes in the hope of gaining admission. Sir Oswald had requested seats in the gallery for '54 intimate friends' – it was agreed that he could bring twelve, who were members of his Union Movement. Rising to his feet, Mosley spoke for 42 minutes. He put the case 'cleverly and ably' but his oratorical spell did not work on the House, whose forensic behaviour Mirfin proudly reported in a letter home the following morning:

The great audience of young men did not greet him with insult or violence – although they made no doubt of the loathing in which they held him. They did not catcall or raise a riot. They sized him up, they applauded his debating points, they gave him his due, as the Devil deserves. And then, having formed their estimate, they poured on him the scorn, disgust and ridicule which so vile a man merits ... By the end of the debate, the arrogant cast of the jaw had fallen away, his proud self-assured air had withered; he looked exhausted, deflated, disillusioned.[11]

When the House divided, the motion was resoundingly defeated: Ayes 54; Noes 704. The voting figures omitted the many other members who sat in the gallery and left by the fire escapes, or listened to the debate via loudspeakers in the bar.

———

The biggest Union controversies, of course, were those relating to its termly elections, long a test of the dark political arts as well as the nobler ones. In the early 1950s these were often split along party lines, with each of the main political clubs whipping up their members to support favoured candidates. For a while, a 'gentleman's agreement' between the three parties put an end to the practice – but in Easter 1952, with the number of their supporters in the Union dwindling, the Labour Club made sure that their preferred candidates were successful and once again employed 'a thorough whip.' This reversion to old practices spelt disaster to Derick Mirfin, president of the Liberal Club:

The upshot is that the Tories are furious. The Labour whip is an affront to public taste, and the Labour success an insult to Toryism. At the next election, the Tories will come out strong against [the] opposition by using their own whip. They have 800 Union members and could if organised sweep the whole Society with Tory candidates.

This thought is appalling. Not only will it spell disaster for the Liberals and even the Socialists. It will entail the entire degradation of Union politics.[12]

In fact, it was not disastrous as far as Mirfin's own Union career was concerned. At the end of November 1953, he was elected President without any opposition. But there was trouble for the other two parties in relation to the rest of that term's elections: leading members of the Conservative Association and Labour Club were accused of colluding to influence the vote. A select committee was formed, and met over the weekend of 27–29 November. As well as the President and the Treasurer, it comprised several senior members of the University – including the economist John Vaizey and the jurist Eli Lauterpacht. Nigel Hammond, by now a trustee, acted as chairman. The committee considered written statements from various candidates, and called in a number of witnesses for questioning. It was 'an event which left an indelible imprint on all of us,' says Tam Dalyell, one of those embroiled in the row.[13] After its three-day hearing, the select committee delivered its unanimous verdict. Three people implicated in the allegations (including the future Presidents Giles Shaw and Nicholas Tomalin) were acquitted. In relation to the others – Dalyell, Allen Molesworth, then CUCA chairman, D.A. Gohl and Christopher Norwood, later Labour MP for Norwich South – the committee returned the equivocal verdict: 'not proven'. Its report noted conduct which, 'while not technically a breach of the Society's laws[,] certainly does represent a flagrant violation of the spirit of those laws and a regrettable departure from the standards of conduct which should prevail in relation to the affairs of the Society'.

Dalyell was to have further brushes with controversy during his three unsuccessful bids to win the presidency. He made his first attempt in Michaelmas 1954, running from what should have been a strong position as Vice-President and as the sitting chairman of CUCA. But he faced a six-way contest, his opponents including

Alan Watkins of Queens' and the Labour Club, later political columnist of the *Observer*; Philip Hobsbawm of Downing, cousin of Eric and later professor of English at Glasgow; John York of Clare, another Conservative who was a 'large, bubbly man of great bonhomie'; and Richard Moore of Trinity, a Liberal whom Dalyell had beaten to the vice-presidency in 'a needle election' the previous term.[14] After the elimination of the low-polling candidates, the votes split clearly in Moore's favour: he won 251 to 183 in the final round. Dalyell says that Moore 'deserved to win. I'd made a dreadful paper speech at the beginning of term ... and was punished for it.' As CUCA chairman, Dalyell was asked to oppose the annual No Confidence motion. Speaking immediately after him was Hugh Gaitskell – and the soon-to-be leader of the Labour party clearly detected the first inklings of the young Dalyell's political conversion. 'Gaitskell simply got up and said, "I wondered why the previous speaker was speaking in the Conservative interest, because all his ideas fitted in with those of the Labour Party" – and it was true.'[15] Nonetheless, Shaw recalls, the defeat was 'a very severe blow to Tam'.[16]

Moore, like Mirfin, was a firm Liberal. The two served successively as secretary-general of the Liberal International after Cambridge, and both stood as Liberal parliamentary candidates from the 1950s to the 1970s. Mirfin's candidacies included the Stratford by-election which followed John Profumo's resignation in 1963. Moore stood in Norfolk, Devon and Northern Ireland; his son, Charles, followed him to Trinity and became editor of the *Daily Telegraph*.

The great controversy of Moore's term arose from the visit of Jawaharlal Nehru, the Indian Prime Minister. Nehru, who had been an undergraduate at Trinity, was proposed for honorary membership of the Society at a private business meeting at the start of term. The motion was moved by the Vice-President and the Secretary, but a rearguard action was mounted by Tertius Metcalf, an eccentric historian from Downing. Though an ardent Liberal, Metcalf had a complex collection of beliefs. A Jesuit and a Jacobite, his obituarist in *The Times* noted his 'curious combination of an eclectic intellect, a profound piety, a sartorial fastidiousness and a tendency towards misogyny'.[17] In later life, he continued to revel in the disputes of private members' clubs as a vocal opponent of women members at the Travellers and the Reform Clubs; when members of the Oxford and Cambridge Club resigned after a bid to admit women failed, Metcalf promptly joined in order to show his support for the decision.

On this occasion he did not defeat the honorary membership motion, but he did prevent it attaining the three-quarters majority required. With Nehru's visit to Cambridge already arranged, this was a great embarrassment – especially as the Union's laws prevented a failed motion being resubmitted in the same term. A special motion had to be brought to suspend that part of the laws and put the original motion again. Again Metcalf led the opposition, but a much larger House had been summoned, and the honorary membership was agreed by 161 votes to 9. Nehru was officially welcomed at his visit on 10 February. Moore ceded his chair to the ex-President, Mirfin, and presented the guest with a copy of Cradock's book. A debate followed, on the motion that virtuosity is preferable to virtue, but no division was taken. Mirfin showed Nehru around the Union before the meeting, finding him 'quite at ease and v. curious to know what had befallen the Society since he was a member years ago'. The building looked more prosperous, he concluded, 'but not half so comfortable'.[18]

Having missed the opportunity to play host to the Indian Prime Minister, Tam Dalyell made his second bid for the presidency in Michaelmas 1955. This time he faced a straight fight – against a Liberal, Martin Rosenhead of St John's. Dalyell remembers Rosenhead as 'a tremendous go-getter' and 'an exceedingly ambitious undergraduate' – though 'there was no personal animosity' in their election.[19] It was closely pitched, but Rosenhead came out on top by 39 votes, winning 258 to Dalyell's 219.

Undeterred, Dalyell made a third attempt the following term. If he had hoped it would prove third time lucky, he was to be cruelly disappointed. This time he had two competitors: Ronald Peierls, a Labour man from Caius, and the colourful Metcalf of Downing, running as an independent. It was a fascinating contest, complicated by the single transferable vote system. In the week before the poll, the Society was rife with rumours of Conservative-Labour pacts over second preferences, and of a Conservative split – the 'machine men' for Dalyell and 'whimsicals' for Metcalf.[20] Liberal leaders largely pledged themselves to Metcalf, but a good many rank and file supported Peierls. Numerous constituencies were rallied, both for and against each candidate – Peierls was Jewish, Metcalf Catholic and Dalyell an Old Etonian.

After an intensely fought campaign, the votes were counted. Dalyell led the first round, with the battle to escape elimination decided by a single vote:

Dalyell	223
Metcalf	201
Peierls	200

The ballot was checked four times, then Peierls was eliminated. But his was not the only fortune affected by the result: most of Peierls's second preferences went to Metcalf, who pulled ahead of Dalyell, beating him to the presidency by 285 to 270. Deprived of victory for a third time, Dalyell requested two further recounts of the first round, neither of which produced any change in the result between Metcalf and Peierls. He then demanded a full 'scrutiny' of the vote, to which he was entitled under the electoral rules. The Society's staff and counting agents worked until midnight, checking each member on the voting register against the Society's full membership list. This process revealed that five reciprocal members had voted without being so entitled: two for Dalyell, two for Metcalf and one for Peierls. This left the new first-round figures as a tie:

Dalyell	221
Metcalf	199
Peierls	199

No one knew what to do. The rules about the process in the event of a tie were unclear, and no precedent could be found. Rosenhead, the President, was in a fix. It was by now the small hours of the morning, and some argued strongly that another election should be called. As a friend of Metcalf's, Rosenhead was also conscious of the need to demonstrate impartiality. He ruled that the stalemate should be decided by the drawing of lots. Metcalf and Peierls, 'under the pressure of an almost hysterically exhausted committee room', agreed.[21] Two billiard balls – one red, one white – were placed in a bag. Each candidate drew a ball. Peierls picked the winning one, and went through to the second round. Metcalf, who had earlier celebrated his presidential victory, was eliminated. But the new outcome was no better for Dalyell. Metcalf's second preferences were counted and gave the victory to Peierls – by just one vote.

Every candidate lost out. Metcalf was humiliated in the press as a 'deposed' President; Peierls was condemned to an unhappy term after his Pyrrhic victory; and Dalyell was pilloried for losing twice more in one night because of his constitutional pedantry. The press were bemused by the Union's Byzantine electoral practices, and suspected a stitch-up. Mirfin drafted a letter of clarification to the *Daily Telegraph* with Evelyn Ebsworth, an ex-standing committee member from King's (and later Vice-Chancellor of Durham), but did not send it after being dissuaded by Metcalf's friends and family. A statement was drawn up for *Varsity* and approved by the standing committee. The repercussions of the election continued for months: three separate schemes making provisions for tied ballots were brought to a PBM in May. A sub-committee was established to review the electoral laws. It reported back in Michaelmas 1956, but its proposals failed to win sufficient support at another PBM at the end of that term. Clarifying amendments were finally approved at a special meeting held in February 1957 – almost a year after the 'billiard ball' election.

But if Ronald Peierls was elected under a cloud of controversy, he was a well-respected figure at the Union. His father was Sir Rudolph Peierls, the German-born nuclear scientist and member of the

Manhattan Project, and Ron spoke memorably on scientific topics. As an eighteen-year-old freshman, he spoke with the astronomer Fred Hoyle on the motion 'That the progress of science has upset our sense of values' – it was a *tour de force* without notes', remembers Dalyell.[22] In Easter 1955, Peierls attracted attention by *opposing* a motion that the manufacture of the hydrogen bomb was morally and politically justified. Though there was a poor House, as it was Easter Term, there were 22 floor speeches and the motion was narrowly defeated, 49 to 47.

A welcome respite from the controversies of the period came in Michaelmas 1954, when Giles Shaw was President. A proud Yorkshireman of diminutive stature, Shaw was 'one of the most favourably and best-remembered undergraduates of the first half of the 1950s,' according to Tam Dalyell, a long-standing friend.[23] 'Endowed with a delicious and unusual wit, devoid of malice, never, ever coarse', he was 'a sparkling and authoritative President.'[24] As a long-serving Conservative MP, representing Pudsey from 1974 to 1997, he won similar plaudits in Westminster, where he was 'probably the most popular man of his time in the Commons'.[25] He served as a minister in the Home Office and the Department of Trade and Industry, and was knighted in 1987.

By his own admission, Shaw 'set out to become President of the Union'. To this end, he 'accepted invitations to other College debating societies ... and also proposed toasts at many good dinners in aid of many good causes, one of them being to become known in other colleges as a likely Union performer'.[26] It worked: he was elected unopposed for the Michaelmas Term 1954. One of the highlights of his term was the first Union ball, held in the chamber. The benches were all removed to make way for a dance floor and orchestra, and members bought tickets for £2 10s 0d for themselves and their lady guests. Shaw recalled the night as 'a fabulous success ... a sell-out which provided not only a first-class evening but also a substantial contribution to Union funds'.[27] Sydney Elwood, demonstrating the realism of an ex-chief clerk rather than the effusiveness of an ex-President, remembers a slight loss – but the evening was deemed a success, and one to be repeated.

Another 'first' of Shaw's term came when he persuaded his mother to speak in one of his debates. Lady Isobel Barnett, star of the popular television panel show *What's My Line?* had been due to speak in the debate 'That this House deplores the disappearance of the chaperon', but had been forced to cancel at the very last moment. A large audience had come to see her – including Shaw's mother and father, both fans. With no time to arrange an alternative speaker, Shaw prevailed upon his mother to take Lady Isobel's place. She appeared on the order paper as 'Alderman Mrs Shaw, JP', and was summoned by the President with the words: 'I now call upon my Mum to address the assembly'. She spoke impromptu for about five minutes and won a rousing ovation when she sat down. Her proud son 'came down from the Chair and gave her a big kiss and presented her with the carnation from my buttonhole to rapturous applause'.[28] She had the added pleasure of helping to win the debate, which was carried 385 to 277.

Shaw enjoyed the opportunities that the Union offered. He went on a debating tour of Canada with another President, John Waite of Corpus (later knighted as a High Court judge and a Lord Justice of Appeal), and attended a number of formal debates around the country. At one, held at Lloyd's of London, he debated with his Oxford counterpart, Michael Heseltine. Shaw invited him to speak in his retirement debate at the end of term but was disappointed when, expecting a return invitation to Heseltine's presidential debate, 'I received two tickets for the Strangers' Gallery'.[29]

———•———

The autumn of 1956 abruptly turned the focus of undergraduate opinion away from internal squabbles and back to international affairs. Three weeks into term, a peaceful demonstration by students in Budapest sparked the Hungarian uprising. John Nott, a former Gurkha officer and future Defence Secretary, had just come up to

Trinity, and recalls the mood that Michaelmas in his contribution to this volume. Initially, the Hungarian revolution divided undergraduates 'between those who did not care to see an outside event distract them from their studies and their fun, and those who followed it with intense concern'.[30] After news of the Soviet intervention spread, however, there was greater attention – a private business meeting in January 1957 voted unanimously to open Union membership to the Hungarian refugees who had been received in Cambridge, and to use £50 of the Society's funds to pay their subscriptions. Perhaps fittingly, the President that term, Noël Marshall, made his career in the Foreign Office, as an Ambassador and the UK's permanent representative to the Council of Europe. He retired in 1993 and, at the age of 60, skippered his own yacht in a circumnavigation of the world. Marshall's successor-but-one as President, Keith MacInnes, had a similar diplomatic career: he was Ambassador to the Philippines, then the UK's permanent representative to the OECD. The Hon. Julian Grenfell, of Eton and King's, who followed in Lent 1959, also made his work in an international organisation. After a stint as a television reporter, he worked for the World Bank in Washington and Paris, and as its representative to the UN in 1974–81. He entered the House of Lords as the 3rd Baron Grenfell in 1976, and was created a life peer in his own right in 2000.

Whereas Hungary at first grabbed the attention of only the worldlier members of the University, the second international crisis of that term – the Suez débâcle – 'galvanised opinion' and threw Cambridge into 'turmoil'.[31] A requisition demanded a special meeting on the crisis, which was held on 1 November 'in a packed and tense House'.[32] The original motion – 'That this House doubts the wisdom of the Government's hasty intervention in the Middle East' – was replaced by a tougher one 'oppos[ing] the armed intervention of the Government in the Middle East without the authorisation of the United Nations', and carried 218–136. The following evening, the Union chamber was the venue for a massive protest meeting sponsored by sixteen different clubs and societies. Among the speakers were Kenneth Younger, the Shadow Home Secretary, and an ex-President of the Oxford Union now in his second term as a Labour MP, the Hon. Anthony Wedgwood Benn. He recorded the experience in his diaries:

> The Union debating hall was absolutely packed tight with crowds round it trying to get in through the windows and jamming the entrance thirty deep. We struggled to reach our places. The UN flag had been stolen and there were wildly noisy scenes and shouts. Great posters hung from the gallery reading, 'Support Eden, not Nasser' and 'We are now committed and must support our troops'... The uproar and noise and silly funny remarks when the world was on the brink of disaster were completely revolting, disgusting and shameful.[33]

There was worse to come, as Nott reveals in his recollection. One Egyptian student present was heckled with cries of 'wog' when he rose to speak; a *Varsity* editorial on 10 November lamented that 'during the past ten days Cambridge opinion, basically sincere and honest, has been ruled by the mob'.[34]

As well as providing topics for heated debates, the Suez crisis affected the Union in more prosaic ways. By Lent 1957, the Vice-President, David Fairbairn – later a successful businessman and Freeman of the City of London – reported that the petrol shortage was restricting travel, making the President's task of persuading guest speakers to come to Cambridge 'doubly difficult'. But with Eden's resignation in January the heat of the crisis passed, and it was soon over.

After such an exciting first term, the rest of John Nott's time at Cambridge 'was a bore ... Had it not been that I met my wife there it would have represented the three most wasted years of my life.'[35] As President in Easter 1959, he organised a transatlantic radio debate with Harvard – inevitably dubbed a 'Cambridge-Cambridge' debate. The motion, 'This House thanks God for the Atlantic', was narrowly passed – with 240 for the Ayes and 231 for the Noes.

Nott was one of three ex-Presidents of the late 1950s to enter the House of Commons as a Conservative. Terence Higgins, his predecessor in Easter 1958, was a member of the British athletic team at both the 1948 and the 1952 Olympics, an economics lecturer at Yale, and a businessman for Unilever, before his election as MP for Worthing in 1964. He served as Financial Secretary to the Treasury, 1972–4, and was knighted in 1993; he retired in 1997 and was raised to the peerage. John Cockcroft, who followed him as President in Michaelmas 1958, had a shorter spell in the Commons, as MP for Nantwich between 1974 and 1979. He also made a career as an economic journalist for the *Financial Times* and the *Daily Telegraph*, and as a political and corporate adviser.

Despite their successes, the end of the 1950s showed signs of an emerging anti-Conservative mood. In April 1959, the motion 'Three cheers for the Young Conservatives' was defeated 21–20 on Nott's casting vote. The previous term, a motion considering the Conservative party 'to be the most truly progressive party in the country' was passed, though only by a majority of four (115 to 111). In Michaelmas 1959, the traditional No Confidence motion was replaced with one regretting the result of the general election held on 8 October, which had seen Macmillan returned with a majority of over 100. The Vice-President, Christopher Tugendhat, noted the slight change of mood in his end of term report: 'As so often happens here, Conservatism triumphed, though by a far smaller margin than in recent years.' Macmillan may have won a third term for the Tories, but it was clear that the tide was turning among the undergraduates of Cambridge.

It is all the more surprising, then, that just around the corner was one of the most successful Conservative generations the Union has ever known.

RECOLLECTION: THE RT. HON. SIR JOHN NOTT KCB

(Mr J.W.F. Nott, Trinity College)
President, Easter Term 1959

Sir John Nott was a lieutenant in the 2nd Gurkha Rifles in Malaysia before coming up to Trinity to read law and economics in 1956. He was called to the Bar in 1959 and went into merchant banking before his election to Parliament as the MP for St Ives in 1966. He joined the Cabinet as President of the Board of Trade in 1979, and was made Secretary of State for Defence in 1981. He offered his resignation to Margaret Thatcher the following year, after the invasion of the Falkland Islands, but it was not accepted. He left politics in 1983 to return to the City, and was chairman and chief executive of Lazard Brothers & Co. (1985–90).

My first term at Trinity in 1956 was the most interesting and intense of all the time that I spent at Cambridge because it was the autumn of Hungary and Suez.

I had started life as a regular soldier with the Gurkhas in Malaya and was extracted from the jungle to act as ADC to the Commander-in-Chief Far East Land Forces in Singapore. The Foreign Office telegrams (which I hastily binned when I became a Cabinet minister) fascinated me as they passed across my desk on the way to the general. As I read the telegrams, I thought that politics is where I must be, not carting around the world fighting 'forgotten wars' as a soldier. So, arriving at Cambridge, I visited the Union where I intended to make my mark. But far more immediate than the events in the Union was the invasion of Hungary by the Soviets. I was deeply upset that the West offered no logistical or even much moral support to the Hungarians. In my then idealistic state, I even considered a foolish journey to Budapest – and talked quite widely about my concern. I suppose the then President, Ken Post, heard about this mature undergraduate – at 23, I was a couple of years older than the majority who had completed their national service – and, to my intense surprise, he visited me in my rooms in Great Court.

'I want an unknown freshman to open a debate on Hungary,' said Post. 'I know your background as a soldier and you are just the man to do it.' I hesitated and protested that I had never spoken in a debate before, but he insisted.

The debate took place on Tuesday 6 November 1956 and I proposed the motion that 'This House would risk a Third World War for the sake of a Communist satellite in revolt'. It was a passionate debate on both sides and I, of course, placed a lot of emphasis on the word 'risk': 'Only by confronting aggression, with all the risks involved, would we ever sustain freedom and democracy.' I suppose similar sentiments occupied me when I took responsibility for the introduction of Trident.

Anyhow, the Union members showed their maturity by rejecting the motion at around midnight. We lost. Three hundred and one votes were cast against and 271 for the motion, but it was quite a debate. I doubt if 570 undergraduates attend debates today.

The press reported that 'it was a serious-minded and often deeply held debate on the dilemma of the West. John Nott's poise and debating skills won the support of the House.'

The Suez invasion followed – and I was sickened that it distracted the attention of the world away from Hungary. Suez divided Cambridge in a way that Hungary had not. The public school contingent, led by the Hooray Henrys of the Pitt Club, of which I am ashamed to say I was a member, arranged to let loose the Trinity Foot Beagles into the chamber during a passionate speech by the

'Honourable Anthony Wedgwood Benn'. Benn's diaries contain the extract:

> My notes were carried away by a rotten tomato and stink bombs, and lavatory paper was thrown all over the place. One did not mind that but it was the flippancy on such a grave issue that was so completely horrifying ... The crowd of students laughing and screaming for war gave me an icy hatred of them.[36]

My goodness, Tony Benn was correct – how did I ever become a Tory? It amazes me to this day! Tory support for the invasion of Iraq is equally astonishing.

Surprisingly, the Hungarian debate was the only occasion, during my entire Union career, when I made a serious speech, except perhaps when I successfully proposed the motion that 'This House has no confidence in Her Majesty's Opposition'. It was seconded by 'Brigadier J. Enoch Powell'. *Plus ça change.*

Later I proposed the motion, and still believe every word of it, that 'Man fulfils himself most fully when uselessly employed'. It was carried overwhelmingly of course. The motion 'This seat of learning needs darning' followed, as did my presidential debate, when I proposed the age-old motion 'That oratory is the harlot of the arts'. There isn't oratory any more, so it showed considerable premonition of the way that public speaking would go. As did the motion that 'The age of chivalry is dead'. Chivalry certainly is dead, made impossible by the independent-minded career women who crave chivalry, but have not the time or inclination to hang around encouraging it.

My election was a close-run thing. In the way these things go, my contemporary, John Cockcroft, stayed on an extra year in order to take the presidency in Michaelmas 1958. This meant that the next three in line were in trouble, and far and away the most brilliant of us was someone called Roger Warren Evans, who stepped down for reasons that no one understood. I slipped in for the summer term, one month after my marriage and just before the final Tripos.

Sadly, I cannot say that I enjoyed debating in the Union; it was a means to an end, and I suppose that when I eventually did my rounds to find a seat in Parliament it looked good on my CV, but then no one has ever asked me if I was President of the Union, where I went to school, or what degree I obtained – which I suppose is rather fortunate.

1960–67:
THE 'CAMBRIDGE MAFIA'

At the end of 1958, the Hon. Julian Grenfell recorded in his vice-presidential report: 'The term's debating has been marked by the emergence of an encouraging number of maiden speakers of considerable promise'. The following term his successor, John Nott, noted: 'There are, at least, 10 freshmen who show great promise'.

In Michaelmas 1960, the new President issued an edict to make it easier for members to speak from the floor. Henceforth, only paper speakers would speak from the despatch box, and the speakers' book – in which anyone wishing to contribute registered their interest before the debate – would be discontinued. Instead, they could just catch the President's eye by standing up.

It seemed to work. In the first debate of his term, the annual motion of no confidence in Her Majesty's government, there were a healthy number of floor speeches. Because of a last-minute cancellation on the government side, the President himself had to open the case for the opposition. A glance at the record of the debate shows that he was supported by consecutive floor speeches from the chairman of the University Conservative Association; a second-year Caian; a lawyer from Peterhouse making his maiden speech; and a historian from Selwyn. When they were written into the debate book in October 1960, their names were unfamiliar to all but a few political devotees in Cambridge. But they stand out from the page four decades later. For the President that term was Leon Brittan, and the

137

speakers joining him in defending the government were Norman Fowler, Ken Clarke, Michael Howard and John Gummer. Together – and with Norman Lamont, who came up the following year – they all went on to serve in government themselves, and have become known as the 'Cambridge Mafia'.

For all their later political success, however, the group was unable to defend the Macmillan government successfully that evening. The motion was proposed by Tony Firth, 'one of the most brilliant of our Cambridge generation', remembers Fowler.[1] President the following term, Firth had a successful career in television after Cambridge, sadly cut short when he died at the age of 42. He was joined in proposition by George Brown, deputy leader of the Labour party. Representing the government was Hugh Fraser, at the time a junior defence minister, who made 'one of the most disastrous speeches' Fowler ever heard at the Union.[2] He misjudged the mood of the audience, threatening that Labour would reintroduce rationing. Then he compounded his humiliation by knocking his glass of water over the Secretary and dropping his whole speech on the floor. When the House divided, it was a resounding defeat for the government – 394 to 245 – the first time a Conservative government had lost the debate since Churchill returned to power in 1951.

The nascent Mafia took this result very seriously. A couple of days after the debate, Fowler was working in his rooms in Trinity Hall (which he shared with another future Tory MP, Peter Viggers). There was a knock at the door, and two undergraduates from the year below him – Clarke and Howard – appeared. 'They were worried at the damage the Union debate had done to the Conservative cause and they wanted urgent action to correct the position,' Fowler recalls.[3] Fortunately, he was able to provide it: the centrepiece to his term as CUCA chairman was a visit by the Prime Minister himself, Harold Macmillan. A row with the Labour Club – who had booked the chamber for a meeting with Barbara Castle and refused to move – meant it could not take place in the Union, but Macmillan's visit was a great success. In a characteristic display of the Mafia's independence (some would say arrogance), Fowler politely refused the suggestion of the Master of Trinity Hall that the Prime Minister should dine at high table there, taking him instead to Brittan's rooms at Trinity – which had been furnished with a new carpet for the occasion.[4]

It was precocious, perhaps, but the young men who ran CUCA and the Union in the early 1960s were confident in their own ability – and excited by a world which seemed to offer them the chance to succeed based on that alone. They knew what they wanted, and knew how to get it. Of the half dozen who made up the 'Mafia', all but Fowler served as President of the Union, and all but Howard were CUCA chairman. They carved up Cambridge politics between them in the early '60s, and seemed to do the same in the Cabinet in the '80s and '90s. Brittan, Howard and Clarke were all Home Secretary; Lamont and Clarke both Chancellor of the Exchequer. Fowler and Clarke both served as Health Secretary, and Gummer and Fowler were two Chairmen of the Conservative party. 'Occasionally,' Clarke told an interviewer in 1993, 'you can look round the Cabinet and think it looks like a CUCA committee meeting.'[5]

Other Cambridge contemporaries of theirs went on to success in Conservative politics. Two others sat around the Cabinet table: John Nott and David Howell. Brittan served as a European commissioner, as did another Union President of the same year, Christopher Tugendhat, after six years as MP for the Cities of London and Westminster. Both now sit in the House of Lords. Eight consecutive CUCA chairmen – from Peter Lloyd in Michaelmas 1959 to Hugh Dykes in Lent 1962 – became Members of Parliament (although two – Dykes and Peter Temple-Morris – later defected from the Tory party). Other prominent Conservative MPs played little role in either society. Peter Lilley 'never had the courage to speak' in the Union, while Michael Spicer – who, as chairman of the back-bench 1922 committee, would officially declare Michael Howard leader of the party in November 2003 – was more involved in his own pressure group, PEST (Pressure for Economic and Social Toryism), than in CUCA.[6]

It is tempting, knowing what glittering prizes lay in store for this Union generation, to view their undergraduate years as a precursor to what followed. Peter Riddell, in a thoughtful analysis of the career politician, warns us against such teleological temptations: 'Later achievement can, of course, make the earlier activities look more glittering in retrospect. Every half-remembered remark is treated as a pointer to future brilliance.'[7] Certainly, the Cambridge politicians in question did not seem so outstanding to many of their contemporaries. One of the first journalists to examine the Cambridge Mafia was Andrew Rawnsley – a Cambridge man himself, and a former *Varsity* editor – in an extended article for the *Guardian* in October 1988. 'As a group,' Rawnsley wrote, 'they appear to have struck most of their university contemporaries as a curiosity: fag-ends of the conservative Fifties, when the rest of student Britain was about to make a sharp left turn into the Sixties.'[8] He quotes John Dunn, a driving force behind the University Labour Club and Vice-President of the Union, now professor of political theory at King's:

> It didn't strike me that I was in the presence of people that would run the country. They were all tremendously unformidable. The most impressive, in an out-of-date sort of way, was Leon Brittan, who was clearly very bright and a fluent orator. But most of them seemed to be in a stage of prolonged adolescence. It was inconceivable that they would be running the country, even scary.[9]

The graduates of this era were not the first group to move from Oxbridge to prominence in national life. The Young England movement of the 1830s has been mentioned elsewhere in this volume, and Martin notes that Gladstone's third Cabinet contained three ex-Presidents of the Cambridge Union, and the Attlee Cabinet of 1945 two – with two other Union veterans.[10] Riddell observes how groups of the politically interested seem to cluster together, pointing to Cambridge of the 1920s (Rab Butler, Geoffrey Lloyd, Selwyn Lloyd and Hugh Foot), and Oxford of the 1930s (Denis Healey, Ted

Heath, Julian Amery, Hugh Fraser, Roy Jenkins and Tony Crosland). But these are not cohesive groupings. Five years separate Butler and Foot's presidential terms – more than a full Cambridge generation – and seven Heath and Crosland's at Oxford. Moreover, they come from different points on the political spectrum.

A more salutary point is that the Mafia were not atypical among their peers of that period in becoming leading characters in their chosen field. Cambridge fizzed with talent. In the Footlights, David Frost and Peter Cook were prominent figures – along with Humphrey Barclay, John Bird, the Goodies Tim Brooke-Taylor, Graeme Garden and Bill Oddie, and three Pythons: John Cleese, Eric Idle and Graham Chapman. At the Amateur Dramatic Club, Derek Jacobi, Miriam Margolyes and Ian McKellen trod the boards under the direction of Richard Eyre and Trevor Nunn. The student press was edited by future journalists and presenters: *Varsity* by Peter Pagnamenta and Richard Whiteley; *Granta* by David Frost.

A number of those in CUCA who did not wish to climb the greasy pole became successful academics. Colin Renfrew was a close friend of the Mafia, and was President of the Union in Easter 1961. Rawnsley reports the widely-held opinion that he was 'potentially the brightest star of their generation'.[11] But after briefly dabbling in national politics – standing in the Sheffield Brightside by-election in 1968 and slashing the Labour majority by 14,000 votes – Renfrew returned to an illustrious academic career at Cambridge. He was Disney Professor of Archaeology from 1981 to 2004, and Master of Jesus College, 1986–97. As such, he was the first of the group to enter the House of Lords, in 1991. He also served as chairman of the Union's trustees from 1994 to 1997. Two friends of Ken Clarke's at Caius became historians. John Barnes taught government at the LSE from 1964 to 2003 and has written extensively on the twentieth-century Conservative party; he contested the safe Labour seat of Walsall North three times in 1964–70. Norman Stone stayed in Cambridge until 1984, when he was appointed professor of modern history at Oxford. Though he was not active in CUCA, he hosted long bridge sessions in his rooms for leading lights of the Conservative

Association – and later became a speechwriter and adviser to Margaret Thatcher. Another historian, David Starkey, shared digs with Norman Lamont but wasn't active in the Union because he 'found it too silly'. Simon Schama, whom Starkey remembers looking 'like a fruit sundae' in his apricot bow tie, appears in the Union records among the proposers of the motion 'This House would support a violent revolution in South Africa' in Michaelmas 1964.[12] The motion was overturned 272–131, but Schama stayed involved in the Union, serving as Steward in 1972–74.

In short, Cambridge was an exciting place to be in the early 1960s, whatever your chosen *métier*. David Frost – who chose numerous *métiers* as secretary of Footlights, editor of *Granta* and a member of the Union's standing committee – wonders what made it so:

> Perhaps there was an atmosphere that valued extra-curricular involvement as more important than narrow academic success, or that was particularly conducive to creative endeavour. Maybe talent does have a knock-on effect, inspiring and creating more talent.

But the best answer comes from Peter Cook, whom Frost asked to 'explain the extraordinary cross-section of people who were up at Cambridge with us at one and the same time':

> Peter leaned forward conspiratorially. 'Rationing,' he said sagely. 'Put it all down to rationing'.[13]

Whatever the reason, Norman Fowler agrees that this was a golden age in many fields: 'I make no claim, then, of exceptional merit for the so-called "Cambridge Mafia" of politicians. I would claim, however, that they symbolized some of the important changes taking place in Britain at the time.'[14]

What were these changes? For one thing, Cambridge – like society at large – was becoming more middle-class. The proportion of former public school boys at Cambridge fell significantly during the years the Mafia were there – from some two-thirds to about half.[15] Taking their place were former grammar school pupils. The future Cabinet ministers were among the first cohort to profit from the 1944 Education Act. To Christie Davies, President in Michaelmas 1964, and later a professor of sociology, 'they belonged to that golden age in British Society between R.A. Butler and Shirley Williams … the only truly meritocratic period in British education'.[16] Fowler had attended his local grammar school in Chelmsford; Michael Howard his in Llanelli. Ken Clarke had gone to Nottingham High School (actually an independent school, but he had been there on a scholarship). Leon Brittan went to the direct-grant Haberdashers' Aske's and, like Howard, was the son of Jewish immigrants. Many of them were the first in their families to attend university. Riddell suggests this spurred them on and 'resulted in a commitment to success'.[17] Fowler would concur: 'Undergraduate careers were taken seriously. Having reached university, we were anxious to make the most of it and were ambitious about what we wanted.'[18]

If getting into Cambridge was one of the factors which drove the Mafia on, they had all the more reason to feel like the *crème de la crème* at that particular time. Michael Crick, in his biography of Michael Howard, points out that the years they came up coincided with the phasing out of national service – and therefore increased competition for places. In 1957, the government announced that no one born after 1939 should expect to be called up; in 1960, it was ended completely. So for two years between 1959 and 1961 those who had been spared national service were competing for places at Cambridge with those who had deferred their entry to do it. 'Two generations overlapped, and those who were successful in getting a place were often of higher calibre.'[19]

But high calibre alone is not a guarantor of success. The matriculands of 1959–61 may have been a particularly good vintage, and dominated Cambridge politics with their distillation of talent, but what explains their continued rise to the top beyond the Cambridge bubble? A number of factors can be suggested. The first is that

Cambridge politics – especially then – can be a useful springboard to the national scene. It offers unheralded exposure to senior figures, providing not only useful contacts but also an educative glimpse into the prosaic reality of political life. As Fowler notes: 'There is nothing like getting close to politicians to make politics appear more accessible.'[20] Riddell advances the theory that undergraduate politics are a sort of apprenticeship for the real thing – an opportunity to learn some of the skills, and a test of aspirants' ability to survive in debates and to win elections.[21] Certainly, when the young Ken Clarke arrived in Parliament, he told his local paper that his experience in Union debating was a useful preparation for the Commons chamber: 'It seemed very much the same in layout, except the Union is shabbier'.[22] Fiona Graham, an anthropologist who has made a fascinating study of the Oxford Union, agrees that Union politics can serve as a useful grounding:

> The considerable responsibility that the President has to take on may be part of the reason that these ex-Presidents seem to excel in later life. Having felt such weight of responsibility already they are able to deal with it when it comes to them later ... But quite apart from this, the mere fact that they have attained something remarkable gives them a sense of privilege and confidence that is with them for life.[23]

Crick argues that student politics were more prominent in the early '60s. There were fewer universities, with fewer students, and the British Establishment was more tightly knit. 'As a result, the activities of Oxbridge students were far more visible. *Varsity*, for instance, was read by the news desks of the national press. A successful student career could readily open doors to a future in politics, law or the media.'[24] But while it could open them, these doors did not open directly onto the corridors of power: other factors must have played a part in the unusual success of the so-called Mafia.

One was luck. Timing is a key element to any political career, and the Cambridge Mafia were particularly fortunate in theirs, as

Riddell notes: 'They entered Parliament during the 1970s and reached an age when they might become ministers ... just when the Tories started a long period in office ... People with their astuteness, speaking abilities and, above all, ambition are always likely to thrive in such conditions.'[25] John Dunn thinks they were especially fortunate to have Margaret Thatcher as their patron: as she swept aside the old, aristocratic paths to advancement within the Conservative party, it 'became a more readily permeable membrane'. But Dunn does not intend this as a compliment: as far as he is concerned, CUCA was 'full of ambitious men of no great or striking ability. Thatcher created the conditions in which they could make it.'[26]

It was probably a mixture of ability, apprenticeship and luck which enabled the Union Presidents of 1960–64 to follow their Cambridge triumphs with success on the national stage. But perhaps it is better to look at the relationship from the opposite point of view – for it is easy to succumb to the *post hoc, ergo propter hoc* fallacy. It is tempting, but probably wrong, to imagine that Union alumni go on to later success *because of* their Union triumphs. A more probable relationship is that those who are interested – and likely to succeed – in politics in general are likely to be interested and succeed in the Union *en route*.

Instead, a better thing to ponder may be why the Cambridge Mafia were all Conservatives – 'in many ways the most striking feature' of the group, says Fowler.[27] Very few politicians from other parties emerged from Cambridge during this period. David Owen, the future Labour Foreign Secretary and co-founder of the SDP, steered clear of student politics. Although he took out life membership of the Union, 'the one debate I attended put me off.'[28] Brian Walsh was a rare Liberal President in Michaelmas 1959. He contested Hugh Gaitskell's old seat after his sudden death in 1963 but subsequently concentrated on his legal career. As a criminal silk and leader of the north-eastern circuit, he defended the ten-year-old killers of James Bulger in their high-profile 1993 case. The only prominent Labour politician to emerge was Gareth Williams, 'a wild Welsh figure with unkempt hair', a member of the Union's standing committee, and later Leader of the House of Lords as Lord Williams of Mostyn.[29] Compared to the great number of future Conservative politicians at Cambridge in these years, the disparity is striking.

Again, of course, luck plays a role. While Conservative graduates of this generation found their party in power for much of their adult life, Labour hopefuls were either defeated or simply deterred from standing. Certainly, the atrophied state of the Labour party in the early '60s was enough to demoralise many. The 1959 general election was held in the same week that most of the Mafia and their year-group arrived in Cambridge. It was a third successive victory for the Tories, and the worst defeat for Labour since the war. The split in the party which opened up nationally was mirrored in Cambridge. The Labour Club was dominated by the left, with an active CND faction run by the historian Angus Calder. From this, the centrist Campaign for Social Democracy broke away during the 1960–61 academic year. The Labour Club was so badly organised that one future Labour MP who was up at the time, Mark Fisher, chose to join the city branch of the party instead.[30] But it was more than just undergraduate disorganisation which exacerbated the imbalance between the parties. Labour were much slower than the Conservatives to come to terms with the education revolution and 'did virtually nothing to recruit undergraduate talent', recalls Fowler. 'At times Labour and the unions seemed deliberately to turn their backs on the universities … In contrast the Conservatives welcomed the chance to get their hands on what they saw as able new recruits.'[31] One embodiment of this recognition was Mrs Cusforth, 'a slim, silver-haired woman' from Conservative Central Office who came up to Cambridge every Wednesday in term-time to train young Conservatives in debating and public speaking.[32] Central Office also operated a speakers' list of party figures who could be called upon to address party meetings, or serve as warm-up acts. As one journalist has noted: 'Humbler university groups might ask for speakers from the list, but at Cambridge, undergraduates expected to be on it.'[33] It was good training for the future ministers among them.

Some of the Mafia's contemporaries doubt the strength of their Conservatism. Peter Hill, an editor of *Varsity*, says his 'impression of these chums … is that they were greatly ambitious, but they didn't believe in anything very strongly. They wanted to become MPs rather than change society.'[34] Fowler admits that 'we were not automatically Conservative and thirty years earlier you would have found some of us in other parties.'[35] Ken Clarke recalls joining the Bow Group, the Campaign for Social Democracy, a Liberal club and 'practically everything that was in sight'.[36] But this was just to hear their guest speakers. For the Mafia, CUCA was the real focus of their political attention – and the radical group of the time. The 1960 *Varsity* handbook told students that CUCA was 'as progressive as its well-developed sense of decorum permits'.[37] In the following year's edition, it reported: 'Most leading members are moving rapidly leftwards … The right wing Tory is not over popular in the Conservative Association.'[38] The club proudly displayed its new credentials. It published a magazine called *New Radical* and boycotted South African sherry. Such moves brought it prosperity – and some 1,500 members, more than the Labour and Liberal clubs combined. A *Varsity* article on the Cambridge political societies in May 1961 declared that 'the Tories have altered out of all recognition … from solidly right wing and upper class, CUCA has become radical and middle class.' Now, its author noted, 'a considerable and influential number of people, genuinely calling themselves radicals, are finding a not too uncomfortable niche in CUCA.'[39] That they could do so was down, in no small part, to the efforts of the Association's leading figures.

Whatever external factors and social trends one acknowledges, they should not detract from the central fact: that this was an outstandingly successful group of political alumni. They achieved much, and they achieved it quickly. Ken Clarke was adopted as a parliamentary candidate less than a year after graduating, and was elected an MP in 1970, two weeks before his 30th birthday. Fowler, Gummer and Tugendhat entered Parliament at the same election, and most of the rest were in by 1974 (the only exception was Michael Howard, who took until 1983 to enter the Commons). Each rose to high ministerial office, and together they clocked up an impressive 88 years in government. They are all Privy Counsellors, and all still in one of the two Houses of Parliament. As their contemporary John Barnes observes, 'it's by far the largest and most successful group of its kind'.[40]

One final remark must be made about the 'Cambridge Mafia'. The sobriquet they have gained gives a misleading impression of how closely they interacted. Though they were friends, they did not operate as a 'Mafia'. Nor were they exact contemporaries: Leon Brittan graduated in 1961, for instance – a term before Norman Lamont came up. Though they did help each other out – such as Brittan and Fowler's successful efforts, as ex-chairmen, to ban fourth-years from taking the CUCA helm in order to make room for Clarke and Howard – they were also competitors.[41] Fowler makes clear: 'We were certainly not a Mafia in the sense that we spent all our time together ... Nor, when we left, did we act as an entirely self-supporting group. Given that we spent a good deal of time competing with one another for the same constituencies, that was impossible.' Fowler beat Brittan to the nomination for Nottingham South in 1970, for example – and when the seat subsequently disappeared under boundary changes, he attempted to wrest the neighbouring Rushcliffe from Clarke. 'Yet,' he continues, 'we have remained friends in spite of the inevitable vicissitudes of politics.'[42] Gummer was Clarke's best man when he got married; Lamont and Howard had the same honour for each other.

The greatest schism within the group was probably between Clarke and Howard during their second and third years at Cambridge. To Crick, their relationship was 'part friendship, but mostly rivalry'. In Peter Temple-Morris's opinion, 'they both knew they were rather good and wanted to be better than the other'.[43] Howard was the slower of the two to start in the Union, and didn't make a single speech in his first year. He recalled years later: 'It took a bit of time … I think it probably took most of my first year to find my feet'.[44] When he did, many of their contemporaries thought that he outshone Clarke. To Barnes, Howard was 'a very polished speaker' and the superior of the two; Oliver Weaver, President between Clarke and Lamont in Michaelmas 1963, remembers Clarke as 'really quite narrow and rather dull' – unlike Howard, who 'was always interesting and entertaining and funny. He was mischievous; he was witty; he was clever without being stylised.'[45] John Dunn disagrees: Clarke was 'warm and buoyant', while Howard was 'a stiff and uncharismatic figure, who contrived to speak at length, smoothly and with considerable emphasis, without ever saying anything even faintly memorable'.[46] One thing all can agree on is that Howard, whose parents were tailors, was always 'carefully dressed … and much better tailored than Ken Clarke'.[47] Despite his one-year handicap, Howard won election to standing committee ahead of Clarke at the end of Lent 1961. Clarke, meanwhile, was quicker to rise through the ranks of CUCA: while Howard was beaten for Treasurer and then Secretary, Clarke became chairman in the Michaelmas of their third year (1961) – succeeding John Gummer.

It was during this term that the Clarke-Howard rivalry came to a head. The occasion was Clarke's decision to invite Sir Oswald Mosley to speak to CUCA. His biographers offer slightly differing verdicts on the episode: to Malcolm Balen, it was 'the defining moment of his Cambridge political career'; to Andy McSmith, it was 'a reckless piece of exhibitionism which dogged him for the rest of his time at university'.[48] In itself, it should not have been so controversial. As already noted, Mosley had spoken in Cambridge before – indeed, he had last visited CUCA only eighteen months earlier for a meeting in the Union chamber, when he had been heckled by a rowdy audience and had had a jelly thrown in his face.[49] But to invite him back again so soon was considered provocative, as Clarke appreciated: 'I did it partly because he would be a good draw,' he has admitted: 'and partly I suppose because it wasn't a safe thing to do. I wished to have controversial speakers.'[50] There was probably also an electoral motive. The Michaelmas CUCA chairmanship was a great springboard from which to run for Union Secretary. CUCA operated a formidable election machine, known as the 'crocodile', which would turn out in force for its favoured candidates in Union elections. A controversial speaker, and a well-publicised row, would galvanise the machine and secure Clarke a solid electoral base. Michael Crick (no stranger to the murky calculations of student politics: he was President of the Oxford Union) thinks that 'it was probably not coincidence that the Mosley meeting was scheduled for the night after the Union elections'.[51] Clarke got his controversy. Howard resigned from the CUCA committee in fury, and was never active in CUCA again – until appointed its honorary president in the 1990s. His resignation made the front page of *Varsity*. On 18 November, the newspaper printed a photograph of the two men sitting next to each other but staring in opposite directions, under the caption: 'We used to be friends …' (Clarke insists they remained 'extremely good friends' throughout.)[52]

If Clarke had invited Mosley in order to boost his personal profile, Howard was suspected of resigning for similar reasons. It struck many as odd that he should have resigned then, and not when Mosley had visited four terms earlier – although, as Crick points out, he was a more senior figure in CUCA by this time, and the repetition of the invitation was an aggravating factor. John Barnes remembers that a lot of his friends 'saw it as a move to secure the presidency of the Union … I think Michael used that issue as a way of distancing himself from CUCA' – though he notes it was a 'perfectly genuine affront' to Howard as a Jew.[53] But while his grandmother and cousins had died in the Holocaust, and his father had lived in the East End when Mosley's Blackshirts held their marches there, Howard did not bring any of these personal reasons up at the time of the CUCA row.

He had plenty of chance to do so at a special meeting of the Union convened on 1 November 1961, and chaired by the ex-President, Colin Renfrew. A motion calling upon CUCA 'to withdraw the invitation extended to Sir Oswald Mosley' was proposed by Brian Pollitt, the Vice-President, and seconded by Barry Augenbraun, the Secretary. Howard spoke in favour of the motion, along with seven other speakers including David Rubadiri, a mature student from Nyasaland (now Malawi), who was at King's on a scholarship. He had previously been imprisoned with the future Malawian leader Hastings Banda as a result of his strong nationalist views, and later became a poet, Vice-Chancellor of the University of Malawi and his country's permanent representative to the United Nations. 'The only way in which CUCA's reputation can be enhanced,' Howard declared, 'is for it to withdraw the invitation'.[54] Eight people joined Clarke to defend it – including John Gummer, Simon Rocksborough Smith and the Indian Mani Shankar Aiyar – but the motion was passed, by 49 votes to 36. Clarke shrugged the result off, reminding people: 'The Union can't dictate to CUCA.'[55] So the meeting went ahead as planned. Under the careful watch of the police and proctors, more than 1,000 people heard Mosley clash with Clarke and Gummer.

But the real clash happened in the Union elections. 'Napoleon Boot', the pseudonymous political columnist in *Varsity*, smacked his lips: 'The battle for Secretary will be a hot one'.[56] Many of Boot's columns seem to have been written by Clarke, Gummer and Renfrew for their own amusement and advancement. If they were designed to promote Clarke that term, they were unsuccessful: Howard won the election, and Clarke finished third out of four. Clarke has no doubt that the Mosley affair was to blame for his defeat: 'I should have won it but the row over my inviting Sir Oswald Mosley was tremendous. It was a huge controversy. I fell out with everybody.'[57] If Howard's resignation was calculated, Crick believes, it showed shrewd thinking. With Clarke running, he could not have banked on securing enough Tory votes; by leading the row against CUCA, he could instead pick up votes from everyone to the left of Clarke, including most Liberal and Labour voters. Another race in that term's elections may also have influenced Howard's positioning: Brian Pollitt, a Communist from King's, was running for President, so was likely to bring out more left-wing voters than usual – and, as

Napoleon Boot suggested in his electoral *post mortem*, 'the left had to vote for someone' as Secretary.[58]

Pollitt's candidacy aroused much greater controversy than Howard and Clarke's battle for Secretary. The son of Harry Pollitt, the late leader of the Communist Party of Great Britain, he had left school at sixteen and come up to Cambridge as a mature student in his early twenties. The Communist party had high hopes for him in the Union, and paid his membership fee for him. He had already attracted controversy when, in his election to the secretaryship in March 1961, cards bearing the words: 'Union Elections Wednesday 8th' were distributed to all Union members in King's. A select committee was convened to investigate, but it was not clear who was responsible for distributing them. Two other Kingsmen were also standing in the elections that term and, as the President Tony Firth told the national press, who picked up on the story: 'there is some evidence that [King's] was by no means the only college' affected.[59] Pollitt narrowly beat John Gummer to the secretaryship, and beat him again to the vice-presidency the following term – by 174 votes to 150 – 'despite considerable pressure to get Conservatives to the polls'. To stop him attaining the Presidency, 'CUCA's "crocodile" went into overdrive'.[60]

The details of the election are charted in Pollitt's contribution to this volume and that of Barry Augenbraun, the Columbia graduate 'diametrically opposed to communism' who challenged him.[61] It was a hard-fought election and, pitting an American against a Communist at the height of the cold war, attracted considerable attention. When Peter Hancock announced the result in the Union bar on 29 November, BBC cameras were there to record it. In the biggest election for over a decade, Augenbraun had snatched victory by 24 votes. But Pollitt suspected canvassing, and challenged the result. On 5 December, just hours before Augenbraun was due to take the chair as only the third American President of the Union, the election was declared void. Pollitt issued a statement announcing that he would not recontest the election, since he had brought the challenge 'and since, inevitably, my motives for doing so are open to misinterpretation'. He continued: 'I personally do not wish to become President next term by default, and it is my opinion that the best interests of the Society would not be served if I achieved this office in this way.' A by-election was therefore held on 7 December, disrupting the usual progression of officerships. John Gummer, who had been elected Vice-President the week before, now became President. He was pilloried in *Varsity* as 'the Union's third choice for the Presidency' and one of 'the quiet, career men who have slid in to political seats of power in the shadow of the Union's greatest hulla-baloo'.[62] Meanwhile, Howard retained the secretaryship, and there was brief hope for Ken Clarke, still without a foothold on the Union ladder. He ran for the vice-presidency which Gummer vacated, but was beaten by John Dunn.

Once the dust had settled, Gummer was left to salvage what term he could from the aftermath of the contentious election. Affectionately known as 'Gum-Gum', he was seen by many as the most fluent speaker of the Mafia – especially in religious debates, in which he spoke frequently. (One *Varsity* review reported wearily: 'With Gummer playing us his gramophone from God again, the sanctity of the Union chamber may be restored.'[63]) But his Vice-President, Dunn, is not so complimentary: 'It was certainly not obvious at the time that he was destined for higher things,' he told Rawnsley. 'I don't think anybody took him very seriously.'[64] One thing that was certainly not meant to be taken seriously was Gummer's penultimate debate as President: to accompany a debate re-running the motion discussed at the Union's first ever meeting, the retiring President got the rest of the officers to dress up in Regency costumes.

Taking the chair the following week was Michael Howard, making a smooth transition from Secretary to President. Having burnt his bridges with CUCA, he was now studiously ecumenical, as 'Napoleon Boot' noted:

Our new secretary is nothing if not ambitious; he has set himself the task of ensuring that his attendances at CUCA and Labour

Club meetings are in exact balance; that he shows at all times a keen interest in Liberal affairs; and all this while retaining the goodwill of the CND and worse.[65]

As well as being aided by this non-partisan approach, Howard's progression to the presidency was sped up by a term when John Dunn resigned as Vice-President and then declined to run for the presidency, choosing instead to concentrate on his exams and hopes of an academic career. So Howard ran for the Easter presidency, challenged by Gareth Williams. Howard's parents watched from the gallery as he and Williams spoke against each other in the final debate before the poll; the following day, he beat Williams comfortably by 208 to 158. Howard was therefore elected President for his Finals term, while Clarke had still never won a post in the Union. The new President drew sarcastic praise from 'Napoleon Boot':

> Step forward Michael Howard and take a bow. Show us all exactly how it should be done. First of all you run with CUCA until Ken Clarke beats you. Then Mosley gives you a few cheap votes. A loud approach to the Labour club, a public promise to speak on their platform, is followed by an agonising reappraisal.[66]

But Howard was humble about his victory: when his local paper reported that he was the first Llanelli boy to reach the presidency of the Cambridge Union, Howard wrote in to correct their error. Elwyn Jones, another local man, had sat in the President's chair 30 years earlier – and would later give the young Howard a pupillage in his legal chambers.[67]

It being an Easter Term, attendance was mixed. The future Home Secretary's first debate was on the motion that 'Law and Justice are incompatible in Britain today' (the House decided that they were not, by 39 to 30), and the hottest debate of term brought Pollitt and Augenbraun back together to clash over the motion that 'Latin America should look to Castro not Kennedy'. Howard ceded his chair to speak last in opposition, and helped to defeat the motion by 108 to 87.

But Pollitt saw victory later in the term. He was mounting a second bid for the presidency, against Howard's Vice-President, Simon Rocksborough Smith, who later became a circuit judge. Again, the election aroused strong comment. During the term, Pollitt received anonymous letters and telegrams threatening violence if he persisted in his plans to contest it.[68] The week of the election, and the night before the first examination of his Finals, he was attacked in his rooms in the small hours of the morning and severely beaten about the head. The attack drew attention from the national media, but Pollitt was kept strictly incommunicado, even to the police, until after his exams.[69] He sat his Tripos in isolation, dictating his answers in the sick bay at King's, and was unable to campaign for the Union election in person. But outrage at the attack probably helped his candidacy, and propelled him to victory by 122 votes.

Pollitt did not appear in public until the Saturday after the attack – when he told a press conference in Cambridge what little he could remember. He had been woken by a bright light shining in his face. He tried to get up, but suspected someone was lying on his chest:

> They stamped on my right hand, [he said]. I think I was hit on the head four or five times. I had a tattoo on my ribs, my legs and shins, and someone performed a slow foxtrot on my right wrist and hand.[70]

Remarkably, Pollitt not only won the Union presidency, but also took a first in his exams, finishing in the top eight in his year. To this day, he does not know the identity of his attackers. Alan Watson put it down to fascist elements in the undergraduate body, about which he wrote an article in the student press the following year. He, too, received a threatening letter and had to be moved out of his college lodgings – until it transpired that the letter to him was a hoax.[71]

Pollitt's election caused great excitement – Oliver Weaver, who had topped the poll for standing committee, resigned rather than serve under a Communist President – and aroused considerable press interest. The handover from Howard to Pollitt took place on 12 June. ITN sent a television crew to cover the accession of the new President, and Michael Howard played to the cameras. In carefully rehearsed Russian he hailed the new President as the 'Socialist hero and successor to Marx and Lenin, Comrade Brian Pollitt'. Pollitt replied in Russian: 'Many thanks, comrade,' before telling the busy House, 'I'm glad to see one or two glum faces here tonight.'[72] With the new President in the chair, Howard lost his retiring motion – 'Neutralism will get us nowhere' – by 116 to 81.

Pollitt's first debate in Michaelmas 1962 after the traditional No Confidence motion was the mischievous 'This House would put Mosley inside'. He spoke in proposition himself, with Clarke in opposition, but the Noes had it by 91 to 39.

A special meeting of the Society was held on 25 October to discuss the Cuban missile crisis, which had erupted ten days earlier. After 'several hours of heated and illuminating discussion, which produced some of the best speeches of the term', two motions were passed. The first, holding the American naval blockade 'to constitute not only a grave breach of international law, but also to imperil world peace' called on Her Majesty's government 'to use all reasonable means in its power' to dissuade the USA from pursuing its 'dangerous and illegal course of action'. That drew speeches in proposition not only from Pollitt and Dunn on the left but also figures from the right like John Barnes and Ken Clarke – and was passed by 130 to 118. A second motion, condemning the 'unilateral action' taken by America and calling upon all parties 'to refrain from further provocative action', was passed by 86 to 28 – the smaller House perhaps the result of such prolonged debate.

Ian Binnie succeeded Pollitt as President in Lent 1963. The previous March, he had beaten Ken Clarke in his second bid for the secretaryship, and risen smoothly up the officerial ladder. He became a justice of the Supreme Court of his native Canada, for which he has appeared as a counsel before the International Court of Justice. After the further blow of losing to Binnie, as well as to Howard and Dunn the previous term, Clarke asked to stay on for a fourth year to take an LLB (Bachelor of Laws) degree. He says he did so partly because he wanted a first: 'I was annoyed with myself for not getting one, and I also decided I'd have another year enjoying Cambridge before going out and earning my living.'[73] In the event, he got an upper second – as he had in Parts I and II – but the extra year did enable him to achieve success in the Union. He was finally elected to office on his fourth attempt in the first term of his fourth year, becoming Vice-President to Binnie. The presidency was now within Clarke's grasp, and he was determined not to lose it. Balen reveals that Clarke and Binnie suspected a canvassing campaign had been mounted to try to defeat his run for the presidency in favour of Alan Watson – who, as secretary of JAGUAR (the Joint Action Group for Understanding Among Races), had crossed swords with Clarke over the Mosley visit. The student blamed for the canvassing was a freshman at Watson's college, Jesus, called Martin Short. Short recalls being woken up by Clarke and Binnie banging on his door one evening: 'They proceeded to interrogate me about my role in the suspected affair.'[74]

But any canvassing which occurred did not hold Clarke back: he beat Watson by 42 votes in a three-way fight, becoming President in the final term of his extra year, Easter 1963. Watson, meanwhile, became president of the Liberal Club – a post he later held in the Liberal party nationally. He was Vice-President of the Union in Michaelmas 1963 and, after Cambridge, was a BBC presenter for *The Money Programme* and *Panorama* and a successful businessman. He was raised to the peerage in 1999, and spent six years as chairman of the English-Speaking Union.

The night Clarke assumed the presidency, the Treasurer, Kenneth Scott, and the ex-President and trustee, Lord McNair, proposed a motion to grant the chief clerk Sydney Elwood honorary member-ship of the Society, in recognition of his 40 years' service to the Union. As Ian Binnie told *The Times*, 'This is the highest honour we have it in our power to pay, but it cannot compensate for the enormous debt the Society owes to Mr Elwood.' He was, said *Varsity*, 'more august than any President, more lasting than any cause'.[75] After accepting the honour, Elwood proposed the evening's motion, 'They'll none of them be missed', against the retiring Binnie and David Frost. In Lent 1965, he was given the further award of an honorary MA by the University.

The Secretary during Clarke's term was Mani Aiyar – 'by miles the best speaker of our time', recalls Lamont, whom Aiyar defeated to the position in a close contest.[76] He ran directly for President at the end of term, against the sitting Vice-President Chris Mason, but both were beaten by the Trinity lawyer Oliver Weaver. That, too, was a close-run thing: Weaver led Aiyar by just five votes in the first round, and won after the transfer of Mason's votes by twelve. While his Cambridge contemporaries worked their way up the British political establishment, Aiyar returned to India, spending 26 years in the Indian foreign service. After working as a special assistant to Rajiv Gandhi, Aiyar entered politics in his own right. In 2004, he too became a Cabinet minister – as minister for petroleum and natural gas, then for youth affairs and sports.

Weaver, a 'right-wing Trinity lawyer', later became a Queen's Counsel.[77] He appeared before a judicial committee of his own during his term, when a motion of censure was brought against him for a telegram he had sent to the President of the United States of America. A member of the Union studying at Yale, Nicholas Bosanquet, had been arrested with a black classmate by the Mississippi state police: the Royal Philharmonic Orchestra was due to appear before a whites-only audience in Jackson, and Bosanquet had tried to dissuade them from playing. He was arrested on his way to the concert and spent three days in custody. Back in Cambridge, Weaver – 'after reading an unsubstantiated report in a newspaper, and without consulting the opinion of the Society', or so the motion of censure ran – sent an appeal to President John F. Kennedy, asking him to intervene in the matter personally. Jeffrey Littmann, the Union's college secretary for St Catharine's, accused Weaver of 'irresponsible, party action, aimed at attracting publicity', and organised the move to censure him.[78] The judicial committee met on 11 November 1963 (eleven days before Kennedy was assassinated) but threw out the motion by 96 votes to 42.

After Weaver came the final President of the so-called Mafia, Norman Lamont. Michael Latham of King's – later the Conservative MP for Rutland and Melton – remembers Lamont as 'brilliant in technique but, as someone said, his content was what he had read in the *Economist* the previous Friday'.[79] John Dunn recalls him as 'something of a smoothie' in his corduroy jackets, whilst 'Napoleon Boot' said he was 'rumoured to be a cherub expelled from the Vatican ceiling'.[80] Lamont was somewhat disadvantaged because his college, Fitzwilliam, had no building of its own at that stage. But, as Sebastian Faulks reported when Lamont became Chancellor of the Exchequer, this left him more time for politics. 'He was,' Faulks wrote, 'an indefatigable coffee-room and spaghetti-bar politician, a tremendous planner of "slates" and campaigns for elections.'[81] Indeed, his appointment as Chancellor was a reward for his successful running of John Major's Tory leadership campaign in 1990 – along rather similar lines to a CUCA or Union election, some thought.[82] Among his debates in Lent 1964, Lamont chose 'Fornication is of more harm to society than smoking' (passed 201–163), 'Tory radicalism is a contradiction in terms' (defeated 309–133) and 'Trade unions are not a force for progress' (defeated 110–98).

The end of Lamont's term marked the end of the future Cabinet ministers' domination of the Union. Some of the Presidents who followed were also Conservatives. Peter Fullerton (Lent 1965) was a good friend of the Mafia – and some say 'the most serious about becoming a politician' – but went off instead to write novels and eventually became a lawyer in Los Angeles.[83] Adrian Vinson (Easter 1966) was also CUCA chairman but drifted from the party, standing for the SDP/Liberal Alliance in Southampton, where he lectured in modern history for over 30 years, and serving as the leader of the city council from 2003 to 2007. But most of their successors were less politically ambitious. Charles Lysaght, an Irish law postgraduate who succeeded Lamont, became a barrister in Dublin, worked for the Irish Department of Foreign Affairs and wrote a biography of Brendan Bracken. A vivacious speaker from County Clare, Lysaght made his exit at his retirement debate 'in a blaze of blarney,' said *Varsity*. 'It was as if the breath he had been saving between polite presidential quips at the term's debates had finally found outlet.'[84] Christie Davies, who followed him, took a double first in economics and, after a spell as a producer on the BBC Third Programme, returned to academia.

Other economist Presidents were Robert Perlman (Lent 1966), a postgraduate at St Catharine's, and Vincent Cable (Easter 1965). Cable worked as an economist for the Kenyan government and for the Commonwealth Secretariat, was head of the economic programme at Chatham House and then chief economist for Shell, but is better known now as a politician. A Liberal at Cambridge, he joined the Labour party after graduation, stood as the Labour candidate for Glasgow Hillhead in 1970, and was a special adviser to John Smith as Secretary of State for Trade. He joined the SDP after its formation in the early 1980s, standing in his native York in 1983 and 1987. He was elected as the Liberal Democrat MP for Twickenham in 1997 and became the party's deputy leader in 2006.

Jeremy Burford, Michael Horowitz, and Nicholas Wall, Presidents in Michaelmas 1965 and Lent and Easter 1967 respectively, went into the law – Burford and Horowitz as QCs and circuit judges; Wall as a High Court judge and Lord Justice of Appeal. Paul Crossley (Michaelmas 1966) became a lecturer in the history of art, and is now a professor at the Courtauld Institute.

In 1959, the city council made a compulsory purchase order on the Union to buy and demolish its properties in Ram Yard and at 6 Round Church Street in order to merge the two narrow streets into one and make way for a multi-storey car park. Also demolished was Prziborsky's, a popular barbers' shop which had stood in the middle of Round Church Street since 'Count' Joseph Prziborsky, reputedly barber to the Austrian imperial court, had emigrated to Cambridge in 1879.[85]

This redevelopment on the Union's doorstep focussed the Society's collective mind on two approaching milestones – the 150th anniversary of the Society in 1965, and the centenary of the Union buildings the following year. The standing committee and trustees agreed in May 1961 that these combined events 'make this an opportune time to launch an appeal'. They envisaged a new extension to the Union on the land behind Round Church Street – ideally 'a large hall properly equipped for use as a gymnasium' which could also be used for meetings, dances and plays or films, as well as eighteen bedrooms for visiting life members. A committee of ex-Presidents was formed to co-ordinate the appeal: chaired by Lord Birkett, it included Rab Butler, Selwyn Lloyd, Michael Ramsey, Sir Geoffrey Crowther and Sir Geoffrey de Freitas. An appeal to raise £150,000 was formally launched at a meeting in Gray's Inn on 7 June 1962. The President, Michael Howard, sat flanked by his predecessors the Archbishop of Canterbury and Denzil Freeth MP. An organiser of the appeal, Charles Scott-Paton, was appointed; he had raised £7,800 by the end of October 1962, and £12,000 by the following year.

Meanwhile, the plans for the Union's sesquicentenary were made. The lucky President to serve in the anniversary term was Peter Fullerton. A celebratory debate and dinner were held on the exact anniversary, Saturday 13 February 1965, when a packed House, many in evening dress, considered the question: 'Should this House move to further business?' The speakers, all for the affirmative, were a galaxy of ex-Presidents: the former Foreign Secretary and Chancellor Selwyn Lloyd, the Attorney General Sir Elwyn Jones, the editor of the *Economist* Sir Geoffrey Crowther and the colourful MP Humphry Berkeley. But it was another ex-President, Alistair Sampson, who delighted the chamber most with a typically self-effacing contribution. Speaking alongside his illustrious predecessors, Sampson told the House how his five-year-old daughter had asked: 'What does Daddy do?'

'Hush, child,' Sampson's wife had replied: 'Daddy is an ex-President of the Cambridge Union.'

'What is an ex-President of the Cambridge Union?' continued
the inquisitive child.

'The Archbishop of Canterbury is one,' Sampson told her.

'Oh,' she said. 'Is the Pope one too?'

'No,' replied her father, dryly. 'He didn't go to Cambridge.'

· 1815   1965

150th Anniversary Debate

Saturday, 13th February

7.0 p.m.

Question for debate

"Should this House move to further business"

Speakers for the Affirmative

RT. HON. SELWYN LLOYD, M.P., *Magdalene College*, Ex-President.

RT. HON. SIR ELWYN JONES, M.P., *Gonville & Caius College*, Attorney
General, Ex-President

SIR GEOFFREY CROWTHER, *Clare College*, Ex-President.

MR. HUMPHRY BERKELEY, M.P., *Pembroke College*, Ex-President.

MR. ALISTAIR SAMPSON, *Selwyn College*, Ex-President.

Teller for the Affirmative

RT. HON. LORD ALPORT, *Pembroke College*, Ex-President.

GONVILLE AND CAIUS COLLEGE   PETER FULLERTON

10 *February*, 1965   *President*

The teller for the Ayes was another ex-President, Lord Alport, though he had an easy task: the motion was carried unanimously by acclamation. Many other former officers joined the speakers and the Archbishop of Canterbury at the dinner held afterwards at St John's. Jeremy Burford recalls drinking an 1815 Madeira which had been laid down after the Battle of Waterloo, and evidently gone past its prime: 'it was like eating a slightly alcoholic Crunchie bar'.[86] The following Tuesday, a more light-hearted motion – 'That this Union be consummated' – was passed, 280–152.

Satisfyingly, the anniversary term was a highly successful one, drawing the largest attendances since 1946 for two of its debates. The first, on 19 January, was 'This House deplores the Labour Party's hypocritical attitude towards immigration policy'. The main speaker was Peter Griffiths, who had just notoriously unseated the new Foreign Secretary, Patrick Gordon Walker, in Smethwick – allegedly with the help of the slogan: 'If you want a nigger for a neighbour, vote Labour'. Despite four Labour MPs and one peer refusing to speak alongside Griffiths, Fullerton pressed on with the debate. There was a large demonstration against Griffiths outside the Union – 40 policemen posted around the building tried to hold back some 200 protesters waving banners and placards – but some still managed to burst through the gates, knocking them from their hinges. Inside the chamber, the atmosphere was highly charged. At one point, Fullerton had to suspend the debate while parts of the overcrowded gallery were cleared.[87] The House did not adjourn until 12.23 am – when it did, it was clear that Griffiths had won the motion easily. The Ayes had 552; the Noes 326.

The second largest House that term was also for a motion which dealt with race. By 544 to 164, the House agreed that 'The American dream is at the expense of the American Negro'. William F. Buckley Jr spoke against the motion, televised on both sides of the Atlantic, but was unable to outdo the writer and civil rights activist James Baldwin, whose speech that evening was reprinted in the *New York Times*. Its most famous passage made the *Oxford Dictionary of Quotations*:

It comes as a great shock around the age of five, six, or seven to discover that the flag to which you have pledged allegiance, along with everybody else, has not pledged allegiance to you. It comes as a great shock to see Gary Cooper killing off the Indians and, although you are rooting for Gary Cooper, that the Indians are you.

In October 1964, the annual No Confidence motion had been disrupted by the general election. By 387 to 324, the Union decided it still had confidence in a Conservative government – but the country narrowly disagreed. In February, Fullerton chose to run another No Confidence debate. Just 100 days into the new Wilson administration, the House decided it had no confidence in Her Majesty's government by a majority of two votes. But this was the end, not the beginning, of a Conservative era at the Union. Although the House still leaned to the right in 1965 – disagreeing that 'The Americans should get out of Viet Nam' and agreeing with Enoch Powell that 'Aid to developing countries does more harm than good' – there was a sense that the times, they were a-changing.

In particular, a clear shift in the Union's social attitudes can be seen. In Michaelmas 1962 Stephen Winnard, a freshman at Clare, had been sent down for 'misconducting himself' after being found in bed with a nurse from Addenbrooke's. On 22 November – against the strong wishes of the proctors – the Union met to debate the motion: 'This House deplores the action of Clare College in sending down an undergraduate for conduct which concerns private morality alone.' Though the motion was passed, it was only a slender victory: 108 to 104. Interestingly, four members from Clare spoke against the motion, and only one in favour.

Despite the increasingly liberal morals of the time – exemplified for many by the trial of *Lady Chatterley's Lover* in 1960 – there are further signs that they were not immediately shared in the Union. The first debate of John Gummer's term, 'Adult sexual morality is no concern of the law', was defeated with 179 Ayes to 236 Noes; in

Ian Binnie's term, the proposition that 'Christian sexual ethics are absurd' was overwhelmingly negated by 276 to 68.

The change, when it came, was swift. In Michaelmas 1964, Christie Davies (later author of such works as *Permissive Britain* and *The Strange Death of Moral Britain*) re-ran Gummer's motion on adult sexual morality verbatim and the result was dramatically reversed. This time, the Ayes secured 222 and the Noes 95. In Easter 1966, the ex-President Humphry Berkeley spoke movingly in support of the motion that 'Private morality is no concern of the law', which demonstrated the Union's support for reform of the laws on homosexuality by 123 to 101. David Steel came to persuade the House, as he was attempting to persuade Parliament, that 'The law on abortion must be reformed'. After a debate which the Vice-President thought 'remarkable for the high level of sustained argument both by undergraduates and guests', the motion was passed by 300 to 143.

The Union also changed its mind about another social issue during these years. In 1967, after passing the age of 60, Sydney Elwood retired as chief clerk. The Change of Officers debate on 8 June 1967 also took the form of his retirement debate, and a dinner was held in his honour afterwards. Elwood spoke in the debate with five other Presidents covering each of the decades in which he had been in the Union's employment: Lord Butler from the '20s, Kenneth Adam from the '30s, Norman St John-Stevas from the '40s, Alistair Sampson from the '50s and the outgoing President, Nicholas Wall. The motion, which was carried 'unanimously', was a phrase Elwood had uttered many times over the years: 'This way please, sir, if you want to join'. But it was a phrase which was already out of date. For the President who took the chair that evening, for the first time in the Society's history, was a woman.

CAMBRIDGE UNION SOCIETY

EASTER TERM, 1967

PRESIDENTIAL DEBATE AND
MR. ELWOOD'S RETIREMENT DEBATE

THURSDAY, 8th JUNE, 1967
at 7.15 p.m.

"This way please, sir, if you want to join"

Proposed by Mr. SYDNEY ELWOOD, Hon. M.A., Retiring Chief Clerk.

Seconded by Mr. NICHOLAS WALL, Trinity College, Retiring President.

Dr. NORMAN ST. JOHN-STEVAS, M.P., Fitzwilliam College,
Ex-President, will speak third.

Mr. ALISTAIR SAMPSON, Selwyn College, Ex-President,
will speak fourth.

Mr. KENNETH ADAM, C.B.E., St. John's College, Ex-President,
will speak fifth.

The Rt. Hon. LORD BUTLER, P.C., C.H., Pembroke College,
Master of Trinity College, Ex-President, will speak sixth.

Before the Debate a presentation will be made to Mr. Sydney Elwood,
retiring Chief Clerk, by the Rt. Hon. Selwyn Lloyd, C.H., C.B.E.,
T.D., Q.C., M.P., Magdalene College, Ex-President.

FOR THE AYES	*Tellers:*	FOR THE NOES
Mr. MICHAEL HOROWITZ, Pembroke College, Ex-President.		Mr. PAUL CROSSLEY, Trinity College, Ex-President.

Trinity College,
12th May, 1967.

NICHOLAS WALL,
President

RECOLLECTION: THE RT. HON. MICHAEL HOWARD QC MP

(Mr M. Howard, Peterhouse)
President, Easter Term 1962

Michael Howard was educated at Llanelli Grammar School and Peterhouse, Cambridge, where he read economics and law. He was called to the Bar in 1964, specialising in employment and planning law, and took silk in 1982. He contested Liverpool Edge Hill in the 1966 and 1970 general elections, and was elected to Parliament for Folkestone and Hythe in 1983.

He joined the government in 1985, became a junior minister at the Department of the Environment after the 1987 election, and entered the Cabinet as Secretary of State for Employment in 1990. He served as Secretary of State for the Environment (1992–3) and as Home Secretary (1993–7), during which time crime fell by an unprecedented 18 per cent. In the 1997 contest for the leadership of the Conservative party he finished last, but was elected unopposed in November 2003 and became Leader of Her Majesty's Opposition. He led the Conservatives into the 2005 general election, securing the party's largest number of gains for 22 years. He stepped down in December 2005, and announced that he would leave the House of Commons at the next election.

He married Sandra Paul in 1975, with whom he has a son and a daughter.

I came up to Peterhouse in October 1959 straight from school – part of the first intake which did not have to do national service.

167

Peterhouse had required everyone to do national service before they came up, so my intake was a mixture of those who had done it and those like me who hadn't.

I had come from a Welsh grammar school. Cambridge was a completely new and different world for me. I'd heard of the Union and agreed to become college secretary for Peterhouse, but I did not speak there at all in my first year. A lot of people who become President come up to Cambridge with the idea of becoming President – nothing was further from my mind. The Union's main debates were on Tuesday nights and, in the second term of my first year, they clashed with a course of lectures on existentialism: I went to those instead.

I did, however, become active in CUCA, the Conservative Association, and at the end of my first year I was elected to the committee. I thought then that if I was to make a go of CUCA I ought to speak at the Union. Ironically, I never became chairman of CUCA.

Debating was something I had only done a bit of at school. We didn't have a formal debating society at Llanelli Grammar School but I had been chairman of something called the Sixth Form Forum which invited guests to speak, and I had taken part in a couple of moot trials. So debating at the Union was my first real experience of public speaking.

I made my first speech from the floor in the No Confidence debate of Michaelmas 1960. Hugh Fraser was defending the government but made a terrible job of it. Somehow he managed to knock the jug of water between the despatch boxes all over the unfortunate Secretary. The other memorable thing about his speech was to do with a very popular recording at that time made by Peter Sellers. It was a pastiche of a politician's speech and included every cliché known to man. The pastiche ended with the words: 'And now … finally … in conclusion … may I just say this …' That evening Hugh Fraser – I fear probably totally oblivious to this Peter Sellers record – ended his speech: 'And now … finally … in conclusion …' The whole House collapsed.

Experiences like that helped to disabuse us of any notion that Cabinet ministers were gods from another land. The Cambridge Union was – and still is – a very cruel forum with absolutely no respect for politicians, and Cabinet ministers not infrequently came a cropper. Seeing them do so enhanced our view of our own abilities – which was already grossly exaggerated.

It worked both ways, of course: I remember a later No Confidence debate when I spoke from the paper defending the government and Dick Crossman was on the paper against us. I made what you might have called in those days a typically moderate Conservative, 'Bow Group'-type speech. Crossman was absolutely devastating. He got up and he said:

> We've heard from the honourable gentleman who opposed this motion. We heard him say it's perfectly all right if you want to vote Conservative but you care about the poor – because *we* care about the poor *almost* as much as the Labour Party does! It's perfectly all right if you want to vote Conservative but you care about social services – because *we* care about that sort of thing *almost* as much as the Labour Party does! And it's all right if you want to vote Conservative and you care about the Health Service – because *we* care about the Health Service *almost* as much as the Labour Party does!

It was an absolutely devastating approach. It completely ripped me apart.

There was a sort of tradition that one President a year was usually a funny speaker, not particularly involved in politics. Lorenzo Giovene di Girasole, at the end of my first year, was one such President. Another example was Peter Hancock, and I suppose the supreme example of my generation was Tony Firth, who was the most brilliant speaker – and most brilliant mind, really – of my generation. It was an absolute tragedy that he died so young. Although he did achieve a lot – he was controller of programmes for Scottish Television and wrote a play which was staged in London's

West End – he never wholly fulfilled the potential that he demonstrated at Cambridge. I recall one speech he made in a debate about religion. I forget exactly what Tony's point was – I think it was to do with God's attitude towards sin – but Colin Renfrew intervened and asked him: 'Well, suppose you're wrong. What would you expect God to say when you arrive at the Pearly Gates?' Quick as a flash Tony Firth said: 'I'd expect Him to say: "Come on in, I'm a Trinity man myself!".'

I ran for office in the Union during a very fractious term. Ken Clarke was CUCA chairman and had invited Oswald Mosley to come and speak. I don't think it was anything to do with Union politics at all. I think he just thought it would attract a lot of attention to the start of his term. My objection to it was that it was not the first time Mosley had been invited. He'd been to speak the previous year and I hadn't really got all that exercised about it. But when Ken invited him it seemed to me as though this was going to be an annual event: this was setting a precedent that every CUCA year should start with Oswald Mosley. That, I thought, was quite unacceptable, and that's why I resigned from the committee – although I remained a CUCA member.

Ken and I were great friends – we still are friends – but it was portrayed as a great falling out at the time. We both ran for Secretary at the end of that term, and Ken was certainly the favourite. I think it was a bit of a surprise when I won.

The election for President that term – between Brian Pollitt and Barry Augenbraun – was much more controversial. I think Barry Augenbraun was very hard done by. Whatever may be the truth or otherwise about his canvassing, there was at least as much canvassing done on behalf of Brian Pollitt. Brian, having assured everyone that he was not going to challenge the election, waited until the very last minute before putting in his requisition. I remember him absolutely assuring me he wouldn't do that: I spent hours drinking whisky with him, I think the night before he actually put the requisition in. The consequence of that was that no counter-requisition could be made in respect of his campaign. That meant that when the select committee was investigating the requisition, we were all called to give evidence before it and we said, 'Well, you know, if there was any canvassing on behalf of Barry Augenbraun there was just as much on behalf of Brian Pollitt.' But Bill Wedderburn, who was on the committee, would say: 'Oh, but we can't look at that – that's outside our terms of reference. There hasn't been any requisition against Brian Pollitt.' I've no doubt at all that Brian knew exactly what he was doing.

So Barry Augenbraun was disqualified. There was an election for President which John Gummer as the sitting Vice-President won, and there was then an election for Vice-President which I might have been expected to put in for, but I knew that John Dunn wasn't going to stand for President in the Easter Term – he always intended to have an academic career and thought that it would be a distraction – so I was quite content for him to be elected Vice-President.

Brian Pollitt stood for President again at the end of the academic year, by which time I was serving as President. Shortly before the election he was mysteriously attacked in his rooms at King's, which some people suggested was a put-up job. There was a great burst of sympathy for him after that happened. Indeed, a lot of people suggested it was monstrous that anyone should think to contest the election against him. A lot of very unfair criticism was made of Simon Rocksborough Smith who was my Vice-President and who, perfectly naturally, was standing for the presidency as he was entitled to do. The left certainly did rise up in arms in support of Brian Pollitt in a very big way. Large numbers of life members came up from London to vote for him in that election, which was very unusual.

The police never found out the identity of his attackers: I think they closed their enquiries. It was a very odd episode.

I was opposed for President by Gareth Williams. He was on the standing committee – he had been very active and he was a very good speaker, so it wasn't a complete surprise that he decided to stand: contested elections were quite common. He was a friend of mine too. Even when he was a Labour minister in the House of Lords we used to meet and have lunch from time to time. In the early days when he went down from Cambridge he started practising at the Bar in Swansea. I used to go home to Llanelli quite often, and almost every time I went home I got in touch with him and we would go out and have dinner together.

Mine was an Easter Term, and Easter Terms are always slightly low-profile. We had a very interesting debate on Kennedy and Castro. The guest speakers included Lord Lambton and a woman called Manuela Sykes. She was a great liberal figure of the age. She'd just come back from Cuba and she was banging on about how wonderful things were in Cuba, how happy people were, what a great man Castro was – this was over dinner beforehand – and Tony Lambton looked at her rather quizzically.

'Tell us,' he said, 'do you speak Spanish?'

'No,' she replied, 'what's that got to do with it?'

'Presumably all the answers that were given to you by these supposedly happy people had to be translated by interpreters who were friendly to the regime,' he said. She got terribly cross and flummoxed.

The greatest thing I got out of the Union was probably the chance to go on the debating tour of America in the year after I left Cambridge. I spent a year there, the first part of which was on the Union debating tour, and that was one of the great experiences of my life. It was a very dramatic year in the United States – I was there when John F. Kennedy was assassinated. I'm sure the fact that I spent that year there – rather than, say, France, which I think Tony Blair did – had a huge influence on my thinking. I was immensely grateful for that opportunity.

My Cambridge generation produced a striking number of Conservative MPs. Ken Clarke was an exact contemporary of mine; John Gummer had come up the year before. Leon Brittan was Secretary of the Union when I came up and was chairman of CUCA the following term. Christopher Tugendhat was President of the Union in my first year; Norman Lamont came up at the start of my third year.

We're all still in touch – John Gummer organised a great reunion dinner recently because it was 50 years since he went up – and we've all stayed friends. Obviously, we've disagreed with each other – Ken and I, as is well known, differ very strongly on Europe – but despite those differences we have all stayed friends.

After the 2005 general election, Ken wrote me a very charming letter saying how sad it was that it looked as though none of the 'Cambridge Mafia' would ever actually make it to Number Ten. When you look at the lists of people involved – not just in my generation, but over the best part of 200 years – it is extraordinary that, in sharp contrast to Oxford, there hasn't been a Cambridge Union President who went on to become Prime Minister.

RECOLLECTION:
BRIAN POLLITT

(Mr B.H. Pollitt, King's College)
President, Michaelmas Term 1962

Brian Pollitt was born in London in 1936. After completing military service and working for Unilever for two years, he was admitted to King's College to read economics.

After completing his degree at Cambridge, he moved to Cuba in 1963 where he worked for five years, training a research team in the conduct of rural surveys. After further research and teaching at Cambridge and Yale, he was a visiting professor at the University of Concepción, Chile, from 1971 until the military coup of 1973. After a spell at the Australian National University and the University of Adelaide, he took up a post at Glasgow University in 1975 where he taught and researched development problems in Latin America and elsewhere. He was also a visiting professor at the University of Massachusetts from 1977 to 1978 and a visiting Fellow at Trinity College, Cambridge from 1982 to 1983.

His main publications concern the society and economy of agrarian Cuba and the contributions to political economy of the Marxist Maurice Dobb. Now retired, he is an honorary senior research Fellow at Glasgow University.

I went up to Cambridge in October 1959. After watching a Union Society debate from the visitors' gallery, I decided not to join. Membership was, for me at least, expensive and I was repelled by the sartorial rigmarole of dinner jackets for undergraduate and visiting paper speakers, with a yet more ornate formality for the Society's officers: Presidents wore full evening dress and customarily sported a flower – an orchid perhaps – in a lapel. All this was entirely alien to me.

My father, Harry Pollitt, had been the general secretary and ultimately chairman of the British Communist Party from 1929 until his death in 1960 and my teenage years were thus passed in the geopolitical context of the cold war. At school this meant coping with occasional hostilities expressed not so much to me personally but to me as my father's son. I encountered more menacing threats during my years of military service from 1954 to '56. The War Office classified me as a 'security risk' and, having been warned against involvement in acts of 'subversion', I was confined to Royal Artillery postings in both more and less remote parts of Wales. Not all officers and NCOs were amiable. Such experiences naturally strengthened, rather than weakened, my feelings of personal and political loyalty to my father and to the party he led, and I inherited from him strong left-wing political convictions that I was well-practised to defend in the most diverse circumstances. I had also perforce developed a skin toughened by some of the more adverse circumstances of my formative years. When I was admitted to Cambridge as a mature student at the age of 23, the only entirely novel phenomenon that I encountered was the day-to-day conduct of the more deplorable products of British public schools.

I sought admission to King's College. King's had a well-established (if not notorious) liberal tradition of providing a safe haven for homosexuals, recently released prisoners from Britain's colonial detention camps in Africa – and the likes of me. Indeed, I was not so much interviewed at King's as grabbed, being admitted without the benefit of a College examination and with my prospective 'A' levels – then being taken part-time at the Manchester College of Commerce – being entirely irrelevant.

I was joined in Cambridge by a number of other undergraduates whose politics had been formed within Communist households and together we formed a student branch of the Cambridge University Communist Party, of which I became chairman. After paying £10 to hire the Union debating chamber for a Communist party meeting, it occurred to us that we were mistaken to lack any representation in what was, after all, the University's best-known forum for political discussion. At a branch meeting, Stephen (now Lord Justice) Sedley and I discussed which of us might perform that particular task and, in the event, my life membership in the Union Society was paid from our CP branch funds.

The prominence that any individual Union member might attain within the debating chamber was powerfully shaped by the President's power to pick the speakers of his choice, initially from the floor of the House and then, perhaps, to open the debates by proposing or opposing the motions formally tabled before it. I was fortunate in that my swift transition from a 'floor' speaker to a 'paper' speaker occurred under the auspices of three outstanding successive Presidents: Leon Brittan, Tony Firth and Colin Renfrew. They were very different characters. Leon Brittan read law and was both a smooth Tory political operator and a polished speaker – but I felt quite unable to penetrate the personal carapace he seemed most comfortable to inhabit. Unlike others later to form Margaret Thatcher's so-called 'Cambridge Mafia', his subsequent rise to high political office did not surprise me.

Tony Firth was a more idiosyncratic individual, not least because he rose to the Union's presidency while unattached to any of Cambridge's political associations. Seeming most comfortable when privately wrestling with Kierkegaard, he could affect a strangely artificial mode of speech in debate but deployed a wit of devastating rapidity. I saw him bested only once in the exchange of spontaneous sallies or ripostes: during the Michaelmas Term of 1960 Sir John Wolfenden, a visiting speaker, referred to the routine of eating breakfast before chapel. Vice-President Firth rose to make the point of information that he 'neither took the one nor attended the other', to which Wolfenden's retort was that he thus 'could promise [him] a short life in this world and an unhappy one in the next'. There was a sad prescience in this for, after a successful career in the media – for some years he headed ITV in Scotland – he suffered from both a disabling physical accident and a debilitating tropical ailment, and took his own life. Colin Renfrew, who wrote Firth's obituary in *The Times*, described him as one of the 'most intelligent men [he] had ever met' which, given the lofty intellectual company subsequently kept by (the then Professor and later Lord) Renfrew, was an accolade of note. Renfrew himself was also a distinctive personality. Like Brittan, he was a prominent Conservative, but could be an unexpectedly exuberant one, capable of bursting into song while delivering a paper speech. He was a considerable socialite whose mantelpiece was crowded with invitations to diverse fashionable Cambridge functions. I recall him concluding an amiable chat in his rooms in St John's College with a self-deprecatory: 'But I'm afraid I must leave you now, Brian: I have to take tea with Princess Margrethe of Denmark ...' In contrast to their more humdrum presidential successors, Brittan, Firth and Renfrew all secured first class honours degrees in, respectively, law, English, and archaeology and anthropology.

I joined the Union only in the Easter Term of 1960, securing exactly one vote – not my own – in the end-of-term elections for membership of the standing committee. Leon Brittan, nonetheless, gave me my first paper speech the following Michaelmas Term, to propose the motion that 'Religion is the opium of the people'. He posed no objection to the fact that I declined to wear a dinner jacket although David Saunders – Easter Term's Vice-President and (a rarity in the Union Society) a prominent member of the University Labour Club – had, on 30 May 1960, proposed and carried *nem. con.* a private business meeting (PBM) motion confirming that these were to be worn by paper speakers and tellers. The subject of religion was then debated every term – the 'God debate' – and I was opposed on this occasion by John Gummer. Though slight in physical stature, he was a vigorous speaker much prone to emphasising his points by jabbing his finger. (This was a habit he maintained in standing committee meetings where, at a later date, I felt constrained to advise him that if he poked his finger at me one more time, I'd be obliged to break it off.) Well known as both Christian and Conservative, he lacked gravitas – as indicated by his long-lived nickname of 'Gum-Gum' – and this impression was reinforced by his practice of commuting to the Union from Selwyn College on a small BSA 125 cc motorcycle wearing a peaked protective helmet. Predictably I lost the motion but in that term's standing committee elections, my single vote was multiplied by 124 and I took my place as a committee member for the Lent Term of 1961 under the presidency of Tony Firth.

During that term I had my first major debate with Kenneth Clarke when I moved that 'Britain needs a planned economy'. Clarke – like most Cambridge Conservatives who later climbed greasy poles to high office in the House of Commons – was reading law, not economics. I therefore sought to anticipate the predictably more formidable arguments of the visiting speaker for the opposition, Enoch Powell.

I clashed with Clarke on quite a different subject during the Michaelmas Term of 1961, for which I had been elected Vice-President. Clarke was then chairman of the University Conservative Association (CUCA) and, in my view as a publicity stunt, invited Sir Oswald Mosley to address a CUCA meeting. This was a mistake. Peter Hancock, then Union Society President and a man of no strong personal political views, allowed a special meeting of the House to be held on 15 November 1961, to call on CUCA to withdraw its invitation to Mosley. I proposed the motion – carried by 49 votes to 36 – and was seconded and supported by two Union members better known for their conservative views. One was Barry Augenbraun – an American who was Union Secretary during that term – and the other was standing committee member Michael Howard. The three of us had in common only our detestation of Mosley's role as the 1930s leader of the British fascist 'Blackshirts'. Augenbraun and Howard evidently attacked Clarke's decision – in which they were opposed, incidentally, by most of the leading Conservative lights who attended the Union special meeting –

179

because both were Jewish. Clarke, however, as he was to demonstrate many times during his later political career, had a thick skin and held CUCA's Mosley meeting anyway. This damaged his immediate prospects in the Union Society. By contrast, Howard resigned from CUCA in protest and adopted a distinctly ambiguous political position from which his Union career was later to reap considerable personal benefit.

As my election as both Secretary and then Vice-President indicated, significant changes were occurring in the Union membership then attending debates and voting in elections. The University's socialists, for instance, began to take a more active interest in the Society's affairs and a number of left-wing figures became prominent in debates. John (now Professor) Dunn, for example, was then chairman of the University's CND, and was elected first to the standing committee and, in December 1961, to Vice-President for the following Lent Term. Only his academic priorities precluded a successful pursuit of the presidency for the Easter Term of 1962. Angus Calder – later the author of the highly-regarded *The People's War* – was also elected to the standing committee while being a prominent CND activist. Dunn, Calder and I were all members of King's College, many of whose more radical representatives now began to take an interest in Union Society affairs.

An important mobilising factor amongst left-wing and liberal-minded undergraduates was the issue of women undergraduates' membership of the Union. Barred from this 'gentlemen's club', perennial efforts were made to carry motions to admit them to full Union Society membership. Frequently carried at PBMs of the House, such motions failed, either there or in subsequent polls of the entire membership, to surmount the formidable obstacle of the three-quarters majority required to change the Society's constitution. It was clear to me that the key to securing women's admission lay not in passing a motion to that effect in a PBM but in reducing the majority required to effect constitutional change from three-quarters to two-thirds. I proposed this first to the standing committee and then, as Vice-President, to a PBM on 27 November 1961. My

180

idea was that, if standing alone and subsequently put to a poll, the measure would fail to attract the kind of attention from the national press that traditionally provoked elderly life members to emerge from their Colleges or to entrain for Cambridge from their London clubs to oppose women's admission. My plan was thwarted by a less tactically astute enthusiast (or, if one prefers, a less Machiavellian one) who proposed an accompanying motion on women's admission. This doomed both measures to failure in a poll held on 5 December 1961. But six months later, my original scheme was copied by – and, indeed, erroneously credited to – John (now Professor) Barnes and Norman (now Lord) Lamont.[88] On 7 May 1962, with an attendance of only 23 members and against the opposition of Clarke, John Gummer, Leon Brittan and Colin Renfrew, they carried a PBM motion that was concerned solely with reducing to two-thirds the majority required for constitutional change. Then-President Michael Howard controversially (and perhaps unnecessarily) refused to grant a poll, and while this measure failed to make the admission of women to the Union immediate, it made it inevitable.

The presidential election for the Lent Term 1962 was probably the most controversial in the Society's history. By long custom, the keenest competition had been among standing committee members for the post of Secretary. The latter then proceeded more or less routinely to the post of Vice-President and then President, their election being contested only by ordinary members or, on occasion, by a committee member with poor prospects in the elections for Secretary. This tradition was broken with Barry Augenbraun's decision, when Secretary, to oppose me, as Vice-President, in the presidential elections held on 29 November 1961. Other matters aside, this opened up the offices of both Secretary and Vice-President for competition, offering not one but two standing committee members the opportunity for further promotion.

I understood why Augenbraun chose to break this tradition. He would have become President as a matter of course after serving a routine term as Vice-President. But as a conservative American, and viewed from a US standpoint (where the contest was also publicised), the prospect of becoming President by defeating a well-known Communist was far more attractive. It was, in short, a decision reflecting cold war, not Cambridge, conditions. His electoral prospects were enhanced, moreover, by his membership of St John's, which was both one of the largest colleges in Cambridge and one adjacent to the Union Society's buildings. In the largest electoral vote for many a year, Augenbraun won narrowly by 389 votes to 365. In a post-election interview published by the *Cambridge Daily News* the following day, he declared himself to be 'very exhausted'. This puzzled me since standing for an election in the Union Society was – or should have been – a physically undemanding affair. But reports soon reached me of Augenbraun's personal exertions in rounding up his College vote, culminating in his positioning himself at his JCR bar to offer drinks in exchange for votes. This was a particularly crass violation of the Society's rules that prohibited candidates from canvassing for votes.

It was widely known that canvassing in one form or another was commonplace. There was a mysterious reptile called the 'CUCA crocodile', reputedly able to turn out loyal Conservatives to support CUCA candidates. Candidates' friends might also tap the wellsprings of individual college loyalty. And there was an anonymous weekly column in *Varsity*, penned by one 'Napoleon Boot', whose witty and/or malicious comments on Union affairs could help or hinder the electoral prospects of particular candidates. But these were generally accepted as part and parcel of the Society's normal electoral milieu, whereas Augenbraun's activities in my view were not. I accordingly alleged electoral malpractice and on 5 December 1961, in an unprecedented decision, a select committee comprising six of the Society's officers (of which four were senior members of the University) unanimously found the new President-elect to have breached the Society's laws on canvassing and declared his election void. Under the Society's rules, he was also barred from standing for office again for at least three terms. In a commendably candid observation, Augenbraun himself was later to remark: 'Hell, in the States we *run* for election. In Cambridge you just *stand*.'

I had already decided to withdraw from the new election for President that was immediately held on 7 December 1961. This election, combined with the unusually simultaneous vacancies for Secretary and Vice-President in the election held just three days before, completely disrupted the hierarchical ranking and prospects of several candidates for office, both then and in future terms. John Gummer was precipitately elevated to President, with John Dunn as Vice-President and Michael Howard unexpectedly finding himself as Secretary. With John Dunn's decision not to stand for President the following term, the hierarchical confusion was complete, and it is entirely likely that more than one member of Mrs Thatcher's so-called 'Cambridge Mafia' owed their position as President of the Cambridge Union Society not so much to any very distinctive individual merit as to the unprecedented turmoil associated with both the preamble to and aftermath of the presidential elections of December 1961.

I largely withdrew from Union affairs until Michael Howard's presidency in the Easter Term of 1962. With the approach of examinations and other diversions, attendance at debates during his period in office was comparatively low. But he began well, having had the canny idea of injecting personal needle into his opening debate of 1 May by pitting me against Barry Augenbraun in a motion that 'Latin America should look to Castro, not Kennedy'. That there would be some palpable animosity appeared to have contributed both to an above-average attendance and to the *Varsity* reviewer's opinion that the conflict brought 'Union debating back to sparkling form'.[89]

I derived greater pleasure that term from authoring a sub-committee report on the Society's finances. This recommended an increase in the membership subscription, primarily to finance improved salaries and wages for the Society's staff. Its recommendation that these should be index-linked in future to the rate of inflation was also approved, but was later quietly shelved by the chief clerk who naturally failed to see why the Society should not take advantage of the fact that Cambridge was a low-wage area.

On Thursday 7 June I stood once more as a candidate for President in the elections for the Michaelmas Term, 1962, opposing Howard's Vice-President, Simon Rocksborough Smith of St John's College. The election was held in unfortunate circumstances. In the early hours of Monday 4 June – the day I was to begin my Part II Tripos examinations – I was assaulted in my rooms, briefly hospitalised for treatment for head and wrist injuries, and then confined to my college sick bay. From there, over subsequent days, I dictated my examination answers to the college chaplain who also acted as invigilator. My performance was not greatly affected by this – the Union and previous experience had given me plenty of practice in speaking from sparse notes – and the publicity attending my misadventure undoubtedly boosted the turnout in that week's Union elections. I polled 357 votes against 235 for Rocksborough Smith – almost certainly a larger majority than I might have secured in ordinary circumstances. According to the *Daily Telegraph*, the police believed the assault might have been the work of 'an anti-Communist movement'.

When elected President, I was joined by five left-wing or liberal officers or standing committee members who also rejected the traditional formal dress code for House debates. On 16 October 1961, when opening the term's first debate, I also disposed of the requirement for members to wear gowns if they wished to speak. But while I failed to secure the admission of women to full membership during my term of office, I did at least ensure that many more members were obliged to listen to the arguments in favour than had been the case in the past. I disagreed with Michael Howard's refusal the previous term to hold a poll on the motion to reduce the majority required to effect constitutional change, since he had done this at a PBM attended by only 23 members. But I did resent the fact that the total attendance of PBMs considering the admission of women was scanty, with most opponents waiting for the less time-consuming opportunity to reject the motion in the seemingly inevitable poll that would follow. On 6 November, I therefore warned the House that if only a tiny minority of members attended the PBM that would be held shortly to debate the subject, with the number of members opposing the motion not substantially higher than had been the case in the past, then I would refuse a poll. My certainty that this threat would ensure that the opposition turned up was duly confirmed: there was a record attendance of no fewer than 460 at the PBM held on 8 November, with 1,582 voting in the poll I duly called for 15 November. I was disappointed that a two-thirds majority was not secured, but on 20 November I imparted a somewhat unorthodox twist to the House ruling that 'ladies of distinction may speak at any debate' by so describing any women undergraduates who had given the President prior notice of their intention to speak. There were vociferous objections to this, but the regular participation of a small number of women in later debates opened up a major fissure in the walls of the 'gentleman's club', and the subsequent conduct of members could be contrasted with the notorious near-riot provoked by the unauthorised presence of a handful of women undergraduates before a debate held the previous year on 17 October 1961.[90]

I also supplemented the regular Tuesday debates with special Thursday meetings to consider matters of pressing current interest. The latter – usually critical political events – had previously been treated less felicitously as emergency 'motions of condolence', briefly considered by the House before ordinary debates. Now they had their own forum, and well-attended meetings considered Cuba's missile crisis and – against the formal objections of the University proctors and the Master of Clare College – the sending down of an undergraduate for the offence of being found in his rooms early one Saturday morning in the company of a young woman. With a measure of hyperbole, Ian (now Canadian Supreme Court Justice) Binnie's vice-presidential report for Michaelmas 1962 described all such activities during my presidency as acts of 'the Revolutionary Government'.

My programme of Tuesday debates did not depart significantly from their traditional format, but the crushing defeat of Her Majesty's government in the annual 'No Confidence' motion – by

520 votes in favour to 335 against – confirmed the growing shift in undergraduate opinion against conservative views. That motion was ably proposed by the Rt. Hon. George Brown, then the Shadow Home Secretary, but I found his private conduct beforehand to be deplorable. Angus Calder was the undergraduate paper speaker and chose to wear his CND badge in his lapel. I found Brown in the washrooms immediately before the debate berating him for this. When he threatened to withdraw from the debate if the offending badge was not removed, I intervened to inform him I would be 'delighted' to inform the House of his reasons for withdrawing if he chose so to do. His objections were promptly dropped. My presidential debate aroused the greatest public attention, however, since the motion I chose to propose was Khrushchev's notorious remark that 'We shall bury you.' Prominent journalists were invited as visiting speakers and much press attention was given to the participation of Vikenty Matveev, the Soviet columnist for *Isvestia*, who flew from Moscow to second me. Reflecting the cold war ethos of the day, however, the Washington bureaux of both *Time* magazine and *Newsweek* vetoed the participation of their London correspondents, much to their frustration. Such a provocative motion was, of course, heavily lost by 344 to 114, but I was glad to have ended my term with a bang, as it were.

Oft neglected, however, were the many debates outside Cambridge to which the Union Society sent representatives. These were disparate in nature, ranging during my term of office from the Oakington Women's Institute to the traditional presidential exchange with the Oxford Union. One of my more enjoyable visits was to the London School of Economics where I proposed that 'This House would fiddle while Oxbridge burned'. Clive James attended that debate and delivered himself of more radical opinions than my own, but he was later to conclude that whereas I had been speaking with my 'tongue in [my] cheek and knew it', he had 'had [his] head up [his] arse and didn't'.[91]

But by far my most memorable debate outside Cambridge was proposing that 'The West is fighting a losing battle' in Wandsworth

186

prison. This was personally poignant since my father had been imprisoned there in 1925–26 for seditious libel and infringing the Incitement to Mutiny Act of 1797. I was accompanied by Vice-President Binnie (opposing) and Secretary Mark Cantley (seconding) and, after a tea of slabs of bread, margarine and jam, the debate took place in a hall packed with prisoners, well-stewarded by prison officers. I was able to open my speech by recounting my father's previous attendance at that very establishment. At that time he had been asked by a professional burglar of high standing as to the length of his sentence. The disgusted rejoinder to the answer 'twelve months' was: 'You ought to be shot. You've no respect for private property!'[92] The anecdote was well-received, but predictably enough there were several speeches from 'the floor' in praise both of private enterprise and of the liberty of the individual enjoyed in the West. One prisoner also invited me to remain behind to enjoy their company for an indefinite period after the debate. I cannot recall which side actually won the debate, since a number of recounts were needed given the penchant of several prisoners for voting twice either by raising both arms, rearranging their seats or by other manoeuvres calculated to confuse the tellers (who themselves had to be replaced by prison officers because of their unreliable performance). I regretted that this debate at Wandsworth prison failed to become a regular fixture for the Union Society since it appeared to have considerable educational value for the visiting speakers, if not for the inmates.

RECOLLECTION:
BARRY AUGENBRAUN

(Mr B.S. Augenbraun, St John's College)
President, Michaelmas Term 1961

Barry Augenbraun went up to St John's in September 1960 on a Kellett Fellowship from Columbia University. He took first class honours in history in 1962; after graduating cum laude from Harvard Law School, he was a practising lawyer and business executive for 41 years, retiring in 2006. He lives in St Petersburg, Florida with his wife of more than 40 years, and has two children: William, who lives in Philadelphia, and Leslie, who lives in Austin, Texas.

The quality of debate during my time at the Union – 1960–2 – was outstanding; indeed, so formidable that at my first Union debate I almost resolved to forget about trying to participate. It was the opening debate of the Michaelmas Term 1960 – traditionally, the motion of no confidence in Her Majesty's government. Tony Firth opened for the motion – he was the most brilliant of a brilliant group. His opening salutation – 'COMRADES' – brought cheers and jeers in equal measure, but set the tone for his 'take no prisoners' approach. I had yet to learn that the traditional salutation was 'Mr President, sir' – but I certainly knew what 'comrades' meant, and how it galvanised the start of a No Confidence debate.

Leon Brittan followed – on very short notice, since the original paper speaker had taken ill that afternoon, and Leon, as President of the Union, stepped into the breach at the last moment. His speech was forceful, coherent and well structured, even though put together at the shortest notice.

Speaking for the motion was a legendary Labour party figure, George Brown: we are not talking about 'New Labour' here, this was Clause Four, and socialism red in tooth and claw. He had the House roaring with his pointed attacks on the government's deficiencies: 'Britain – with the poorest health care in Europe; Britain – with the least effective transportation system; Britain – with the lowest GDP ...' at which point Leon Brittan rose on a 'point of information' – 'and the lowest rate of unemployment in Europe,' he commented. Without blinking an eye, Brown responded, 'Yes, I give you that, and what it tells us is that in Britain today we need more and more people to produce less and less ...'

Then the guest speaker for the Conservatives – Hugh Fraser, a man who, until that evening, appeared to have led a charmed life: President of the Oxford Union, MP, junior minister in the government – and he was savaged by the House. Beset by questions and points of information that he could not deal with, he grew increasingly incoherent and flustered – until finally, as he turned to respond to a questioner, he knocked over the glass of water that used to sit on the despatch desk, drenching the Secretary who sat behind it. Rising, and dramatically wiping himself down, the Secretary looked over at him and said: 'That's all right, sir, we don't use that desk much anyway.' Disaster was now complete.

After that display – of both brilliance and the consequences of less-than-brilliance – I had decided to leave the House without speaking. But as the evening wore on, I became comfortable that even mere mortals were able to express themselves with reasonable support from the House, and I decided to make my maiden speech.

One of my Union colleagues, with whom I have stayed in touch over the years, has kindly told me from time to time that of the thousands of maiden speeches he has heard since then, mine is the only one whose opening line he can still repeat to this day – so I offer it here.

'Mr President, sir, as no doubt you can tell from my accent, I come from a long and honoured tradition of having no confidence in any of Their Majesties' Governments ...' It was well received, and I went on to oppose the motion because I believed the Labour Opposition did not have a serious programme for addressing the many ills that had been identified by the proponents of the motion.

The premier speakers of that era were Leon Brittan, Colin Renfrew and Tony Firth. I did not really get to see much of Leon's debating skills, since he was already President in my first term – but his aura of distinction and leadership already marked him as a future political figure of the first rank. Colin Renfrew was a polymath: as much at home in the world of modern French art and the classics as in his field of archaeology. His speaking style was marked by effervescence and verve, as well as powerful rhetoric.

Repartee was highly valued by the House – and nobody was ever better than Tony Firth. He was like a world-class bullfighter – toying with a questioner, pirouetting around him, then pinning him with a rapier – and he could do it time after time. I know that I was the subject of Tony's rapier on more than one occasion – one I particularly recall came during his term as President. Taking a lead from his approach, I tried to evade a hostile questioner by deprecating his question and remarking that 'I have given the other side a chance, Mr President'.

'But not an answer,' came the acerbic response from the chair, preceded by that ominous 'ding' of the President's bell.

On one occasion, his sally turned into a group effort: '*odi profanum vulgus*,' Tony sneered at a bemused questioner seeking to put a point of information during the course of his speech. Seated on the committee bench, I jumped to my feet to provide the next line of Horace's Ode: '*et arceo*, Mr President, *et arceo*'. At which point Colin Renfrew rang his President's bell, and continued with the next line: '*favete tibi linguis*'. As the House roared with delight, a wonderful man named Wallace – a brilliant orientalist – scrambled to his feet and rattled off the next several stanzas of the poem.

(I should add that, of the many displays of rhetorical swordplay that I experienced at the Union, this was the only one that later gave rise to mutterings that it must have been rehearsed. I am happy to say, over the distance of 45 years, that it was not – while I may have been considered by some to be an American cowboy, I did study Latin for six years, including a graduate-level class in the poetry of the Augustan Age with Gilbert Highet, the distinguished Oxford man of letters who was chair of the classics department at Columbia for many years.)

Politics was very serious at the Union of my day, and the impact of the cold war was very much a part of Cambridge politics – understandably so, since we prided ourselves on debating the key issues of the day.

Probably the most famous cold war debate of the time took place in the Michaelmas Term of 1961. I was travelling in France in August 1961 when, on 13 August, the Kremlin began to seal off the border of East Berlin and erect what became known, infamously, as the Berlin Wall. While *en route*, I sent a telegram to Peter Hancock, then President of the Union, stating that I wished to propose the following motion in the Michaelmas Term: 'This House would fight for West Berlin'.

The debate was set for November 1961, and took place before a packed House, with both the BBC and *The Times* of London covering it. The line-up of speakers was interesting: the student speaker opposing me was Ken Clarke, then chairman of CUCA. My guest adjutant was Reginald Paget, a prominent Labour party spokesman on defence issues; on the other side of the motion, seconding Clarke, was the Revd John Collins, Canon of St Paul's Cathedral, a leader in the Campaign for Nuclear Disarmament, and then often referred to as the 'Red Dean'.

I concluded my speech by reminding the House of the infamous Oxford Union motion, 'This House would not fight for King and Country'. While, I said, I was confident that most members would abjure that pledge today and recognise their loyalty to their country, I argued that they would never have the chance to face that simple challenge again. Life had moved too far, and they must now be prepared to stand for the cause of freedom and loyalty to Britain's commitments even when it appeared in the guise of defending their former enemies.

After the paper speakers concluded, the debate went on to near midnight, and the motion was carried, 284 to 258. I thought it was an extraordinary outcome, given that it was only fifteen years since the end of the war brought on by Germany that had taken so much British life and treasure. And it was also extraordinary in the light of the increasing power of the left in Union politics.

My decision to challenge Brian Pollitt for the presidency of the Union was prompted by the urging of many members who felt that communist leadership of the Union would be a mistake – while there were some who considered that it would be a charming novelty (I found that particularly true among a number of undergraduates of aristocratic lineage), many others felt that in the political climate of the times it would send a message that would be wrong for Cambridge, and wrong for Britain. It was a very closely contested election; in a turnout of over 700 members, I received a majority of some 24 votes. Brian decided to challenge the election on the grounds that I had violated the rules against 'canvassing' for votes – he was shocked, shocked, to learn that there was electioneering going on in this election! Of course, there was no lack of electioneering on the other side, as the left had mobilised around Brian's candidacy as never before. One of the charges levied against me was that I had been buying votes for drinks in St John's – a claim that was, obviously, laughable. St John's College was not Old Sarum, and votes were not for sale there or anywhere else at Cambridge.

Of course, canvassing, or 'electioneering', could take many forms. In October 1961, during the course of a debate on an unrelated subject, a group of women (then prohibited from debate or entry to the floor during debate) marched into the chamber to stage a demonstration. One of the women appeared to faint as a result of the confusion and tumult – and, fortuitously, Brian Pollitt was there to sweep her up in his arms to rescue her, and again – quite fortuitously – a photographer from *Varsity* just happened to appear on the chamber floor, camera at the ready, to capture the moment. And so, three weeks or so before the election, the front page of *Varsity* featured a huge photo of a firm-jawed Brian Pollitt, looking for all the world like Gregory Peck, gallantly carrying to safety this recumbent casualty of the opposition to women in the Union. Brilliant. I had to admire it. We all did.

I think the reality is that Brian was unable to accept so small a margin of victory on my part – had the margin been greater (had I bought more beers for voters?) he would not have raised the canvassing issue. But, as the special committee convened to investigate his complaint pointed out to me, the by-laws were quite specific: 'canvassing' for votes was prohibited, period, even though it had been commonplace for decades, and even though the other side was equally at fault – and once someone complained, there was nothing to be done but enforce the rules. After the decision to invalidate the election was announced, I received many warm notes of support and regret at the injustice of the outcome – most from students whom I did not know and had never met.

While politics was the stuff of many debates, there were other subjects that were regularly on the paper list. Religion – in one form or another – was debated virtually every term: in my first term up, when a debate on the US election was held a week or so after the religion debate, *Varsity* commented caustically that 'Kennedy carried the House by a greater majority than God'.

I have particularly fond memories of the humorous debates. I think humour was much more difficult to do. On substantive subjects – whether political or social – I could always do some serious homework and find the information needed to make a credible presentation. But to be funny on demand – ah, that was a challenge.

Two debates I remember with great vividness. In May 1961, the House debated: 'Let's do it!' The final guest speaker was James Robertson-Justice, a well-known actor of distinguished bearing. One of the earlier speakers had made some off-colour comments about spying Mr Robertson-Justice in questionable circumstances at

Inverness station. When it came his turn to speak, Mr Robertson-Justice rose with great dignity, turned to the prior speaker and firmly asseverated: 'Let me make one thing perfectly clear, *I have never done it at the Station Hotel in Inverness.*' Great cheering and applause.

But the best of the lot was the evening that Bernard Bresslaw, a well known stage comedian, appeared as the final guest speaker. I forget the motion, but the earlier speakers had all made a point of urging us not to allow Mr Bresslaw's comedic talents and drollery to divert us – and charm us – and captivate us. On and on they went, warning us of the comic wiles of this man Bresslaw – so that when he finally arose to speak, we were fully primed with expectation.

Bresslaw stood, began to fuss with his papers – and raised a quizzical eyebrow at the prior speaker; at that, our anticipation gave way to a roar of laughter, even though he hadn't said anything yet. And for the next several minutes, he said nothing – simply gestured, appeared ready to speak, changed his mind, referred to his notes – and with each new movement the laughter grew louder and more unrestrained.

Finally, the House settled down, waiting for him to begin – Bresslaw surveyed us, turned, and then reached for the glass of water on the Secretary's desk, ostensibly to soothe the throat parched by his oratorical efforts to that point. Once again, the House was consumed with laughter.

My biggest regret during the course of my Union years was in joining in the opposition to admitting women to full membership. I treated the subject as less than serious, and joined in the debate on women by making a frivolous speech in opposition. I see now that I was wrong, and I am glad that some years later that injustice was remedied. One highlight of that debate that I recall, though, was a brilliant speech opposing the admission of women given by Gay Turtle, then the fiancée, later the wife, of Tony Firth (the rules were suspended to permit women guest speakers for that debate). To the argument that participation in Union debates was an important preparation for later life, Gay responded: 'The only thing in life that being President of the Cambridge Union prepares you for … is being President of the Oxford Union!'

While I have vivid memories of some of the giants and future political leaders who dominated in the Union at that time – Brittan, Firth, Renfrew, Michael Howard, John Gummer, Ken Clarke – there were many others who provided verve and interest to Union debates. I am told that there is less of an emphasis on the student speakers at both the Oxford and Cambridge Union debates today, and more focus on the guest speakers. That seems to me unfortunate, and a misplaced emphasis. In my time there was generally only one guest speaker to a side, rarely two. And while there was frequently a movement out of the House after the paper speakers concluded, most stayed for at least a while to assess the quality of the speeches from the floor. When standards were high, or the subject was highly controversial – or, as happily was often the case, when both conditions were met – the House remained strong to the end of the debate, as total votes that often ran over 200 or 300 demonstrated.

I have strong memories of some of those who made the floor debates so compelling. John Dunn was a man of great personal modesty and sweetness, whose charm and understated manner of presentation belied the extreme radicalism (or so it seemed to me) of his views. One of the favourites of the House was Gareth Williams, the late Lord Williams of Mostyn. The 'Welsh Firebrand' could be histrionic and overly aggressive in his approach – but his passion and intensity often carried the House with him. It seemed to me quite ironic that with all the Tory aspirants who trod the Union floor, it was the Welsh Firebrand – whose politics were often far to the left of the Labour Club – who was among the first of our generation to enter the House of Lords, ultimately becoming the Leader of the House.

I had the pleasure of dining with Gareth when, as a successful barrister, he would visit Florida on his occasional tours of American Bar Associations, instructing us provincials in the time-honoured British barrister's approach to 'beating up a witness' – and I was one among many who mourned his untimely death in 2003.

Another favourite of the House was the Revd Myles Appleby, a Benedictine priest who attended Christ's and served on the Union committee with me. He had a kind and generous nature, and his sincerity and warmth endeared him to the House – and made him, for me, a boon companion at The Pickerel and many other Cambridge pubs of the time.*

Jonathan Tinker, another committee member, was a favourite of the House – even though his ingenuous enthusiasm often made him an easy target for some of the more caustic questioners. John Toulmin (now Judge Toulmin) and Chris Mason were two other popular speakers – as was Wallace, whose first name I do not recall, whose seemingly encyclopaedic knowledge and unique perspective on subjects always made for a distinctive, if sometimes esoteric, presentation. And one of my favourites (and an early rival for a place on the Union committee) was Simon Rocksborough Smith, now a retired judge. Simon had a whimsical way of looking at even serious subjects. I remember the opening for one of his speeches: 'You, Mr President, are standing on your head...' – so that one anticipated an adventure in oratory whenever he rose to a subject.

I am sure that there are wonderful debaters in each Union generation, and that each is a golden age. I know that mine was.

---

* As Dom Raphael Appleby, he was head master of his old school, Downside, 1975–80, and returned there again in 2003 as a chaplain.

RECOLLECTION: THE RT. HON. THE LORD LAMONT OF LERWICK

(Mr N.S.H. Lamont, Fitzwilliam House)
President, Lent Term 1964

Norman Lamont was born in the Shetland Islands and educated at Loretto School and Fitzwilliam House, Cambridge, where he was elected President of the Union and chairman of the University Conservative Association. After Cambridge he spent two years in the Conservative Research Department and eleven as a merchant banker with N.M. Rothschild & Sons.

He contested Hull East at the 1970 general election, and was elected to Parliament in a by-election in Kingston-upon-Thames two years later. He served in Margaret Thatcher's government at the Departments of Energy, Trade and Industry, and Defence, and as Financial Secretary (1986–9) and Chief Secretary (1989–90) to HM Treasury. He was Chancellor of the Exchequer under John Major from 1990 to 1993. After his departure from the Cabinet he unsuccessfully contested Harrogate and Knaresborough at the 1997 general election, and was raised to the peerage the following year. He continues to be politically active in the House of Lords and holds a number of company directorships.

The early 1960s were a highly political time in Cambridge, the height of the cold war. The Berlin Wall had gone up and we lived through the Cuban missile crisis, when there were large demonstrations on Parker's Piece and a fear, not confined to the left, that we were on the brink of a nuclear war.

This period in Cambridge is often thought of as one of Conservative dominance but politics in the Union were highly polarised. The left, including the Campaign for Nuclear Disarmament (CND), was strongly and effectively represented by Brian Pollitt, John Dunn, Angus Calder, Mani Aiyar and Gareth Williams. It was a time when the Macmillan government was tottering, and the old order was yielding to a more meritocratic one. We Conservatives were almost all Butskellites, liberal Conservatives. Our hero was Iain Macleod, we admired Edward Heath but were unenthusiastic about Alec Douglas-Home. However, when Lord Home, as he then was, as Foreign Secretary, addressed a Conservative meeting in the Union chamber, he made a masterly speech and was warmly received.

The so-called 'Cambridge Mafia' shared the Butskellite view but after Cambridge, we did not act together and our views diverged, particularly on Europe. Michael Howard and I became Eurosceptic; Leon Brittan, Kenneth Clarke and John Gummer more Europhile. At times there was rivalry between us. Ken Clarke replaced me as Chancellor of the Exchequer. That may not have been the happiest moment of my life but both of us took trouble to remain friends.

Of course, not all the debates at this time, by any means, were political. Many of the best-attended debates were on religion or social issues. Oliver Weaver, who was President immediately before me, confined himself to highly whimsical, funny speeches. Charles Lysaght, an eloquent, experienced debater who succeeded me, again was non-political and more interested in projecting his Irishness than being political.

I made my first speech from the floor, opposing the motion, 'This House would fight for West Berlin'. I am embarrassed today that I should have held such wrong views. After my speech, I was approached by Angus Calder to see if I would join the Campaign for Nuclear Disarmament. He could not believe I was a Conservative.

I made a few other speeches and was beginning to feel I was getting nowhere when I was invited to speak against a motion that 'Germany should remain divided'. I still remember the thrill of opening that letter from Brian Pollitt, the Communist President, and I have retained a warm feeling towards him ever since. Richard Crossman was to support the motion and Sir Edward Boyle was to oppose. My undergraduate opponent was John Toulmin, later a QC and circuit judge. I was completely terrified. I knew nothing about the subject and spent the whole of the long vacation preparing.

I discovered that Crossman had once said that the division of Germany should be 'permanent but not for ever'. During the debate, I produced this apparently ridiculous quotation with great fanfare. Crossman was with me. Ingeniously, he justified his remark and ended each point by repeating 'so that is why I say to Mr Lamont, the division of Germany should be permanent but not for ever'.

My next paper speech was as a defender of Israel. I was supported by John Connell, the journalist and biographer of Wavell. Today, my views are less sympathetic to Israel, though I defend its right to exist. Looking back on that debate, what strikes me today is that, at that time, Israel was only fourteen years old. I had little comprehension of the newness of Israel or why its creation was so resented by Arabs.

I became President in Lent 1964 and vividly remember the anxieties of trying to arrange a programme. I wrote to everyone, including Evelyn Waugh. My letter was written a few weeks after eggs had been thrown at Henry Brooke, the Home Secretary, at a CUCA meeting. Waugh replied 'Dear Lamont. I fear I would be unable to defend myself. Why don't you try Baroness Summerskill, who is a skilled pugilist?' (Baroness Summerskill was a campaigner against boxing.) 'Or better still, try my son, Auberon, who is a war cripple.'

The big debate of my term had Iain Macleod supporting the motion: 'Tory radicalism is a contradiction in terms'. He was opposed by Sydney Silverman, the Labour MP. Macleod had recently resigned from the government in protest at the election of Alec Douglas-Home as Prime Minister, and become editor of the *Spectator*. He was labelled 'too clever by half' by Lord Salisbury. Needless to say, Macleod made an electrifying speech, giving us a dissertation on the history of the Tory party right back to the seventeenth century and adding as an aside 'nothing much changes in politics – including the opinions of the Cecils'.

During this time, there were many who did not hold Union office but were effective and regular speakers: Peter Lilley, John Wilkinson, Hugh Dykes, Michael Latham and Peter Bottomley all became colleagues of mine in the House of Commons. There were others who later made their mark as successful writers such as Robert Lacey, John Costello and David Eady, now Mr Justice Eady and scourge of the *News of the World*.

I did a fourth year and saw the presidencies of Christie Davies, Peter Fullerton and Vince Cable, then, as now, an eloquent spokesman on economics.

Peter Fullerton oversaw the most dramatic term of all. There was a fierce, disorderly debate on immigration and one on the situation of – as it was then put – 'the American Negro', when James Baldwin, the black American novelist debated with William Buckley, the owner and editor of the *National Review*. The evening was televised by CBS and Norman St John-Stevas was the commentator in the gallery. Baldwin spoke with great power and received a prolonged standing ovation. William Buckley had a task that would have daunted many, but he coolly informed the House that he had 'no desire to ingratiate' himself. He compared the standard of living of the average black American with that in Europe. At one point, he asked the House 'What would you have us do?'. That prompted the predictable response: 'Why not give the Blacks the vote?' He replied, at his most Whiggish: 'I agree completely. But the problem is not just that too few Blacks have the vote, too many Whites have the vote'. Predictably, he lost massively but was quite unperturbed.

Peter Fullerton oversaw the celebrations of the 150th anniversary of the Union, which included dinner at Trinity and a debate attended by numerous ex-Presidents including the Archbishop of Canterbury. The speakers included the maverick MP Humphry Berkeley and Selwyn Lloyd, lately Chancellor of the Exchequer, who had had to implement very unpopular policies. Berkeley paid Lloyd a backhanded compliment by saying, 'he bears as much responsibility as anyone for the position in which the Conservative party finds itself today'. At the time the Conservative party was plunging in the polls. The House was much amused but Selwyn Lloyd was really quite offended.

In Vince Cable's term, Enoch Powell won the motion 'Aid to underdeveloped countries does more harm than good'. Powell was opposed by David Ennals MP, the minister for overseas development. The House was by no means on Powell's side from the start. He developed a formidable case and the audience wanted an answer. I don't think it had ever occurred to Ennals that there could be any arguments against overseas aid. He was reduced to saying, 'this is not a very Christian motion'. The longer he spoke, the more he lost votes.

Powell was not always well-received by Conservatives in Cambridge. I remember him being barracked at a Conservative dinner for his free-market views. On another occasion, after a CUCA meeting, he and Kenneth Clarke had a heated exchange about immigration. This was several years before Powell's famous 'Rivers of Blood' speech.

Christie Davies and I represented the Union on an ESU debating tour of the United States, covering the mid-West and the east coast and lasting nearly three months. We spoke in about 30 debates on six or seven different subjects. It could have been invaluable training for an election! That wasn't in Christie's mind. He was a double-first economist, then on the left, but later one of the few right-wing professors of sociology in the country. The subject we debated most was the war in Vietnam, which he opposed and I supported. I don't know whether Christie realised it but the more we debated, the more I had doubts about the position I was advocating. A low point came when, in one mid-West university, I received the first standing ovation of my life from students, some of whom must have gone on to fight in Vietnam. On my return to England, I decided that I had been completely wrong.

Debating is taken very seriously in America. There were coaches and professors of debate. Our opponents carried card indices with quotations. We were approached by one professor of debate and asked to write a book about debating, including sections on English humour. The book never happened, but Christie later wrote what could have been part of it in his entertaining study *Ethnic Humour Around the World*.

Mention should also be made of our exchanges with other universities. Tariq Ali came across from Oxford and charmed everyone with his revolutionary fervour. We had a debate with the Yale Union. Years later Peter Fullerton said to me, 'You remember when we spent an evening with John Kerry'. He had also spent a whole day in New York with the future presidential candidate. My memory must be at fault as I do not recall it. But I do remember debating in the Leeds Union with Jack Straw, later President of the NUS.

Today when I come back to speak in the Union, I am surprised how recognisable it all seems. The rules of order are perhaps not as strictly enforced as they should be, but otherwise it appears surprisingly unchanged.

Recently I took part in a debate opposing the motion 'Islam is incompatible with Liberalism'. From the number of women with headscarves in the chamber, it was clear that there were many who were not Union regulars. It was a passionate and unusual debate. When I was back at the House of Lords, Kenneth Baker asked me, 'Why do you bother?' I replied, 'Because it makes me think.'

What is the value of a Victorian debating society today? Oratory is in decline, out of fashion and replaced by TV interviews. Even in the House of Commons, people talk of the 'chamber being in decline' and the real work being done in committees. But debate is still how decisions are formally reached in legislatures around the world. Debate is about organising one's thoughts while at the same time responding to others and communicating the outcome to an audience. As long as there is democracy and argument, there will be a need for such debating skills.

It is certainly possible for student debating societies to take themselves too seriously. 'Little pifflers spouting big piffle' is one description. Nonetheless, I feel a debt of gratitude to the Union. I may have neglected my studies but I learnt a considerable amount listening to the often well-chosen motions which encapsulated issues. No doubt one listened to a lot of nonsense as well, some of it brilliantly put, some of it not. Echoes of the arguments I heard remained with me sometimes for years. And one was able to acquire some of the skills of debating. But more than anything else, I am grateful for the friendships. Enoch Powell once remarked that friendship is not possible in politics. Fortunately, that has not been my experience.

1912–63: THE BATTLE
TO ADMIT WOMEN

Two women's colleges were founded at Cambridge within two years of each other in the late nineteenth century. Girton College was established in 1869, originally at Hitchin, and moved nearer to Cambridge (only relatively nearer, some would say) in 1873. Newnham began as a residence for women who came to attend lectures in 1871. It was not until much later that women won equal footing in the University, however. They had to wait until 1947 before they could take their degrees and become full members; as the University's official historian has noted, 'Cambridge was to prove the most reluctant of all British universities fully to accept the presence of women'.[1]

The Union was no quicker to welcome women into its fold, despite strong connections with both of the original women's colleges (Newnham was founded by an ex-President, Henry Sidgwick, and Girton by Emily Davies, the sister of another). In the nineteenth century, the Union generally displayed a conservative attitude towards the question of women's admission – either to the University or to its own proceedings. Two motions proposing that women be allowed to hold degrees secured less than a quarter of the vote at debates in 1863 and 1867.[2] In 1868, a motion admiring women's efforts to establish colleges 'on the principle of those existing for men' was rejected 33–19. The foundation of Girton the following year obviously changed some opinions, for the Society 'view[ed] with interest and sympathy the career of the Ladies' College at Hitchin' by 78 to 26. (An amendment to strike 'sympathy' and substitute 'amusement' was defeated.) There were some signs of support in the 1870s: the Union voted comfortably in favour of the principle of higher education for women in 1877 and 1879, but did not necessarily include Cambridge in that sentiment.

When, in 1881, the Senate House decided to allow women to sit Tripos examinations, the Union defeated a motion of approval which hoped that this was 'only a step towards granting them degrees'. There were narrow majorities in favour of admitting women to Cambridge degrees in Easter 1880 (109–92) and Easter 1887 (71–65), but opinion had swung strongly away again by Lent 1888, when a motion deprecating the 'continued refusal of Degrees to properly qualified women students' was rejected by 135 to 55. Martin points out the event which seems to have contributed to that swing: in 1887, Agnata Frances Ramsay of Girton outperformed all the 'official' candidates for the classics Tripos. Although this highlighted the injustice of denying degrees to women who scored more highly than men, the immediate reaction of many men would seem to have been indignation, not humility. Martin also points out Miss Ramsay's Union links: after her strong Tripos result, she married the widowed ex-President H.M. Butler, then Master of Trinity. Two of their sons, James and Gordon, also became Union Presidents.[3]

For the rest of the nineteenth century, the Union remained opposed to female emancipation. Degrees for women were rejected again in 1889 and 1891 – and in 1896, when one of the proponents was the future President and suffragist Frederick Pethick-Lawrence. Only the more virulent anti-feminist motions, such as the 1893 suggestion that the ladies' colleges were 'useless and dangerous and ought to be abolished', were defeated – that one by 145 to 86.

In 1897, the Women's Degree Syndicate which the University had established mooted a compromise solution: women could be given the 'title' of BA degrees, though not the degrees themselves. In the event, the Senate House rejected the proposal by 1,707 votes to 661 – but the debate which it provoked in the wider University was arresting. A referendum of undergraduates held on the eve of the Senate House vote showed that they were more opposed to the proposal than the senior members of the University – voting was 2,137 against and 298 in favour – and a debate at the Union was more hostile still. The Society opened its doors to all junior members of the University on 11 May and carried a motion 'strongly condemn[ing]' the recommendation by 1,083 to 138. Far from holding more progressive views than their elders, Union members exhibited a stronger degree of their conservatism. Martin provides an interesting analysis of the Union's attitude towards women *vis-à-vis* the House of Commons. The Union rejected women's suffrage on 28 of the 31 occasions on which it debated it between 1866 and 1914. The exceptions were slender majorities of three, four and one. Most strikingly, he finds that Union members were not only more conservative than the House of Commons as a whole on the question of women's suffrage, but generally more opposed than most Conservative MPs.[4]

The Union came round to the idea of women's degrees more clearly in the first decade of the twentieth century – at first by a tentative 131–121 vote in Lent 1905, then by a more definitive 147–55 four years later. By Michaelmas 1929, the Union wanted to see women given full rights within the University. But the University itself proceeded more slowly. Oxford admitted women to full university membership in 1920, and the Royal Commission on Oxford and Cambridge Universities, which reported two years later, recommended that Cambridge follow suit. But still it held back. In 1921, the 1897 compromise – granting women titular degrees but not the real thing – was resuscitated and this time approved. A Union debate was held suggesting that this arrangement did not meet the legitimate aspirations of women. Surprisingly, it was defeated heavily: by 375 to 185. The main reason for this backward step seems to have been the eloquent opposition of W.R. Sorley, the professor of moral philosophy to whom Rita McWilliams-Tullberg ascribes the dramatic turnaround between two debates on the admission of women to the University in 1920. In May that year, the Union voted

365 to 266 in favour of admitting women – but almost completely reversed its opinion in another debate at the end of November. On that occasion, with Professor Sorley leading the charge, the result was 423 to 337 against.[5]

If the Union was – except on occasions when Professor Sorley spoke – happy to imagine women as members of the University, it was certainly not so willing to imagine them as members of the Union. In 1912, a proposal to open membership of the Society to Girton and Newnham was rejected by a two-to-one majority (127–63). The matter was laid to one side as the First World War interrupted the normal running of the Society. In Lent 1920, a motion to allow members of Girton, Newnham and the Cambridge Training College for women to participate in debates was brought forward by a Mr W.A. Harris of St John's, but it was opposed by the standing committee and failed at a private business meeting (PBM). That October, following the decision to admit women to Oxford and anticipating their eventual admission to Cambridge, a committee formed by the Steward, Sydney Castle Roberts, amended the Union's laws to state explicitly that membership was limited to 'male' members of the University. If women were to be admitted to the Union, it would not be through the back door.

In fact, women had been allowed into the Union from at least as early as the opening of the new building and chamber in 1866.[6] As guests, they could watch debates from the gallery – though this caused some sensitivity, such as at a debate on birth control in Lent 1924. Lord Dawson, the King's physician, was supporting the motion and sent a telegram to the President asking that women be excluded from the gallery that evening. The President, Vyvyan Adams, diplomatically closed the gallery to non-members of either sex.[7]

Letting women into the building raised problems beyond the chamber – most notably the lack of ladies' lavatories. With typical urgency, a sub-committee was formed in Easter 1923 to consider the practicalities of addressing this problem. In due course it reported, but the only practical result of its deliberations was the decision to

Theodore Roosevelt addresses the Union in Easter Term 1910. Geoffrey Butler of Trinity, future MP for the University, sits in the President's chair; Norman Birkett of Emmanuel, one of the judges at Nuremburg, sits on his right.

Palmer Clarke

In Michaelmas Term 1939, the Union agreed that women at Cambridge should have the same rights as men – but a rooftop prank on the day of the debate showed what some members thought of the suggestion.

Cambridge Daily News

Photo]   [Cambridge Daily News
UNDIE-GRAD HUMOUR ?
A 'Varsity version of the Siegfried Line discovered on the top of the Cambridge Union Society building to-day. On the pole is a domestic utensil. To-night the Society are to debate a motion dealing with women students' status in the University!

Damage caused by the Luftwaffe in July 1942. The Union was the only building connected to the University to suffer a direct hit.

Several fire bombs hit the library, starting a huge blaze. The Union still has a number of volumes which bear the scars of the explosion.

Douglas Hurd (Trinity) takes the President's chair from Greville Janner (Trinity Hall) at the end of Lent Term 1952. Alistair Sampson (Selwyn), the new Vice-President, stands behind Hurd.

HRH the Duke of Edinburgh accepts honorary membership of the Society, Michaelmas Term 1952. Percy Cradock (Trinity Hall) sits in the chair as an ex-President.

Ronald Reagan is presented with a Cambridge University sweater after delivering an address to mark the Union's 175th anniversary. The President, Martin Harris (Corpus Christi) looks on, wearing the Union officers' tie.

Linda MacLachlan/Martin Harris

amend the wording of the booklet for prospective members. After explaining that ladies could be introduced as guests, a new sentence was added warning that 'no general accommodation for ladies is provided at present'. Female guests had to wait ten years for a more concrete solution, when the modernisation of the building in 1933 included the construction of a ladies' cloakroom.

The main champion of female participation in the 1920s was Viscount Ennismore of Magdalene, who preferred to go by his family name of W.F. Hare. He tried three times in 1928 to allow female guests to speak in debates. His best result came at a special PBM before the main debate on 15 May – 136 voted for his motion, and 102 against – but under the Union's constitution any proposal to make new laws, or to alter or rescind existing ones, needed a three-quarters majority to pass, so his proposals were still defeated.

This constitutional threshold was to become a regular stumbling block in the struggle to admit women to the Union. Like much of its internal wrangling, the Society's constitutional mechanisms were often as contentious as the issues being discussed. Whether or not the supporters of a motion won the necessary majority at a PBM, they could request a poll of all life members, which it was at the discretion of the President to grant or deny. Such polls also required a three-quarters majority to pass, but to many reformers they seemed an easier way of securing change than persuading supporters to sit through interminable private business meetings. But they were as open to abuse as any other channel. At one poll in the late 1920s, an inventive opposition to women's admission was organised by Hugh Foot and Gilbert Harding: 'They circulated an appeal to members purporting to come from its proponents, dirtily stencilled, with the names on the envelopes misspelt. For good measure their circular was couched in ungrammatical English and adopted an unpleasantly superior tone.'[8] The true proponents of the change were no more persuasive, for nothing came of the poll.

The issue receded somewhat in the 1930s. In June 1931, the laws were amended so that women could be brought as guests for luncheon, tea or dinner. But no further efforts were made to admit them as members in their own right: 'interest seemed to have flagged', says Elwood.[9] In Easter 1934, another attempt to allow women to speak in debates failed to attract the quorum of 30 to the discussion – though there were signs that apathy, not misogyny, lay behind the flagging interest. A debate that term disagreed that the power of women 'has increased, is increasing, and ought to be diminished'; an earlier motion in Easter 1932, 'This House prefers Girton to Newnham because it is farther away', was also defeated.

In Michaelmas 1935, whether to revive interest in the matter or simply to gauge opinion, a full debate – 'That this House would welcome the admission of women to full membership of the Cambridge Union Society' – was held by the President, Arnold Kean. Proposing the motion, Mr V.H.H. Green of Trinity Hall asked those on the other side of the House to throw off their cloak of inhibitions: 'We don't want to think of the day when members of Newnham or Girton will strap themselves to the seats of this House in order to compel the passing of this motion', he said, with some perspicacity.[10] Opposing, the future President P.R. Noakes of Queens' said he 'would be the last to deny that woman has a place in the Union, but that place is in the gallery'. Another opposition speaker, J. Lloyd McQuilty of Trinity Hall, worried that Union elections would become beauty contests if women were involved. 'Imagine a woman sitting there on your chair,' he cautioned the President: 'like a bad photograph, under-developed and over-exposed'. When the House divided, the motion was lost by 274 to 193.

Undeterred by this loss, Leonard Miall of St John's proposed at a PBM three weeks later to permit 'ladies of distinction' to speak in one debate per term. His motion failed to achieve sufficient support, either at the meeting or in the subsequent poll. He tried again, unsuccessfully, as Secretary the following term, and as Vice-President in Easter 1936, when he once again failed to win the three-quarters majority needed.

In January 1939, another Vice-President, Peter Hague, introduced a similar motion. But 'this chivalrous and useful gesture' – as he described it in his end-of-term report – was 'counted out', there being only nineteen people present at the meeting to discuss it. One of the nineteen was a Mr H.D. Catling of St John's, a retired civil servant and life member who used the premises almost daily. He was, in Elwood's recollection, 'the current inveterate anti-feminist in the Union'.[11] When Hague made a second attempt to put his motion at the end of term, Catling led the opposition. But Hague had ensured a better turnout for this meeting, and the motion was carried 'by a large majority'. Catling secured two concessions: an amendment that the word 'ladies' be replaced by the word 'women', and agreement from Hague, who was chairing the meeting, that a poll should be taken. This was held on 13 March, at the same time as the termly elections, and succeeded in defeating the proposal.

When the Second World War was declared and the normal Union offices suspended, the first chairman of debates, R.R. Pittam, held a motion suggesting that female university students should have the same rights as men. It was carried by 99 votes to 60 – but the opponents of the motion made their point dramatically. On the morning of the debate, a pair of stockings, a brassiere and a pair of knickers were found suspended between a stone finial and the flag-pole on the roof of the Union. The *Cambridge Daily News* carried a picture of the spectacle, under the headline 'Undie-grad humour'.[12]

The status of women changed between the two world wars. At a special private business meeting held on 3 June 1943, with Neville Sandelson in the chair, it was proposed that women resident in the University be granted 'associate membership' of the Union 'as a war-time emergency measure only'. After the bomb damage the previous year, the Society had just recorded its lowest wartime intake, and the proposal to admit women, at a special rate of five shillings a term, seemed a useful expedient. But it was not to be: after 'a lengthy discussion', the question was dropped because there was an insufficient number of members present.

After the war, when life had returned to normal, the question of admitting women could be put again. In Lent 1946, yet another Vice-President, Jack Coventon of Magdalene, assumed the mantle of his predecessors Miall and Hague by proposing a motion to allow women of distinction to be invited to one debate a term. This time, the effort was successful. The motion passed at a PBM and was aided by the President, Godfrey Carter – another Magdalene man – who exercised his discretion in refusing to grant a poll. This decision provoked a 'minor constitutional crisis', according to Coventon's account of it: 38 members signed a petition criticising Carter's decision and asking for the matter to be brought before a committee of the whole House. Thereafter, Coventon records, 'the position became somewhat confused':

> The Chairman [of the meeting of the whole House] found that the Committee was out of order and the whole business was referred to a Select Committee. The members of this Committee after some painstaking and most conscientious deliberation presented a report, ruling that the original petition was inadmissible and that the matter must be left to stand.

Whatever the confusion and controversy, Coventon and Carter's efforts resulted in the first victory for women's involvement in the Union. Coventon succeeded his friend as President the following term, and made the most of the change he had helped enact. His retirement debate on 11 June 1946 was the first to include female speakers in the Society's 130-year history. The motion, 'This House views with grave disfavour the theories and practices of the Conservative Party', was proposed by Lady Violet Bonham Carter, president of the Liberal party, and opposed by Viscountess Davidson, the Tory MP for Hemel Hempstead – who, the press noted with some interest, chose not to wear a hat. Coventon delightedly welcomed the two ladies in his opening speech, and won prolonged applause when he added that he would like to see another amendment allowing 'all women studying in this University, if they choose, to come to this Society and give expression to their opinions'. Lady Violet was the first of the two to rise, and expressed her pride at being 'the first woman to break down the barriers of your purdah ... the first woman to raise her voice in your assembly in all its long and sheltered history'. She went on: 'Heavy is our responsibility and black will be our guilt if by our performance here tonight it takes another 130 years ...' – the rest of her remark drowned out in laughter and applause.[13]

In the wake of this triumph, Elwood recalls, 'it was then thought inevitable that the next step, that of women's membership, would be pursued more vigorously'.[14] But the incoming officers were not so enthusiastic for further change. Granger Boston, Bill Richmond and Ian Lloyd – the new President, Vice-President and Secretary – quelled the expectations of the *Cambridge Daily News* on the day of Coventon's retirement debate with a joint letter pointing out that 'the Union is both a debating chamber and a man's club. While the admission of women students to the former may be a desirable aim,' they wrote, 'the fact the membership of the one involves membership of the other raises problems ... The absurdity of having women officers of a man's club is evident.'[15] When the Society met again in the Michaelmas Term, an attempt to procure membership for women won a majority of just ten – far short of the three-quarters required. There was another attempt the following Michaelmas – after another successful debate featuring a lady of distinction, this time the Duchess of Atholl – but it was defeated on a show of hands. There was felt to be no point requesting a division, let alone a poll.

That term was, nonetheless, to prove a significant one for women at Cambridge. In December 1947, a congregation of the Regent House approved a Grace – a formal motion put before the University's decision-makers – admitting women to full status within the University. It received Royal Assent in 1948 and at the end of Easter Term – 28 years after Oxford – the first women graduated from Cambridge.

Now that women were finally full members of the University, there was renewed pressure on the Union to admit them too. In the new year, the future President George Pattison of St John's proposed a motion allowing women to attend – and to speak and vote at – three debates a term. The debate spilled on to the pages of *Varsity*,

Pattison writing a head-to-head article against Norman St John-Stevas. Pattison outlined his arguments in favour of reform. It was absurd that a woman could become Prime Minister, he said, but that no member of Girton or Newnham could speak in the Cambridge Union. Conversely, it was a shortcoming for members of 'this school for politicians' that they could not hear the views of the other sex in a Union debate or have the experience of addressing a mixed audience. 'There is something highly absurd,' he concluded, 'in the sight of the Cambridge Union ... solemnly endorsing opinions which our own grandfathers began to consider untenable, and which our own fathers rejected before we were born.'

St John-Stevas, on the other side, dismissed the 'misguided enthusiasts' who fought in the feminist cause, whose motives lay 'in a muddled form of chivalrous humanitarianism'. The Union, he pointed out, 'is not a society which everyone has a right to enter at will. It is a man's club.' Holding debates may be 'one of the most spectacular activities of that club', but this side of Union life 'cannot be cut off and placed in a watertight compartment.' It would be 'illogical' to allow women to take part in debates and yet exclude them from membership – and it would be a 'grosser absurdity to suggest that a man's club should be open to women'. Besides, he concluded, there was no great demand among women to be allowed entry to the Union: 'The whole agitation has been worked up by a few demagogues whose enthusiasm has blinded them to the actual facts of the situation.'[16]

St John-Stevas may have had the satisfaction of seeing his side win the day – the proposal was defeated at a poll – but Pattison had his reward too. At the end of that term he was elected Secretary, beating candidates from each of the three political clubs.

The following Michaelmas there was an attempt to win full membership for women on the same terms as men. This was proposed by N.T.D. Kanakaratne of Trinity Hall, who had raised the subject three times before and been defeated at each attempt. He was seconded on this occasion by Percy Cradock, but to no avail. Seventy-one members supported their motion, but 115 voted against. They were not helped by a *Varsity* survey of Newnham and Girton. Held to coincide with the meeting, it revealed no great desire among women for membership of the Union: at Girton, less than half of those surveyed – 49 per cent – were in favour of admission, and 31 per cent against it. Sixteen per cent didn't care, while the remaining 4 per cent simply felt it should be left to the men. Said one: 'I enjoy seeing men make fools of themselves, but I don't like seeing my own sex doing it.'[17]

One woman who did speak out was Rosalind Henn, the chairman of Newnham College Debating Society. After Kanakaratne's motion for full equality was defeated once again, she wrote to *Varsity* suggesting that a separate class of 'debating membership' for women would be a fair compromise. Her cause was taken up at a PBM the following term by Benet Hytner of Trinity Hall, the future judge and father of the National Theatre director. 'I only wish to see women as members of the debating society,' Hytner explained to *Varsity*. 'Any move to give them equal facilities in the club might lead to the Union becoming like the unions in the provincial universities.'[18] But even this reassurance was not enough to win approval for the proposition: it was put to a poll and defeated by 182 votes to 166.

Cradock tried to reintroduce the 'debating membership' scheme in Michaelmas 1949 with an emollient preamble 'to preserve the character of the Cambridge Union Society as a male club while at the same time making all members of the University eligible to participate in the debates'. The motion passed by a single vote – 63–62 – far short of the requisite three-quarters majority. The same proposal was made in each of the next five Michaelmas terms, each time unsuccessfully. Jack Ashley tried in 1950, winning leave to put the motion by 146 to 102 – but the meeting ran on until nearly midnight and was adjourned until the following afternoon, when the substantive part of the proposals were defeated 52–48. Thereafter, the motion to consider the proposals did not achieve even a simple majority. In 1951, Greville Janner secured 36 per cent; in 1952, D.H. Macintosh of Fitzwilliam House just 26 per cent; and in 1953,

S.H.J.A. Knott of Trinity, 33 per cent. A slightly broader motion in Michaelmas 1954, proposed by Alan Watkins, lost 22–13 on a show of hands, and 26–11 in a division.

So many times was the question of women's participation discussed in private business meetings that one member, D.G. Rice of King's, grew tired of it and suggested (in vain) that the matter should be limited to one meeting a year. It also formed the basis for main debates: Greville Janner presided over a debate on the motion that 'Woman has come into more than her own and this House regrets it'. Though it was not an entirely serious motion, it was passed by an overwhelming 370 votes to 73. But it was clear where Janner's own views lay: he persuaded the House to suspend the law preventing him from inviting female speakers on more than one occasion that term, and welcomed Lady Astor to his retirement debate.

It was clear that women had very limited support inside the Union; outside it, there was little they could do themselves. There were occasional letters to the student press such as Rosalind Henn's, and a small demonstration was held outside the Union before a debate in Michaelmas 1950. A group of women stood by the front gate on Bridge Street holding placards bearing such slogans as 'We want to debate' and 'Why are we waiting?'. But the protest was a small one, and they were easily persuaded to disperse.[19]

Instead, those women who wished to debate had to find their own fora in which to do so. In October 1950, the 'Boadiceans Debating Society' of Newnham sought permission to hold a joint debate with a Girton society in the Union chamber, open to members of the University and with guests in the gallery. The standing committee cautiously agreed that the debate could be held, but set two conditions: the Boadiceans' chairman would not be permitted to use the President's chair, and it would have to be made clear 'by previous advertisement' that this was not a debate under the auspices of the Cambridge Union. Another proposed condition, that men attending the debate not be allowed to speak, was not insisted upon.

In 1954, a third female college – New Hall – was founded in Cambridge. In the Lent Term that year, the Union debated whether or not this new arrival should be viewed with foreboding – and only decided by one vote that it should not. But the foundation of New Hall gave a boost to the establishment of another entity – a separate Women's Union Society. It began as 'a ghastly after-dinner joke' in Derick Mirfin's rooms at Magdalene in the early hours of a January morning in 1955.[20] It would have gone no further were it not for the colourful character of Robin St John Shurley, who – to Mirfin's great surprise – decided to see the idea through and named himself chairman of the foundation committee. By February, an inaugural committee of four women had been formed, including the President and Steward of New Hall, a medical student at Girton called Andrea Langford, who became its first president, and a Miss J. Ronald of Newnham. These women were much more serious about the society's purpose than the men who had joked about it over their port. It was intended to be more than a debating society, Langford explained: she hoped it would unite women from across the three female colleges and foster the kind of fellowship without which women in Cambridge 'can't hope to get anywhere'.[21]

There was considerable interest in the establishment of the new society: *The Times* thought it a 'brave venture' and devoted a leading column to it.[22] Coverage in *Varsity* was comprehensive – the editor that term, Michael Winner, had volunteered to serve as the new society's press officer.[23] But others were less welcoming. The President of the Union that term, Richard Moore, scoffed: 'The whole thing will probably prove only that women cannot debate.'[24] Nevertheless, the Union voted on 28 February 'to send the Society's fraternal greetings to the newly formed Women's Union Society'. The motion was proposed by Ron Peierls, a future President, and carried *nem. con.*, although a number of frivolous amendments – such as to delete 'fraternal' and insert 'platonic', or to delete 'greetings' and insert 'love' – were suggested and lost.

The Women's Union Society held its first debate on St George's Day 1955. It chose as its motion 'That woman's place is in this House', and met in the Red Lion Hotel, the site of the first meeting of the main Union Society in 1815. The room they had booked was packed with an audience 'which, although predominantly feminine, contained a distinct leavening of males curious to learn of this challenge to their supremacy', reports Elwood.[25] The BBC sent cameras to cover the debate, which was preceded by a foundation feast. Among the speakers was Lady Violet Bonham Carter, chosen because of her recent history-making speech at the Union; also attending the debate was Nehru's sister, Vijaya Lakshmi Pandit, although her role as the Indian High Commissioner precluded her from speaking. But the debate was not a women-only affair. Two ex-Presidents of the Union were invited to speak: Giles Shaw and, fittingly, Derick Mirfin. This arrangement, *The Times*'s special correspondent noted, 'resulted in a debate which started on the high level of spirited address perfected by the Union Society but degenerated into plain dullness'. Though he thought it 'fair not to expect too much', 'any but the most self-deluded feminist must have been disappointed at the lack of sparkle [and] the generally pedestrian quality of most of the later speeches'.[26] Even with Lady Violet's support, the motion was only carried with Langford's casting vote – not an auspicious start for the new society.

By the end of the academic year, it claimed to have enrolled as members a quarter of the women at Cambridge. But Dinah Hutchinson, its president in Michaelmas 1956, was dismayed to find that subscriptions (of five shillings) had only been collected in the first term. She set about finding suitable premises for the new society in central Cambridge, renting a second-floor room above a fishmonger's in Petty Cury with a loan from her ex-suffragette grandmother. A social membership for men was created 'partly to raise funds'. But her success was short-lived. By January 1958, the Newnham College Roll Letter was reporting the 'retrenchment' of the Women's Union: it 'will continue debating activities in hired rooms,' the college said, 'but its own premises hired a year ago proved too expensive to be kept up'. There is no further record of the society, and it seems to have disbanded shortly thereafter.[27]

In the short term, however, the establishment of a separate women's society gave the Union a brief hiatus in the debate over its

THE UNIVERSITY WOMEN'S UNION
CAMBRIDGE

EASTER. TERM, 1955

FOUNDATION CEREMONIES

(Recorded by the B.B.C. for the Third Programme and Television)

SATURDAY, 23rd APRIL, 1955, at 8.15 p.m.

The Lion Hotel

Admission to Honorary Membership of :

H.E. MRS. VIJAYA LAKSHMI PANDIT, High Commissioner for India

Motion of Congratulation :

Proposed by : THE CHAIRMAN, The Foundation Committee, C.U.W.U.
Mr. R. I. A. St. John-Shurley

The Motion for Debate reads :

"That Woman's Place is in this House"

Proposed by Mr. D. MIRFIN, Magdalene College, Ex-President,
Cambridge Union Society

Opposed by Mr. J. G. D. SHAW, St. John's College, Ex-President,
Cambridge Union Society

There will speak Third LADY VIOLET BONHAM CARTER

There will speak Fourth Mrs. SHEILA PRIOR PALMER

There will speak Fifth Miss M. J. ROBERTS, Newnham College

There will speak Sixth Miss J. APPLETON, Girton College

From the Floor of the House Delegates from the Universities of the
United Kingdom and Members

Tellers :

FOR THE AYES
Miss B. MASON, Girton College

FOR THE NOES
Miss E. MARPLES, Newnham College

A. M. D. LANGFORD,
President.

Girton College,
9 *April*, 1955.

own membership. For a while, the only feminine question it had to ponder was what relationship to have with the Women's Union. In Easter 1955, there was some controversy at standing committee over an 'invitation' from the Women's Union to a joint debate in the Union chamber, which the women had hired. The President, Neil Crichton-Miller, thought the Union should accept; other members of the committee thought it 'improper'. The Vice-President, Martin Rosenhead, described opposition to the proposal as 'stubborn, childish and prudish'. Ken Post, a member of the committee and future President, 'implored the Secretary to place him on record as "all those things".' A motion was brought to the first PBM of Michaelmas Term 1955 directing the standing committee 'not to hire the debating chamber, or any other part of the Society's premises, to the University Women's Union during the current term'. It was lost, but voting was slim on both sides.

By the end of the decade, however, the Women's Union had fizzled out and the old issue was taken up again. In Lent 1958, Christopher Norman-Butler interpreted the term 'ladies of distinction' rather more loosely and invited Jennifer Platt of Newnham, president of the University Liberal Club (and, it seems, the last president of the Women's Union), to speak in one of his debates. Miss Platt's appearance – as the first female undergraduate to speak in a Union debate – attracted attention from outside Cambridge. The *Sunday Times* published a half-page picture of the scene inside the debating chamber as she stood at the despatch box.[28] The following Lent, Julian Grenfell held a main debate – 'This House would welcome women undergraduates to full membership of the Union Society' – vacating the President's chair during it in order to speak for the proposition. Joining him on that side of the House were Norman Fowler and John Nott; among the opposition were Colin Renfrew, Leon Brittan and Brian Walsh. Two female students were invited, one speaking on each side: Miss Angela Mills of Girton in favour of the motion, and Miss Pamela Stent of Newnham against. Perhaps the presence of a woman arguing against female membership contributed to the crushing 131–64 defeat for the motion –

though it was, once again, a mixture of serious and light-hearted debate, not a faithful indication of Union opinion.

———

The dawning of a new decade and the demise of the Women's Union led to 'a renewed and more vigorously conducted campaign for women's advancement in the Union' in the 1960s.[29] In Lent 1961, a group led by Brian Pollitt organised a survey at Newnham and Girton to find out whether or not women wanted to join the Union. Their findings were different to those of the *Varsity* survey twelve-and-a-half years earlier – three quarters thought they should be allowed to join, and 34 per cent said they would certainly do so.[30] The survey was part of a concerted campaign to change the Union's laws. A week earlier, Pollitt had seconded a series of motions proposed by Jonathan Tinker of Peterhouse to open Union member-ship to both sexes. They had been carried by 48 to 22 – over the three-quarters threshold – but a poll had been requested so it had to be met again, this time against a larger and freshly provoked opposi-tion. The poll was held on 13 March 1961, and the proponents of change went all-out. *Varsity* devoted its whole front page to the vote: under the headline 'It's time we woke up', an open letter urged all members of the Union to 'Use your vote and vote for women'. Almost 5,000 leaflets signed by seven members of the standing committee were delivered to Union members calling for 'a vote of sanity' in support.[31] These efforts secured the support of 591 members – but also drove out 447 to vote against, leaving a majority of just 57 per cent.

After the disappointment of the poll, supporters of women's membership turned to more devious tactics the following term. In Easter 1961, the standing committee set up a sub-committee to review the Union's list of affiliated societies. Led by the Revd Myles Appleby, its recommendations included some minor changes to the Society's laws, which were brought to a PBM on 29 May. Here, Appleby's proposals were hijacked by a series of amendments moved by David Saunders of Trinity, which would have had the effect of opening Union membership to women. Saunders and his supporters divided the House, winning 37 votes to 18 in favour of his amendments. Appleby then moved to withdraw his motion, but was outvoted 40–14. The President, Colin Renfrew, then announced he was dissolving the meeting. His decision was contested, and a requisition was later sent to him demanding a committee of the whole House to reverse his decision. Here, he was defended by the ex-President Leon Brittan – but the motion, proposed by Saunders, failed to win the support of sufficient members to be valid.

A less underhand attempt was made to advance the cause of women at a later PBM that term, when a Mr P.H.S. Hatton of Christ's proposed that honorary membership of the Union should be open to 'men *or women* of distinction'. He had also cleverly tabled a motion suggesting that Her Majesty the Queen Mother be invited to become an honorary member, perhaps hoping to divide the strong Tory element in the Union. But his tactic was wasted on a small House: fourteen supported Hatton's proposals, with seven opponents (including John Gummer) denying him the necessary majority and rendering his second motion invalid.

The campaign for women's membership got off to a dramatic start at the beginning of the new academic year in Michaelmas 1961. Immediately after the official party for the No Confidence debate had entered the chamber – including the President, Peter Hancock, the student speakers Brian Pollitt and Michael Howard, and the guest MPs Richard Crossman and Peter Thorneycroft – five women and several members sprang from the cellar door in the main lobby of the Union and ran the few paces to the chamber doors. Three women made it into the chamber, where they were given seats 'obviously by prior arrangement with supporters who were expecting them'.[32] Initial reports suggested the intruders, all from New Hall, were 'swept on' by male members and 'pushed to the ground'.[33] But Pollitt denied that they were treated roughly: 'There was quite a lot of excitement,' he said, 'but no anger'.[34] One of the women, Gill Boulind, dramatically fainted and was carried out by Pollitt. A doctor was called, and she was taken to hospital for overnight observation. In the face of the drama Hancock adjourned the debate for ten minutes, during which the other two women, Elizabeth Gunn and Jennifer Daiches, left peacefully.

The intrusion had clearly been carefully planned – although no hint had reached the Union's officers. Some suspected Pollitt's involvement: as Barry Augenbraun's recollection in this volume suggests, he certainly profited from his gallant role in it. 'As a suffragist exercise,' Sydney Elwood thought, 'the escapade perhaps had some merit. It was, however, a widely held opinion that the incident did little to further the women's cause and may even have stiffened the opposition'.[35] But it certainly succeeded in grabbing attention. Hancock invited Jenni Daiches back to a main debate later in the term to argue for the admission of women as full members, against another female student, Gay Turtle of Hughes Hall. The motion was carried by a substantial margin – 225 to 125 – with John Gummer this time supporting the women's cause, against an opposition which included Augenbraun, Hugh Dykes and Ken Clarke. Turtle, it has been said, spoke 'with such style and wit that the nonsense of the case she was advocating became apparent to everyone'. She later worked for the Equal Opportunities Commission during its formative years – revealing where her true sympathies lay.[36] Whether she was arguing against her beliefs or not, her appearance at the Union was fortuitous: there, she met the recent ex-President Tony Firth, whom she later married. He became a writer and broadcaster, she a writer and journalist with a wide range of interests – particularly in her native Northern Ireland, where she was involved in the establishment of the Alliance party.

After the protest and the debate, this eventful term ended with an attempt to change the laws at the final PBM before the Christmas vacation. Pollitt, writing his vice-presidential report shortly before the meeting, anticipated 'fireworks'. Well he might, for he was bringing one of the motions himself – an attempt to lower the threshold for motions put to a poll from a majority of three-quarters to one of two-thirds. Pollitt explains in his recollection how he hoped this would make it easier to win a subsequent poll to admit women – and how his plan was scuppered when another motion proposing just that was brought to the same PBM by Chris Mason of Magdalene. Both motions were defeated at the PBM and at the subsequent poll, held on 5 December. Voting was very similar across the two issues. The motion to admit women won 295 votes, but 186 denied it a three-quarters majority; the motion to lower that threshold to two-thirds in the future was slightly less successful – it won 274 to 181 so was also defeated.

If Pollitt's plan had failed, however, its 'tactical value' was 'undoubtedly' recognised by others, says Elwood. The following term, Michael Howard reintroduced the proposal for a two-thirds threshold in Union polls. He obtained a ten-to-one majority for the change at a PBM on 5 March, but a poll granted by the President, John Gummer, and held two days later reversed the decision.[37]

The following week, this poll defeat once again precipitated renegade action at a run-of-the-mill PBM. The meeting, held on 12 March 1962, had been specially called to make a minor alteration to the laws in order to comply with new licensing regulations, and was due to be chaired by John Dunn, the Vice-President, while Gummer attended another meeting in the Union. A small group on the standing committee, it seems, decided to seize this opportunity. The rules made clear that such meetings were held 'to deal solely with some specified business' and that no new motions could be introduced without prior notice. But instead of closing the meeting after the housekeeping motion had been passed, Dunn allowed Gareth Williams, a member of the standing committee, to propose a series of new motions suspending the restrictions on moving to new business, and the requirements to give notice for new motions. Williams, who later showed greater adherence to protocol as Leader of the House of Lords, recalled the meeting 30 years later: 'There were just three or four of us there … so we simply suspended the standing orders of the Union generally and of the business meeting itself.'[38] Indeed, the only opposition in the chamber seems to have come from Michael Howard, who, the minutes record, was 'suspended by the chair at 5.10 for grossly disorderly conduct'. In this acquiescent

House, Williams's proposals were all carried *nem. con.*, as was a final motion – the *coup de grâce* – declaring that 'notwithstanding any words to the contrary in the laws of the Society, women members of the University shall henceforth be eligible for full membership of the Society'.

Its 'business' concluded, the meeting was adjourned at 5.28 pm and the next step in the coup was effected. Twelve female members of the University were enrolled immediately in the new members' book in the office. When Gummer came downstairs from the other meeting shortly afterwards, he was presented with a *fait accompli*. When he discovered what had been done, recalled Williams, 'he ran into the chamber screaming – you can't do that!'[39] There then erupted an evening of 'intense argument'.[40] Gummer, after consulting his predecessors, declared that the business had been unconstitutional. He placed a notice on the boards advising members that at the meeting that day 'the only motion to be put and carried within the terms of the constitution was the substantive motion shown on the order paper'. The women's names in the new members' book and the record of the meeting in the minute book were all crossed out with an explanatory note signed by the President. The offending pages still bear, in thick blue ink, Gummer's correction across the top:

> This was unconstitutional and therefore did not take place officially – J. Selwyn Gummer.

But the matter was not settled as easily as that. Pollitt and Dunn resigned from the standing committee in protest the following day, and a meeting of the whole House was called to consider a motion of censure against Gummer. The motion was proposed by a Mr C.S. Robinson and seconded – surprisingly – by John Barnes. But, although the meeting was held at the very end of term (and two days after Gummer's final debate as President) it drew a large attendance. While the rebels might have been inventive, their actions were clearly unconstitutional, and the motion was thrown out by 392 votes to just 5.

The following term Michael Howard, now President, succeeded in lowering the poll threshold to two-thirds. His Vice-President, Simon Rocksborough Smith, brought the motion to a PBM on 7 May 1962. The record of the meeting in the minute book gives no voting figures: it simply recorded that the motion was passed by a three-quarters majority and that 'the President, in his discretion, declined to grant a poll'. Howard's decision was a controversial one. Though it was within his powers, the Vice-President's report at the end of term made clear that 'a bare twenty-three members were scraped together' for the meeting, which some thought a very small mandate. 'It seems strange that a change involving the procedure of a poll should itself not be put to a poll,' Howard's predecessor, Colin Renfrew, told *Varsity*.[41]

But the change had been made – and later that term the first attempt was made to take advantage of the new threshold. On 21 May, John Barnes and Norman Lamont proposed a motion to admit women to full membership of the Society. Their motion passed with the three-quarters majority still needed at a PBM, and Howard announced that it would be put to a poll on 24 May. But when the votes were counted – 371 in favour, and 220 against – it was clear that even the new two-thirds majority had not been achieved. 'The result,' *Varsity* said, 'must come as a great disappointment to the President, Michael Howard ... A victory for the feminists would have been a memorable ending to his term in office.'[42]

Howard's successor, Brian Pollitt, was just as keen that the victory should finally be won during his term. He fixed a PBM for 8 November, but warned at the main debate two days before that he would not grant a poll if the three-quarters majority was attained and those insisting on a poll were simply the same small number of vocal opponents. Pollitt's warning – and an unofficial notice of the meeting which was reported to have been circulated to many members – had a clear effect. An impressive 460 people attended the meeting, where Chris Mason proposed the same motion that Barnes and Lamont had brought in May. After some discussion, the House divided: 318 in favour of the motion; 142 against. This was below the three-quarters threshold. Now it was Mason and the supporters of the motion who called for a poll, and Pollitt granted their request. It was held a week later, on 15 November, and a strong campaign was waged. Pollitt himself drove round Cambridge during polling day, drumming up support for the motion.[43] There was a huge turnout – 1,582 votes were cast. Frustratingly for Pollitt, they gave a majority of just 60 per cent: 952 in favour, 627 against, with three papers spoilt. The opposition, Ian Binnie noted wryly in his Vice-President's report that term, owed much 'to a truly astonishing revival of political interest in the Pitt Club'.

The new term, Binnie's own, was dominated by the news on 8 February 1963 that the Oxford Union had voted to admit women. There, the battle had run a parallel course: female Oxonians had been granted 'debating membership' of the Union a year earlier, and a similar two-thirds majority had eluded efforts to grant them full membership by just five votes the previous term. Binnie welcomed the news, and hoped that Cambridge would soon follow suit: 'I do not see any reason why women should not be accepted as members,' he said. 'We have been trying very hard to get them in here and I am glad to hear of the Oxford result.'[44]

In the meantime, Oxford's decision raised an interesting question: would female members of the Oxford Union be permitted to exercise their reciprocal membership rights at Cambridge? This issue was raised by Nora Beloff – whose nephew, Michael Beloff, had moved the motion to admit women in Oxford – when she spoke in a debate at Cambridge later that term. She told the chamber that a group of women would soon be coming to Cambridge 'to assert their rights'. The chamber 'clapped and roared their approval' at this news – though when the cheering had died down, Binnie quipped: 'From what I have seen of them, they will pass for men anyway.'[45] In the end no women made the journey from Oxford, but it certainly encouraged women at Cambridge to push the issue. Binnie showed his support by inviting two women to speak on the paper in a debate the following month. One of the speakers was Susan Strickland of New Hall, a campaigner for women's admission. Seeing her in the

Union lobby the morning after the debate, Binnie pulled down a copy of the debate poster from the noticeboard and gave it to her as 'something for your grandchildren'. He could have given it to them himself: he and Susan married two years later and are now proud grandparents.[46]

Another attempt was made to admit women that term, this time proposed by Angus Calder of King's – who later married one of the New Hall intruders of 1961, Jenni Daiches. But the news from Oxford was not enough to sway opinion in Cambridge. At a poll on 11 March, 438 members (59 per cent) voted in favour, and 299 against.

Binnie's successor, Ken Clarke, was unsupportive of women's membership. As the incoming President, he told *The Times* he had 'always' opposed it, and told *Varsity*: 'The fact that Oxford has admitted them does not impress me at all. They will soon realise what a mess they are in.'[47] Speaking before his first debate in the chair, however, he wished to make it clear that stories about his wholesale opposition were 'extraordinary' and 'entirely mythical ... the invention of a man in the *Cambridge Daily News* service':

> Various people said they were rushing through urgent polls to get women in the chamber before I and the forces of darkness behind me are here ... I hope that members will hurriedly assure their suffragette friends that all the assassination attempts, all the boycotts and all the sit-down strikes are quite unnecessary and will bear that in mind in future.[48]

Nonetheless, Clarke's term was not to see any progress on the question of female admission. Chris Mason, his Vice-President, reported at the end of term that 'the House has preserved intact its reputation for futility in Private Business Meetings. Various brave attempts at revolution were made,' he continued, but these were 'thwarted by the low cunning of the political clique who run this Society.' One such attempt was John Costello's proposal that female members of the University be allowed to speak if they entered their name in a book provided for that purpose before the start of the debate. Each lady would have to be introduced by a full member, and the President would have the power to restrict the number of such women entering the House – but neither of these safeguards was enough to carry Costello's motion.

CAMBRIDGE UNION SOCIETY

MICHAELMAS TERM, 1963

SPECIAL PRIVATE BUSINESS MEETING

THURSDAY, 31st OCTOBER

at 8.15 p.m.

ON

THE ADMISSION OF WOMEN MEMBERS OF THE UNIVERSITY TO MEMBERSHIP OF THE SOCIETY.

For full details of motion see notice board in Society.

Trinity College,
29th October, 1963.

OLIVER WEAVER,
President.

At the end of Clarke's term, then, women were still not able to join the Union. But his successor, Oliver Weaver, was 'an ardent supporter of their struggle' and the new standing committee was supportive of him.[49] At a special PBM in place of the advertised undergraduate debate on Hallowe'en 1963, the now familiar motion to admit women to full membership was debated once more. As was customary for committee motions, it was proposed by the Vice-President, Alan Watson, and seconded by the Secretary, Norman Lamont. It was carried by 166 votes to 43 – easily enough to surpass the three-quarters threshold. But the opposition fell back on their second line of defence, and requested a poll. This Weaver granted, and it was held on 4 November 1963. A ban on canvassing ensured a calmer atmosphere than had surrounded the poll the previous Michaelmas, and the turnout was lower. But the result was clear: 449 voted in favour; 180 against. The supporters of women's membership had won 71 per cent of the vote. The battle was over.

Within seconds of the announcement, five women joined up. The first to sign the members' book was Janet Hogg of New Hall. Another, Lois Radice of Girton, declared: 'This is a wonderful night for all the women in Cambridge.'[50] Nevertheless, there was no great queue of women waiting to join the Union: only 41 had signed up by the end of term, and just 63 by the end of the year. Nor was their presence strongly felt: only nine women had spoken in debate by the end of the academic year, delivering just 25 speeches between them. After the struggle of half a century, Sydney Elwood noted, this 'had almost an air of anti-climax ... Their impact on the Society was so slight that many old members wondered what all the fuss had been about'.[51]

There are some signs that the admission of women had a negative effect on membership in the immediate term. Only 745 new members were signed up that year, compared to 1,065 the previous year. 'In no year since 1945 has the number of new members been so low,' noted the Treasurer, Kenneth Scott – 'and this in spite of the ... widening of our potential membership to include all members of the University.' Membership recovered to see a record intake in

Michaelmas 1965 – but this was boosted by a number of factors, such as the wide coverage of the Union's 150th anniversary, no fewer than nine televised debates in the previous year, and innovations such as pre-paid envelopes to persuade more freshers to join before coming up.

For those struggling to adjust to the new arrangements, there remained one final bastion of masculine sanctity in the Union: the smoking room was still closed to women. But there were signs that the change was more welcome to other members of the Society. In November 1964 – only a year after the vote to admit women – the standing committee considered a motion which had been tabled for the next PBM 'to make a contraceptive machine available in the Union, should it be economically feasible'. (It was later decided that this proposal be dropped 'for fear of offending potential benefactors'.)

There was considerable interest in the new, mixed-sex Union. In Michaelmas 1964, television cameras came to watch as the Union debated whether or not 'emancipated woman has proved a disappointment' (she hadn't). The following term, Anglia TV screened a Union debate on the motion: 'Be good, sweet maid, and let who will be clever'. Barbara Cartland spoke in favour, and the opposition was led – unsuccessfully – by a young PhD student from Newnham, Miss Germaine Greer.

There was further proof that the presence of women failed to usher in an era of unfettered feminism in Michaelmas 1965, when the contestants in the 'Miss World' competition visited the Union. Two of them – Miss Australia and Miss South Africa – spoke in a debate, 'Beauty is only skin deep', which was defeated overwhelmingly by a large House. The others, recalls Jeremy Burford – who was President that term – were rather preoccupied. 'While they were interested in seeing all the sights of Cambridge, they were all desperately worried that the cold would affect their complexion and it would hinder their chances in the competition.'[52]

Women's early impact on the Union in electoral terms was also limited. Two women – Susan Crombie of Girton and Laura

Kaufmann of Newnham – ran in the first elections after women were admitted at the end of Michaelmas 1963, but neither won enough votes to join the standing committee. Interviewed on the radio after she had become the first woman to make a speech as a member, Crombie was pessimistic about the chances of a woman becoming President: 'Not for another one hundred years,' she replied.[53] Sheena Matheson of Girton was more successful at the end of Easter Term, becoming the first woman on standing committee in Michaelmas 1964. Also active in the Labour Club, she failed in her bid to be elected Secretary at the end of that term, but beat John Costello to the Easter vice-presidency by 24 votes. This lined her up to make the first female run for the presidency in Michaelmas 1965. There was much to commend her, as Vince Cable recalls: 'she was immensely talented, a potential political star and very beautiful'.[54] But she was opposed by Jeremy Burford of Emmanuel, running from the position of Secretary. Burford, who had gone straight into the second year of a law degree after a BA in his native Cape Town, was only going to stay on for a third year if he won, so felt he had nothing to lose. But he was confident of victory: 'I knew that the Union wasn't ready for a woman President, and in particular wasn't ready for a Labour woman President.' Although there was certainly an added interest in the first election to involve a female candidate, Burford would be hard pressed to say whether it was Matheson's sex or her politics which was the bigger factor in her defeat: 'I couldn't go better than say fifty-fifty.'[55] Another contemporary is fairly certain that Matheson's defeat was a question of merit rather than misogyny.

The election was also contested by a third candidate, Peter Bottomley of Trinity, who 'stood absolutely out of the blue. He hadn't spoken in any debates ... No one knew why the devil he was standing.'[56] Had they known his familial links to the Union, his contemporaries might not have been so surprised: he was the son of James Bottomley, chairman of debates in Easter 1940. He finished third in the contest that term and was unsuccessful in two further bids for the Presidency. He entered Parliament in 1975, where he was followed by his wife Virginia. A likelier bet to follow in their father's footsteps was Peter's sister Susan, who was also up at Cambridge at the time. 'Exceptionally beautiful' and 'a very good speaker', she was elected to the standing committee in her second term. 'Everybody thought she would be the first lady President,' recalls Burford, 'but she got married in her second year, so that took her out of the running.'[57]

In fact, the first female President came two years later, in Michaelmas 1967. This was Ann Mallalieu of Newnham, daughter of the Labour minister (and ex-President of the Oxford Union) J.P.W. Mallalieu. Her uncle was also an MP, as her grandfather had been. She followed a conventional route to the President's chair, serving as Secretary in Lent 1967 and Vice-President in Easter. She became a well-known personality in the University, foreshadowing her role as president of the Countryside Alliance by riding to hounds and regularly attending the Newmarket races. She was also helped by her glamorous good looks. Speaking opposite her in a debate on abortion law in Lent 1967, the Catholic priest Fr Joseph Christie described her as 'a grave threat to the celibacy of the Catholic Clergy'.

Mallalieu's opponent for the Presidency, Robert Jarman, had held no office in the Union and she beat him by a comfortable 190 to 104 the week after sitting her Finals. Her election made the front page of *The Times* and, to the surprise of the new President-elect, attracted huge interest from around the world. A modest Mallalieu told reporters her election was 'a great thrill', but that she was aware of the pressure on her: 'I think people would expect me to be twice as good as a man in the President's chair just because I am a girl.' The question of dress, she said, was 'quite simple. I will be wearing at each debate a long, formal dress. The question of sitting up here in a mini-skirt to direct debates will not arise.'[58] She celebrated by opening champagne for friends – but drank only orange juice herself – and posed for photographers wearing a deep blue pyjama suit. But not everyone joined in the celebrations: the Principal of Newnham did not even congratulate the first President from her college.[59]

Although they had admitted women earlier, the Oxford Union had still not had a female President when Mallalieu was elected. There, her victory was held – in a thoroughly Oxbridge pun – to be *'mal à l'autre lieu'*. Their first female President was Geraldine Jones, elected on her second attempt for Hilary (i.e. Lent) Term 1968, the term after Mallalieu. She later married a German diplomat and 'disappeared completely from the public eye in Britain'.[60]

Record recruitment in Mallalieu's term made amends for the dip after the admission of women. Over 1,300 new members were signed up that Michaelmas – although Ian Martin, the Vice-President, was unsure 'how far this success was due to the considerable publicity following the election of the Society's first lady President, or to the nature of the recruiting campaign.'

Lady Mallalieu recalls her term as President, and the doors which it opened to her, in the recollection which follows. After Cambridge she trained for the Bar, joining Elwyn Jones's chambers in 1970. There, she struck up a relationship with fellow ex-President Michael Howard, whom she had met on his visits back to Cambridge. Nowadays, the Labour peer is admirably coy about her relationship with the future Tory leader. 'We went out together for about six months,' she recalls: 'it was very pleasant and ended with no acrimony at all, and it wasn't of great significance in either of our lives.'[61]

The successful conclusion of the first term with a woman at the helm marked the final victory in the battle to include women in the Union Society. After Girton's decision in 1970 to admit men as well as women, the Union showed itself to be an early supporter of co-residence, passing a resolution urging 'the men's colleges to follow the same line'. That motion was proposed by the Girtonian Arianna Stassinopoulos, who became the third woman President the following year. At the time of her election, she mentioned in press interviews that she was against women's lib; a point picked up by the publishers of Germaine Greer's *The Female Eunuch*, who suggested she write a 50,000-word reply. The outcome was the lively and successful *The Female Woman* (1973). Stassinopoulos rehearsed some of the arguments in her final debate as President – 'This House would explode the myth of women's liberation' – in which she was joined by Professor C. Northcote Parkinson, Auberon Waugh and the editor of *Penthouse*. The motion was tied by acclamation, and the new President gave his casting vote in favour. Sixty years after first rejecting the idea of women's membership, the Union had entered a phase of post-feminist revisionism.

———•———

One coda must be added. While it may have taken the best part of a century after the foundation of Girton and Newnham for the Union to admit women, the Society was actually rather progressive compared to the rest of Cambridge. It should be noted that the Union opened its doors to both sexes before any of the colleges – as well as many University societies, such as Footlights – did.* The first mixed-sex college was University College (later Wolfson), founded in 1965. Other colleges followed at an erratic pace: the last all-male college, Magdalene, admitted women in 1988, and two female colleges remain single-sex. Even at King's, that bastion of progressive radicalism, women had only just been allowed to dine as guests in 1963 (and even then, a maximum of 22 were admitted on alternate Saturdays, and for the second sitting of high table only).[62] If the Union's attitude towards women was held back by the slow pace of change in the wider University, it also played its role by breaking away and challenging that hesitation.

---

* Eric Idle, president of Footlights in October 1964, wrote to the club's senior treasurer, noting that 'it is rather sad that the Footlights lag behind even the Union' in admitting women (R. Hewison, *Footlights! A Hundred Years of Cambridge Comedy* (London: Methuen, 1983), p. 151).

Recollection:
Baroness Mallalieu QC

(Miss A. Mallalieu, Newnham College)
President, Michaelmas Term 1967

Ann Mallalieu was educated at Holton Park Girls' Grammar School and Newnham College, Cambridge, where she was the first woman to be elected President of the Union. She was called to the Bar of the Inner Temple in 1970, and was elected as a Bencher in 1992. She took silk in 1988 and sat as a Recorder between 1985 and 1993.

Active in the Labour party (her father and uncle were both Labour MPs), she was elevated to the House of Lords in 1991, where she served as an opposition spokesman on home and legal affairs. A vocal champion of foxhunting, she has been president of the Countryside Alliance since 1998.

I went up to Newnham in 1964 to read history. I don't think I would have mustered the money to join the Union but my father paid my subscription because he had been President of the Oxford Union and he thought I should at least be a member. I started to go regularly and enjoyed it every week. I had debated very little at school, so when I started debating in the Union I was complete rubbish. I used to stand up and read every word, and I certainly couldn't have coped with an interruption of any sort. The Union was really where I learned to speak – whether I ever mastered it is another matter! But it was certainly a very good grounding. Just sitting, watching other people was a wonderful way to learn: to see what went down well and what didn't, and what was an irritating characteristic. I saw some really incredible debates and heard some wonderful speeches. I can vividly remember the ones in my term which really made the hair stand up on the back of the neck, and there certainly were a number in my early terms which made me want to keep going week after week.

I arrived in Cambridge just after women had finally been allowed to join the Union as full members. Sheena Matheson was the Vice-President at the end of my first year: she was the first woman to have become an officer in the Union. So the battle was over in a sense, and women were starting to climb up the Union ladder.

I had paid no attention to the struggle to admit women, or indeed to the Union, before I came to Cambridge, and I have to say that when I came up most of my close friends in college weren't interested in the Union at all. I went along because my subscription had been paid and I thought I would see what it was like. I became more and more interested, and then I made friends in the Union and it became a priority to go along each week. I didn't go intending to speak, and certainly didn't go intending to stand for any sort of office.

I suppose all that began to change towards the end of my first year. I had been pressed to speak and had done it. Then people said: 'Well, why don't you stand for election? You should stand.' It was friends saying that which made me do it. At that stage, I think there was an enormous advantage in being a woman. The important thing was to be remembered – it mattered not what for – and there were sixteen men to every woman at Cambridge at that time, so women stood out as beacons whatever they did.

There certainly weren't many women involved at the Union. There were very few – perhaps only half a dozen – who actually spoke. I suppose, looking back now, one would say it was like a boys' public school in a way – although it wasn't actually populated by public school boys: it was a complete mixture. I don't know what it was that kept women away: it may have been the formality of the arrangements and so on; the way the debates were conducted, which wasn't part of the Sixties style at all. Formal debates and formal rules were all slightly old-fashioned.

There had been a strong Conservative leaning in the Union in the years just before I was up. By the time I was there, it was moving away from that. There had always been quite a marked difference between the two Unions: Oxford was very much about points of order and formality; Cambridge was less so. But there were undoubtedly people in the period just before me who regarded the Union as the stepping stone to a political career. I think those who were active and held the offices in the Union during my time on the whole weren't in that category. Very few of them went on to become politicians. For the most part, they have become academics or lawyers.

Similarly, although there were obviously the standard political debates every year, there was a much wider range of motions in my time. I think political motions wouldn't have attracted the audiences. Being President in Michaelmas, your main job was to recruit members who would pay for the Union to continue. If you didn't recruit members in that term, things were rather serious. I have to say I think that was one of the factors which led to my being elected. There were people who certainly said to me that they thought it would be good for recruitment to have a woman.

I became Secretary in the Lent of my third year, which put me on track for the presidency in the first term of my fourth year. Having switched to law for Part II, I decided to stay on for a fourth year to do an LLB. I couldn't bear to leave Cambridge apart from anything else. I was longing to find an excuse to have another year there – but the Union was also certainly worth staying for.

Ian Martin was Secretary when I was Vice-President, and if Ian had chosen to stand against me for President he would have beaten me, I have no doubt at all. He was extremely able, he was very popular, he spoke very well, and he very decently said he wasn't going to stand. So I owe Ian Martin a great deal – but his decision didn't leave me a completely free run. I didn't ever have an unopposed election that I can remember. I don't think that was because

I was a woman: there was always somebody who was ready to stand, whether they had a reasonable chance or not.

When I ran for President, my opponent was Robert Jarman. He was a good speaker, but he wasn't in the Union hierarchy and that did make a difference. Even though one couldn't canvass, there was no question that people whom members saw week in week out in the Union, speaking and playing a part, had an advantage.

I was also at an advantage as my father was a minister in the Wilson government at the time – so the papers would pick up little stories here and there, which happened all through my time at Cambridge. Ghastly things like the 'William Hickey' column used to have little things in them, so there was a little bit of national publicity, which obviously got reflected in the Cambridge and the University press. But the University press also had a very gossipy, University-celebrity dimension to it, and you became known in the University if you were a girl.

Once Ian Martin said he wasn't going to stand against me, I'd realised that it was in the bag, and it was very exciting indeed – but I had absolutely no idea of the incredible publicity that would result – from all over the world. It was the most incredible international effect. I was absolutely besieged by television, radio, newspapers – all wanting me to go and do wonderful things: to appear on the David Frost show, and *Desert Island Discs*, and goodness knows what. I did all of them, and it did me enormous good later in life – far better than any amount of work I could have done to get a decent degree! But I think I was not alone in my surprise at the way in which the Cambridge Union was known, and in which the presidency was in some way symbolic. I never thought it would have any impact beyond Cambridge. I think it was a symbol of something: it was the old order – the male order in a way – and to have a woman was a milestone.

Perhaps it was a sign of the times: everything was changing, and the Union was just the first to go. The very next term, of course, the Oxford Union elected a woman, Geraldine Jones, and the two of us used to be sent around doing joint turns. Poor old Robert Jackson, who was her predecessor – he got left out. I got to know Geraldine a bit because of the things we did together: we were both photographed by David Bailey, which was wonderful.

I had so many really marvellous opportunities, all of which led on to even better things and ultimately led to my being in the House of Lords, I have no doubt. I did quite a bit of broadcasting, starting with little interviews, and then things like *Any Questions*, which I became a regular on, and for the next twenty years I did little bits and pieces of journalism and broadcasting which, in a sense, kept my name about as someone who was a Labour sympathiser. I had also taken silk as a criminal barrister. The Labour party needed a criminal barrister for the opposition benches in the Lords and I got a call from Lord Irvine saying, 'Are you still a member of the People's Party?'

The first debate of my term was 'The present law on drugs is an unnecessary infringement of the liberty of the individual' – Jonathan Aitken spoke in favour. That was an interesting debate because two years before, a rather long-haired chap who was known to be someone who took drugs had come to me and said, 'Why don't you have a debate on drugs?' And I remember thinking, 'That's ridiculous. No one would be the slightest bit interested in drugs. It's of no relevance to anyone here except one or two weirdoes.' Anyway, by 1967 clearly times had changed. The motion was defeated, but not by much: 292 supported it, with 353 against.

I also held some political debates, of course – though the Wilson government was very unpopular at that particular time and didn't come out of them very well. Barbara Castle came to the No Confidence debate as a favour, as she was a friend of my father's. She became a really great friend when I came to Westminster because we were neighbours as well, so I used to drive her up and down to the House of Lords until she died, and she always regretted coming to my debate. She was transport minister at the time, and the members in the debate *howled* her down. They behaved appallingly. I've always slightly regretted it, because I didn't try to be more restraining. But I took the view that she was a government minister, it was an unpopular government, and she was going to have to take it! She lost the debate heavily – by a majority of nearly 300.

Later in the term I ran a debate deploring devaluation as 'a humiliating reversal of Government policy', and calling for the Prime Minister to resign. But it was a fill-in debate, not one of the main ones, so only undergraduates spoke in it. It was an interesting set of undergraduates nonetheless: there was Christopher Clarke, who's now a very eminent QC; Mary Arden, who is a High Court judge; and Peter Riddell from *The Times*. I suppose it was a rather contentious motion for the daughter of a government minister to put forward, but I don't remember any suggestion that I was doing things in order to help the government, or to hinder it.

The debate which I think was by far the best of the whole lot was 'This House would rather have written Grey's "Elegy" than taken Quebec', which was a debate about different kinds of glory. Clive James, who was then doing quite a lot in the Footlights and was an Australian postgraduate, was his usual self. As he is now, he was then: very, very funny, with a quick-fire delivery. Jonathan Sacks, now Chief Rabbi, also spoke – as did George Steiner, who was brilliant. He painted a picture of Quebec, and read from chronicles of the time about the ghastly blood and guts of the fight, and he said, 'No matter how bad a poem Grey's "Elegy" is' – and he tore it to bits – 'I would rather have done that than been responsible for this sort of carnage.' Then Bernard Braden gave a very funny speech about Canada and what would have happened if Quebec had not been taken, and so on. The whole debate was a perfect mixture of comedy and seriousness – and all four speeches were just superb.

There were, of course, one or two difficulties to contend with during the term. The big controversy came when Peter Kellner, the political pundit, ran for President as a protest against the Union's ban on written canvassing. He took over the window of the Copper Kettle in King's Parade to put up advertisements for his campaign. He flagrantly broke all the rules just to show that this was a ridiculous way of conducting things. He was probably right, actually. But he had broken the rules, and had to be disqualified. It was a difficult matter, because he had quite a lot of support from people who totally agreed with him. Peter did speak regularly, but he was seen as a troublemaker – and he chose to be seen as that. If he'd stood in the ordinary way, he might have done rather well.

The other main worry of the term was the financial position of the Union, which is why recruitment was so crucial every autumn. It was vital to have a President who put on a popular programme, so it had to be someone who it was thought could attract well-known speakers; there was much less emphasis in those days on the other aspects of the Union. There was the bar and the awful Union cellars where the dances took place, but there was really nothing to sustain the Union apart from the debating, and people joining for the purposes of coming to hear debates. So people wanted a really good programme for that first term each year. Luckily we had good recruitment figures in my term. I think part of that was the publicity I received as the first female President. It did all help.

I'm ashamed to say I haven't been back to the Union now for some time, and it's not because they haven't asked me – they have. I went back quite a bit early on, and to Oxford too. I think there's a point at which you become out of touch, and then there's a point at which you can come back as a complete stranger. But I think there's a point where you think you're in touch and you're not, and that's not a good time to return. I think you do need to know the feel of the place, because it does change and you can get it badly wrong. The last time I went, I went expecting to make a speech of twelve minutes or so, and I arrived and was told it was half that. I had just about started when a note came up saying 'Stop'. I'd travelled all the way there and thought '—— this!' So it was slightly frustrating – but the sort of thing one had done to other people oneself, so I suppose I shouldn't have minded about it!

There's a sort of unwitting arrogance, I suppose, to dragging people like Barbara Castle up to Cambridge to be screamed at. You expect people to be honoured to come to your little student do. But it's a major job: you've got to prepare a speech, and you've got to prepare for people being less than pleasant to you. And then you come up to be insulted and go away again.

But the Union continues to have a special draw. I still wonder that it means anything to people outside what is, after all, a very narrow little world. It's symbolic of something far wider than it actually is, as I know. The Union is basically a small debating society of a few members of the University, and a very good place to learn to speak. It's astonishing that so many people associated with it have gone on to have such an amazing range of careers. But it does have a prestige which stretches far beyond what it actually involves to hold the office. I'm extremely lucky to have been in the right place at the right time. It is just sheer luck to get it right.

1967–75:
An 'Open Union'?

While the Cambridge Union was debating the admission of women, students around the world were turning their attention to a whole host of new causes. The late 1960s and early '70s were years of unprecedented student activism – protests and marches spilled onto the streets and, for a time, caused serious anxiety among those who witnessed the newly militant youth. While Cambridge University was never as swept away by the 'Spirit of '68' as were students in Paris or London, nor was it completely insulated from the new political mood. Students demanded greater say in college and University life and employed new tactics to draw attention to their campaigns. In what seemed to be a rapidly changing academic climate, the Union faced some fundamental questions about its place in modern Cambridge – questions which extended to its very existence as an independent institution.

Until fairly recently, 'student' was held to be an alien term in Cambridge. Junior members of the University were 'undergraduates' – and 'student' was reserved for women at Newnham and Girton before their admission to degrees. 'Student,' an earnest *Varsity* pronounced, 'is a word that goes down badly in Cambridge'.[1] But as Cambridge undergraduates identified themselves more closely with the political causes of the late 1960s and assumed a greater sense of solidarity with their peers around the world, so they adopted the terminology of the broader student movement.

There were palpable signs of this changing mood. New magazines and publications appeared, chiefly *Stop Press*, founded in January 1972 to meet the desire for a more radical, campaigning newspaper. It did not pose an immediate threat to the primacy of *Varsity*, which was that term under the editorship of Jeremy Paxman: the new paper lasted only five issues before running out of money. It reappeared in Michaelmas, however, and added a new, stridently political tone to the student scene. By the following year, it was *Varsity* which faced financial difficulty, and the two merged as *Stop Press with Varsity*. Even then, the paper struggled – it was forced to go fortnightly for two terms in 1975, and only managed one edition in Easter 1977.[2]

In the weeks when they were published, however, the student papers had plenty of exciting events to report. Political protests became bigger and more frequent, with sit-ins the latest student vogue. In January 1969 a sit-in took place at the University's administrative centre, the Old Schools. It was held to show solidarity with a similar protest at the LSE, but produced a list of demands which could only have been written in Cambridge – such as gate hour reform and an end to University representation on the city council. The Old Schools were occupied again in 1972, when 600 students stayed there for 48 hours. The catalyst for this protest was a set of proposed reforms to the economics Tripos, but the broader issue was the demand for student representation in University decision-making. The Old Schools sit-in led to an inquiry by the High Steward of the University (and ex-President of the Union) Lord Devlin. It also led to another sit-in at Lady Mitchell Hall and the economics faculty to protest against the lack of progress by the following year. Further sit-ins took place at the Senate House against the lack of nursery provision for students and staff – and, perhaps most oddly, at the University Library, where the complaint was its decision to close at 7.00 pm rather than 10.00 pm.

The most dramatic protest in Cambridge, however, was the so-called Garden House Riot on 13 February 1970. The Greek government – then a military junta – organised a 'Greek Week' in the city with support from local travel agents and hotels. Some 400 demonstrators gathered outside the Garden House Hotel on the Friday evening to stop people attending a dinner hosted by the Greek tourist board. The protesters hammered on the windows and climbed onto the roof in order to disrupt the dinner. As the weather had been wintry, they threw snowballs, which were soon joined by bricks and stones. The protest flared into violence; the dinner was invaded, and the hotel's River Suite was damaged. The *Cambridge Evening News* called it a riot. Six students were arrested, and a total of thirteen people, including a don, were charged. In June, nine of them were convicted of riotous or unlawful assembly: their sentences ranged from short periods in borstal to eighteen months' imprisonment.

The Union held an emergency debate on 23 February condemning the violence, which was passed 'almost overwhelmingly'. But the Society may have been partly responsible for the Greek government's decision to hold a 'Greek Week' in the first place: Andreas Papandreaou, the exiled son of the former Greek Prime Minister, was due to speak at a meeting at the Union in March. 'His opinions of the military junta are unfriendly to say the least,' mused *Varsity*: 'What more natural than that the Greek government might think of getting in first and presenting their own side of the matter?'[3]

This was certainly a left-leaning period at the Union. In 1968, on the night of the American presidential election, a series of speeches were made by students 'on behalf of the American presidential candidates'. Across the Atlantic, Richard Nixon was about to win a narrow victory over Hubert Humphrey. In Cambridge, the result was much less finely balanced: he won just 20 votes, compared to 281 for the Democrat (and three for George Wallace). Debates about the British general elections of the early '70s also saw victories for the left. A debate to coincide with the election in June 1970 produced a majority for Labour, albeit in a small House with a large number of abstentions (perhaps encouraged by the Liberal and Communist speakers also present). The February 1974 election was marked by a debate on the motion that 'Only the Liberal Party offers genuine solutions to the problems of modern Britain'. Appropriately, perhaps, the result was split down the middle, with 117 in favour and 116 against. When the exact nature of the hung parliament was finally determined, the Union decided on 22 April that it welcomed the change in government, giving Labour a slender majority of two.

The Union's internal decisions also reflected its left-wing inclinations. In January 1969, the standing committee decided to name an upstairs room the 'Kennedy Room' – six months after Bobby Kennedy's murder, and despite the fact that none of the family had ever visited Cambridge. The single transferable vote system was adopted for Union elections at the May Week members' business meeting (MBM) of 1971. The standing committee had resolved to oppose the changes at its meeting earlier in the day, but in the event the proposal went through without opposition.*

Many of the Union Presidents of these years were figures of the progressive left. Ian Martin of Emmanuel, President in Lent 1968, became general secretary of the Fabian Society. A human rights activist, he served as secretary-general of Amnesty International from 1986 to 1992, and worked extensively with the United Nations on humanitarian projects in Haiti, Rwanda, Bosnia and Herzegovina, East Timor, Eritrea, and Ethiopia. Ken Jarrold, President the following Michaelmas, was a manager in the National Health Service for 36 years. He was deputy chief executive of the NHS in England for three years, and has been a director of the Serious Organised Crime Agency since 2005.

Hélène Middleweek became the Union's second female President in Easter 1969. Like Ann Mallalieu, she also went into Labour politics – indeed, the two went head-to-head for the party's nomination in Welwyn and Hatfield in 1974. Middleweek won and represented the seat in Parliament until 1979, during which time she became the

---

* The new voting system was extended to committee elections in Lent 1979. It was supported 276–53 in a poll, even though all but one of the standing committee members were opposed to it. The Union's returning officers were so concerned they would not be able to organise the count satisfactorily that they asked the local Liberal party agent to come and help. An attempt to reverse the decision fell one vote short of the necessary majority the following Michaelmas.

first sitting MP to have a baby. She was raised to the peerage in 1995 as Baroness Hayman. After spells as a health minister and as chairman of Cancer Research UK and the Human Tissue Agency, she was elected as the first Speaker of the House of Lords in 2006.

Two lawyers in 1970 were also of progressive opinions. Rajeev Dhavan followed in his father's footsteps to Emmanuel College and then the Union Presidency in Easter 1970. He became a professor of law, and now practises at the Indian Supreme Court. Nick Stadlen of Trinity was President in Michaelmas 1970. He and Dhavan won the *Observer* Mace debating competition in 1969. It was the first time the Union had won the annual competition, and it has only done so twice since: in 2004 and 2007. Stadlen went to the commercial Bar, took silk in 1991, and was voted Barrister of the Year by *The Lawyer* in 2006. He made the longest opening speech in legal history as the leading counsel for the Bank of England's two-year trial against claims of misfeasance – it lasted 119 days, and was described as a '*tour de force*' by the presiding judge.

Others on the standing committee have become well-known figures on the centre-left: the future Cabinet minister Patricia Hewitt made her maiden speech from the floor during Mallalieu's term in a debate on the motion that 'The price of progress is too high'. She served on standing committee alongside Peter Riddell, the political commentator with *The Times*. Of course, there were right-wing Presidents too – the first President of the 1970s was Roger Evans, 'an appalling Tory of the worst kind', according to one future Labour minister who was up at the same time.[4] Chairman of CUCA the year before his Presidency, Evans became a barrister and then went into politics. In 1991 he unsuccessfully contested the Monmouth by-election; he won the seat at the general election the following year, but was defeated again in 1997. He returned to the Bar, and has been a Recorder since 2000. Another CUCA chairman-turned-barrister was Philip Heslop, President one year after Evans. Born in Newcastle, he unsuccessfully contested Vauxhall in 1979, but never found a safer Conservative berth. Instead, he enjoyed considerable success at the commercial Bar. He was appointed Queen's Counsel at 36, and head of his chambers in 1998. A barrister who 'combined acute forensic skills with kindness, courtesy, humour and old-world charm', he died aged 55 in 2003.[5]

There were others, too, who eschewed politics. Ged Martin, President in Easter 1968, took a first in history and stayed at Magdalene to complete his PhD. He spent five years as a research fellow at the Australian National University, then lectured at Cork. He taught Canadian history at the University of Edinburgh for eighteen years, where he received a professorial chair in 1996. On his retirement to Ireland in 2001, the university paid tribute to this 'brilliant lecturer and writer, with a coruscating and hilarious wit'.[6] He maintained an interest in the Union, publishing a study of the Society and its debates on the Irish question from 1815 to the First World War. And Rupert Jackson of Jesus, President in 1971, took silk in 1987 and spent two years as head of his chambers. He has been a Lord Justice of Appeal since 2008.

The towering President of these years, however, was a man unmistakably of the left: Hugh Anderson, President in Michaelmas 1969. The son of Sir Norman Anderson QC, professor of Islamic law at SOAS, Hugh followed in his father's footsteps to Trinity. He had a highly successful Cambridge career, and it was widely anticipated that further success lay beyond. But it was not to be: Sir Norman and his wife suffered the cruel fate of outliving all three of their children. Hugh revealed shortly after his election as President that he had been fighting stomach cancer for the past year. The illness had developed after he had been hit in the stomach by a cricket ball; he had had a couple of operations and believed he was 'virtually cured'. But he died on 12 August 1970, less than a year after his Union term. An obituary in *The Times* noted that 'he won popular acclaim for his vitality and mature approach to student politics'. He had made little of his illness, said a friend: 'The range and intensity of his activities and interests were his only acknowledgement of the term set upon his life.'[7]

Anderson certainly had an intense and active time as President. In addition to the main debates, he held a 'Teach-In' at the Union during his term, which was a symposium on the subject of education. Anderson explained there was 'a feeling within the Union that debates, though very useful in delineating broad disagreement, are not always conducive to an understanding of a complex question in depth'.[8] Forty guest speakers came over the course of one weekend, including ministers, teachers, and professors of education and sociology – Bernard and Shirley Williams, John Vaizey, Sir Edward Boyle, and the ex-Presidents Rab Butler and Lionel Elvin. Together, they provided more than 30 hours of discussion. To spread the debate further, their speeches were recorded and the transcripts published by Heinemann.

But Anderson was a fine debater too. When Stadlen and Dhavan won the *Observer* Mace, Anderson was named the best individual speaker. Outside the Union, he was also chairman of the University Labour Club, and was widely active in the party. He established a new national body, Students for a Labour Victory, with the president of Leeds Students' Union – a young Jack Straw. For his retirement debate, Anderson chose the motion 'Equality of opportunity is not enough', and invited Paul Foot and the Methodist campaigner Lord Soper to speak alongside him. The debate was tied, and passed by the new President (Roger Evans)'s deciding vote.

He also amassed a fine collection of second-hand books – many on left-wing political themes. After his death, his parents presented the collection to the Union library: inside each volume, above the bookplate, is written in Anderson's own hand his name, the place where the book had been bought, and the price. A memorial fund was also opened by the Union in October 1970. A letter to *The Times* announcing this was signed, *inter alia*, by the Archbishop of Canterbury and his fellow ex-Presidents Lords Butler and Caradon. In a sign of the mark that Anderson had already made on the Labour party, it also bore the signatures of Richard Crossman, Michael Foot, Shirley Williams and the then leader Harold Wilson. It raised £3,000 to bring South African students to British universities. A photograph of Anderson was hung in the debating chamber, and it was decided that a Hugh Anderson Memorial Lecture be held each Michaelmas.

The series ran until the late 1980s and attracted a number of prominent speakers including Wilson, Anthony Crosland, Malcolm Muggeridge, Tony Benn and Jim Callaghan. In 1978, it was delivered by the Prince of Wales, on the subject of 'Human Motivation'. According to the Vice-President's report, it was 'one of several occasions which attracted more people than the Union can contain' that term.

Prince Charles had been a contemporary of Anderson's at Trinity. He came up in 1967, and – like his grandfather George VI before him – joined the Union. He made his maiden speech in a debate on 12 May 1970: 'This House believes that technological advance threatens the individuality of man and is becoming his master'. Although the Prince spoke from the crossbenches and made it clear that he was not formally for or against the motion – 'a slightly difficult position', he remarked – he expressed concern at the extent to which people had become creatures of technology, and suggested that there was sometimes a need for the purpose of new developments to be questioned.[9] His speech – one of his first in the public spotlight – sparked a minor controversy by voicing disquiet about Concorde. 'If it is going to pollute us with noise, if it is going to knock down churches, or shatter priceless windows when it tests its sonic boom – is that what we want?' he asked. The British Aircraft Corporation was driven to confirm that the plane would not fly supersonically over land, and gently suggested that Prince Charles 'listen to both sides of the controversy'.[10] The motion was carried 214–184, beating the Prince's great-uncle Lord Mountbatten, who spoke in opposition.

A more controversial speaker was another Trinitarian, Enoch Powell, who visited the Union twice in the year he made his so-called 'Rivers of Blood' speech. In Lent 1968 – before his speech in April – he received a standing ovation along with J.K. Galbraith when they spoke respectively for and against the motion: 'The State can be supported when it regulates the economy but must be condemned when it intervenes.' Despite Powell's ovation, the motion was heavily defeated by 561 votes to 265. In Michaelmas, after his sacking from the Shadow Cabinet, Powell was invited to speak to the University Conservative Association by its chairman, the future Tory MP Howard Flight. Initially, CUCA could find no building in Cambridge to host the visit for fear about what protests might ensue. The police's favoured venue was the Union, whose President that term, Ken Jarrold, made it clear that the Society would uphold its commitment to free speech. 'We feel that whatever happens to the building we have a duty to allow the meeting to take place here', he told the national press.[11] Standing committee agreed unanimously that it was 'desirable to have Mr Powell speaking in Cambridge, but at the minimum risk to the Society'. It was agreed that the building should be closed during the day of the visit – Sunday 27 October – and that the staff were not to come in. Flight 'spent hours with the police organising plans for getting him in and out of the Union safely'. On the afternoon of the meeting, a crowd of 500 demonstrators awaited the contentious guest but were frustrated when, just after four o'clock, loud applause came from the debating chamber: Powell had been smuggled in earlier. He stayed in the Union until 7.15 pm, when a dozen policemen escorted him to a waiting car.[12]

Powell was belatedly condemned in an emergency motion later that term: on 25 November Hélène Middleweek and Peter Riddell proposed, and 'carried by an overwhelming majority', a motion condemning 'the conduct of Mr Enoch Powell as tending to impede the solution of Britain's racial problems'. The Union was evidently in a censorious mood that evening: another motion to 'censure the Beatles on their new LP' was carried – with a speech in support from Patricia Hewitt.

Powell came to the Union again almost exactly a year after his visit to CUCA. Hugh Anderson invited him to speak in a debate on 29 October 1969 on the nationalised industries. The invitation provoked a sit-in, starting the day before the debate. Nearly 100 students occupied the Union chamber in an attempt to prevent Powell speaking there. Some damage was done, and there was mention of Union property being stolen. Anderson made a statement 'utterly deplor[ing]' the action and hoping that the students would leave 'without causing further trouble'. But he defended his decision to invite Powell: 'Having worked in the Indian community in Southall for most of the vacation,' he pointed out, 'I know all too well the harm that Mr Powell has done to the coloured citizens of this country ... The debate, however, is on nationalisation and this seems to me an important issue on which Mr Powell has distinctive views.' Perhaps surprisingly, Anderson was supported by left-leaning student organisations. The president of the Student Representative Assembly, David Beggitt, said the sit-in was 'a blow against freedom of speech, against the right of the Union committee to invite persons to speak on behalf of its members, [and] against the freedom of assembly for private societies.'[13]

On the evening of the debate itself, 400 protesters marched with flaming torches to the Union. Carrying a black coffin, they followed a drummer around the Union building in slow time. Inside the chamber, a motion 'regret[ing] the President's decision to invite Mr Powell to speak here tonight' was introduced before the debate – but Anderson responded to it personally, and it was defeated with only six votes in favour.

The police made two arrests as the result of the protests, and two members were fined after the sit-in: Chris Stevenson, a leading light in the International Socialists, and J.F.H. Bennett of Christ's, who was fined £2. On 5 November, Brian Pollitt – who was in Cambridge at the time as a lecturer at Queens' – exercised his right as an ex-President to attend standing committee to raise some questions about the fines. A requisition was brought for a committee of the whole House to consider reversing Anderson's decision to impose the fines; it was held on 10 November, but quickly dissolved after only 28 members attended. At an MBM also held that day, a motion was brought seeking an assurance 'that in future a speaker who is liable to require such stringent internal security arrangements as to exclude members from the Union premises should not be invited'. It was opposed by the Vice-President, Roger Evans, and 'defeated over-whelmingly'. Even after the turmoil of the recent weeks, the Union's commitment to free speech was unabated.

———

A more equivocal attitude existed towards the nature of the Union itself. With many other universities establishing students' unions and fighting for greater representation in academic decision-making, there was considerable support for such an organisation in Cambridge – and many people thought the Union was the obvious venue for it. Of course, this raised some serious questions. The Union was a private members' club, not a body to which all Cambridge students automatically belonged: should it continue to be so, or should it open its doors to all? While the Union met weekly to debate the burning issues of the day, it never presented itself as a representative body of student opinion: could it take on that mantle, and what effect would that have on its activities and reputation? Unsurprisingly, these questions provoked a wide range of answers.

A number of Cambridge undergraduates had been involved in the establishment of the National Union of Students in 1922 – and, as we saw in the introduction to this volume, the Union was briefly affiliated to it during Rab Butler's term. But the early NUS won little support from Cambridge colleges: those which had joined before the Second World War left soon afterwards. Girton was the last to disaffiliate in 1952. The collegiate system was strongly supported, and most colleges had a Junior Combination Room (JCR) to look after the interests of their undergraduate members. There was, therefore, little enthusiasm for central representation. 'In Cambridge the very concept of "student opinion" is suspect,' wrote *Varsity* in the year of Girton's departure from the NUS. 'To make undergraduates into a separate caste, solemnly holding its annual congresses and uttering mythical "collective opinions" is both pretentious and absurd.'[14] In an effort to rebuild its links with Cambridge, the NUS proposed a looser form of affiliation in the mid-1950s; by February 1964, the last college (Selwyn) had signed up to it.

That month in Cambridge also saw the establishment of the Students' Representative Council (SRC). This new body comprised one representative from each of the 24 JCRs, plus six 'University representatives'. The President of the Union that term, Norman Lamont, was invited to its inaugural meeting; his successor, Charles Lysaght, made a 'reluctant' casting vote against the motion that 'the SRC is unnecessary' at the first debate of Easter term. 'It seems that the House found the SRC a subject of amusement rather than serious debate,' recorded the Vice-President, Bill Treharne Jones. Nonetheless, the standing committee allowed the new organisation to use a room in the Union over the summer, and offered it filing space and use of a noticeboard – so long as it refrained from 'any assaults upon the Union'.

By Michaelmas, it seems the establishment of the SRC had spurred thoughts of a new form of Union membership: allowing colleges to buy 'block membership' for all their undergraduates. An enabling motion was passed that term allowing the Union to consider such a scheme. Peter Fullerton sought to calm nerves in his end-of-term report: this would not mean the Union would become, 'as has been suggested, a students' union'; rather, it was a way of 'stabilising our income and increasing our membership'. After all, 'it is obviously the Society's policy to encourage as many freshmen as possible to join the Union – logically to persuade them all'. The Union's Treasurer, Kenneth Scott, was in favour of block membership arrangements: it would make it easier to budget if numbers were more stable. But there was opposition from some within the Union who feared the current facilities could not cope with a vast increase in numbers – and opposition from outside too, from those who feared it would undermine the JCRs.

Clare was the first college to consider the idea – but rejected it at a JCR meeting early that term. Sidney Sussex and Churchill considered it in Lent 1965, and St Catharine's requested details. But Fitzwilliam House rejected it at the end of February – and there was a greater stumbling block. Interested colleges approached the Ministry of Education to see if they could get increased grants to pay for the block memberships, but were turned down: Oxbridge students were already given substantially higher personal grants than students elsewhere. Under the most recent Education Acts, local

authorities were required to give money for 'obligatory' social societies, so that was another potential source of funding – but a Catch-
22 situation prevented it. The block membership would only be
considered obligatory if *all* Cambridge students were members. That
could not happen until the Union was expanded; and that could not
be afforded without the local authority money. So the plans were
officially dropped at the end of April 1965.

There were moves to revive them two years later. In Michaelmas
1967, Kenneth Scott reported that the financial position of the
Union was 'very serious'. The Society had an overdraft of £8,000
and another £4,000 was owed to its creditors. The 'only salvation'
for the long term, he said, 'would be a system of state-financed automatic membership'. Standing committee unanimously agreed that
'every possible step' should be taken towards such a scheme, and that
the Union should announce this publicly. The situation was so
drastic that membership was even discussed for students at
Homerton, who were admitted as associate members in Lent 1968
and, at Hugh Anderson's suggestion, as full members in Michaelmas
1969. Particular excitement was caused in June 1973 when it was
decided that student nurses at Addenbrooke's should also be
permitted to join. By the end of that year, however, the Union's
financial standing had improved markedly, removing much of the
impetus behind the block membership scheme. 'This year for the
first time in a very long while the Society did not once go into an
overdraft,' the Vice-President happily reported at the end of
Michaelmas. 'The Union is in the healthiest financial position it has
been in for many years.'

This financial turnaround should be seen in the context of the
Union's younger sister at Oxford. There, the financial position dete-
riorated so rapidly that, 'for much of the decade, the Society had a
fight for survival on its hands'.[15] In 1970, the Oxford Union actually
voted to turn its facilities over to a central students' union, but the
idea was rejected by the University. Cambridge looked on with
ambivalence. At a standing committee meeting in October 1970,
'the President reflected – with some relish – on the state of the

259

Oxford Union's finances – a topic from which all present derived manifest satisfaction'. But the committee were all too aware that a similar fate could befall them. Mr Thompson, the chief clerk, reminded them that turnover in the bar had been lagging that term, 'and it was decided to change the subject'.

The SRC disbanded and was reconstituted as the larger Students' Representative Assembly (SRA) in 1969. With a president and 200 elected members, it was hoped that the new assembly would be a more representative and powerful body. But the SRA was 'widely held in contempt' – four colleges pulled out almost immediately, and no one seemed entirely certain what it was for.[16] An emergency debate at the Union on 12 May supporting the SRA in its attempt to establish 'a strong body representing student opinion as a whole' was defeated by 89 votes to 68. By the following February, it had been decided to revert back to one representative from each college, and the SRA gave way to another new organisation, the Cambridge Students' Union (CSU). Like the SRC and SRA, the new body had no official recognition from the University (it would not be recognised until 1984, when it added 'University' to its name and became CUSU). But it attracted considerable attention from the student body. Nine candidates contested its first presidential election in June 1970. The winner was John Newbigin of Queens', the candidate of the Socialist Society. Later a freelance journalist and political adviser, he worked for Neil Kinnock when he was Leader of the Opposition. Another adviser to Kinnock was Newbigin's successor as CSU President, Charles Clarke. One of the priorities he set for his term of office was the merger of the CSU with the Union to form a central students' union, open to all.[17] He was a formidable operator – and he came close to achieving his goal.

At the time of its formation, the Union treated the CSU with broadly the same disdain that it had shown towards its precursors. A debate in October 1970 'deplore[d] the mechanism of student representation proposed by the CSU' by 264 votes to 144. But there was support for a central students' union in some form: another debate the following month – proposed by the President, Nick Stadlen –

agreed that it was 'necessary for the future of the University that there should be a central union with free automatic membership for all students'. Clarke assumed the CSU helm the following Michaelmas, and fired his opening salvo within weeks. At the start of November 1971, the CSU executive, 22 of the 23 JCR Presidents, and three members of the Union's standing committee signed an open letter to *Varsity* calling for an 'Open Union' – a new, central union formed by the merger of the CSU and the Union Society, based in the Union buildings but administered by the CSU. Clarke followed this up with a letter to the President of the Union, asking to set up a joint committee to explore the proposal. Despite the presence of three junior members among the signatories, no one on standing committee supported the establishment of such a committee, and 'all members of the Committee expressed considerable disapproval' that Clarke had approached the Union's trustees and the Vice-Chancellor of the University about a merger without having consulted the Union.

Former Cambridge student Patrick Cosgrave, writing in the *Spectator* that month about a recent visit back to Cambridge, reported that the Union was facing 'a take-over by the unspeakable Cambridge Student Union'. They were, he said:

a democratic gathering of malcontents of various kinds who want a merger with the Union which will give them control over the Union building while the debating society itself is reduced to being a chat show having first call on the chamber twice a week … If the CSU had their way Union dinners would become crusts, debates exercises in radical paranoia, and social life yet another extension of the activities of Lefty brainwashers.[18]

'Fortunately,' he reassured his readers, 'a stout defensive action is being fought by the Union President, the delightful Miss Arianna Stassinopoulos.' If Charles Clarke was a formidable champion for the CSU, he faced in Arianna an equally formidable – and unpredictable – opponent. The rich and glamorous daughter of an Athenian newspaper magnate (whose continued operation under the military junta led to some criticism during her term, as she recalls in her contribution to this volume), she has been dubbed 'the most upwardly mobile Greek since Icarus'.[19] A profile of her in the national press when she became only the third female President of the Union in 1971 gushed: 'She is glamorous with lots of charm; her clothes are stunning ... Her make-up is always impeccable and the long hair and her looks make people think: "Yes, she reminds me of Jackie Kennedy".'[20] Matthew Parris, her Cambridge contemporary, recalls tycoons in London sending helicopters to collect her for lunch: witty undergraduates called her 'The Face That Lunched a Thousand Shits'.[21] Stassinopoulos herself says she was 'a blissfully ignorant outsider' – and claims this naïveté was an asset:

> Since I had grown up in Greece, I had never heard of the Cambridge Union or the Oxford Union and didn't know about their place in English culture, so I wasn't weighed down with the kinds of overwhelming notions that may have stopped British girls from even thinking about trying for such a position.[22]

Be that as it may, she showed an admirable flair for Cambridge politics. Early during her time there she held a party at the Dorchester and invited lots of people from Cambridge who were 'very flattered' to have been asked.[23] Her term as President was a suitably glittering affair: she almost missed one of her own debates when, having been up in Newcastle for the launch of a Greek ship, a traffic jam caused her to miss her train back. So she caught a plane instead. A waiting friend drove her straight from Heathrow to Cambridge, where she made 'a lightning change in the ladies, and she took her presidential seat only five minutes late to a round of applause'.[24]

After Cambridge, she moved in select London circles and was much in demand in the media. She was seen stepping out with her fellow ex-President, John Gummer, then an up-and-coming MP;

another former President of the Union, Leon Brittan, acted for her when she successfully sued *Private Eye* for suggesting she had cheated in a Cambridge exam. She wrote columns for *Punch* and *The Times*, and was a frequent guest on *Any Questions* and game shows like *Face the Music* – where, as a fellow panellist, she met Bernard Levin. She was 21, he 42; but he became 'the big love of my life'.[25] They lived together until 1980, when her desire to start a family drove them apart – and her to America. In 1986 she married Michael Huffington, a Texan oil millionaire. A Republican, he was elected to the US House of Representatives in California, and spent heavily from his fortune in an unsuccessful bid for the United States Senate after one term. The couple divorced in 1997 and he came out as bisexual the following year. When, in 2003, Arianna stood as an independent candidate in the recall election to replace the Governor of California, Huffington backed her rival, Arnold Schwarzenegger. Although she later pulled out of the race, her name still appeared on the ballot and she finished fifth. Once a Republican, she is now an influential liberal commentator in US politics, both in the mainstream media and via her website, The Huffington Post.

Charles Clarke believed Arianna to be in favour of the Open Union scheme. Looking back now, he thinks 'she didn't really care. Once she'd been President of the Union as it was, then that was her thing'.[26] At the time, however, her equivocation provoked greater anger. On 13 November, *Varsity* revealed that she had written to Clarke to say the terms outlined in the open letter were 'quite unacceptable'. She had the full backing of her Canadian Vice-President, David Powell, who Clarke says 'was completely obsessed by Arianna and would do whatever she wanted'.[27] 'With Arianna and her Vice-President David Powell having come off the fence, and taken the whole of standing committee with them,' wrote *Varsity*, 'the present situation begins to resemble open war.'

Instead of forming a joint committee with the CSU, it was agreed that the Union should consult its members with a questionnaire to find out their opinion on an 'Open Union'. Six thousand questionnaires were duly sent to members in Cambridge – but Stassinopoulos was careful to present the issue in a certain light. The circular sent out with the questionnaire mentioned both the site value of the Union building, on which the CSU were keen to get their hands, and the healthy bank balance of the Union Society. Clarke was furious: 'She has displayed total hypocrisy in her approach to the question of the Union Society going open,' he stormed. 'Her previous assurances of support for this idea are now shown to be what they were – empty vote-catching promises.'

Having failed to put pressure on standing committee via the press, the 'Open Unionists' took their fight to the Union's open business meetings. At an MBM on 22 November, Andrew Oppenheimer of Trinity proposed a motion to establish an 'Open Union Committee'. Stassinopoulos was away, so David Powell took the chair. In a small House, Oppenheimer argued that he should be allowed to introduce his motion in a slightly different form to the one in which it had originally been submitted. He was supported by Colin Rosentiel, a regular contributor to MBMs at this time; Powell allowed the new motion to be put, and a vote to set up the new committee was carried 30–11. Stassinopoulos, however, later declared that the vote had been unconstitutional, and it was agreed at the next standing committee meeting 'that it was extremely regrettable that Messrs. Rosentiel and Oppenheimer should have succeeded in misleading the Vice-President'. The matter did not stop there: a requisition was brought, and Stassinopoulos appointed a new MBM on 29 November. Oppenheimer reintroduced his amended motion to establish an Open Union committee, but it was ruled out of order. A second motion, however, proposed by Charles Clarke and demanding that the committee comprise four Union members nominated by the CSU executive, was carried 95–30. Without Oppenheimer's motion being approved, it was meaningless – but the vote put considerable pressure on the Union to consider the Open Union question.

A new controversy helped its opponents to dodge the question for a bit longer. Chris Smith, the future Labour MP and Cabinet minister, had been elected Secretary on 24 November in a four-way contest, but was accused of having canvassed. He responded by requisitioning all the other candidates in the election, and a select committee was convened. This came to the opinion that 'a great deal of canvassing' had indeed taken place; it found the case against Smith not proven, but declared the election for standing committee void, and recommended it be rerun next term. Four days later, the committee issued a second report: despite clearing Smith personally, it found 'clear evidence of members canvassing to affect the results of the Secretarial election' and 'reluctantly' declared that election void too. The select committee commended the successful presidential candidate, David Powell, who 'behaved with common sense and discretion'. It hoped that, despite this inauspicious beginning, his term of office would 'see the calm consideration of the serious issues which face the Society'.

Alas, calm was not to be restored so soon. The elections for Secretary and standing committee were held again on 15 January 1972 and produced the same results with only one change for standing committee – but the controversy spilled over into the new year. Eight undergraduates were requisitioned by Powell following reports of a party held at Downing before the poll at which a list of candidates' names was allegedly read out. Another select committee was convened. By a majority of four to two, it found Chris Smith and Christopher Kenyon guilty of canvassing. The committee's report agreed their behaviour was 'devious', but it could not take further action without unanimous agreement. Smith – who had deliberately left Cambridge on polling day and found the accusations 'ludicrous' – was therefore elected Secretary. 'None of this can do the Union Society or progress towards an Open Union any good,' he said. 'I hope for the Union's sake the charges will be rebutted and then perhaps the Union can begin to mature a bit after its plethora of self-indulgent political intrigue of the last couple of months.'[28] *Stop Press*, meanwhile, implied that candidates favouring an Open Union were 'being victimised to ensure the survival of the present Union Society establishment'.[29] The insinuation was not helped by the select committee's decision to disqualify Kenyon. During interrogation it emerged that he had not read the laws of the Society – a requirement for all candidates – and on this technicality it was declared that he had not been an eligible candidate in the first place. This decision was taken to a committee of the whole House, and Kenyon was reinstated by 80 votes to 31. It was now three months after the Michaelmas elections had first been held. There was to be one last casualty: Ged Martin, the ex-President, resigned as Steward after the overruling of the select committee, on which he had served. He wrote to Powell expressing his 'alarm at this fresh evidence of complete disregard for the laws of the Society'.[30] His position lay empty in the Easter term, but was filled in Michaelmas by another historian: Simon Schama, then a Fellow of Christ's.

The Open Union debate came back to the fore with the publication of the questionnaire results on 15 January. They showed a two-to-one rejection of the CSU's merger proposals: 1,247 members against the terms proposed by CSU, and only 559 in favour. *Stop Press* denounced the results, claiming that many copies had been removed from members' pigeon-holes, and that one well-known opponent of the Open Union at Pembroke was 'seen flushing completed questionnaires down a lavatory'.[31] But the numbers were clear: the vast majority of respondents (1,424 to 399) were in favour of an Open Union 'in principle', but 1,046 to 649 preferred to see a students' union 'on a separate site, totally independent of the Union Society'. Announcing the results, David Powell said it was 'clear that the Society will in no circumstances accept the CSU proposals of last term'.[32]

Powell was, however, willing to establish a group to consider the future of the Society – in part, perhaps, to head off calls for an Open Union committee, but also in recognition that this offered a chance to secure the Union's long-term finances. At the first meeting of his standing committee on 2 December, he established the 'President's Committee on the Future of the Union'. This included supporters of an Open Union like Clarke and Oppenheimer, as well as more sceptical people from the standing committee. The committee met eight times and published a report in February. It noted that there was no financial necessity for the Union to change: its present financial position was 'healthier than it has ever been'. Nor had attempts 'to go open organically' come to anything – not least because 'the traditions and functions of the Union Society are entirely incompatible with those of a student representative body'. Nonetheless, the report envisaged a solution in which the Union would continue to exist as a private club and debating society, while providing space for a new 'students' centre' run by the CSU and financed by the colleges. It proposed the Union 'should limit itself to a defined unit within the present building' – namely the chamber, the offices and what are now the dining room and Mountbatten Room – and lease the rest of the building to the University for 99 years, with a set of doors at the foot of the stairs acting as the partition. The Union would keep its squash courts but lose the library, and the likely cost of a new life subscription to the Society would be £5.

Apart from a minor disagreement about whether the scheme could commence that year, the only voice of dissent was that of the Vice-President, Nicholas Davidson, who issued a minority report. Now a Queen's Counsel and a deputy High Court judge, Davidson was 'an extremely archaic Tory' in Clarke's view.[33] He believed the committee was working from a false premise in accepting that the Union would have to contract. The whole thing, he felt, was too hasty and ill-founded. In short, it was 'a poor report'.

The report was debated at two MBMs on 7 and 17 February. At the second, a motion to accept it and urge its implementation was proposed by Powell and seconded by Clarke. It was 'passed by an overwhelming majority'. Another motion, to implement the scheme as soon as possible, was also passed despite Powell's opposition. It was decided that both should be put to a poll of all members. Yet by the standing committee meeting the following week, Powell had decided the polls could not be held that month – because of a standing committee resolution that polls should not take place within seven days of Union elections. Powell's committee expressed 'its utmost regret' at his decision, but was powerless to overrule it. Chris Smith told *Varsity* that he was 'not aware' of the resolution which Powell claimed was the justification for his delay, and said he thought it was 'simply prevarication'.[34]

In the event, the elections gave people an opportunity to voice their opinions on the report. Nicholas Davidson stood for the presidency, maintaining his opposition to the report; he was opposed by Kevin Carey of Downing, a prominent supporter of the Open Union. Although he had been elected to standing committee at the end of his first term in Cambridge, Carey had never held Union office, but his editorship of *Varsity* that term made him a well-known figure. Davidson led comfortably on the first ballot, 192 to 155 – but the transferral of votes from a third candidate, the Labour Club's Julian Fulbrook, took Carey ahead with 212 to 206. It was a surprise victory for the Downing man, who told his old paper he 'honestly didn't expect' to win: 'precedent was all against me'.[35] But there was an even wider victory for the proposals' supporters further down the ballot: Chris Smith beat the future Energy Minister Tim Eggar to the vice-presidency by more than 100 votes (266–158). It was a clear victory for the left and for the supporters of an Open Union. Even the national press reported that Carey had been 'voted into office on an open union ticket against strong opposition'.[36] Eggar was particularly upset by Davidson's defeat, expressing his sorrow that members had 'treated a person who has served the Society so well so badly'. But Clarke was delighted: 'This unprecedented election demonstrates the strong feeling within the Union Society in favour of an Open Union,' he proclaimed. 'I'm extremely confident this can be achieved for October 1972.'[37]

Another development that term bolstered Clarke's confidence. Active though the CSU was, its members' hopes for an Open Union would amount to little without the official backing of the University. As far back as December 1969, the Council of the Senate – the 'principal executive and policy-making body of the University' – had agreed to set up two committees to investigate the finances of the Union, and to look into the possibility of a central students' union for all undergraduates.[38] Chaired by the Revd Jack Plumley, a professor of Egyptology, this met just three times in 1970 and made no further progress until, at the start of 1972, it was prompted by Clarke to produce its report. This so-called Plumley Report appeared on 24 February and agreed that 'on the evidence, there was a need for a Student Centre in which all students could meet together'. It recommended that the Council of the Senate consider the proposals which had just been unveiled by Powell's 'Future of the Union Committee' – and, particularly, that the willingness of the individual colleges to support the scheme be investigated. The Council of the Senate agreed. 'The University authorities have thus demonstrated their basic approval of the plan,' *Varsity* reported in an article alongside the news of Carey's election.

Kevin Carey was therefore President at a critical juncture in the Union's history. Partially blind, he read his notes in the chamber using Braille. A 'very brilliant man', he won a Knox scholarship to Harvard, where he ran the student radio station.[39] He later became a radio journalist with the BBC and worked around the world with Sight Savers International. He stood for Parliament as an SDP/Liberal Alliance candidate in Brighton in 1987, and has been vice-chairman of the Royal National Institute of Blind People since 2000. True to his electoral mandate, he made strides for greater openness at his first standing committee meeting. It was agreed to pin a summary of the committee's minutes on the Society's notice boards, and to record the way each member voted in the minute book. Such was the reformist zeal of the new committee that all but two of its members voted to share leftover beer and cheese with members after pre-debate dinners.

Most importantly, Carey drove forward the arrangements for a poll on the future of the Union. The date was set for 22 April. A factual report about the proposals was to be released to *The Times*, the *Daily Telegraph*, the *Guardian* and *Varsity*, and, if necessary, classified adverts would be taken out informing life members of the poll. A one-page summary of the report was sent out with the termcard that term, and David Powell wrote a letter to *The Times* to explain its proposals to Union members everywhere. 'I believe the report to be an important positive contribution to the society's future,' he wrote. The scheme would ensure the Society a firm income, as well as relieve it of financial responsibility for part of the building, 'thereby allowing us to concentrate on our main aim – debating.' He urged members 'not to become alarmed. Nothing will be done without the maximum publicity. The poll on April 22 is one in principle; a further poll will have to be held before any possible implementation.'[40] Powell's letter 'surprised many who had thought his enthusiasm for the scheme half-hearted'.[41] But alongside it appeared another letter from a life member – and former Steward – of the Society, the Revd James Owen, who was at this time a chaplain at the University of Nottingham. He questioned the practicability of a central students' union in a collegiate university. 'There is some danger in Cambridge that a students' union would be unrepresentative and would be a playground for a few who "liked that sort of thing",' he cautioned:

> It is certainly true that the Union Society in Cambridge was (and perhaps is) just such a playground (and I enjoyed it very much myself) but at least it did not, and does not, claim to speak with the authoritative (and even authoritarian) voice of 'all students' for it is a free assembly, tied to no coat-tail whether it be 'staff' or 'student' or any political group or party … Those who deplore the collegiate system as a device to divide and rule should honestly examine their own motives (and the real origin of collegiate life).[42]

Meanwhile, on the pages of the *Daily Telegraph*, the Hon. Christopher Monckton – 'a constant "anti" voice' in the Open Union debate – wrote a rather more stringent letter calling on life members to 'come and help us to prevent the dissolution of the Union Society'.[43] Now the 3rd Viscount Monckton of Brenchley, he was educated at Harrow and Churchill, where he took a third in classics. He was an indefatigable conservative voice at the Union, and recalls being 'the only non-socialist on its committee in that post-1968 period'.[44] Later a journalist (including as a leader writer on the London *Evening Standard*) and an adviser to Thatcher in the Downing Street policy unit, he is also the inventor of the 209-piece 'Eternity' jigsaw puzzle. A prize of £1 million was offered for its near-impossible solution; it took eighteen months before two Cambridge mathematicians could provide an answer.

Suitable attention having been drawn to it, the poll was duly held on 22 April 1972. The 'yes' campaign won huge support from *Varsity*. Its edition which came out that day carried an editorial headlined 'Open Union – we want it now' and a fawning interview with the President entitled: 'Carey hits at scaremongers'. For good measure, there was also a front-page story suggesting that Conservative Central Office was trying to influence the vote. A report written by Nicholas Davidson had been circulated to old CUCA members with a letter from Miss Elizabeth Salisbury, the Conservative Eastern Area Agent, stating that 'rather a serious situation' had arisen at the Union and urging members to visit Cambridge to vote. Charles Clarke condemned this interference: 'It's absolutely wrong for the Tory Central Office to get involved in this matter,' he said indignantly. But Davidson claimed he had written the report on his own initiative 'and merely used the facilities made available by the Conservative Party. I felt it was important old Union members should know about this.'

In the event the turnout for the poll on 22 April was high, but not extraordinary – and smaller than for those on the admission of women. Trestle tables were erected on the lawn at the front of the Union, and people 'were queuing up for most of the day to vote', recalls Barry Thoday, then the assistant chief clerk.[45] Both motions from February were on the ballot paper. The first was to accept the report and urge its implementation:

| For | 730 |
| Against | 703 |

The second was the additional motion urging it be implemented 'as soon as possible':

| For | 743 |
| Against | 687 |

Both, then, were clear but not overwhelming victories for the Open Union camp: had they been seeking to do more than explore the question in principle, they would have fallen short of the necessary threshold. The large opposition votes were blamed on the successful effort to whip up older members. Carey said he believed a quarter of those who voted were senior members of the University or non-resident members; one member of the CSU executive claimed between 300 and 500 non-resident members had come up.[46] Nonetheless, standing committee felt it now had a mandate to discuss the proposals in greater detail. Clarke, too, breathed a sigh of relief: 'We now have the full support of the student body,' he said. 'I think we have won.'[47] He predicted the students' union would move into its part of the building by the following year.

Before anything could be done, however, the colleges had to confirm that they were prepared to support the scheme financially. This looked likely at first: fifteen JCRs had already expressed support for the Plumley Report by the time of the poll on 22 April. Some had decided by referenda, others by open meeting; but the majorities were large in every case, the narrowest being a 48–38 endorsement at Jesus. By the end of April, only Selwyn and St John's had yet to commit themselves. But it soon became clear that the college authorities were not as enthusiastic as their undergraduate members. A number of college councils or governing bodies overruled the student votes. Girton JCR was told to hold a new referendum because the original question had implied that it could get the money with relative ease. St Catharine's and Queens' simply said the money could not be found, while Magdalene's amalgamated clubs society rejected the scheme, even though the rest of college had been supportive.

Because of this uncertainty, it was now too late for any scheme to be implemented – let alone any conversions made to the building – in time for the new academic year. It was therefore decided to postpone the proposals to 1973. This carried a risk for the Union: the recruitment of new members – its principal source of income – could suffer because of the uncertainty over the future of the Society. Why pay to join a society which could be dramatically scaled back or thrown open completely within a matter of months? The Union argued that the University should guarantee any shortfall in recruitment income as a result of the delay, but it was not willing to do so. The University did, however, accede to another suggestion. At the standing committee's urging, a committee was set up by the Council of the Senate to look into the practicalities of establishing a student centre so that this could be done in time for Michaelmas 1973. This committee consisted of two students – Carey and Clarke – and two senior members of the University – Roger Andrew, the Union's Senior Treasurer, and Trevor Gardner, the University Treasurer (and later a trustee of the Union). It met over the summer of 1972 and went through several drafts, hoping to present its final report in Michaelmas 1972. Before doing so, it agreed it ought to seek legal advice, so consulted a barrister at Lincoln's Inn. His opinion, when it finally arrived, 'was a complete blockbuster'.[48] A deed of gift was discovered from the time when the land on which the Union stood had originally been bought. The counsel advised the trustees that the building was entrusted to them subject to a law of that time – the Literary and Scientific Institutions Act of 1854 – and that, if it ceased to be used for the purposes of the Society, it would revert to the estate of the man who had signed the deed: one Henry Peto, Vice-President in Michaelmas 1864.

A possible way to overcome this ancient obstacle was for the Union to lease part of the building without carrying out any physical subdivision – so the committee went back to the drawing board to amend its proposals. It finally reported back to the Council of the Senate in January 1973. It suggested that the Union lease approximately two thirds of its space – roughly the same as had been proposed by Powell's Future of the Union committee – to the University on a 99-year lease, to be used as a student centre. This would be administered by a management committee chaired by the Vice-Chancellor of the University, with representatives appointed by the Union and the CSU.

The report included draft budgets for both the student centre and the reconstituted Union Society, whose level of recruitment it anticipated would halve. These required a total annual contribution of over £18,000, which would be funded by a levy on each college of

£2.20 per undergraduate. These could be phased in, with the University covering the shortfall in the first years, but it was clear that these payments were crucial. The draft budgets left an excess of income over expenditure of just £210. Without these payments, the proposals 'could not be implemented'.[49]

The report was well received by the Union hierarchy. Open Union supporters had 'swept the board' in the elections for Lent 1973. Andrew Oppenheimer beat the Vice-President Chris Kenyon, who now opposed the scheme, to the top job, and other Open Union candidates took all but one of the places on standing committee.[50] Together, they quickly agreed the text of a press release welcoming the report 'in the best interests of the Society'. They also prepared a four-page statement setting out their full views on the report – not least to quash what they called the 'spurious claims' and 'imagined figures' being circulated by an unofficial group of members organised by Monckton. Eight thousand copies of the statement were distributed around the University. It argued that the student centre scheme was an opportunity to solve two pressing problems: first, to give the Union the financial security which was 'essential if we are even to stay where we are, let alone expand our facilities'; second, to satisfy the widespread demand beyond the Union for a central student venue. Its authors felt a dual responsibility, they said in conclusion:

> As the Standing Committee of the Union Society it is our duty to safeguard the long-term interests of our members. As Cambridge students, we feel that a Student Centre is a real and long felt need. It is our belief that the present scheme satisfies both these requirements.

With the support of the Union leadership, the mandate of a ballot among all life members, and the backing of an official University committee, the student centre scheme was therefore sent to the college JCRs for confirmation that they would support it financially. This was really the final hurdle.

The Council of the Senate recommended that all colleges use the same wording for their vote or referendum. In particular, it felt it ought to be made clear that the colleges would be committing themselves to providing the money even if they could not squeeze any more out of local authorities – something the Council believed 'would be extremely difficult to obtain'. This may or may not have made the crucial difference. But by the beginning of March, the front page of *Stop Press* warned that an Open Union was 'in the balance'. Nine colleges had voted on the scheme, but four had rejected it – including two of the largest, Trinity and St John's. At John's, a 'major row' had erupted: the proposal had actually been passed in a referendum, but the JCR had voted 4–3 not to provide the money. One JCR member told *Varsity*: 'We have many more facilities here than the new centre would have.' By the following week, nineteen colleges had voted and the tally of rejections had risen to five. Magdalene, Trinity Hall and Queens' had 'voted decisively against the scheme'; in addition, students at St Catharine's had voted in favour, but not by the majority required.[51]

It was too late to try again. Even Clarke and Carey had made clear in their report that it was important for the sake of the Union, its staff and its recruitment figures that the question 'be settled one way or the other as soon as possible. The matter has now been under consideration for some three years ... and the Committee consider that the time has now come when a decision should be reached by the various parties.'[52] The Vice-President's report the following term dolefully pointed out that the student centre proposal had faltered 'because of the unwillingness of a number of colleges to finance any such scheme in the Union, and not because of the unwillingness of Union members'. To Chris Smith, it was 'one of the great "what-nearly-happened" moments of student history'.[53]

Thereafter, the Union's relationship with the CSU settled into the cycle of cooperation, disinterest and hostility which still broadly operates today. From time to time, the Union allowed the CSU to hold its open meetings in the chamber. There was 'a certain amount of disruption' at the first open meeting of Easter 1973: 'a lot of damage was caused', for which the CSU was billed. Someone turned out the lights at another CSU meeting in May. In January 1974, the disruption was rather more serious: *Stop Press with Varsity* carried news of a tear gas attack. 'There was panic in the Chamber as those near the door all tried to leave at once,' the paper reported. 'Mark Broad of the CSU executive saw the man responsible leaving; he kicked the smoking canister into the entrance hall and tried unsuccessfully to catch him.'[54] By the following week's report, however, the 'canister' had been downgraded to a chemical substance left on a saucer; the police were called in, but no one seems to have been held responsible.

There were attempts to revive the Open Union schemes, often with considerable support. When in Easter 1975 the new President, the American David Condit, suggested a joint Union/CSU committee be established to reconsider the viability of the 1973 student centre scheme, the standing committee agreed unanimously. The joint committee was still going in Lent 1976, when another President, Christopher Greenwood (now Professor Sir Christopher Greenwood QC, a Fellow of Magdalene and barrister whose cases have included the Lockerbie disaster and the extradition of General Pinochet), proposed entering into negotiations with the Council of the Senate and the CSU. But the scheme was based on a system of subsidised membership, which once again found little support. By June 1977, almost all the colleges had refused to subsidise their junior members' subscriptions (Trinity and Trinity Hall were the exceptions). Two offers were forlornly recorded in the standing committee minutes that October: Corpus JCR would refund 10 per cent of their members' Union subscriptions, and Christ's would give £3 to members who made paper speeches. But hope had long since been abandoned. In Lent 1978, Daniel Janner 'chaired a meeting to consider re-opening the question of an Open Union scheme ... After considering past schemes it was decided that the idea is still dead because there is not the money available to finance [it].'

Looking back, Charles Clarke was 'very sorry' the Open Union scheme never came to fruition: 'it would have been a long-standing achievement ... It was a lovely solution, it was with the spirit of the times. Could the two have cohabited the building reasonably well? Well, I see no reason to think why not. I actually personally think the debating society would have been stronger as a result.'[55]

———

Another reason for the collapse of the scheme was the ephemeral nature of Cambridge generations: many of those who had provided the impetus for the Open Union scheme had come up at the turn of the decade, between the summer of '68 and what Carey sees as Cambridge's very own 'Bennite' revolution. By the 1973–4 academic year, however, 'the high-water mark of "people's republics" had receded', and most of these student firebrands had either graduated – like Clarke and Carey – or were just about to.[56]

During its height, however, there was no mistaking that this was a left-wing generation. All four candidates in the election which brought Chris Smith the secretaryship were of the left. Smith was unopposed for President two terms later and, after a Kennedy scholarship to Harvard and a PhD back at Pembroke, became a Labour MP – and the first openly gay Member of Parliament. He was Secretary of State for Culture, Media and Sport in Tony Blair's first term, and retired from the Commons in 2005 as Lord Smith of Finsbury. He was one of a number of Labour Presidents in the early '70s. David Grace (Easter 1973) began his Cambridge political career as a moderate Tory but had switched to Labour by the time of his presidency; after graduation he joined the Liberal party, and contested the 1987 general election for them.[57] Mark Goyder, his successor, was another Labour supporter; he now runs a think tank on ethical business.

Harold Carter (Lent 1974) spent two years at Nuffield College, Oxford, worked as a banker and management consultant, and lectured for the Open University. A former vice-chairman of the Young Fabians, he was an adviser to David Owen as leader of the SDP, and was the party's candidate for St Ives in 1983 and 1987. He now teaches history at St John's College, Oxford. Toby Harris

(Easter 1974), was also chairman of the Cambridge Organisation of Labour Students (as the Labour Club had become), and has made his career in Labour politics. He led Haringey Borough Council for twelve years and the Labour group on the London Assembly for four; he was also the first chairman of the Metropolitan Police Authority, and sits in the Lords as Lord Harris of Haringey. David Bean (Lent 1975) took a first in law and went to the Bar, where he was heavily involved in the Society of Labour Lawyers.[58] One of the founder members of Matrix Chambers with Cherie Booth, he established a reputation as a leading silk in employment and discrimination law, and was elected chairman of the Bar in 2002. He was appointed a High Court judge in 2004.

Toby Harris's 1974 retirement debate – although a light-hearted one – perhaps takes on an extra significance in light of the discussions about the Union's future: 'This House believes that the Cambridge Union Society should declare UDI'. It was chaired by Lord Butler, who was made an honorary member to mark the 50th anniversary of his own presidency. Harris proposed the independence motion, along with Sydney Elwood, the former chief clerk. They were opposed by the President-elect Stephen Weil (an Ulsterman and investment banker whose brother Peter had been Secretary two years earlier) and Elwood's successor, Roland Thompson. Lord Butler took the vote by acclamation and declared it a tie; after a moment's deliberation, he announced his casting vote in favour of the motion.

Recollection:
Arianna Huffington

(Miss A.-A. Stassinopoulos, Girton College)
President, Michaelmas Term 1971

Arianna Stassinopoulos was born in Athens and moved to England at the age of sixteen. She read economics at Girton, and was President of the Union in Michaelmas 1971. Much in demand as a panellist on programmes such as Any Questions *in the 1970s, she published* The Female Woman, *a riposte to* The Female Eunuch, *in 1973. She moved to the USA in 1980, and in 1986 married the Texan oil millionaire and Republican politician Michael Huffington, with whom she had two daughters. The couple divorced in 1997.*

In 2003, Arianna stood as an independent candidate in the recall election to replace Gray Davis as Governor of California. In 2005, she launched the internet newspaper The Huffington Post, *which has become the world's fifth most popular weblog, and helped to make her one of the most prominent political commentators in America. Her twelve books include biographies of Picasso and Maria Callas,* Pigs at the Trough, *and* How to Overthrow the Government.

In 2006 she was named one of the hundred most influential people by Time *magazine. Her contribution below is adapted from a piece she wrote for a 1977 anthology entitled* My Cambridge, *edited by Ronald Hayman and published by Robson Books.*

I've always been political, and can't ever remember a time when politics didn't excite me. But it was at the Cambridge Union that I was truly transformed. This was where my political instincts were forged into political convictions. Broadly speaking, the political debate is basically the same whether you are in Athens, in Cambridge, in Timbuktu, in Plato's Greece or in Harold Wilson's Britain. The issues of the day, whether it's the Industrial Relations Act or whether to subsidise the tomato growers of northern Macedonia, are all good testing grounds for principles and ideas.

I threw myself into the Union: my maiden speech was made at the first debate of the year on the traditional Michaelmas Term motion of no confidence in Her Majesty's government. My one great advantage was that I hadn't been weaned on the Union mythology – fighting for King and country, the breeding ground of the great, the toughest House to speak in, the nursery of statesmen. So although I was fascinated, I didn't know enough to be over-whelmed. My one reservation was my accent – a not inconsiderable fear in a speaking contest. Would I be clearly understood?

As I listened attentively to the sparring politicians in that first debate, my fears were put to flight. I became convinced for the first time – though not the last – of the immense value of total incomprehensibility in public life.

If I wasn't overwhelmed by the Union, neither was the Union by me. I can't say that the night of my maiden speech was one of those nights when leaders are discovered and reputations born. In fact, the chief clerk told me later that one of the secretaries, having listened to my speech, was overheard breathing a deep and very audible sigh of relief: 'Thank God! At least I won't have to be typing that funny name any more.' But I stuck with it – the apprenticeship had begun. Every Monday night became Union night. I would stay until the end. And I would wait to be called to speak from the floor, even when the only members left in the chamber were those whose inertia had momentarily got the better of their judgment and, of course, those who had simply fallen asleep.

There was a lot of contemptuous talk against 'speech-makers' and the eloquent Union careerists. And all with, as it happens, an equally eloquent and intellectually impeccable pedigree going back to

Socrates and Montaigne: 'Away with that Eloquence that so enchanted us with its Harmony, that we should more study it than things.' 'Foul. No rhetoric,' cried Rosencrantz. But me, I wallowed in it – in the rhetoric, in the eloquence, in the 'cultured insolence' and even in the verbal savagery – in the whole magic of people's minds being moved by words. These were, of course, rare moments, but I would sit through all the acres of slogans, far-fetched allusions, platitudes, idiotic puns and sub-Wildean witticisms, to live through the good stuff again.

One of these moments came in the second term of my first year. The motion set out for us was one of those omnibus Union motions that sometimes led to the best debates: 'This House believes that technological advance threatens the individuality of man and is becoming his master.' I had been given my first paper speech in a major debate – the Union careerist's dream. This meant that I would be proposing the motion, seconded by George Steiner, with C.P. Snow and Lord Mountbatten opposing and Prince Charles speaking from the crossbenches.

There was enough tension in the packed House to satisfy even the biggest drama queen. And then came one of those magical moments. It was during George Steiner's speech: he stood up after Lord Mountbatten had sat down, a small man with a withered arm but a face that could express every emotion from hatred to amusement and then invent some more. There was only the occasional gesture, and usually with very little emphasis. But there was inspiration and there was charisma, a touch of unconscious magnetism and plenty of conscious strength. Steiner got a standing ovation from a House that, unlike our younger sister at Oxford, is very sparing with them. He'd won the debate for our side.*

But when, in the committee room after the debate, he asked the Prince and the Earl to sign the order paper 'for his children,' I felt uneasy, almost let down. Steiner had, after all, for 35 minutes and only an hour before, transcended all earthly princes – a speaker

---

* Ayes 218; Noes 184.

transformed into a poet. It was the Prince and the Earl who should have asked the professor to sign the order paper – 'for their children.'

After that, my Union life took a rather unexpected turn. Two weekends before the end of my first term, I went down to London and, while I was away, my name was put down in the candidates' book for the upcoming election for standing committee and one of the officerships by Barbara Scott, a Girtonian in her second year. When I was told, I tried to withdraw my name but the ballot papers had been printed. It was not a case of modesty. It was a case of vanity – I simply did not fancy the idea of getting no votes! As it happened, I got enough votes to get elected to the standing committee.

And it was on 26 November 1969, as I sat contemplating the election results, that the idea of becoming President of the Union first took root in my mind. And it seemed to be coming to pass until suddenly, on 23 October 1970, something happened that convinced me that nothing would come of it.

The occasion was the debating equivalent of Ali vs. Fraser – J.K. Galbraith vs. William F. Buckley on 'The Market is a Snare and a Delusion'. It was to be televised by NBC, with two undergraduates opening the debate and two closing it. I was chosen to make the closing speech on Galbraith's side, against the free market, and was sitting next to him. He spoke – badly, very badly in fact – and sat down. Buckley, dripping smoothness, ease and self-assurance, proceeded to tear him into elegant little pieces.

The professor was becoming visibly agitated. He leaned and whispered in my ear, 'Stand up and interrupt him – tell him that the conditions he's describing only apply to the Stock Exchange, and that all other markets are far too imperfect to bear out his case.' Um, perhaps. Maybe. Still, this was a debate, not a seminar. And Bill Buckley was a debating pro. But the venerable professor, prophet and licensed Jeremiah of the 'affluent society' was nudging me on. So I stood up – as tradition dictates at the Union – and interjected. Buckley, giving a new meaning to *reculer pour mieux sauter*, replied: 'Well, Madam, I do not know what market *you* patronise.'

You may think that the Union has a strange sense of humour, but he brought the House down. And me as well. I can still feel my cheeks burning as I sat down, bidding, as I thought, a final farewell to the idea of being President.

Need I say that, after a comedown of that magnitude, my closing speech was not exactly a success? The final nail was put in the coffin by Christie Davies, a 'mature' ex-President who would occasionally pop back in on his way from London to Leeds, where he was teaching. Well, he had popped back that evening, and he popped up immediately after me and gave a virtuoso Union performance – light, paradoxical, effortless, brilliant. He clinched the devastation of our side and, I was sure, of my Union career.*

But even the Union forgets, and a month later I had recovered sufficiently to attempt a comeback, speaking – with more success – with Bishop Trevor Huddleston and former Defence Secretary Denis Healey against the sale of arms to South Africa. At the end of term I was elected Secretary against the then chairman of the Conservative Association, who had been the *Varsity* favourite. Bang went my trust in opinion polls – forever.

If Sitwell got his education 'in vacation from Eton,' I got mine 'in vacation from Economics,' and in preparation for my Union speeches. Even now I can relive the debates I spoke in – Religion and Education, Critics and the Arts, Trade Unions and the State, Censorship and Literature, Racialism and Communism. Every speech became a base camp for exploration. I would start on a reading jaunt around the subject, the more unfamiliar the better, trying to relate the burning issues of the debate to the fundamental ideas behind them, to the past, to what was perennial rather than merely topical. Most of the discoveries were, of course, totally useless for the debate. But not useless for me. As one of my favourite Greek poets put it, 'Ithaca set you on the beautiful journey. Without her you would never have taken the road.' Gradually the skeleton of what I believed began to emerge.

---

* Ayes 118; Noes 200.

The most important thing the Union gave me was not the presidency but the opportunity, the playing field, to 'connect, always connect' – political ideas, religious beliefs, social systems, personal lifestyles. The Union gave me the framework. The presidency – through the national publicity and the then-raging debate on women's liberation – gave me a book commission. The decision to give up my place at the Kennedy School of Government at Harvard, and with it any idea of graduate work in America, followed naturally, as did the decision to make my home in London.

From Secretary to Vice-President, to President – that was the chain, but it was too often broken to provide any guarantees. The evening that the results of the election for Vice-President were coming out, Shirley Williams was giving the Founders' Memorial Lecture at Girton. As secretary of the Junior Combination Room, I had been invited to the dinner the Mistress of Girton was giving after the lecture and was sitting next to Williams. She knew about the election, and if it had been a general election involving the Labour party (of which she was a leading member at that time), she could not have shown more concern. Finally someone came in and passed a piece of paper with the results to the Mistress. That evening solved for me the mystery of why Shirley Williams was one of the most popular politicians in Britain – across parties. Her ability to empathise with someone else's anxiety and someone else's happiness was astounding.

One of my inflationary pre-election promises had been that there would be two debates a week instead of one, and something happening at the Union every evening. There was. But only after a summer holiday spent at my Union office and the routine weekly walk-out by the Union's permanent staff.

I wonder whether other people's presidencies were as studded with gaffes as mine was, right down to the cook choosing pork as the main course when, yes, the Israeli Ambassador was speaking – which, coupled with the fact that members of the Arab delegation refused to sit at the table with the Israelis and instead sat in the billiard room eating Mars bars, gave a new twist to the art of imaginative pairings at dinner parties.

The big successes of the term were our record recruitment figures, and the big flop the 1971 Cambridge Teach-In on Higher Education. Sir Eric Ashby, the Vice-Chancellor of the University, was to open the weekend's proceedings after lunch on the Friday; the list of participants read as a *Who's Who* of the world of higher education. Cambridge was plastered with posters, leaflets and programme cards. Walking with the Vice-Chancellor from the dining room to the chamber, I had to explain why, in that case, he was about to trumpet the opening in the presence of three unhappy-looking undergraduates, two very superannuated education officials and a mass of empty benches.

Over the weekend, I had to explain the same thing to John Vaizey, and Lord Boyle, and Baroness Lee, and Professor Gareth Williams, and Sir Desmond Lee, and Lord Beaumont ... In between, I was running about desperately trying to find someone to explain it to me. *Varsity*'s headline gave the verdict: 'Flop-In at the Union'. All we had to do at the post mortem was provide the moral. 'Eels in the process of being skinned,' murmured the assistant clerk, 'are clearly not interested in a three-day Teach-In on Higher Skinning.' We decided that that would do.

Apart from me, there was only one other Greek undergraduate at Cambridge. Connoisseurs of Greek politics from Alcibiades to today will instantly know that we were therefore inexorably bound to each other by all the traditional bonds of rivalry and suspicion. His reaction when I was elected President was to spread brotherly rumours of my undying support for the Greek junta then ruling Greece.

By the day of the first debate of my term, the rumours had become a front-page story in *Varsity*, complete with all the standard dramatic flourishes – calls for my resignation, confession, retraction, execution. The standing committee met, issued a suitably melodramatic statement on the lines of 'fully behind our President,' and advised me to do nothing.

I did, in future, have many opportunities to regret disregarding their advice. But not on this occasion. I trusted my own gut and decided to face the critics. The chamber was absolutely crammed for the next debate, and so was the gallery when I walked in with the guest speakers. And there are few more exciting sights. There was all the hush and expectancy of a first night, and my sense of theatre – in this case the theatre of the absurd – rose to it: 'Good evening. Before we proceed to the motion before the House tonight, I propose to … I believe … Members have the right … I therefore call on the Vice-President to take my seat and myself to answer members' questions.'

I had arrived with four pre-Watergate tapes of my Union speeches in the last two years against the Greek regime, in favour of the expulsion of Greece from the Council of Europe, against the Garden House celebrations with members of the Greek junta. And by the end of the cross-examination, it was clear that only those for whom evidence is a fetish of the bourgeoisie remained unconvinced. It seems touchingly childish now, but it was one of my happiest moments in Cambridge.

RECOLLECTION:
PETER BAZALGETTE

(Mr P.L. Bazalgette, Fitzwilliam College)
President, Michaelmas Term 1975

Peter Bazalgette was educated at Dulwich College and read law at Fitzwilliam. After Cambridge he was a BBC news trainee, then became a television producer. His shows include Ready Steady Cook, Changing Rooms, Ground Force, *and the UK version of* Big Brother. *He was a non-executive director of Channel 4 (2001–4), chairman of Endemol UK (2002–8), and is a Fellow of BAFTA and the Royal Television Society. He also served as a trustee of the Union Society from 2002.*

One morning at breakfast in 2005, feeling a little ancient, I remarked to my wife that it was 30 years since I had been President of the Cambridge Union Society. 'Yes dear, and now it's time to move on,' she replied. At the risk of ignoring her advice, I'd like to reflect on an institution that's almost 200 years old.

One sunny afternoon in early June 1975 I was standing on a Cambridge lawn enjoying my fifth May Week party of the day. A rather insouciant man came up to me and murmured, 'I say, your place is on fire.' He was referring to the Union Society building, where I had been elected Michaelmas President a few days earlier. Workmen had overfed a basement fire and the flue had ignited, causing considerable damage to Waterhouse's Grade II listed debating chamber and eventually taking much of the roof with it.

Unbeknownst to me the fire brigade had been fighting the fire all morning – how slowly news travelled before mobile phones. By the evening a team of undergraduate volunteers, led by Adair Turner (now Lord Turner of pensions fame), were busy rescuing as many seats and carpets as possible from the residual smoke and dripping water. What was at the forefront of my mind? That in exactly four months' time I had BBC2 televising my No Confidence debate with guests including the Chancellor of the Exchequer (Denis Healey), his shadow (Geoffrey Howe) and Harold Macmillan in attendance to receive honorary membership. Could we do it in the open air? The chamber itself was a shambles.

There followed a crash course for a 22-year-old in loss-adjusters, English Heritage, architects and project management. The worst discovery was a few days later – our insurers, Norwich Union, were to 'apply average'. Yes, I had no idea what it meant either. It was a period of high inflation but before insurance premiums were index-linked. Thus organisations became under-insured without knowing it. Norwich Union pronounced that they would only pay 60 per cent of the renovation cost, leaving us with a bill of several hundreds of thousands – money we neither had nor knew where to find. I immediately launched an appeal but I guessed (correctly) that this would not solve our problem. In addition a young Conservative MP and former President, Norman Lamont, assisted me by chairing an *ad hoc* meeting of ex-Presidents in Westminster to discuss the crisis. One attendee, Christopher Norman-Butler, was a banker and assured us he would put pressure on Norwich Union, via its chairman Lord Mancroft, to pay for the full refurbishment. Quite how he did it I do not know, but he pulled it off and the insurers agreed to pay up. But could we get it ready in four months? In truth, I doubted it.

I spent that summer commuting between my family home on the Kent coast and the Union each week to push the project forwards. I got to know Saffron Walden rather well, before the days of the M11. Whenever I hear 10CC's 'I'm Not In Love', the great hit of the summer of 1975, all I can think of is builders' dust. With help of the architect, James Crabtree, we bought some old Methodist pews to restore the seating in the gallery – all part of a grand restoration of the magnificent chamber. It opened, on time, to welcome Henry Cooper to the opening debate, 'This House regrets the passing of the amateur'. I invited all the craftsmen who had restored the wood carvings and paintwork to the event and I remember them clearly, all scrubbed up, hanging on 'Enery's every word from the gallery. Then, three days later, the Westminster circus descended on us. But the politics had started somewhat earlier.

I inherited Harold Macmillan's honorary membership from a previous President following an earlier clash of dates. The former Prime Minister was also the serving Chancellor of Oxford University (not to mention his tenure as Treasurer of the Oxford Union in 1914). As I planned the visit, I could not decide whether also to invite perhaps the most distinguished living former President – Rab Butler, now Master of Trinity, across the road. I knew of the animosity between the two of them stretching back to Supermac's backing of Alec Douglas-Home for Prime Minister in 1963. In the end I decided to keep quiet. Then I discovered that Lord Adrian, Cambridge's Chancellor (whom I *had* invited) was insisting Macmillan stay with him in his college. His college was Trinity. I hurriedly invited Rab to the Union event and three days later he accepted. Mollie, his wife, later told me that Rab had writhed and agonised for those three days whether to come or not.*

On the day, I went down to Cambridge railway station to meet Macmillan. I had not alerted anyone else, but as I waited for the train I suddenly found the station master at my left elbow, in his best bowler hat, joining the reception party. At Trinity Lord Adrian

---

* Mollie writhed and agonised herself. Macmillan's visit 'was unwelcome to me', she recalls, and, true to a vow she had made years before, she 'refused to have him in the [Master's] Lodge'. But she was unable to avoid her husband's old rival altogether. He was told that Lady Butler was in bed with a cold but, when the taxi due to take the men to the Union failed to turn up, Rab pressed her to drive them in their own car – 'which with a very ill grace I was forced to do' (M. Butler, *August and Rab: A Memoir*, London: Weidenfeld & Nicolson, 1987, p. 114).

greeted us but, as yet, no sign of Rab. The pre-debate dinner took place at Magdalene College, where I arranged a photograph of all the participants, who also included Michael Heseltine and Peter Shore. Just as I had everyone in their correct place I was about to sit down in the middle of the front row, where Presidents belong. But Macmillan suddenly bellowed out that he wanted Adrian ('my fellow Chancellor') next to him and a game of geriatric musical chairs ensued. Just to get the photo done I gave in and beat it to the back row where I am caught forever, looking slightly disgruntled.

On the way down a long Magdalene corridor to the dinner Macmillan and Butler walked arm in arm (as I followed with my ears cocked): 'We're in the corridors of power now, Rab,' observed Macmillan. Rab unsurprisingly grunted in response – a pretty rich remark considering that is exactly what Macmillan deprived Rab of. This sort of low-level sniping went on all evening but I haven't space for the repartee here ... well, perhaps just one more. I had laid on a car to take the older gents down the hill to the Union. Rab decided to walk on Michael Heseltine's arm. When Macmillan found himself the sole occupant of the taxi he asked, 'Where's the Master of Trinity?' I told him that he was walking. 'Walk? He can't walk, he's too fat,' was the extraordinary reply.

The evening was duly televised as a special programme on BBC2. The producer was very anxious that I should secure him a joint interview with Macmillan and Rab. I told him that he was welcome to it but would have to arrange it himself. It never took place. My general memory of the evening is of Supermac ribbing Rab throughout while the latter maintained as dignified an expression as he could.

During the long summer of building works I had felt the need for some sort of distraction. The opportunity arose when our colleagues over at the Oxford Union had their annual fracas over whether candidate A had canvassed, candidate B had held an illicit party and so on. The usual committee of dons had sat, debarred the winner and put her runner-up in office. This was David Soskin (now a successful dotcom entrepreneur). I was aware that Soskin had no programme for his term, having been catapulted into the presidential chair at the last minute. This was my opening. I invented a character called Colonel Roland Wetherby-Johnston and then invited him to give a lecture to the Cambridge Union on his specialist subject: 'Idi Amin, Apostle or Oppressor?' The colonel (from my brother's house in south London) honoured us with an acceptance. I then printed the event in my Michaelmas programme card. Having established Wetherby-Johnston's credentials I warmly recommended him to Soskin, a man badly in need of a few events of his own. He bit. Once again my brother graciously accepted the invitation. The colonel was now down to speak at both Oxford and Cambridge. I thought little more about it. When the colonel was due in Cambridge he cancelled – a nasty recurrence of dengue fever. Soskin got a bit suspicious and told me he wanted to talk to him. My father duly obliged from his office in the City and, in fact, gave Soskin a bit of a roasting for bothering him.

Now I had to decide. Reveal all or cast the colonel and go through with the actual lecture. Encouraged by Nigel Dempster, the legendary *Daily Mail* diarist, I decided to go ahead. I recruited a Cambridge schoolmaster with a fondness for amateur dramatics. I kitted him out with a borrowed Green Jackets regimental tie. A game New Hall undergraduate agreed to be his overdressed wife. Next I needed transport. Andrew Mitchell, now Tory frontbench spokesman for overseas development (and a President of the Union after me) was in his first year at Jesus and, crucially, had a car. He drove us over on the appointed evening. There were some 200 eager students in the Oxford Union library. The colonel, once introduced by Soskin, got up and started to huff and puff about nothing in particular. After a while there was fidgeting. Unfortunately it turned out that there were a number of genuine Ugandan refugees from Amin's brutal regime in the room. They were not amused. They started to heckle and remonstrate. I thought we were all on the verge of being assaulted (and deservedly so, in retrospect).

And then a stroke of good fortune that, even now, I cannot explain. The Oxford Union fire alarms suddenly went off. This was not our doing but proved very welcome. We were all ordered to evacuate. In the confusion all four of us made it to Mitchell's car and escaped under cover of darkness. Dempster did not let me down – he wrote it up under the heading, 'Who Was Dat Man At De Union?' It all sounds a bit politically incorrect today. But the ghastly Amin was treated as a joke at the time by *Punch* and most of the national newspapers.

The debates of my term came and went. More than 30 years later I scarcely remember them, except one: the night I hosted the Scottish aristocrat, Sir Iain Moncreiffe of that Ilk. I had been tipped off by my Vice-President, David Johnson, that the Ilk was a good booking, a man who had performed memorably at the Durham Union. I sent him an invitation to speak. Over the summer this turned into a lengthy correspondence. He communicated from his castle in Scotland, always on cheap postcards and always in red biro. I remember his first card to me ending: 'I am writing this card in my life's blood, which I am disturbed to see is red.' The Ilk had a fetish for genealogy – he was a clan chieftain and claimed the most exotic family tree stretching back to Dracula, amongst others.

When Sir Iain arrived to debate he was in a party of three, consisting of him, Lady Moncreiffe and their chauffeuse for the evening, the Duchess of Newcastle. His wife told me he had been on the wagon for a month and was on no account to be given any alcohol. Apparently when he arrived he took a compliant undergraduate on one side and persuaded him to replace the speaker's water with vodka. Hence throughout the undergraduate paper speeches he was conducting his own clandestine vodka tasting. When I called him to speak he did make it to the despatch box. There he swayed slightly while he searched his pockets for his speech. It was not forthcoming. Those close to him could hear him mumble 'I've lost el speech, thought it was in el pocket ...' Why he employed the Spanish definite article I do not know.

The Ilk then decided to embark on his speech without notes, but all in a slurred whisper so that no one could discern the drift of his argument or whether, indeed, he had an argument at all. At first the members of the Union laughed. Next they were perplexed. And finally they began to slow handclap. I passed a note to the under-graduate paper speaker on his side, Peter Fudakowski (later a President himself). I instructed Peter to wait until I rang my bell and then, with the assistance of the man next to him, to carry Sir Iain out. I rang my bell. They picked him up and, to much cheering, gently carried the supine Scotsman to the chief clerk's office.

Afterwards I instructed the Duchess of Newcastle to bring her car round to the front of the Round Church and promised I would get her passenger to the kerbside. So it was that I and the Secretary, Chris Greenwood, with a Moncreiffe arm each, set off down the steps. Halfway down the path the Ilk stopped us – he wished to relieve himself into the flower bed. Greenwood throughout maintained a respectful attitude, addressing the man we were propping up as 'Sir Iain' at all times. The Ilk turned to him as he continued to empty his capacious bladder. 'What I want to know is why you keep on calling me *Sir* Iain when I'm pissing all over your roses?' It didn't occur to me at the time, but we could have done with the Ilk five months earlier. He could have put the fire out single-handed.

Part of the value of being an officer of the Union is gaining early experience of the responsibility of running an organisation, with employees, that needs to break even. The recruitment of new members in my term was particularly successful, thus we were relatively flush with funds. This gave me the opportunity to sort out the deficit in the Society's contributions to the chief clerk's pension fund. In my day this was Mr Thompson ('Mr T'), a man whose neurosis was only matched by his dedication. He was ably assisted by his deputy, Barry Thoday, though they managed our affairs while seldom speaking to each other. I also managed to set up a small pension for Mr Gates who cleared up at lunch. His chief claim to fame was that he had waited, as a footman in the 1930s, on Edward VIII and Wallis Simpson at furtive dinner parties in Belgravia. Forty years later, as he wiped the Newcastle Brown from the Formica table tops in the Union bar, he maintained an impeccable demeanour at all times.

I have since served as a trustee of the Union and I'm heartened that little has changed over the years. The building retains its decaying charm. The debates can be awful but can still also be brilliant. And although it has always been fashionable to decry the Union Society the debating remains a powerful and valuable education. I know it's true that some successful politicians never got involved (for instance Michael Portillo, Francis Maude and Geoff Hoon in my era), but many others did and cut their political teeth there. To be able to marshal your argument and sway an audience are skills that are useful beyond the narrow confines of politics. I myself have had a career in the media where what the Union gave me has been just as useful as it would have been had I tried to enter politics.

When I stepped down as a trustee I was asked whether I would contribute to the fund they were raising to renovate the garden area in front of the Union Society premises. After the scandalous Scottish irrigation of the rose bed in 1975, I was only too grateful to be given the opportunity to make amends.

Recollection:
Karan Thapar

(Mr K.B. Thapar, Pembroke College)
President, Lent Term 1977

Karan Thapar was born in India in 1955, attending The Doon School in Uttarakhand and Stowe School in Buckinghamshire before coming up to Pembroke in 1974 to read economics and political philosophy. He took a doctorate in international relations at St Anthony's College, Oxford and worked for The Times *in Nigeria and as a leader writer. After eleven years at London Weekend Television, he returned to India and helped to establish HTV, presenting its flagship interview programme,* Eyewitness, *and* The Chat Show – *India's first such programme.*

He has become one of India's leading commentators and interviewers, noted for his combative interrogations of leading politicians and celebrities – from Prime Ministers P.V. Narasimha Rao and Manmohan Singh to the Dalai Lama and the Indian cricket captain Kapil Dev. He also interviewed the Pakistani Prime Ministers Moeen Qureshi and Benazir Bhutto and, in 2000, conducted the first interview with General Musharraf by an Indian journalist.

He has won the Best Current Affairs Presenter trophy at the Asian Television Awards on three separate occasions, and is presently head of Infotainment Television (ITV), which makes programmes for a number of international networks.

The door was ajar. Was that an invitation to walk in or simply care-lessness? Unsure, I knocked. A loud but distant voice responded. 'Come in.'

I entered a square room lined with bookshelves rising to the ceiling. The curtains were drawn and the lights were not bright. The rich smell of cigar smoke hung in the air. It was a comfortable, well-used room but it was empty.

'I'm in the bath.' It was the same voice. 'Sit down and amuse yourself. I'll join you shortly.'

That was how Michael Posner, the man who would become my tutor, introduced himself. I would learn more of his eccentric ways in the years to come but at this first encounter I was flummoxed. I had come to Pembroke for an interview. Although anxious, eager and excited, I was ready for almost anything – but not this.

At eighteen I wasn't sure what to do. I wanted to behave like an adult but the question I could not answer was what would that amount to? I reached for a book and stood by an upright old brass lamp glancing at its pages. I can't remember its name but it had something to do with the Indian economy.

'Ah, there you are.'

I turned to find Michael Posner bearing down on me. He was a large man but his smile was equally generous. He thumped my shoulder and more or less simultaneously pushed me into a cavernous armchair. Then he sat down in another in front of me.

'What's that?'

Posner reached for the book I had just put down. He seemed to know it.

'Well, young man, you want to come up to Pembroke, do you?'

'Yes, Mr Posner.' What else could I have said? The answer should have been obvious.

'In that case, what can you tell me about the Indian economy?'

It was a trick. And I had created the opportunity by choosing that particular book. I wished I had picked up a magazine or a newspaper instead. Now I had to talk about a subject of which I was completely ignorant. Inwardly I panicked but outwardly I started to gabble. It was the only way of covering up. I must have spoken for three minutes or more.

'Hmm.' The sound was enough to stop my flow. But Posner was staring at the documents in his hand. I guessed they must have been part of my application.

'Not knowing the subject doesn't seem to be a handicap for you!'

Ouch! But there was a hint of a smile and his eyes were gleaming. That was the first time I saw Posner embarrass and applaud with the same sentence. It was his trademark style.

Eight months later, my A levels completed, I arrived at Pembroke. It was a dark, sultry October evening and the heavy clouds threatened rain. Having installed myself in my room and unpacked, I headed for the common room. It turned out to be in the same building as Michael Posner's rooms. As I opened the door to enter I noticed a large figure at the top of the stairs heading down.

'Is that the expert on the Indian economy or have I got it wrong?'

I blushed. I had hoped Posner would have forgotten the gibberish I spouted at the interview. But not just his size, his memory was also elephantine.

'Whatever else you do you should join the Union.'

And with that he walked through the door I had just entered, leaving in his wake the warm feeling of a pleasant greeting but also a small niggling doubt that I had been put in my place. But what was the Union? I'd never heard of the place. I was to find out by another series of fortuitous accidents.

During my first days at Pembroke I was, to be frank, a little lost. It wasn't just new, it was strange and also intimidating. But when a fellow freshman, who I assumed was less sophisticated, announced he had joined the Union I rushed to do so. My reason was simple: if he could, so should I. But it was a gamble.

I remember well my first visit. I was one of many undergraduates on an introductory tour. As we were shown around the premises, speaking in hushed if not awed whispers, I heard an announcement about a freshers' debating competition. It not only attracted my attention but whetted my appetite. I decided to try my luck.

I can't recall the first round but, equally, I will never forget the final. The motion was 'This House prefers Marks and Spencer to Spenser and Marx'. I weighed in on the side of the latter, exuding all the deliberate learning of an expensive Indian education. What I lacked in rhetoric – and it was quite a bit – I made up with erudition. And I won.

Two months later a second accident added to my fortunes. It was 14 November 1974 and the undergraduate opposing the sixth debate of term suddenly fell ill. Stephen Weil, the Union President, perhaps inspired by my freshman victory, asked if I would take his place. The motion was 'This House reaffirms its faith in America'.

The other guests were Charles Wheeler of the BBC, Anthony Howard of the *New Statesman* and Birch Bayh, a US Senator. They took the subject seriously. For reasons I can never explain, I decided to be witty. 'America,' I pronounced, 'is a Coca-Cola culture, swamped by ginger ale, 7 Up and Canada Dry.' It wasn't really funny but it had the House in stitches. That was enough to inspire more silly humour. But that night no joke was so poor the audience wouldn't laugh.

By the end of my first term I had attracted enough attention to risk an act of audacious temerity – I stood for election to the Union standing committee. The combination of an English-speaking wog, whose name led many to believe he was a girl, with a talent for daringly speaking out, resulted in a collection of votes – no doubt some mistaken – that proved hard to beat.

I can't say the Union career that followed was political. It was personal. I sought to be independent, hoping that would find favour with all. I tried to be striking, even outrageous, convinced that if I stood out I would be remembered. And, without being provincial, I wanted to be Indian.

I was elected President in an unopposed contest for the Lent Term of 1977. Determined to be different, my first event was not a debate but a concert: Ravi Shankar playing at King's College Chapel. The Union membership and even the city of Cambridge were enthralled. But poor Ravi Shankar froze half to death. On a frosty mid-January night the unheated chapel was more than he could bear.

Of the people I met perhaps the most colourful was Jeremy Thorpe, then leader of the Liberal party. I was 21 and Thorpe was a star guest at one of our debates. Afterwards I invited him to accompany a group of friends to my digs for a nightcap. To my surprise he agreed.

At the time Thorpe was deeply enmeshed in the coils of the crisis that was to destroy his career a few months later. He had been accused of duplicitous homosexual conduct – including the possible use of force – and his defence had worn thin. Earlier in the evening, when he arrived by train, the national press had besieged him. The Union, and in particular the gallery above the chamber, was packed with photographers and correspondents. There must have been several hundred. Thorpe was not just at the centre of a dreadful scandal, he was also the biggest story around. But if any of this was cause for tension, he showed no sign of it that evening.

Of course, we were eager to discuss his problem. That was the obvious motive behind the invitation. No doubt Thorpe realised this, but his reason for accepting was quite different. He either wanted to get away and relax or to show his complete control over the looming crisis. Adversity can bring forth strange responses.

Whatever his motive, Thorpe succeeded admirably. Within minutes he was telling stories, making us laugh and playing the good-natured fool. Maybe it was an act but, if so, it was a superlative one. I'll never forget the challenge he threw at me. By then it was well past midnight and the bottle of port I kept in my room lay empty.

'Can you do yoga?' he asked.

'Of course not!' I replied, appalled that anyone should think I could.

'Well, I can' – and without further ado he got up to show us.

Now, Thorpe was wearing a well-cut double-breasted dinner jacket which he kept buttoned. Yet dressed as he was he squatted in the *padmasan* position and raised his body a full six inches off the floor using only the palms of his hands. A perfect *uththitpadmasan*. We were hugely impressed.

When he left I walked with him down King's Parade and Trinity Street to his hotel. It was an inn called The Blue Boar. On the way he started to talk about his troubles.

'It's a funny world,' he said. I kept silent. After a bit he continued at his own pace.

'You know, a man can only be himself. Say what you feel and mean what you say. If the world misunderstands, so be it. But be true to yourself.'

At the time I understood him to be speaking about his personal crisis. Today I realise his words have far greater application. Candour wins respect, sincerity commands admiration. It's also the only honest way for a politician to behave. That was the real point Jeremy Thorpe wanted to make. I mistook it for a *mea culpa* but it was a lot more than that. His words constitute a motto that is worth remembering: 'Say what you feel and mean what you say. If the world misunderstands, so be it. At least you will be true to yourself.'

Of course, Union Presidents are blissfully unaware of such virtues. At the time, so was I. Like my predecessors, I was more concerned with being witty or, at least, clever. Rhetoric mattered more than reality. Consequently the debate I was most proud of is a perfect example of this. I dreamt up a motion that had the audience at the Union laughing long before any of the speakers began. It was: 'A drink before and a cigarette after are three of the best things in life.' Everyone interpreted the middle bit differently! No one agreed with me. *The Times* devoted an entire diary to it, claiming it was doing so because the paper was thoroughly perplexed!

The Lent Term of 1977 ended with my presidential debate, just days before the elections in India, Indira Gandhi's defeat and the end of the Emergency. Perhaps I had sensed change in the air. Or perhaps I was risking my luck. But instead of handing over to my successor I staged a mock coup, declared my own emergency and announced I would continue in office!

Alas, I spent so much time on this gimmick that I was poorly prepared for the debate that followed. I fear I was a disappointment. That the motion 'Equality should be the first principle' was carried is a tribute to the generosity of the House and the large-heartedness of the Union tradition that always ensures the retiring President wins.

1975–90: 'The Passion
for Free Expression

After the unrest and uncertainty of the early 1970s, the Union approached its 175th anniversary in 1990 on a rather more stable footing. The radical Conservative governments of the 1980s inspired new and heated topics for discussion, but these were – generally – kept to the confines of orderly debate. The Thatcherite spirit can perhaps also be detected in the career paths of Union alumni from this period – a striking number chose the corporate world as their destination after Cambridge, many with great success. The Union itself sought to bring its finances in order, with mixed results.

A number of ex-Presidents at the end of the late '70s made their careers in the media. Peter Bazalgette, who helped the Union rise from the ashes of the fire which threatened to overshadow his term, has forged a very successful career in television. He came to Cambridge after failing to get into Oxford. Taking a year out and teaching at a 'cheerfully insane prep school', he applied to Cambridge to read law and was pooled to Fitzwilliam. There, he 'made a beeline' for both the Union and Footlights. His *entrée* to the Union came when he reached the final of the freshers' debating competition. Tam Dalyell was invited to judge the competition, and selected four members of the audience at random to help him. One of them was a friend of Bazalgette's from Fitzwilliam: 'He did not declare his interest – and argued ferociously for me to win. I won.' Thereafter, he started to climb the Union ladder and was elected President for

Michaelmas 1975 – somewhat to the detriment of his studies. His tutors 'were very nice about the fact that I spent all of my time at the Union and socialising,' and he graduated with a third.[1] But if the Union hindered Bazalgette's academic performance, it made up for it by providing the location for an early career opportunity. Coming back to speak in a debate as a BBC news trainee, he made a great impression on his fellow speaker Esther Rantzen. 'It was clear here was a creative talent and a very bright young man,' she later recalled. 'I found out he was a BBC news trainee and persuaded News and Current Affairs to let him leave and come to work on *That's Life*.'[2] It was the beginning of a lucrative career in TV. Shows which Bazalgette has helped to bring to the screen include *Ready Steady Cook, Changing Rooms* and the UK version of *Big Brother*.

The President the following Michaelmas, Peter Fudakowski, became a film producer. After an MBA at INSEAD, he worked in the film financing department of the First National Bank of Chicago. He left in 1982 to set up his own production company, Premiere Productions Ltd., with his wife. Among the films they have produced is the South African drama *Tsotsi*, which won an Oscar for best foreign language film in 2006. Fudakowski became President rather by chance. The sitting Vice-President, Sarah Nathan, was not very popular with the right-wingers of Magdalene, who scrambled round for a candidate to put up against her. Fudakowski, who had served his three terms on standing committee and 'more or less given up the Union' was persuaded to run, recalls Barry Thoday, who took over as chief clerk that summer. Fudakowski had booked a skiing trip and then planned to go to America – but he won the election, so hastily had to organise a term with Thoday's help. Thoday recalls: 'I was new to the job, he hadn't expected to do it, he hadn't done anything at all, so we had a really hectic summer.'[3] It all came together, and the Michaelmas Term opened with a debate on the motion 'This House would have sex before marriage'. Among the proposers was the future Prime Minister of Pakistani Benazir Bhutto, then Treasurer of the Oxford Union. The motion was resoundingly carried, 519–218.

At the end of term, Fudakowski irreverently welcomed his Indian successor, Karan Thapar, with the motion 'This House believes that Britain is going to the wogs'. The motion was tied by acclamation, and the new President cast his vote against. Now one of India's leading broadcasters, Thapar worked for *The Times* and London Weekend Television before returning to India to found HTV. He has won critical acclaim – and numerous awards – for his interviews with leading politicians, celebrities and heads of state.

It was evident from early on that Robert Harris, President in Easter 1978, planned a career in journalism. The 'superfluity of speakers' already lined up for his retirement debate – 'Journalism is an honourable profession' – was noted at his second standing committee meeting, and the President's career prospects were discussed. 'He was always the outstanding member of our generation at Cambridge,' says his predecessor Andrew Mitchell, 'through sheer ability and decency'.[4] He worked as a researcher with Jeremy Paxman on *Panorama*, then on *Newsnight* and later as political editor of the *Observer*. He resigned in the early 1990s to write a novel, *Fatherland*, which became a bestseller on both sides of the Atlantic. Since then, Harris has sold over 10 million books, including the thrillers *Enigma*, *Archangel* and *The Ghost*, and the historical novels *Pompeii* and *Imperium*. He had a lively term at the Union: Michael Palin spoke in a comedy debate, and the Great Train Robbers came to be interviewed in the chamber. The prospect of their visit caused some consternation from the Union's former Senior Treasurer, the Revd Stanley Booth-Clibborn, who asked Harris to justify his invitation at an MBM on 2 June. Harris promised to consult the standing committee and withdraw the invitation if they felt it necessary, but he had their support, and the visit went ahead.

Another journalist was Ed Stourton, President in Lent 1979. Born in Nigeria and educated at Ampleforth, where he was head boy, Stourton had done a lot of debating at school and 'was determined to speak' at the Union when he came up to Trinity. He 'just failed' to get on standing committee at his first attempt, but was successful the second time.[5] After Cambridge, he was a graduate trainee at ITN and presented the *One O'Clock News* on the BBC for six years until, in 1999, becoming a presenter on Radio 4's *Today* programme. When, at the end of 2008, his tenure was abruptly cut short, a public campaign was mounted to save him – which included a motion in Parliament. (Another *Today* presenter, Brian Redhead, who worked on the show between 1975 and 1993, had also served on the Union's standing committee.) As an undergraduate Stourton proposed, alongside Hugh Thomas and Mary Whitehouse, a motion suggesting that 'The mass media are abusing their freedom'. It was defeated by 472 to 293.

Two Presidents from the late 1970s have forged successful business careers. Adair Turner (Michaelmas 1977) took a double first in history and economics and became a management consultant with McKinsey & Co. As director general of the Confederation of British Industry (CBI) from 1995 to 1999, he was one of the leading voices of British business. At Cambridge, he had been chairman of the University Conservative Association, but he joined the SDP in the 1980s and later developed close links to New Labour, for whom he chaired government commissions on low pay and pensions. He became Lord Turner of Ecchinswell in 2005, and is chairman of the Economic and Social Research Council, the council of the Overseas Development Institute, and the Financial Services Authority. Dominic Casserley (Easter 1979) has stayed with McKinsey & Co. and is now their managing partner for the UK and the Middle East. He joined the company in 1983, working in New York and Hong Kong. At the end of 1987, he was asked by Ronald Reagan to serve on the staff of a presidential task force, the Brady Commission, which reviewed the causes of that year's market crash.

Of course, politics and the law continued to be popular career paths for other ex-Presidents. Andrew Mitchell (Lent 1978) came up to Cambridge after a short service commission in the Royal Tank Regiment; he joined Lazard Brothers after graduation, but was keen to join his father in the House of Commons. He fought Sunderland South in 1983 and was elected MP for Gedling in 1987, but lost his seat in the 1997 Labour landslide and went back to the City. He returned to Parliament in 2001, succeeding his fellow former CUCA chairman Norman Fowler in Sutton Coldfield. (Before Fowler that seat had been held by Geoffrey Lloyd, another ex-Union President.) Mitchell held two light-hearted debates on feminism during his term. The first, 'Female emancipation has gone too far', was proposed by Fanny Cradock and opposed by Clive James; the Noes won, 234–172. The following month, Princess Anne attended a charity debate on the motion 'The woman's place is in the harem'. Despite the royal presence – and a strong line-up of guests including Robert Morley and Stirling Moss in favour, and Felicity Kendal and Derek Nimmo (with a young Rory McGrath) against – the debate caused quite a furore. A large number of people, it seems, failed to see the motion in a humorous light: some 200 came to protest outside the Union on the evening of the debate, and very nearly managed to break into the chamber. 'As I saw the doors bulging, I saw my life pass before my eyes,' recalls Mitchell. Luckily the police were outside to maintain order, so the President – and his royal guest – 'just insouciantly carried on'.[6]

Finding the debate tied by acclamation, Mitchell declared it carried. A less troublesome debate was Mitchell's retirement debate, to which he invited his father and Lord Thorneycroft. The motion, 'Socialism will not solve the problems of society', was carried by acclamation.

Three other Presidents went to the Bar. Andrew Dallas (Easter 1977) practises as a criminal barrister in Leeds, where he is also a Recorder. Michael Booth (Michaelmas 1979) came up to Trinity from Salford on a scholarship; he became a chancery and commercial barrister and took silk in 1999. Daniel Janner followed in the footsteps of his father, Greville, by reading law at Trinity Hall and becoming President of the Union in Michaelmas 1978. He invited his father to speak alongside him in his retirement debate, 'The art of advocacy is dead'. Speaking with the Janners was Peter Cook; against them were Greville's Cambridge contemporary Sir Geoffrey Howe and his Labour colleague Lord Elwyn-Jones. Although Daniel stood as a Labour candidate in the 1983 general election, his politics were rather more ambiguous than his father's; more recently, he has been active in the Society of Conservative Lawyers. Even at an MBM during his term it was pointed out that some order papers had been swapped for ones bearing the motion: 'The nearest thing to a Tory in disguise is Janner in power.' The President asked for a member of the standing committee to own up to the joke, but no one did.

One President of the late 1970s is rather harder to categorise. On the face of it, the Revd Fr David Johnson (Easter 1976) followed the most traditional career path of all – he was ordained in 1979 and was a curate in Fulham and a rector in Northamptonshire. But his career in the Church was not helped by his fondness for ecclesiastical satire. There was an 'explosion' when *Not The Church Times*, a spoof magazine he produced (with the aid of Christopher Monckton), outsold the genuine article – but its editor saw the funny side and gave him a job as TV critic for the real version of the paper. A series of hoax letters he sent to bishops, however, were not taken so well. Following the form of the 'Rochester Sneath' letters of another ex-President, Humphry Berkeley, they fooled more than 70 members of the Establishment, and were subsequently published as *The Spiritual Quest of Francis Wagstaffe* (1994). Unfortunately for Johnson, his own bishop found them 'contemptible'.[7] Now retired from the Church, Johnson has found a safe berth for his eccentricities at the Oxford Union, where he is fondly known as 'the Vicar'. Indeed, he has even scored electoral success there. Running for standing committee in the Hilary (i.e. Lent) Term 2002, he submitted a manifesto in which he was pictured in old-fashioned military dress, complete with a feathery hat. Next to him were the words:

> Manifesto of the Reverend father Sir David William Johnson, Knight of St John of Beverly (first class); Order of St Rombart (silver); Master of Arts (Cantab.); ex-President, The Other Place; ex-Standing Committee, Oxford Union; Champion Debater; 'Vicar'. I will be good.[8]

He came top of the ballot.

Johnson's time at Cambridge was scarcely less colourful. As Vice-President, he was kidnapped and taken hostage by members of the Oxford Union. He received a telephone call asking him to come to the church in Grantchester at ten to three (after the Rupert Brooke poem) in his Selwyn blazer and boater to have his photograph taken for *Cherwell*, the Oxford student newspaper. More than happy to oblige, he turned up at the appointed hour, was bundled into a car with a bag over his head and was whisked off to Oxford. There he was held, blindfolded, until the Change of Officers debate two days later, when he was wheeled into the chamber bound up in a shopping trolley. The incoming Oxford President thought it was a stunt by Johnson 'until he saw that I hadn't shaved for two days'.[9] But Johnson got his revenge in 1980 when Churchill's grandson, the Hon. Rupert Soames, was President at Oxford. With the help of two guardsmen, Johnson took him off to Cambridge in the back of a van and tied him to a chair in the window of the academic outfitters' Ryder & Amies on King's Parade, with a sign round his neck saying 'President of the Oxford Union'. Soames was finally rescued when the Master of Jesus, Sir Alan Cottrell, passed the shop window. Sir Alan, a former chief scientific adviser to the government, was due to be speaking at the Oxford Union that evening, and offered the hostage a lift back. 'Rupert still talks to me,' Johnson is relieved to say – 'he didn't for a bit'.[10]

In 1975 Johnson captained a Union cricket team against the Oxford Union with John Hastings Bass, the CUCA chairman. The Oxford team was led by Benazir Bhutto and John Monckton, the financier who was stabbed to death in his Chelsea home by burglars in 2004. The match took place at the Leys School in Cambridge and 'was said by those who witnessed it to have been hilarious, though history does not record the result'.[11]

One clergyman of a much more orthodox kind was the Revd (later Canon) James Owen, who served as the Union's Steward for nearly two decades until his death in 1993. Owen had a long association with Cambridge: he had been an undergraduate at Trinity Hall in the early 1950s, and served as the chaplain of Jesus College in the early '60s. In 1974, he was appointed by Peterhouse to serve as the vicar of Little St Mary's; at the same time, he was invited by the Union to serve in 'the secular-cum-pastoral office (for that was how he saw it) of Steward'. Few, it was said of him, had 'a shrewder sense of what was in the university air or more friends in colleges and town alike'.[12] He was made an honorary canon of Ely cathedral in 1986, and also became a trustee of the Union in 1992. He died, a bachelor, in the summer of the following year, bequeathing to the Union a collection of parliamentary and political pictures and £10,000 for a travel fund.

———•———

The improvement in the Union's finances in the mid-1970s proved to be short-lived. In Easter 1975 the Junior Treasurer reported that, 'during the third week of this term, rather earlier than usual, the Society was forced to fall back for financial support on an overdraft granted by the bank.' This was expected to reach £10,000 by the end of the summer vacation, when revenue from the annual membership drive would start to come in. The situation became dramatically worse when, at the end of Easter Term, the fire broke out in the Union. The cost of repairs was estimated at £50,000. It was clear that a number of measures were needed to put the Society's finances back on an even footing.

The price of life membership was substantially increased from £14.85 to £18.50 in time for that Michaelmas, but thankfully this did not seem to dent recruitment figures. Roland Thompson, the chief clerk, ought to have retired at the end of June 1975, but was asked to stay on for a bit longer – not least because of the difficult situation in which the Union found itself. He finally retired in September 1976 and was made an honorary member of the Society. He was succeeded by Barry Thoday, who had started working for the Union in August 1950 and served as chief clerk until 1995 – a 45-year commitment to the Union broken only by two years' national service. Thompson continued to work at the Union as an accounts clerk for another two years, when he was replaced by Sandra Finding – who would, in turn, succeed Thoday as chief clerk.

The ageing Thompson had moved out of the chief clerk's house behind the Union three years earlier, making it available to let. It was agreed in June 1975 to lease the premises to a language school, Anglo World, for five years. This would bring in a rent of £2,000 per annum – plus more for the occasional hire of other rooms. Another tenant moved into the Union in Lent 1978: the cellars were hired out to the theatrical group Footlights, whose clubrooms had been demolished in the controversial redevelopment of the Lion Yard area in 1972. The Footlights had a long-standing connection with the Union: Oscar Browning had served as President and Treasurer of both societies in the late nineteenth century, and many Cambridge wits had performed to both audiences. A gala 'smoker' event was held to inaugurate the new rooms on 25 February 1978, featuring Jonathan Lynn, Pete Atkin, Clive James and Griff Rhys Jones. There were, however, a number of 'awkward restrictions' for Footlights in the lease, drawn up under Adair Turner. As well as paying an annual rent of £600 and running costs of some £1,800, its members also had to be members of the Union or pay an extra fee. Entrance to the clubroom was via the Union, so the Footlights couldn't keep their own hours – and the Union insisted on supplying the bar and bar staff, removing 'the potentially most profitable side of the club's operations'.[13] Nonetheless, the relationship seems to have been a happy one.

The CSU rented premises from the Union in Round Church Street, and *Stop Press with Varsity* moved in next door in Michaelmas 1979. (The radical *Stop Press* edge gradually faded after the papers' merger; by 1987, it had been subsumed entirely and the paper reverted to *Varsity*.) Both moved to University-owned premises in 11–12 Trumpington Street in 1990.[14]

In January 1977, the library committee proposed selling part of the collection of rare books left to the Union by Col. Fairfax Rhodes on his death in 1928. David McKitterick, the Librarian, said that 'it was with much regret on the part of members both Senior and Junior that this sale was proposed', but many of the books were already inaccessible to members for insurance reasons, and the revenue generated would allow the library to become self-financing. The selection was valued by Sotheby's at £42,000 and put up for auction in May. In fact, by the end of July, £51,000 had been raised, with another 21 lots still to be sold; a further £8,000 had been made by November. The Union was delighted – although it seems that even more could have been made. One of the volumes put up for auction was an album which included etchings by Jacques Callot, a baroque printmaker and a significant influence on Rembrandt. It was sold as a book rather than a collection of prints, and wrongly catalogued, attributing much of the engraving to a lesser artist. The album was bought by a dealer who paid £6,820 for it – more than the estimate, but still well below the true value of the engravings. He sold the other artists' work separately and stored the Callot etchings away until the artist's quatercentenary in 1992. Then, he carefully removed the prints and sold them individually – each one fetching between £200 and £8,000.[15]

The Union had considered applying for charitable status before, but the steep increase in VAT in 1979 made it all the more worthwhile to pursue. The rate rose from 8 to 15 per cent, meaning an additional tax bill of about £3,000 on subscription fees – in other words, an extra 200 members would have to be recruited just to cover the difference. The Charity Commissioners turned down the Union's first application in the autumn of 1980; they suggested some changes to the Society's constitution, which were all passed at an MBM in February 1981, and the Union finally became a charity that Michaelmas.

At the same time, the Union was pursuing a scheme which would help with the upkeep of the building. The Societies Syndicate – a body representing all the University's clubs and societies – pointed out that student groups were paying hefty sums for room hire, and pressed the University to investigate the provision of a cheap, reliable source of accommodation. An obvious possibility was the Union and, early in 1980, the Council of the Senate formed a committee to investigate a partnership in which the University would help with the maintenance of the Union building in return for cheap room hire for student societies. It was made explicit, at the request of the Union trustees, that there was no intention of reopening the question of an 'Open Union' – not least because of the effect this might have on recruitment.

An investigation chaired by the Master of Emmanuel, Derek Brewer, came up with detailed proposals by the end of July 1980. Under a five-year agreement, the Union would retain exclusive use of key rooms like the chamber, library and reference room, and have priority over the use of most others. The rest of the buildings, including numbers 3–5 Round Church Street, would be made available to the Societies Syndicate, who would allow University societies to rent rooms at a reduced rate. In return, the University would undertake to repair and maintain the building, and contribute towards the cost of heating and lighting it, to the value of around £14,000 a year.[16] Two Presidents were instrumental in the drawing up of these plans. Mel Libby of Girton (Easter 1980) hoped to become a Tory MP after Cambridge: she contested the safe Labour seat of St Helens North in 1987, but spent an unsuccessful ten years searching for a winnable seat thereafter.[17] Frustrated by the attitude of many Conservative associations, she gave up and is now a travel writer for the *Daily Telegraph*. Charles Gallagher, her successor, was well qualified to draw up the building arrangement. He went on to chair the family firm, a Dublin-based housing company, and was president of the UK House Builders Federation.

The plans were approved by a Grace on 14 February 1981 and, by April, a substantial start had been made by the University's estate management team on bringing the building up to University standards. The central heating was renovated and extended, and some £2,000 of external painting was planned for the summer.

Once this arrangement was up and running, thoughts turned to a more ambitious scheme to redevelop the site at the back of the Union and on Round Church Street. Sir Leslie Martin, the architect of several important University buildings, was invited to submit a plan.

His design involved demolishing the three houses in Round Church Street and the Anglo World language school, and redeveloping the site as a three-storey arcade of shops with office space above. The project would provide space for the CSU and *Stop Press with Varsity*, as well as other University societies, and would cost some £1.1 million. It was an ambitious scheme, and a search for funding was made over a number of years. The University showed some interest and, in early 1984, a 'Joint Committee on Redevelopment of Part of the Union Society Site' was set up by the Council of the Senate.

After a series of dead ends, Trevor Gardner, now chairman of the Union's trustees, came to standing committee at the end of Easter 1986 with the most promising scheme yet. For some months, he said, the trustees had been in negotiations with Gonville and Caius College to develop the site behind the Union. They had drawn up plans to sign a 300-year lease to Caius in return for a £350,000 lump sum and an annual payment of £15,000, reviewed at 50-year intervals. The college would then build, at its own expense, two squash courts with changing rooms and a viewing gallery, a flat for the chief clerk, and suites for University societies. The proposals had the consent of the Charities Commission and the backing of the trustees. The standing committee approved them unanimously that October and a special MBM was held later that month at which they were given the green light – but sadly the plans came to nought. The reasons were various: in May 1987 the standing committee minuted its concern that 'the Union was faced with additional costs and loss of space of which the membership was not aware'; the following February, the Junior Treasurer 'reported that Gonville and Caius were now reconsidering their Union redevelopment plans'. The trustees sent a letter asking for compensation, as Anglo World had ended their lease of the chief clerk's house in anticipation of the scheme. In March 1988 it seemed that the consensus behind the scheme had broken down: the President 'reminded the Committee that the trustees had virtually forced the Society into the deal'.

By the time the trustees met in June 1991 it was clear that the Union would be in no position to commence work before planning permission on the site expired the following year. Moreover, Gardner questioned the wisdom of proceeding given the poor state of the market. It would be financially more sensible to let the properties. Selling the site at that time might raise £400,000, resulting in a maximum income of £16,000 a year; letting the current properties out, however, could bring in at least £24,000 a year, and would leave the Union with the chance to develop the site at a later date. This the trustees decided to do. The minutes of their meeting on 9 July 1991 end with the recognition 'that barring exceptional circumstances any redevelopment or sale was now put aside for a very long period'. They were right.

———

After the radical climate in which the decade had opened, there was a palpable change of political mood as the 1970s drew to an end. David Condit, filing his vice-presidential report in Lent 1975, noted 'a profound change of atmosphere in the House' since his first term in Cambridge in 1973. Back then,

> left-wing speakers were given rousing ovations for their rhet-oric. Those days have passed, at least for now. In the words of the President, speaking before the Cambridge Union is like 'addressing the Tory Party Conference'. It is extremely difficult for instance to get left-wing student speakers for both emergency motions and main debates. No doubt the pendulum will swing the other way, but at the moment it is a vexing situation for the Officers.

A further problem with this new political mood was the 'hissing and continued vocal interjections' directed towards left-wing guests – such as during a debate that term on the motion: 'The NUS does the student cause more harm than good'.

315

The Callaghan government went down to a thumping defeat at the No Confidence debate in Michaelmas 1976. In fact, every No Confidence debate held during the Wilson and Callaghan governments resulted in a Labour defeat, but that year the motion was particularly decisive. It was proposed by Adair Turner, and the government – represented by Tony Benn, Neil Kinnock and Daniel Janner – was beaten 391–178.

There was further humiliation for the government the following term when the House disagreed 374–331 with the motion that 'Labour is Britain's party of progress'. The following month the suggestion that 'The House of Lords is now an anachronism' was thrown out by 307 votes to 163. Andrew Mitchell led for the opposition, speaking alongside the former Prime Minister Lord Home of the Hirsel.

A number of familiar Tory names appear in the debate records of this period. In Michaelmas 1977 Oliver Letwin proposed the motion: 'This House is opposed to the whole concept of the welfare state', and lost 479–143. Later, the future frontbencher was back, proposing the motion: 'Politicians do no good and our most urgent task is to prevent them from doing harm'. His fellow Trinitarian, Charles Moore, made his maiden speech in the No Confidence debate of Michaelmas 1975.

If the Union had drifted back to the right, however, it was not socially conservative. In Michaelmas 1977 the House agreed strongly with Germaine Greer that 'abortion on demand is the right of every woman' (518–273). The freshers' debate that term was on the motion 'that homosexuality is as natural as heterosexuality'. Ian Harvey, an ex-President of the Oxford Union who had resigned from Parliament after being caught with a guardsman in St James's Park, spoke in favour and persuaded the House to support the motion by 298 to 234. The following Michaelmas, the House decided it would legalise cannabis (400–252) and that it would not obey the law (323–268). At the end of the 1980s, by contrast, the Union was strangely censorious. When, in Lent 1988, the city's environmental health officer offered to install condom machines in the Union free of charge, the standing committee thought it too controversial to be decided without being put to an MBM. Two members of the committee worried it 'would offend Roman Catholics and encourage free sex'. The motion was actually defeated 16–15, and had to be put to a poll of all members. At the same time, members voted 12–9 against selling cigarettes at the Union.

The big political shift, of course, came with the election of Margaret Thatcher as leader of the Conservative party. By 1979 the Union had made up its mind about her and a thinly populated House on the eve of the general election on 3 May 'look[ed] forward to Mrs Thatcher moving into Number 10 Downing Street' by 94 to 54 (with 22 abstentions). At the end of that term, the retiring President Dominic Casserley and Robert Rhodes James, who had been comfortably returned as MP for Cambridge, showed themselves to be out of step with the mood of the new era by proposing that 'British politics should pursue the middle way'. It was defeated by acclamation.

The first No Confidence debate of the Thatcher government was held on 2 November 1979. Two members of the new government who had been Union regulars – Norman Fowler and Sir Geoffrey Howe – returned to the Society and carried the debate 307– 262. Also defending the government that evening were three undergraduates who would go on to become Conservative MPs: David Lidington, Julie Kirkbride and Bernard Jenkin. Lidington had been CUCA chairman; Kirkbride chaired the Tory Reform Group, and Jenkin was Union President in Michaelmas 1982. Son of the Cabinet minister Patrick Jenkin, Bernard raised some eyebrows by printing the family crest on his order papers – and for chairing some of his debates in a kilt. At standing committee at the start of his term, 'an amusing and at times heated discussion followed in response to Mr Jenkin's desire to install a sauna opposite the showers in the shower room ...' The logistics of fitting five people into a sauna measuring 5′ by 8′ were considered: there were also, the Steward remarked, 'questions of propriety'.

Julie Kirkbride was Vice-President of the Union in Lent 1981, and was evidently a popular young lady: a man clad in a frog-suit entered the chamber before a debate that February and presented her with a box of Cadbury's Milk Tray from an anonymous admirer. (It was a Rag Week stunt, but Miss Kirkbride was lucky: another student burst in during the debate and threw a custard pie in the face of the Secretary.) Despite such romantic gestures, she was beaten to the presidency by Peter Sugarman in the elections at the end of that term. She brought a requisition against him for an article which appeared in the student press two days before the poll, arguing that this 'unfairly brought his name to the attention of the reading public of the University'. But her complaint was dismissed by a select committee which concluded that it had no power to declare the election void. Sugarman went on to become an investment banker; he spent sixteen years with JP Morgan and became a managing director of Lehman Brothers' insurance advisory group, and chairman of its subsidiary Libero.

Jenkin entered the House of Commons in 1992, and Kirkbride in 1997. Another ex-President who nearly joined them was Mark Bishop, President in Lent 1980. He was called to the Bar after graduating from Downing, and was selected to succeed Robert Rhodes James when he stepped down as MP for Cambridge at the 1992 election. Rhodes James's majority had been 5,060, but Bishop lost to Labour's Anne Campbell by a narrow 580 votes. He returned to the Bar, became a Recorder in 2001, and is now (fittingly, given his surname) an Anglican priest. During Bishop's term at the Union the positions of 'Director of Ents' and 'Director of Concerts' were merged into one portfolio – held by the improbable figure of Simon Heffer. During his time as the organiser of the Union's social events, the future *Daily Mail* and *Daily Telegraph* commentator arranged such licentious entertainments as a Sixties night, a 'juvenile delinquents party', and a Las Vegas evening, for which he 'hoped that the subtle combination of vices ... would secure a large attendance'.[18]

In common with the rest of the country, the Union's support for Mrs Thatcher ebbed away towards the middle of her first term. It was still there during Bishop's term, when a debate 'regret[ting] the Prime Ministership of Margaret Thatcher and call[ing] for an early general election' was rejected by nearly two to one. But there were some signs of change the following term, Easter 1980: a motion suggesting that 'Government governs best when it governs least' was only narrowly passed 42–41, and another supporting 'the Government's economic policy' was defeated 162–53. The Industry Secretary Sir Keith Joseph was hit by an egg when he came to a debate in Lent 1981. Despite 'rigorous' security arrangements, 30 protesters from 'various left-wing groups' mobbed his car as it pulled up at the back of the Union. As Sir Keith was jostled inside by Special Branch officers, the 'diminutive' President, David Senior, got caught on the wrong side of the police cordon. When he cried out to be let in, the demonstrators responded by pretending he was one of them. There was some confusion before he was eventually let in.[19] Once he was cleaned up, Sir Keith defended the government's economic policies against J.K. Galbraith and Lord Kaldor but, in another humiliation, the motion against the government was carried 264–210. David Senior spent eleven years in industry working for ICI, then tried to enter Parliament. He contested Barnsley Central in 1992 and Luton North five years later.

Despite such incidents, the Tories were still clearly in the ascendant at the Union. The first edition of a short-lived Union newsletter, *The Hackler*, in Easter 1982 carried an article on 'The Union and the Left' by Ed Cairns, chairman of the University Fabian Society. 'It is now eleven terms since we had a President who was a member of the Labour Party,' Cairns complained. The President that term, Simon Baynes of Magdalene, had been CUCA chairman the term before. He became a managing director of JP Morgan Cazenove, and contested Montgomeryshire for the Conservatives in the 2005 general election.

Another CUCA chairman who became President was Simon Milton in Lent 1983. After Cambridge he studied at Cornell University, then became a PR consultant. He was a member of Westminster City Council for eighteen years and its leader between

319

2000 and 2008. He was knighted in 2006, and is now chairman of the Local Government Association. One of the highlights of his Union term was 'An Evening with Dame Edna Everage' held on Australia Day, 26 January. The Antipodean icon was assisted by her *alter ego* Sir Les Patterson, who was presented with an 'honorary degree' by the Society 'for services to Australian culture'. The glowing citation was read in Latin and in English, followed by a pithier Australian version: 'Good on yer, Les'. Sir Les delivered a lecture on Australian culture, the Trinity College Choral Scholars performed 'A Musical Tribute to Australia', then Dame Edna was interviewed by the President.

There was an upsurge in support for the government during the Falklands crisis. A *Stop Press with Varsity* survey found that over 60 per cent of Cambridge students thought the islands were worth fighting for. Eighty-five per cent approved of sending the task force to back up diplomatic moves. Simon Baynes hastily rearranged one of the debates in his term to discuss the conflict: on 3 May 1982 – the day after the sinking of the *Belgrano* – Tam Dalyell confronted Admiral of the Fleet Sir Michael Pollock in the Union chamber.

It was not until the end of the decade that the Union's opinion really turned against Thatcher. When, in Michaelmas 1989, the No Confidence debate was heavily lost (574–331), it broke a three-year run of success for the Tory government. Norman Tebbit, the former Party Chairman, spoke that evening; he was due to be joined by the ex-President Ken Clarke, then Health Secretary – but he had to return to London 'only minutes after arriving in Cambridge' because of the mounting ambulance pay dispute.[20] Another ex-President, Chris Smith, joined the former standing committee member Peter Shore to win the debate resoundingly.

Of course, there was no shortage of people who never had any sympathy for the right. Andrew Rawnsley – now associate editor of the *Observer* – edited *Stop Press with Varsity*, and was named student journalist of the year in 1982. He recalls taking to 'the nursery slopes of political journalism sketching the tyro posturers of the Cambridge Union and reporting the skulduggeries of the Conservative

Association'.[21] The front pages for which he was responsible featured regular exposés of the two societies. The Cambridge Organisation of Labour Students (COLS) and the University Left ran an anti-Union campaign to hinder the Society's annual recruitment drive. Arguing that the Union was elitist and expensive, the campaign included boycott stalls at the Freshers' Fair. Their efforts were not particularly damaging to recruitment, however: they were met with mirth one year when a leading anti-Union campaigner, Tom Shakespeare, was revealed to be the grandson of an ex-President, Sir Geoffrey Shakespeare (and the heir to his baronetcy).

In fact, the extra publicity may have helped the Union. In 1978–9, the Society recorded its highest ever number of new members (still unsurpassed), when 2,278 signed up – or 72 per cent of all freshers that year. In Michaelmas 1981 the Union took the rare step of circulating a leaflet to counter the claims made in another, issued by the anti-Union campaign and entitled 'The Union Rip-Off'. This set out all the benefits of Union membership, which were available for the equivalent of just 41p a week. In Lent 1986 the President, Tom Oliver of St John's, went as far as holding an open debate on the worth of the Union. Inviting two speakers from CUSU to put the case against, Oliver spoke in defence of the Society himself, along with his fellow Johnian Martin Tod. Oliver was another President of the centre-right: also chairman of the Tory Reform Group at Cambridge, he worked for six years in advertising before moving to the National Trust, the Council for National Parks and the Campaign to Protect Rural England, where he is head of rural policy.

Martin Tod, meanwhile, took a unique course in Cambridge politics. After sitting on the Union's standing committee, he served as deputy president of CUSU for one year. This sabbatical position – and the many campaigns he ran during his year – gave him a high profile in the student press. He returned to the Union, editing the Society's newsletter with Matthew Lindsay, and ran straight for the vice-presidency, beating the Secretary, Anne McLauchlan of Newnham, by 250 to 177. Lindsay, later a partner at the corporate law firm Mischon de Reya, was elected Secretary by an even greater margin, and the two were consecutively President in Lent and Easter 1987. Tod, a leading member of the Liberal Club and now a Liberal Democrat parliamentary candidate in Winchester, showed a reformist zeal during his time as President. He proposed that the black tie dress code for debates should be made optional, and that anyone chairing a debate or meeting should ensure 'that as far as possible as many women as men are called to speak'. The first suggestion was defeated 24–13 at an MBM, but the second was amended to an avowal that 'no sexual or racial prejudice should be practised when calling members to speak' and passed without objection. Tod further displayed his Liberal credentials by choosing 'Britain needs a new electoral system' as one of his debates. Roy Jenkins was due to propose the motion but pulled out at short notice: it was the first day of voting for the Oxford University chancellorship, and he thought he had better not be seen in 'the Other Place'.[22] Even without him, the Ayes had it, beating the ex-Presidents Michael Howard and Leon Brittan.

Negotiations with COLS led to the dropping of their boycott stall in Michaelmas 1990 and the disappearance of the Anti-Union Society entry from the CUSU handbook. In return, COLS requested that the Union approve a statement recognising the need for a central students' union in Cambridge and acknowledging that, 'as a fee-paying society, [the Union] does not meet this need'. The Union had little cause to sign even this innocuous statement: it had signed up 2,051 new members the previous year despite the COLS campaign. The latter was finally wound up altogether in 1994.

Certainly, compared to the fervent activism of the '60s and '70s, student politics in the 1980s seemed rather sedate. In 1984, even the University proctors said they were 'disappointed at the very small amounts of peaceful dissension that we have seen this year' and expressed their concern 'about the current political apathy on the part of the students in the presence of numerous national and international problems'.[23] The undergraduates of the mid-1980s had more material concerns, as one President of CUSU noted: 'I think the increasing apathy results from more pressure to get a good degree these days in order to get a good job when you leave here.'[24]

One subject which did stir passions throughout the decade was the anti-apartheid movement. In Michaelmas 1979, Action Against Apartheid scrawled 'AAA' on the front door of the Union and sent a letter 'issuing threats of action if the Union Society did not remove its account from Barclays Bank by the first day of the Lent Term 1980' (a vote on disinvestment had been heavily defeated at standing committee the previous year). Barry Thoday contacted the police, but nothing came of the threats. More attention was drawn to a debate in Michaelmas 1984 to which the South African Ambassador had been invited. At an MBM on 14 November, Martin Tod proposed that the invitation be withdrawn and that 'no further invitation should be issued whilst South Africa is governed under the Apartheid system'. The Revd James Owen took the chair while the President, Laura Chapman Jury, spoke against Tod's motion and defended her invitation. Some twenty people spoke in all; when the House divided, 65 voted to rescind the invitation, but 200 thought it should stand. The debate duly went ahead on 26 November. There was further controversy the following term when it transpired that Lance Anisfeld, Chapman Jury's successor as President, had visited the South African embassy in Michaelmas. Chris Steele, a 'confirmed socialist' from Girton who was later President himself – and subsequently joined the Foreign Office – raised the matter at standing committee in January 1985. The new President replied that 'just because he had been to the South African Embassy did not suggest that he was a racist – any more than a visit to *Stop Press*'s offices would suggest that he held Communist tendencies'. Anisfeld went on to become an adviser to Peter Lilley at the Department for Trade and Industry, having worked at the Adam Smith Institute and in Price Waterhouse's privatisation unit. He later worked as a real estate developer in eastern Europe, before joining the family business: H. Forman & Son, the salmon smoker and gourmet food supplier.

The question of free speech fuelled a series of controversies in this period. Andrew Mitchell opened his term with a debate on the motion: 'This House would ban the National Front'. It was proposed by Robert Harris and opposed by the president of the CSU and Viscount Stormont. Unsurprisingly, it was a huge victory for free speech: the Ayes had 50 votes; the Noes 393. Later that year, Nick Griffin of Downing – the future chairman of the British National Party – sent a letter to the President 'asking that a National Front speaker be invited to debate at the Society'. The President, Daniel Janner, made it clear that there was no policy to block National Front speakers; 'however,' it was explained, 'there is no debate envisaged this term to which such a speaker might be expected to make a relevant contribution.' His judicious handling of the issue may have been in recognition of his father's views on such speakers: when the National Front organiser Martin Webster was invited to a debate in Michaelmas 1981, Greville Janner, president of the Board of Deputies of British Jews, had led the opposition to the event. He called on his fellow MPs to boycott the Union, and the invitation was eventually dropped.[25]

The controversial historian David Irving visited the Union twice in the early '80s. In Easter 1980 he proposed the motion 'History is bunk', speaking opposite Simon Heffer and the Cambridge historians David Cannadine and Geoffrey Elton. They trounced him 284–42. Irving returned to the Union for a 'stormy visit' in January 1982, and does not seem to have been too impressed with his reception. The audience, he said, were 'on the one hand scrofulous pink-haired specimens from the Socialist Workers Party' and 'on the other, a sea of shining, characterless faces'. Later that year, he was banned from attending the Oxford Union.[26] Two weeks after Irving's visit another contentious guest – Nabil Ramlawi, the PLO's representative in London – came to a debate on Israel and Palestine. His invitation attracted much criticism, but the debate itself 'passed off without incident'.

The President who was compelled to rethink his invitation to the National Front organiser was Giles Kavanagh, now a leading aviation lawyer. He was President in Michaelmas 1981, the Union's 500th term. A celebratory feast was held at King's on 28 November with the ex-President and former Archbishop of Canterbury, Lord Ramsey, as guest of honour. Messages of congratulation were received from HM the Queen Mother, the Prime Minister and the Leader of the Opposition, and many others as diverse as Dr Henry Kissinger, Professor Milton Friedman, Norman St John-Stevas, Lord Snowdon and Arthur Scargill. It was decided to launch a fund-raising appeal to tie in with the celebrations, chaired by another ex-President, Sir Geoffrey de Freitas. In the end, because of Sir Geoffrey's ill health, the appeal was merely announced in Lord Ramsey's speech, with a formal launch to follow. The appeal had an inauspicious start: Roland Thompson, the former chief clerk, died on the day of the feast, and Sir Geoffrey died during the summer of 1982. Lady de Freitas kindly gave the Union £4,000 in a covenant, but the appeal had to be delayed. Letters were finally sent out to ex-Presidents in Easter 1983 signed by Lord Ramsey and Melanie McDonagh, President that term and now a leading Catholic journalist. A brochure was sent to 35,000 life members over the summer and had brought in £42,000 by the start of Michaelmas. By the following July, this had risen to £62,000 – but was still far short of the £250,000 it was hoped the appeal would raise.

It was also decided in Michaelmas 1981 that the Union should enter the World Debating Competition, a new tournament which had held its inaugural event earlier that year in Glasgow. The Union sent a team to Toronto for the following year's competition, but it was to be many years before Cambridge won its first world title – not until Stellenbosch in 2003, when Jack Anderson and Caleb Ward won 'probably the best and tightest final' in the competition's history.[27] An ex-President, Wu Meng Tan, was named best individual speaker at the same time; the following year, two former Union officers, Jeremy Brier and Alex Deane, won the competition for Middle Temple having both gone there after Cambridge to read for the Bar.

The Union was also in competitive mood when it arranged a re-enactment of the 1950 boat race against the Oxford Union. Thirty years after the original contest, this time it was held in London over part of the University Boat Race course on the Thames. Jeremy Thorpe, a member of the original Oxford Union crew, started the race with the samurai sword Lord Mountbatten had given to Cambridge. The race lasted fifteen minutes and was followed by a champagne party – and the traditional ducking of the two Presidents, Charles Gallagher and Rupert Soames. In a sign of the changed times, however, it seems the evening dress worn by the rowers was not their own. One of the Oxford crew told a journalist: 'I do not think Moss Bros. will be too happy about this.' The Oxford team won – but then they had the advantage of the ex-President Colin Moynihan, who had just won a silver medal at the Moscow Olympics. He put their victory down to 'hard training, complete dedication, and the right university'. The race was held in aid of the RNLI – although Moynihan 'thought we might have to call them out to help us'.[28]

Two later races against the Oxford Union took place on dry land. In Lent 1981 British Leyland sponsored a 'Mini Metro Marathon', in which the teams competed for the best mileage per gallon. The teams set off from their respective Unions and met at the halfway mark, Woburn Abbey, where they were treated to lunch by the Marquess of Tavistock. The Oxford Union won, beating David Senior and Simon Baynes. A similar event was held in Michaelmas 1982, this time with Ford Sierras.

Andrew Lownie, President in Lent 1984, explored the possibility of a political career by contesting Monklands West in 1992. He was vice-chairman of the Conservative Group for Europe and proposed, for his retirement debate, 'This House has faith in the EEC and hopes for greater European unity' along with Shirley Williams and Roy Jenkins. On the other side of the debate, which was filmed by the BBC's *Newsnight* programme, were Teddy Taylor and Enoch Powell. Finding the Conservative party of the 1990s too Eurosceptic, Lownie dedicated himself to a literary career. He was helped on his way by the Union. John le Carré and his agent came to do a reading during Lownie's term: 'They were on the lookout for a junior agent and I was interested in going into publishing.'[29] He founded his own agency in 1988 and has written a number of books himself, including a biography of John Buchan (1995). His interest in espionage was evident from the forum on the Cambridge spies he organised during his Union term. He even secured an acceptance from Michael Straight, the former Union Vice-President who had recently published a memoir of his Communist activities, but he did not attend in the end.

Lownie's interest in intelligence history also led him to John Costello, a comprehensive school student who had been elected 'by the sheer force of his personality' as Secretary of the Union in Lent 1965.[30] Lownie became literary agent for Costello, a former television producer who had written a number of books on naval history, including successful studies of the Pacific War and Pearl Harbor. He had, says Lownie, a great ability to follow paper trails in archives, but it was hampered by 'a tendency to overplay the evidence he discovered' and a fondness for conspiracy theories.[31] He also had a taste for dramatic publicity stunts. When his book on Anthony Blunt, *Mask of Treachery*, was published in 1989, Costello took out a full-page advert in *The Times* depicting Margaret Thatcher reading the book with her hair standing on end. He also arranged a debate at the Union in October 1988: 'This House would keep an official secret'. He spoke against the motion, which was proposed by Lownie and the spy writer Nigel West. It was defeated by two votes. During the debate, Costello had the passages he had been asked to remove from his book under the Official Secrets Act printed on red paper and scattered from the balcony into the audience.[32] His later books – suggesting that Rudolph Hess was lured to Britain by MI5, and delving into the KGB archives behind the Cambridge spy ring – irked professional historians and the intelligence community alike. He found a loophole to access classified British documents by requesting American copies of them under the US Freedom of Information Act. When he died, aged 52, in the middle of a transatlantic flight, some thought it slightly mysterious.

Andrew Ground, President in Michaelmas 1987, chose a thoroughly modern career as a brand manager and strategy consultant. After a number of senior marketing roles at Sainsbury's, he became managing director of the subscription TV service Homeserve. He is now the UK director of the online DVD rental firm Love Film. Ground was a Conservative councillor for ten years in Hammersmith and Fulham; his successor as President of the Union, Stephen Greenhalgh, has been leader of the borough council since 2006. Following him in Easter 1988 was an Australian postgraduate. Chris Kelly came up to Trinity with glowing credentials: degrees in classics and law from the University of Sydney; a university medal for history and another for 'academic excellence and contribution to University life'. Having won the World Debating Championships in Edinburgh in 1984, it was little surprise that he made his way to the Union. His first debate was splendidly of its era: 'This House would nuke Sloane Square, ok yah'. During his time at Trinity Kelly also organised a re-enactment of the *Chariots of Fire* race around Great Court in aid of Great Ormond Street hospital. He won three prizes for his PhD and became a research fellow at Pembroke; he was senior tutor at Corpus between 2000 and 2004, and is still there as director of studies in classics. His final debate as President was on a fittingly classical theme: 'This House regrets the decline and fall of the Roman Empire'. Sir Geoffrey Elton, the Regius Professor of History, proposed the motion – but Frankie Howerd, star of *Up Pompeii!*, and *Private Eye* editor Ian Hislop ensured it was defeated 297–145.

Two Union officers in 1988 became successful businessmen. After Cambridge, Union Treasurer Simon Wolfson joined the retailer Next, where his father, Lord Wolfson of Sunningdale, was chairman. In 2001, at the age of 33, he became the company's chief executive – the youngest CEO of a FTSE 100 company at the time. He was one of two Cambridge teams to reach the play-offs at the World Debating Championships in 1989, and was named sixth best speaker overall. Kelly's Vice-President, Karan Bilimoria, was a Parsi Indian and mature student at Sidney Sussex who also rowed for the University and won a Blue for polo. On leaving Cambridge he founded Cobra Beer – the firm now has a turnover of well over £100 million. He was appointed CBE in 2004 and elevated to the House of Lords two years later; he sits there as a crossbencher, and is Chancellor of Thames Valley University.

Bilimoria was involved in a row with Kelly during his term. An emergency debate concerning Jean-Marie Le Pen, the ultra-nationalist politician who had just won 14 per cent of votes in the first round of the French presidential election, was scheduled for 3 May 1988, but cancelled at the last minute. Kelly explained why at standing committee the following day. Such 'offensive motions' should be stopped 'not only as a matter of principle but also to respond to the left['s] boycott', he said. 'Had the debate gone ahead COLS would have used it against the Society in Michaelmas.' Kelly referred to a statement of policy which had been drawn up by Martin Tod and amended by the later Presidents Ground and Greenhalgh, balancing the Union's commitment to freedom of speech with a desire to combat racism and sexism. Kelly asked for the standing committee's support in his decision and said 'he would reconsider his position as President' if it was not forthcoming. In fact, the issue escalated to a special MBM called for Friday 6 May. David Turner of Trinity proposed that 'The cancellation of the Emergency Debate on the motion: "This House believes that France needs Le Pen" is contrary to the principles of free debate upon which this Society was founded'. The meeting went on for nearly two hours, during which more than twenty people spoke. One of those to speak against the President's decision was Bilimoria, his own Vice-President. When the House finally divided, the motion was narrowly defeated 37–35, with five abstentions.

At a meeting of the standing committee later that afternoon, the matter was discussed again. Kelly said that since the motion had been defeated he would not be resigning. He was 'appalled' by the behaviour of those supporting the motion at the MBM and felt they were 'an unrepresentative rump and minority of Union members'. He was also 'bitterly disappointed with the behaviour of Standing Committee at Wednesday's meeting' for failing to back his policy.

Moreover, Kelly felt that in light of his support for the defeated motion Bilimoria should resign as Vice-President. Bilimoria, for his part, 'felt that the President was blackmailing the Committee and members into supporting him'. The situation was defused when, at Simon Wolfson's suggestion, standing committee passed a motion affirming its support for the policy statement.

The cancellation of the debate did not do much to appease COLS anyway: at a standing committee meeting later that month Kelly announced he had received a letter from them and that, although they congratulated him for cancelling the Le Pen debate, they were not prepared to improve relations with the Society. The chief clerk remarked that COLS would be satisfied with nothing less than the complete destruction of the Union. Bilimoria ran for President at the end of term, but was beaten by Piers Pressdee, the Secretary whom he had defeated for the vice-presidency the term before.

Pressdee, from St John's, was called to the Bar and is now a children's law specialist in Oxford. During his term, the Union was struck again by a fire. Thankfully, it was a much smaller one than in 1975 and, like the earlier conflagration, was discovered by Barry Thoday. 'It was a Sunday morning and I was walking out to buy my Sunday papers,' he recalls. 'I looked up, and there was smoke coming out of the library chimney.' Thoday ran over to St John's to wake Pressdee up and tell him what was going on: he remembers it well because when Pressdee answered the door 'he'd got a nightgown on and a nightcap'.[33] The cause of the fire was probably a discarded cigarette. The damage was restricted to the reception room at the end of the bar, which was gutted, some charring in the bar itself, and the library, the floor of which had been damaged. The cost of repairs was fully covered by insurance but, as a consequence, some of the more valuable books and archives were moved to the University Library. The fire also provided an opportunity to redecorate the bar, including the removal of its false ceiling. This was done over the summer of 1989.

A happier incident in Pressdee's term was the visit of King Hussein of Jordan, who accepted honorary membership of the

Union. Thoday's stock answer, whenever a President asked his opinion on a possible guest, was: 'Yes, it's worth a stamp'. This was his advice to Pressdee and it evidently paid off. It was also helped by the fact that His Majesty's nephew, Prince Ghazi bin Muhammad, was at Trinity at the time: the King and Queen came to pick him up at the end of term and 'jumbled two jobs together'.[34] Members were asked to cover their arms and wear full-length trousers or skirts for the packed meeting at the end of term.

Pressdee's successor, Anand Aithal, was an economist at Trinity and joined Goldman Sachs as a financial analyst. He became the bank's chief strategist in Asia and is now managing director of Amba, an investment research firm he co-founded. He did not seem so business-savvy as President, however. During his term, it was suggested that the Union invest in Sky TV for its members. Aithal told the standing committee that Sky 'was not very high quality' and said that the Union should 'wait to see how successful the channel was'. Many other Presidents of the decade, like Pressdee, went into the law. Julian Lloyd (Michaelmas 1983) is a barrister in Chester specialising in family law. Clive Blackwood (Easter 1985) resigned as chairman of CUCA after one of the association's regular election scandals; he was called to the commercial Bar the following year. David Walbank, his successor, was called a year later and specialises in the field of serious fraud. Graham Earles, President the following Michaelmas, is now a partner at Slaughter & May, while Chantal-Aimée Doerries (Easter 1989) is a commercial barrister specialising in construction. She studied at the University of Pennsylvania after Cambridge, was called to the Bar in 1992, and took silk in 2008. Cameron Robson of St John's (Lent 1990) established a solicitors' practice in Chester; his successor David Willink is a barrister at Lamb Chambers.

One lawyer who escaped from the Bar is Graham Davies (Lent 1984). He now makes a lucrative living as a professional after-dinner speaker. Describing himself as 'a recovering barrister with a silver tongue, a brass neck and a Platinum Amex card', Davies got his break from Nicholas Parsons, who remembered him from a Union debate. Unable to make a speaking engagement, Parsons recommended Davies as a last-minute replacement: 'Nobody had a clue who he was, or why he was there, but they loved his speech,' said the *Independent*. 'He realised there was a market for someone non-famous who could be funny.'[35]

The decade drew to a close with the Union's 175th anniversary in 1990. A party was held in March, with a disco in the cellars until 1.00 am and a band in the bar. The 'Cantab. Group' was set up in the same month. Intended as 'an association of old members of the Society in industry, commerce and politics', it aimed to keep alumni in touch with the Union's activities and assist with fundraising. An inaugural dinner for the group was held at the Savoy Hotel in October, but the turnout was disappointing. It had been hoped that up to 200 would come: in the end, it was less than half that number. A more successful endeavour was the Schools Debating Competition which was established that year. Still running on an annual basis, it has helped to promote debating in schools around the country, in both the state and private sectors.

The highlight of the anniversary celebrations, however, came at the end of Michaelmas Term, when Ronald Reagan addressed the Society. Martin Harris, the President that term, had written to him wishfully using the anniversary as a hook: '175 was not a terribly round number,' he admits, 'but we thought it had some cachet.'[36] It evidently worked: the Oxford Union had also extended an invitation, but Reagan chose to go to Cambridge instead. The visit was arranged for 5 December, the day after the Change of Officers debate – although Harris was clear that he would stay at the helm for the extra day.

The former President of the United States brought five security personnel with him, and sent an advance party to check out the building a few days beforehand. Members queued from early in the morning to get a good seat in the chamber; by the time he arrived, the queue stretched for nearly a quarter of a mile. There were some banners and protesters outside the building, but these were low-key and were 'subsumed by the enthusiasm for having him there'. When Reagan entered the chamber he was treated to 'a prolonged and enthusiastic standing ovation'.[37] The room was packed to the eaves, with the audience spilling over into the bar. Harris – now a diplomat whose career has taken him to Russia and Ukraine – welcomed the ex-President as a fitting guest for the end of this anniversary year. When the Union was founded in 1815, the world was being reshaped after the Napoleonic wars; now, the world was being reshaped again after the end of the cold war, thanks in no small part to the man who stood before the chamber today. Reagan spoke for 40 minutes before walking to a special lunch at St John's. His speech was covered by national and international media. Devotees of the 'Reagan gaffe' were eventually rewarded when he congratulated the Society on its '775th anniversary'.[38] But nothing could mar the generous tribute he paid the Union: 'For a century and three-quarters now you have passionately debated the issues of the day,' he said. 'Many of your members have gone on to positions of leadership in government and the professions.' Moreover, he continued, the Union stood for something deeply venerable:

> The free and open expression of ideas – and debate over these ideas – is a heritage that Britain has given all of us in the democratic world. It has been an integral process of the long evolution of representative democracy since the knights confronted King John at Runnymede. It is an essential part of the British spirit, seemingly ingrained in all of you. I think I hear it in the music of Benjamin Britten, Elgar and Handel. I read it in the poetry of Shakespeare, Donne and Milton and the prose of Dickens. The passion for free expression seems to permeate your culture just as it does your Union here.

The President also congratulated the Union on a project it was planning with Princeton to teach debating at universities 'in the lands that were once behind the Iron Curtain':

As you celebrate your 175th anniversary, nothing could be more fitting than to undertake a project such as this, taking the British spirit of freedom of expression into lands which have known so little of it in the past.

Concluding, he wished the Union 'year upon year of continued success and vigorous debate of issues yet unknown. It has been a pleasure and an honour to be with you today. Thank you and God bless you'.[39]

———

Two weeks before Reagan's visit, standing committee had met to discuss some necessary changes to the debating programme. 'The economics debate would go ahead,' it heard, 'but Norman Lamont and Nick Brown would be unable to attend because of the Prime Minister's resignation.' As the Union welcomed President Reagan to Cambridge, a new government was being formed. The new Cabinet included no fewer than five ex-Presidents of the Cambridge Union (and another four from Oxford). Here – with the Union celebrating its 175th year and another generation of its former officers reaching the top of the ladder – seems an appropriate time to end our account. Undoubtedly, the years since 1990 have produced many more who will go on to do the Union proud. But they are still climbing the rungs. As the Union approaches its third century, it has every reason to remain confident in the potential of its offspring, and the promise of its future.

Appendix I:

Officers of the Society, 1815–

Lord Thomas of Swynnerton: My Lords, a lifetime ago, it seems, I came up to London in the company of a distinguished Cambridge graduate, Percy Cradock ... He was just about to launch his publication on the history of the Cambridge Union. That admirable volume had as an appendix a list of ex-Presidents of the Cambridge Union and against some of them Percy Cradock had put an asterisk. I asked him the meaning of the asterisk, particularly as I was in the list as a President, but I did not have an asterisk. He said, 'Ah, you must realize, those who have asterisks are those who can be found in the Oxford *Dictionary of National Biography*'. We all aim for that. More important than the K, the G or the OBE, the asterisk for Percy Cradock was the centre of our ambitions.

House of Lords Hansard, *10 September 2004, Col. 880*

Lent 1815
President	*Mr E. Gambier, Trinity
Treasurer	*Lord Normanby, Trinity
Secretary	Hon. C.J. Shore, Trinity

Easter 1815
President	*Lord Normanby, Trinity
Treasurer	Hon. C.J. Shore, Trinity
Secretary	Mr G. Stainforth, Trinity

Michaelmas 1815
President	Hon. C.J. Shore, Trinity
Treasurer	Mr G. Stainforth, Trinity
Secretary	Mr E. Leycester, St John's

Lent 1816
President	Mr G. Stainforth, Trinity
Treasurer	Mr E. Leycester, St John's
Secretary	Mr R. Whitcombe, Trinity

Easter 1816
President   Mr E. Leycester, St John's
Treasurer   Mr R. Whitcombe, Trinity
Secretary   *Mr W. Whewell, Trinity

Michaelmas 1816
President   Mr R. Whitcombe, Trinity
Treasurer   *Mr W. Whewell, Trinity
Secretary   Mr W.G. Graham, Trinity

Lent 1817
President   *Mr W. Whewell, Trinity
Treasurer   *Mr H.J. Rose, Trinity
Secretary   *Mr C. Thirlwall, Trinity

Easter 1817
President   *Mr C. Thirlwall, Trinity
Treasurer   Mr C.B. Sheridan, Trinity
Secretary   ---

Michaelmas 1817
President   *Mr H.J. Rose, Trinity
Treasurer   Mr H. Waddington, Trinity
Secretary   Mr T. Thorp, Trinity

Lent 1818
President   Mr B.H. Malkin, Trinity
Treasurer   Mr T. Thorp, Trinity
Secretary   Mr T. Baines, Trinity

Easter 1818
President   Mr T. Thorp, Trinity
Treasurer   Mr T. Baines, Trinity
Secretary   Mr S. Hawkes, Trinity

Michaelmas 1818
President   Mr T. Baines, Trinity
Treasurer   *Mr T. Platt, Trinity
Secretary   Mr J. Fisher, Trinity

Lent 1819
President   *Mr T. Platt, Trinity
Treasurer   Mr S. Hawkes, Trinity
Secretary   Mr W.M. Praed, St John's

Easter 1819
President   Mr S. Hawkes, Trinity
Treasurer   Mr J. Cooper, Trinity
Secretary   Mr J. Cooper, Trinity

Michaelmas 1819
President   Mr J. Cooper, Trinity
Treasurer   Mr E.D. Rhodes, Sidney Sussex
Secretary   Mr J.D. Glennie, Trinity

Lent 1820
President   Mr E.D. Rhodes, Sidney Sussex
Treasurer   Mr J.D. Glennie, Trinity
Secretary   Mr E. Whiteley, Jesus

Easter 1820
President   Mr E. Whiteley, Jesus
Treasurer   Mr T. Sheepshanks, Trinity
Secretary   *Mr T.B. Macaulay, Trinity

Michaelmas 1820
President   Mr T. Sheepshanks, Trinity
Treasurer   *Mr E. Strutt, Trinity
Secretary   Mr J. Punnett, Clare

Lent 1821
President   *Mr E. Strutt, Trinity
Treasurer   Mr J. Punnett, Clare
Secretary   Mr J. Furnival, Queens'

Easter 1821
President   Mr J. Punnett, Clare
Treasurer   Mr J. Furnival, Queens'
Secretary   *Mr C. Austin, Jesus

Michaelmas 1821
President   Mr J. Furnival, Queens'
Treasurer   *Mr C. Austin, Jesus
Secretary   *Mr A. Stapleton, St John's

Lent 1822
President   *Mr C. Austin, Jesus
Treasurer   *Mr A. Stapleton, St John's
Secretary   *Mr T. H. Villiers, St John's

Easter 1822
President   *Mr C. P. Villiers, St John's
Treasurer   Mr W.H. Ord, Trinity
Secretary   Mr J.H. Pattisson, St John's

Michaelmas 1822
President   Mr W.H. Ord, Trinity
Treasurer   *Lord Howick, Trinity
Secretary   Mr W. Blunt, King's

Lent 1823
President   Mr W. Blunt, King's
Treasurer   *Mr T.B. Macaulay, Trinity
Secretary   Mr G.O. Townsend, King's

Easter 1823
President   Mr G.O. Townsend, King's
Treasurer   Mr R.C. Hildyard, St Catharine's
Secretary   *Mr W.M. Praed, Trinity

Michaelmas 1823
President   Mr J.J. Rawlinson, Trinity
Treasurer   *Mr W.M. Praed, Trinity
Secretary   Mr R. Steele, St John's

Lent 1824
President   Mr R.C. Hildyard,
               St Catharine's
Treasurer   *Mr A.J.E. Cockburn, Trinity
               Hall
Secretary   Mr J. Haughton, Pembroke

Easter 1824
President   *Mr A.J.E. Cockburn, Trinity
               Hall
Treasurer   Mr J. Haughton, Pembroke
Secretary   *Mr E.G.L. Bulwer, Trin. Hall

Michaelmas 1824
President   Mr J. Haughton, Pembroke
Treasurer   *Mr E.G.L. Bulwer, Trin. Hall
Secretary   *Mr E. Beales, Trinity

Lent 1825
President   Mr W.E. Tooke, Trinity
Treasurer   *Mr B.H. Kennedy, St John's
Secretary   Mr R.D. Boylan, Trinity

Easter 1825
President   *Mr B.H. Kennedy, St John's
Treasurer   Mr R.D. Boylan, Trinity
Secretary   Mr V. Vyvyan, Trinity

Michaelmas 1825
President   Mr J. Stock, Peterhouse
Treasurer   Mr J. Wilson, Trinity
Secretary   Mr E. Romilly, Christ's

Lent 1826
President   Mr J. Wilson, Trinity
Treasurer   Mr E. Romilly, Christ's
Secretary   Mr J.H. Smith, Corpus Christi

Easter 1826
President   Mr J.H. Smith, Corpus Christi
Treasurer   Mr R. Hutt, Trinity
Secretary   Mr C. Lillingston, Emmanuel

Michaelmas 1826
President   Mr C. Lillingston, Emmanuel
Treasurer   *Mr C. Buller, Trinity
Secretary   Mr J. Jordan, Clare

Lent 1827
President   *Mr C. Buller, Clare

Treasurer   *Mr J. Sterling, Trin. Hall
Secretary   *Mr J. Kemble, Trinity

Easter 1827
President   *Mr J. Sterling, Trin. Hall
Treasurer   Mr T. Sunderland, Trinity
Secretary   Mr J. Leigh, Trinity

Michaelmas 1827
President   *Mr S.H. Walpole, Trinity
Treasurer   Mr J. Leigh, Trinity
               *Mr R.C. Trench, Trinity
Secretary   Mr J.H. Cameron, Trinity
               Mr C. Templeton, Trinity

Lent 1828
President   *Mr J Kemble, Trinity
Treasurer   *Mr J.W. Blakesley, Corpus
Secretary   Mr H.H. Luscombe, Clare

Easter 1828
President   *Mr R.C. Trench, Trinity
Treasurer   Mr H.H. Luscombe, Clare
Secretary   *Mr J.P. Simpson, Corpus

Michaelmas 1828
President   Mr H.H. Luscombe, Clare
Treasurer   *Mr J.P. Simpson, Corpus
Secretary   Mr W.G. Ponsonby, Trinity

Lent 1829
President   *Mr J.W. Blakesley, Corpus
Treasurer   Mr C. Chapman, Corpus
Secretary   Mr P.H. Crutchley, Magd.

Easter 1829
President   Mr C. Chapman, Corpus
Treasurer   Mr P.H Crutchley, Magd.
Secretary   Mr H.P. Hope, Trin. Hall

Michaelmas 1829
President   Mr P.H. Crutchley, Magdalene
Treasurer   Mr H.P. Hope, Trin. Hall
Secretary   Mr H.W. Lloyd, Magdalene

Lent 1830
President   Mr L.S. Orde, Queens'
Treasurer   Mr C. Lloyd, Magdalene
Secretary   Mr J. Carne, Trinity

Easter 1830
President   Mr H. Matthew, Sidney Sussex
Treasurer   Mr J. Carne, Trinity
Secretary   *Mr H. Alford, Trinity

Michaelmas 1830

President	Mr L.S. Orde, Queens'[1]
Treasurer	*Mr H. Alford, Trinity
Secretary	*Mr W.H. Brookfield, Trinity

Lent 1831

President	Mr A.S. O'Brien, Trinity
Treasurer	*Mr W.H. Brookfield, Trinity
Secretary	Mr W. Bailey, Trinity

Easter 1831

President	Mr J.W.D. Dundas, Magdalene
Treasurer	Mr J.R. Gardiner, Trinity
Secretary	Mr R.G.L. Blenkinsopp, Trinity

Michaelmas 1831

President	*Mr W.H. Brookfield, Trinity
Treasurer	Mr R.G.L. Blenkinsopp, Trinity
Secretary	Mr R. Sale, St John's

Lent 1832

President	Mr C.R. Kennedy, Trinity
Treasurer	Mr R. Sale, St John's
Secretary	Mr R.A. Johnstone, Trinity

Easter 1832

President	*Mr H. Alford, Trinity
Treasurer	Mr R. A. Johnstone, Trinity
Secretary	Mr K. Macaulay, Jesus

Michaelmas 1832

President	Mr R.A. Johnstone, Trinity
Treasurer	Mr F.S. Williams, Trinity
Secretary	Mr W.F. Dobson, St John's

Lent 1833

President	Hon. C.W. Henniker, St John's
Treasurer	Mr W.F. Dobson, St John's
Secretary	Mr J.C. Walker, St John's
	Mr T.J. White, Magdalene

Easter 1833

President	Mr E. Warburton, Trinity
Treasurer	Mr T.J. White, Magdalene
Secretary	Mr B. Stocks, Trinity

Michaelmas 1833

President	Mr J.E. Heathcote, Trinity
Treasurer	Mr G. Ferguson, Trinity
Secretary	Mr C.G. Burke, Christ's

Lent 1834

President	*Mr W.H. Brookfield, Trinity[2]
	Hon. C.W. Henniker, St John's[3]
Treasurer	Mr T.J. White, Magdalene
Secretary	Mr C.G. Burke, Christ's

Easter 1834

President	Mr T.J. White, Magdalene
Treasurer	Mr C.G. Burke, Christ's
Secretary	Mr G.F. Townsend, Trinity

Michaelmas 1834

President	Mr C.G. Burke, Christ's
Treasurer	Mr G.F. Townsend, Trinity
Secretary	Mr W.A. Mackinnon, St John's

Lent 1835

President	Mr G.F. Townsend, Trinity
Treasurer	Mr W.A. Mackinnon, St John's
Secretary	Mr H.B. Jones, St John's

Easter 1835

President	Mr K. Macaulay, Jesus
Treasurer	Mr J.H. Timins, Trinity
Secretary	Mr H. Roberts, Magdalene

Michaelmas 1835

President	Mr W. A. Mackinnon, St John's
Treasurer	Mr H. Bullock, Christ's
Secretary	Mr S. Spranger, Trinity

Lent 1836

President	*Mr W.F. Pollock, Trinity
Treasurer	Mr J. Kirkpatrick, Trinity
Secretary	*Mr W.G. Romaine, Trinity

Easter 1836

President	Mr T. Spankie, Trinity
Treasurer	Mr H.R. Goldfinch, Trinity
Secretary	Mr W. Mackenzie, Trinity Hall

Michaelmas 1836

President	Mr H.R. Goldfinch, Trinity
Treasurer	Mr W. Mackenzie, Trinity Hall
Secretary	Mr J.A. Hardcastle, Trinity

Lent 1837

President	*Mr A. Baillie-Cochrane, Trinity
Treasurer	Mr C. Tower, St John's
Secretary	Mr R.N. Philipps, Christ's

---

[1] For the second time
[2] For the second time
[3] For the second time

Easter 1837

President	Mr A.J. Ellis, Trinity
Treasurer	Mr R.N. Philipps, Christ's
Secretary	Mr S. T. Bartlett, Clare

Michaelmas 1837

President	Mr R.N. Philipps, Christ's
Treasurer	Mr S.T. Bartlett, Clare
Secretary	*Mr J.G. Maitland, Trinity

Lent 1838

President	Mr J.C. Tindal, Trinity
Treasurer	*Mr R. Baggallay, Caius
Secretary	Mr E. Banbury, Trinity

Easter 1838

President	Sir J. Lighton, St John's
Treasurer	Mr H. White, Trinity
Secretary	*Mr W.J. Butler, Trinity

Michaelmas 1838

President	Mr S.T. Bartlett, Clare
Treasurer	Mr F. Thackeray, Caius
Secretary	Mr T. Frere, Trinity

Lent 1839

President	*Mr A.J.B. Hope, Trinity[4]
	*Mr J.W. Donaldson, Trinity
Treasurer	Mr C.J. Ellicott, St John's
Secretary	Mr B.H. Drury, Caius

Easter 1839

President	Mr C.J. Ellicott, St John's
Treasurer	Mr E.H.J. Craufurd, Trinity
Secretary	Mr P. Wright, Trinity

Michaelmas 1839

President	Mr E.H.J. Craufurd, Trinity
Treasurer	Mr A.S. Eddis, Trinity
Secretary	Mr J.A. Beaumont, Trinity

Lent 1840

President	Mr T.H. Bastard, Trinity
Treasurer	Mr J.W. Sherringham, St John's
Secretary	Mr W. Cunliffe Brookes, St John's

Easter 1840

President	Mr W. Werge, St John's
Treasurer	Mr J.A. Beaumont, Trinity
Secretary	Mr J.R. Stock, St John's

Michaelmas 1840

President	Mr J.A. Beaumont, Trinity
Treasurer	Mr J.R. Stock, St John's
Secretary	Mr M. Ware, Trinity

Lent 1841

President	Mr J.R. Stock, St John's
Treasurer	Mr W. Cunliffe Brookes, St John's
Secretary	Mr H.L. Young, Trinity

Easter 1841

President	Mr W. Cunliffe Brookes, St John's
Treasurer	Mr E. Rudge, St Catharine's
Secretary	Mr J. Slade, St John's

Michaelmas 1841

President	Mr T.H. Bullock, King's
Treasurer	Mr J. Slade, St John's
Secretary	Mr J. Hardcastle, Peterhouse

Lent 1842

President	Mr G. Crawshay, Trinity
Treasurer	Mr J. Hardcastle, Peterhouse
Secretary	Mr T.S. Western, Trinity

Easter 1842

President	Mr J. Hardcastle, Peterhouse
Treasurer	Mr A. Chisholm, St John's
Secretary	Mr H. Cox, Jesus

Michaelmas 1842

President	Mr T. S. Western, Trinity
Treasurer	Mr H. Cox, Jesus
Secretary	Mr J.C.H. Ogier, Trinity

Lent 1843

President	Mr F.W. Gibbs, Trinity
Treasurer	Mr J.C.H. Ogier, Trinity
Secretary	Mr G.W. King, Trinity

Easter 1843

President	Hon. F.S. Grimston, Magd.
Treasurer	Mr G.W. King, Trinity
Secretary	*Mr J. Kay, Trinity

Michaelmas 1843

President	Mr G.W. King, Trinity
Treasurer	Hon. A. Spring-Rice, Trinity
Secretary	Mr T.H. Tooke, Trinity

Lent 1844

President	Mr J.C.H. Ogier, Trinity
Treasurer	Mr T.H. Jones, Pembroke
Secretary	Mr J. Brame, St John's

[4] Resigned, 20 March 1839

Easter 1844

President	Mr W. Blake, Trinity
Treasurer	Mr E.F. Fiske, Emmanuel
Secretary	Mr A.B. Hemsworth, Pembroke

Michaelmas 1844

President	Mr E.F. Fiske, Emmanuel
Treasurer	Mr T.H. Tooke, Trinity
Secretary	Mr H. Lindsay, Trinity

Lent 1845

President	*Mr C. Babington, St John's
Treasurer	Mr J. Brame, St John's
Secretary	*Mr H.W. Thomson, Jesus

Easter 1845

President	Mr H. Lindsay, Trinity
Treasurer	*Mr H.W. Thomson, Jesus
Secretary	Mr T. Dealtry, Trinity

Michaelmas 1845

President	*Mr R.A. Cross, Trinity
Treasurer	*Mr H.W. Thomson, Jesus
Secretary	Mr T. Dealtry, Trinity

Lent 1846

President	Mr J.F. Baird, Trinity
Treasurer	Mr A. Garfit, Trinity
Secretary	Mr A. Codd, St John's

Easter 1846

President	Mr T. Dealtry, Trinity
Treasurer	Mr A. Garfit, Trinity
Secretary	*Mr J. Ll. Davies, Trinity

Michaelmas 1846

President	Mr A. Garfit, Trinity
Treasurer	*Mr J.Ll. Davies, Trinity
Secretary	*Mr D.J. Vaughan, Trinity

Lent 1847

President	Hon. W.F. Campbell, Trinity
Treasurer	*Mr J.Ll. Davies, Trinity
Secretary	Mr E. Prest, St John's

Easter 1847

President	*Mr J.Ll. Davies, Trinity
Treasurer	Mr E. Prest, St John's
Secretary	Mr A.A. VanSittart, Trinity

Michaelmas 1847

President	Mr A.A. VanSittart, Trinity
Treasurer	Mr A.G. Day, Gonville & Caius
	Mr R.H. Parr, Trinity
Secretary	*Mr J.F. Thrupp, Trinity

Lent 1848

President	Mr R.H. Parr, Trinity
Treasurer	*Mr J.F. Thrupp, Trinity
Secretary	Mr F.H. Colt, Trinity

Easter 1848

President	*Mr J.F. Thrupp, Trinity
Treasurer	Mr F.H. Colt, Trinity
Secretary	*Hon. A.C.H. Gordon, Trinity

Michaelmas 1848

President	Mr F.H. Colt, Trinity
Treasurer	*Hon. A.C.H. Gordon, Trinity
Secretary	Mr W. Finnie, Trinity

Lent 1849

President	*Hon. A.C.H. Gordon, Trinity
Treasurer	*Mr W.V. Harcourt, Trinity
Secretary	Mr A.H. Louis, Trinity

Easter 1849

President	*Mr W.V. Harcourt, Trinity
Treasurer	Mr A.H. Louis, Trinity
Secretary	Mr R. Temple, Trinity

Michaelmas 1849

President	*Mr J.Ll. Davies, Trinity
Treasurer	Mr A.H. Louis, Trinity
Secretary	Mr R.S. Lane, Caius

Lent 1850

President	Mr A.H. Louis, Trinity
Treasurer	Mr R. Temple, Trinity
Secretary	Mr R.S. Lane, Caius

Easter 1850

President	Mr R. Temple, Trinity
Treasurer	Mr R.S. Lane, Caius
Secretary	Mr H. Leach, Emmanuel

Michaelmas 1850

President	Mr R.S. Lane, Caius
Treasurer	Mr H. Leach, Emmanuel
Secretary	Mr S.P. Butler, Trinity

Lent 1851

President	Mr H. Leach, Emmanuel
Treasurer	Mr P. Laurence, Trinity
Secretary	*Mr H.A. Bright, Trinity

Easter 1851

President	Mr P. Laurence, Trinity
Treasurer	*Mr H.A. Bright, Trinity
Secretary	Mr R.J. Cust, Trinity

Michaelmas 1851

President	*Mr H.A. Bright, Trinity
Treasurer	Mr R.J. Cust, Trinity
Secretary	*Mr J. Payn, Trinity

Lent 1852

President	Mr R.J. Cust, Trinity
Treasurer	*Mr J. Payn, Trinity
Secretary	Mr R.J. Livingstone, Trinity

Easter 1852

President	*Mr J. Payn, Trinity
Treasurer	Mr R.J. Livingstone, Trinity
Secretary	*Mr A. Cohen, Magdalene

Michaelmas 1852

President	*Mr F.J.A. Hort, Trinity
Treasurer[5]	Mr S.P. Butler, Trinity
Secretary	Mr S. Gedge, Corpus Christi
Librarian	Mr V. Lushington, Trinity

Lent 1853

President	*Mr J. Lloyd, Trinity
Treasurer	Mr S.P. Butler, Trinity
Secretary	Mr V. Lushington, Trinity
Librarian	Mr J.W. Wilkins, Trinity Hall

Easter 1853

President	*Mr A. Cohen, Magdalene
Treasurer	Mr S.P. Butler, Trinity
Secretary	Mr J.W. Wilkins, Trinity
Librarian	*Mr E.J.S. Dicey, Trinity

Michaelmas 1853

President	*Mr E.J.S. Dicey, Trinity
Vice-President	Mr C.T. Swanston, Trinity
Treasurer	Mr A.G. Marten, St John's
Secretary	*Mr H.M. Butler, Trinity

Lent 1854

President	Mr C.T. Swanston, Trinity
Vice-President	Mr H.W. Elphinstone, Trinity
Treasurer	Mr A.G. Marten, St John's
Secretary	Mr G. Bulstrode, Emmanuel

Easter 1854

President	Mr H.W. Elphinstone, Trinity
Vice-President	Mr G. Bulstrode, Emmanuel
Treasurer	Mr A.G. Marten, St John's
Secretary	Mr C.S. Grubbe, Jesus

Michaelmas 1854

President	Mr V. Lushington, Trinity
Vice-President	Mr F. Kelly, Trinity

[5] From this date the office of Treasurer was made annual.

Treasurer	Mr A.G. Marten, St John's
Secretary	*Mr W.C. Gully, Trinity

Lent 1855

President	Mr F. Kelly, Trinity
Vice-President	*Mr W.C. Gully, Trinity
Treasurer	Mr A.G. Marten, St John's
Secretary	Mr H.E.F. Tracey, St John's

Easter 1855

President	*Mr W.C. Gully, Trinity
Vice-President	Mr H.E.F. Tracey, St John's
Treasurer	Mr A.G. Marten, St John's
Secretary	*Mr H. Fawcett, Trinity Hall

Michaelmas 1855

President	*Mr H.M. Butler, Trinity
Vice-President	Mr H.E.F. Tracey, St John's
Treasurer	*Mr J.E. Gorst, St John's
Secretary	Mr E. Latham, Trinity

Lent 1856

President	Mr W.D. Gardiner, Peterhouse
Vice-President	*Mr E.E. Bowen, Trinity
Treasurer	*Mr J.E. Gorst, St John's
Secretary	Mr E.H. Fisher, Trinity

Easter 1856

President	Mr J.W. Dunning, Trinity
Vice-President	Mr W.L. Heeley, Trinity
Treasurer	*Mr J.E. Gorst, St John's
Secretary	Mr C. Puller, Trinity

Michaelmas 1856

President	*Mr E.E. Bowen, Trinity
Vice-President	Mr E. Bell, Trinity
Treasurer	Mr T.M. Gilbert, Trinity
Secretary	*Mr W.S. Smith, Trinity

Lent 1857

President	Mr C. Puller, Trinity
Vice-President	Mr J.J. Lias, Emmanuel
Treasurer	Mr T.M. Gilbert, Trinity
Secretary	Mr C.A. Jones, St John's

Easter 1857

President	*Mr J.E. Gorst, St John's
Vice-President	Mr C.A. Jones, St John's
Treasurer	Mr T.M. Gilbert, Trinity
Secretary	Mr H.J. Matthew, Trinity

Michaelmas 1857

President	*Mr W.S. Smith, Trinity
Vice-President	*Mr R. O'Hara, Caius
Treasurer	*Mr C. Trotter, Trinity
Secretary	Mr B.H. Alford, Trinity

Lent 1858
President	Mr C.A. Jones, St John's
Vice-President	Mr J.M. Moorsom, Trinity
Treasurer	*Mr C. Trotter, Trinity
Secretary	*Sir G. Young, Bt., Trinity

Easter 1858
President	*Mr R. O'Hara, Caius
Vice-President	*Mr O. Browning, King's
Treasurer	*Mr C. Trotter, Trinity
Secretary	Mr W.S. Thomason, Trinity

Michaelmas 1858
President	Mr E.H. Fisher, Trinity
Vice-President	Mr J.J. Cowell, Trinity
Treasurer	Mr T.W. Beddome, Trinity
Secretary	*Mr G.O. Trevelyan, Trinity

Lent 1859
President	*Mr H.C. Raikes, Trinity
Vice-President	*Mr C. Trotter, Trinity
Treasurer	Mr T.W. Beddome, Trinity
Secretary	Mr E.T. Arden, Christ's

Easter 1859
President	*Mr O. Browning, King's
Vice-President	Mr A. Ainger, Trinity Hall
Treasurer	Mr T.W. Beddome, Trinity
Secretary	Mr H. Hanson, Trinity

Michaelmas 1859
President	Mr T.W. Beddome, Trinity
Vice-President	Mr F.E. Kitchener, Trinity
	Mr J. Salwey, Trinity
Treasurer	Mr F.Ll. Bagshawe, Trinity
Secretary	Mr C. Dalrymple, Trinity

Lent 1860
President	Mr C. Trotter, Trinity
Vice-President	Mr H. Geary, Corpus Christi
Treasurer	Mr F.Ll. Bagshawe, Trinity
Secretary	Mr D.M. Home, Trinity

Easter 1860
President	Mr H. Geary, Corpus Christi
Vice-President	Mr W.J. Laurance, Trinity
Treasurer	Mr F.Ll. Bagshawe, Trinity
Secretary	Mr W.M. Lane, Trinity

Michaelmas 1860
President	*Sir G. Young, Bt., Trinity
Vice-President	Mr C. Dalrymple, Trinity
Treasurer	*Mr A.H. Hill, Trinity Hall
Secretary	Mr R.F. Woodward, Trinity

Lent 1861
President	*Mr H. Sidgwick, Trinity
Vice-President	Mr W.M. Lane, Trinity
Treasurer	*Mr A.H. Hill, Trinity Hall
Secretary	Mr R.H. Wilson, Trinity

Easter 1861
President	Mr F.Ll. Bagshawe, Trinity
Vice-President	Mr G.A. Skinner, Trinity
Treasurer	*Mr A.H. Hill, Trinity Hall
Secretary	Mr W. Everett, Trinity

Michaelmas 1861
President	*Mr G.O. Trevelyan, Trinity
Vice-President	Mr W. Everett, Trinity
Treasurer	Mr M. Powell, Trinity
Secretary	Mr E.L. O'Malley, Trinity

Lent 1862
President	Mr W.M. Lane, Trinity
Vice-President	Mr E.L. O'Malley, Trinity
Treasurer	Mr M. Powell, Trinity
Secretary	Mr E.H. McNeile, Trinity

Easter 1862
President	Mr W.J. Laurance, Trinity
Vice-President	Mr A. Sidgwick, Trinity
Treasurer	Mr M. Powell, Trinity
Secretary	Mr H. Lee-Warner, St John's

Michaelmas 1862
President	Mr W. Everett, Trinity
Vice-President	Mr H. Lee-Warner, St John's
Treasurer	Mr A. Clowes, Trinity
Secretary	Mr R.D. Bennett, Trinity Hall

Lent 1863
President	Mr E.L. O'Malley, Trinity
Vice-President	Mr R.D. Bennett, Trinity Hall
Treasurer	Mr A. Clowes, Trinity
Secretary	Mr J.B. Payne, Downing

Easter 1863
President	Mr E.L. O'Malley, Trinity[6]
Vice-President	Mr W. Whitworth, Pembroke
Treasurer	Mr A. Clowes, Trinity
Secretary	Mr T. Beard, Jesus

Michaelmas 1863
President	Mr A. Sidgwick, Trinity
Vice-President	*Mr C.W. Dilke, Trinity Hall
Treasurer	Mr E.E.W. Kirkby, Trinity
Secretary	Mr A.G. Shiell, Peterhouse

[6] For the second time

Lent 1864

President	Mr R.D. Bennett, Trinity Hall
Vice-President	*Mr C.W. Dilke, Trinity Hall
Treasurer	Mr E.E.W. Kirkby, Trinity
Secretary	Mr H. Peto, Trinity

Easter 1864

President	*Mr H. Jackson, Trinity
Vice-President	Mr B.K. Woodd, Trinity
Treasurer	Mr E.E. W. Kirkby, Trinity
Secretary	Mr H.D. Jones, St John's

Michaelmas 1864

President	*Mr C.W. Dilke, Trinity Hall
Vice-President	Mr H. Peto, Trinity
Treasurer	Revd E.E.W. Kirkby, Trinity
Secretary	Mr J.R. Holland, Trinity

Lent 1865

President	Mr H. Peto, Trinity
Vice-President	Mr R.C. Greene, Trinity
Treasurer	Revd E.E.W. Kirkby, Trinity
Secretary	*Mr E.S. Shuckburgh, Emmanuel

Easter 1865

President	Mr J.R. Holland, Trinity
Vice-President	*Mr E.S. Shuckburgh, Emmanuel
Treasurer	Revd E.E.W. Kirkby, Trinity
Secretary	*Lord E. Fitzmaurice, Trinity

Michaelmas 1865

President	*Mr E.S. Shuckburgh, Emmanuel
Vice-President	*Lord E. Fitzmaurice, Trinity
Treasurer	Revd E.E.W. Kirkby, Trinity
Secretary	*Mr S. Colvin, Trinity

Lent 1866

President	*Mr C.W. Dilke, Trinity Hall[7]
Vice-President	Mr H.L. Anderton, Caius
Treasurer	Revd E.E.W. Kirkby, Trinity
Secretary	*Mr W.R. Kennedy, King's

Easter 1866

President	*Lord E. Fitzmaurice, Trinity
Vice-President	*Mr S. Colvin, Trinity
Treasurer	Revd E.E.W. Kirkby, Trinity
Secretary	Mr G.C. Whiteley, St John's

Michaelmas 1866

President	Mr H.L. Anderton, Caius
Vice-President	*Mr W.R. Kennedy, King's

[7] For the second time

Treasurer	Revd E.E.W. Kirkby, Trinity
Secretary	Mr W.A. Lindsay, Trinity

Lent 1867

President	*Mr W.R. Kennedy, King's
Vice-President	Mr G.C. Whiteley, St John's
Treasurer	Revd E.E.W. Kirkby, Trinity
Secretary	Mr H.A. Rigg, Trinity

Easter 1867

President	Mr W.A. Lindsay, Trinity
Vice-President	Mr F.T. Payne, Trinity Hall
Treasurer	Revd E.E.W. Kirkby, Trinity
Secretary	*Mr A.S. Wilkins, St John's

Michaelmas 1867

President	Mr G.C. Whiteley, St John's
Vice-President	*Mr A.S. Wilkins, St John's
Treasurer	Revd E.E.W. Kirkby, Trinity
Secretary	Mr E.A. Owen, Trinity

Lent 1868

President	*Mr A.S. Wilkins, St John's
Vice-President	*Mr J.F. Moulton, St John's
Treasurer	Revd E.E.W. Kirkby, Trinity
Secretary	*Mr W. Lee Warner, St John's

Easter 1868

President	*Mr J.F. Moulton, St John's
Vice-President	*Mr W.K. Clifford, Trinity
Treasurer	Revd E.E.W. Kirkby, Trinity
Secretary	Mr R.T. Wright, Christ's

Michaelmas 1868

President	Mr E.A. Owen, Trinity
Vice-President	Mr R.T. Wright, Christ's
Treasurer	Revd E.E.W. Kirkby, Trinity
Secretary	Mr J.E. Foster, Trinity

Lent 1869

President	Mr R.T. Wright, Christ's
Vice-President	Mr F. Watson, St John's
Treasurer	Revd E.E.W. Kirkby, Trinity
Secretary	Mr S. Leeke, Trinity

Easter 1869

President	Mr F. Watson, St John's
Vice-President	Mr S. Leeke, Trinity
Treasurer	Revd E.E.W. Kirkby, Trinity
Secretary	Mr J.D. Fitzgerald, Christ's

Michaelmas 1869

President	Mr J. Kennedy, King's
Vice-President	Mr I. Davis, Christ's
Treasurer	Mr J.E. Foster, Christ's
Secretary	Mr A. Foster, St John's

Lent 1870
President   Mr G. Warington, Caius
Vice-President Mr A. Foster, St John's
Treasurer   Mr J.E. Foster, Christ's
Secretary   Mr C.V. Childe, Corpus

Easter 1870
President   Mr A. Foster, St John's
Vice-President Mr J.E. Symes, Downing
Treasurer   Mr J.E. Foster, Christ's
Secretary   Mr J. De Soyres, Caius

Michaelmas 1870
President   Mr J.E. Symes, Downing
Vice-President Mr J. De Soyres, Caius
Treasurer   *Mr J.F. Moulton, Christ's
Secretary   Mr W.B. Odgers, Trinity Hall

Lent 1871
President   Mr W.B. Odgers, Trinity Hall
Vice-President Mr G.C.W. Warr, Trinity
Treasurer   *Mr J.F. Moulton, Christ's
Secretary   *Mr A.W. Dilke, Trinity Hall

Easter 1871
President   Mr J. De Soyres, Caius
Vice-President Mr W.F. MacMichael,
              Downing
Treasurer   *Mr J.F. Moulton, Christ's
Secretary   Mr C.G. Kellner, King's

Michaelmas 1871
President   Mr C.G. Kellner, King's
Vice-President *Mr A.W. Dilke, Trinity Hall
Treasurer   *Mr J.F. Moulton, Christ's
Secretary   *Mr W. Cunningham, Caius

Lent 1872
President   Mr W.F. MacMichael,
              Downing
Vice-President *Mr W. Cunningham, Caius
Treasurer,   *Mr J.F. Moulton, Christ's
Secretary   Mr W.J. Scott, Trinity

Easter 1872
President   *Mr W. Cunningham, Trinity
Vice-President Mr T.O. Harding, Trinity
Treasurer   *Mr J.F. Moulton, Christ's
Secretary   *Mr F.W. Maitland, Trinity

Michaelmas 1872
President   Mr T.O. Harding, Trinity
Vice-President Mr W.J. Scott, Trinity
Treasurer   *Mr J.F. Moulton, Christ's
Secretary   *Mr T.R. Warrington, Trinity

Lent 1873
President   *Mr F.W. Maitland, Trinity
Vice-President *Mr T.R. Warrington, Trinity
Treasurer   *Mr J.F. Moulton, Christ's
Secretary   *Mr A.W. Verrall, Trinity

Easter 1873
President   Mr W.J. Scott, Trinity
Vice-President *Mr A.W. Verrall, Trinity
Treasurer   *Mr J.F. Moulton, Christ's
Secretary   Mr F.J. Lowe, St John's

Michaelmas 1873
President   *Mr A.W. Verrall, Trinity
Vice-President Mr T.J. Lawrence, Downing
Treasurer   Mr R.T. Wright, Christ's
Secretary   Mr J.H.W. Torr, St John's

Lent 1874
President   *Mr C.S. Kenny, Downing
Vice-President Mr P.M. Laurence, Corpus
Treasurer   Mr R.T. Wright, Christ's
Secretary   *Mr W. Leaf, Trinity

Easter 1874
President   Mr P.M. Laurence, Corpus
Vice-President Mr G.H. Rendall, Trinity
Treasurer   Mr R.T. Wright, Christ's
Secretary   Mr R.W. Jameson, Trinity

Michaelmas 1874
President   Mr R.W. Jameson, Trinity
Vice-President Mr J.E.C. Munro, Downing
Treasurer   Mr R.T. Wright, Christ's
Secretary   Mr H.N. Martin, Christ's

Lent 1875
President   Mr J.E.C. Munro, Downing
Vice-President Mr H.N. Martin, Christ's
Treasurer   Mr R.T. Wright, Christ's
Secretary   Mr J.F. Skipper, St John's

Easter 1875
President   Mr H.N. Martin, Christ's
Vice-President Mr J.F. Skipper, St John's
Treasurer   Mr R.T. Wright, Christ's
Secretary   *Mr J.E.C. Welldon, King's

Michaelmas 1875
President   Mr J.F. Skipper, St John's
Vice-President Mr J.F. Little, Downing
Treasurer   Mr R.T. Wright, Christ's
Secretary   Hon. H.N. Waldegrave,
              Trinity

Lent 1876
President	*Mr J.E.C. Welldon, King's
Vice-President	Hon. H.N. Waldegrave, Trinity
Treasurer	Mr R.T. Wright, Christ's
Secretary	Mr R.C. Lehmann, Trinity

Easter 1876
President	Mr J.F. Little, Downing
Vice-President	Mr R.C. Lehmann, Trinity
Treasurer	Mr R.T. Wright, Christ's
Secretary	Mr J.F. Main, Trinity

Michaelmas 1876
President	Mr R.C. Lehmann, Trinity
Vice-President	Mr J.F. Main, Trinity
Treasurer	*Mr C.S. Kenny, Downing
Secretary	Mr A. Gwynne James, Trinity

Lent 1877
President	Hon. H.N. Waldegrave, Trinity
Vice-President	Revd A.G. Tweedie, *no college*
Treasurer	*Mr C.S. Kenny, Downing
Secretary	Mr T.D. Hart, Downing

Easter 1877
President	Mr J.F. Main, Trinity
Vice-President	Mr T.D. Hart, Downing
Treasurer	*Mr C.S. Kenny, Downing
Secretary	Mr W.B. Milton, Trinity

Michaelmas 1877
President	Revd A.G. Tweedie, Caius
Vice-President	Mr W.B. Milton, Trinity
Treasurer	*Mr C.S. Kenny, Downing
Secretary	Mr T.R. Hughes, Trinity

Lent 1878
President	Mr T.D. Hart, Downing
Vice-President	Mr T.R. Hughes, Trinity
Treasurer	*Mr C.S. Kenny, Downing
Secretary	Mr W.R. Phillips, Trinity Hall

Easter 1878
President	Mr W.B. Milton, Trinity
Vice-President	Mr E.J.C. Morton, St John's
Treasurer	*Mr C.S. Kenny, Downing
Secretary	Mr M. Reed, Trinity

Michaelmas 1878
President	Mr T.R. Hughes, Trinity
Vice-President	Mr F.P. Lefroy, Trinity
Treasurer	*Mr C.S. Kenny, Downing
Secretary	Hon. J.W. Mansfield, Trinity

Lent 1879
President	Mr E.J.C. Morton, St John's
Vice-President	Mr S. G. Ponsonby, Trinity
Treasurer	*Mr C.S. Kenny, Downing
Secretary	*Mr T.E. Scrutton, Trinity

Easter 1879
President	Mr F.P. Lefroy, Trinity
Vice-President	*Mr T.E. Scrutton, Trinity
Treasurer	*Mr C.S. Kenny, Downing
Secretary	*Mr J.P. Whitney, King's

Michaelmas 1879
President	Mr S.G. Ponsonby, Trinity
Vice-President	*Mr J.P. Whitney, King's
Treasurer	*Mr C.S. Kenny, Downing
Secretary	*Mr J.K. Stephen, King's

Lent 1880
President	*Mr T.E. Scrutton, Trinity
Vice-President	Mr E.V. Arnold, Trinity
Treasurer	*Mr C.S. Kenny, Downing
Secretary	*Mr J.W. Welsford, Caius

Easter 1880
President	*Mr J.P. Whitney, King's
Vice-President	*Mr J.K. Stephen, King's
Treasurer	*Mr C.S. Kenny, Downing
Secretary	*Mr A. Strachey, Trinity Hall

Michaelmas 1880
President	*Mr J.K. Stephen, King's
Vice-President	*Mr H. Cox, Jesus
Treasurer	*Mr C.S. Kenny, Downing
Secretary	Mr E.A. Parkyn, Christ's

Lent 1881
President	Mr N.C. Hardcastle, Downing
Vice-President	Mr E.A. Parkyn, Christs
Treasurer	*Mr C.S. Kenny, Downing
Secretary	Mr O. Rigby, St John's

Easter 1881
President	*Mr H. Cox, Jesus
Vice-President	Mr O. Rigby, St John's
Treasurer	*Mr C.S. Kenny, Downing
Secretary	Mr R. Temperley, Queens'

Michaelmas 1881
President	Mr E.A. Parkyn, Christ's
Vice-President	Mr T. Beck, Trinity
Treasurer	*Mr O. Browning, King's
Secretary	Mr J. Peiris, St John's

Lent 1882
President   Mr O. Rigby, St John's
Vice-President   Mr J. Peiris, St John's
Treasurer   *Mr O. Browning, King's
Secretary   Mr F.L. Lucas, Trinity

Easter 1882
President   Mr T. Beck, Trinity
Vice-President   Mr F.L. Lucas, Trinity
Treasurer   *Mr O. Browning, King's
Secretary   Mr H. F. B. Lynch, Trinity

Michaelmas 1882
President   Mr J. Peiris, St John's
Vice-President   *Mr J.R. Tanner, St John's
Treasurer   *Mr O. Browning, King's
Secretary   Mr G S.W. Jebb, Trinity

Lent 1883
President   Mr F.L. Lucas, Trinity
Vice-President   Mr G.S.W. Jebb, Trinity
Treasurer   *Mr O. Browning, King's
Secretary   Mr H. Harley, King's

Easter 1883
President   *Mr J.R. Tanner, St John's
Vice-President   Mr H. Harley, King's
Treasurer   *Mr O. Browning, King's
Secretary   Mr W. Blain, St John's

Michaelmas 1883
President   Mr G.S.W. Jebb, Trinity
Vice-President   Mr W. Blain, St John's
Treasurer   *Mr O. Browning, King's
Secretary   Mr W.H. Stables, Trinity

Lent 1884
President   Mr W. Blain, St John's
Vice-President   Mr W.H. Stables, Trinity
Treasurer   *Mr O. Browning, King's
Secretary   *Mr W.A. Raleigh, King's

Easter 1884
President   Mr W.H. Stables, Trinity
Vice-President   *Mr W.A. Raleigh, King's
Treasurer   *Mr O. Browning, King's
Secretary   *Mr E.A. Goulding, St John's

Michaelmas 1884
President   *Mr W.A. Raleigh, King's
Vice-President   *Mr E.A. Goulding, St John's
Treasurer   *Mr O. Browning, King's
Secretary   Hon. W.G. Scott, Trinity

Lent 1885
President   Hon. W.G. Scott, Trinity
Vice-President   *Mr J.A. Chamberlain,
                  Trinity
Treasurer   *Mr O. Browning, King's
Secretary   Mr J.T. Bell, Trinity Hall

Easter 1885
President   *Mr E.A. Goulding, St John's
Vice-President   Mr J.T. Bell, Trinity Hall
Treasurer   *Mr O. Browning, King's
Secretary   *Mr E.J. Griffith, Downing

Michaelmas 1885
President   Mr J.T. Bell, Trinity Hall
Vice-President   *Mr E.J. Griffith, Downing
Treasurer   *Mr O. Browning, King's
Librarian[8]   Mr J.D. Duff, Trinity
Secretary   *Mr L.J. Maxse, King's

Lent 1886
President   *Mr E.J. Griffith, Downing
Vice-President   *Mr L.J. Maxse, King's
Treasurer   *Mr O. Browning, King's
Librarian   *Mr M.R. James, King's
Secretary   Mr H. Boyd Carpenter,
                  King's

Easter 1886
President   *Mr L.J. Maxse, King's
Vice-President   Mr H. Boyd Carpenter,
                  King's
Treasurer   *Mr O. Browning, King's
Librarian   *Mr E. Jenks, King's
Secretary   *Mr W.H. Wilkins, Clare

Michaelmas 1886
President   Mr H. Boyd Carpenter,
                  King's
Vice-President   *Mr W.II. Wilkins, Clarc
Treasurer   *Mr O. Browning, King's
Librarian   *Revd J.H. Moulton, King's
Secretary   *Mr F.E. Garrett, Trinity

Lent 1887
President   Mr L.G.B.J. Ford, King's
Vice-President   *Mr F.E. Garrett, Trinity
Treasurer   *Mr O. Browning, King's
Librarian   *Revd J.H. Moulton, King's
Secretary   *G. Strickland, Trinity

[8] From this date the office of Librarian was made annual and was held by a resident Senior Member of the University.

Easter 1887
President   *Mr F.E. Garrett, Trinity
Vice-President   *G. Strickland, Trinity
Treasurer   *Mr O. Browning, King's
Librarian   *Revd J.H. Moulton, King's
Secretary   Mr G. Ince, Trinity

Michaelmas 1887
President   *G. Strickland, Trinity
Vice-President   Mr W.W. Grantham, Trinity
Treasurer   *Mr O. Browning, King's
Librarian   Mr W.G. Monkton, Trinity
Secretary   Mr R.R. Ottley, Trinity

Lent 1888
President   Mr W.W. Grantham, Trinity
Vice-President   Mr R.R. Ottley, Trinity
Treasurer   *Mr O. Browning, King's
Librarian   Mr W.G. Monkton, Trinity
Secretary   *Mr R.J. Wilkinson, Trinity

Easter 1888
President   Mr R.R. Ottley, Trinity
Vice-President   *Mr R.J. Wilkinson, Trinity
Treasurer   *Mr O. Browning, King's
Librarian   Mr W.G. Monkton, Trinity
Secretary   *Mr F.H. Maugham, Trin. Hall

Michaelmas 1888
President   *Mr R.J. Wilkinson, Trinity
Vice-President   *Mr F.H. Maugham, Trin. Hall
Treasurer   *Mr O. Browning, King's
Librarian   Mr N. Wedd, King's
Secretary   Mr C.H. Bompas, Trinity

Lent 1889
President   *Mr F.H. Maugham, Trin. Hall
Vice-President   Mr C.H. Bompas, Trinity
Treasurer   *Mr O. Browning, King's
Librarian   Mr N. Wedd, King's
Secretary   Revd E. Grose-Hodge, Trin. Hall

Easter 1889
President   Mr C.H. Bompas, Trinity
Vice-President   Revd E. Grose-Hodge, Trin. Hall
Treasurer   *Mr O. Browning, King's
Librarian   Mr N. Wedd, King's
Secretary   Mr W.E. Brunyate, Trinity

Michaelmas 1889
President   Revd E. Grose-Hodge, Trin. Hall
Vice-President   Mr W.E. Brunyate, Trinity
Treasurer   *Mr O. Browning, King's
Librarian   Mr W.G. Clay, Trinity
Secretary   Mr S.R.C. Bosanquet, Trinity

Lent 1890
President   Mr W.E. Brunyate, Trinity
Vice-President   Hon. M.M. Macnaghten, Trinity
Treasurer   *Mr O. Browning, King's
Librarian   Mr W.G. Clay, Trinity
Secretary   Mr S.R.C. Bosanquet, Trinity

Easter 1890
President   Hon. M.M. Macnaghten, Trinity
Vice-President   *Mr J.McT.E. McTaggart, Trinity
Treasurer   *Mr O. Browning, King's
Librarian   Mr W.G. Clay, Trinity
Secretary   Mr E.A. Newton, King's

Michaelmas 1890
President   *Mr J.McT.E. McTaggart, Trinity
Vice-President   Mr S.R.C. Bosanquet, Trinity
Treasurer   *Mr O. Browning, King's
Librarian   *Mr J.W. Headlam, King's
Secretary   *Mr E.W. MacBride, St John's

Lent 1891
President   Mr S.R.C. Bosanquet, Trinity
Vice-President   *Mr E.W. MacBride, St John's
Treasurer   *Mr O. Browning, King's
Librarian   *Mr J.W. Headlam, King's
Secretary   Mr R.F. Graham-Campbell, Trinity

Easter 1891
President   *Mr E.W. MacBride, St John's
Vice-President   Mr R.F. Graham-Campbell, Trinity
Treasurer   *Mr O. Browning, King's
Librarian   *Mr J.W. Headlam, King's
Secretary   Mr H.W.L. O'Rorke, Trinity

Michaelmas 1891
President   Mr R.F. Graham-Campbell, Trinity
Vice-President   Mr H.W.L. O'Rorke, Trinity
Treasurer   *Mr O. Browning, King's
Librarian   Mr C. Geake, Clare
Secretary   Mr A. Bertram, Caius

Lent 1892
President   Mr H.W.L. O'Rorke, Trinity
Vice-President   Mr A. Bertram, Caius
Treasurer   *Mr O. Browning, King's
Librarian   Mr C. Geake, Clare
Secretary   Mr G. Davidson Kempt, St John's

Easter 1892

President	Mr A. Bertram, Caius
Vice-President	Mr G. Davidson Kempt, St John's
Treasurer	*Mr O. Browning, King's
Librarian	Mr C. Geake, Clare
Secretary	Mr J.H.B. Masterman, St John's

Michaelmas 1892

President	Mr G. Davidson Kempt, St John's
Vice-President	Mr J.H.B. Masterman, St John's
Treasurer	*Mr O. Browning, King's
Librarian	Mr E.E. Sikes, St John's
Secretary	*Mr R. Carr Bosanquet, Trinity

Lent 1893

President	Mr J.H.B. Masterman, St John's
Vice-President	Mr P. Green, St John's
Treasurer	*Mr O. Browning, King's
Librarian	Mr E.E. Sikes, St John's
Secretary	Mr A.A. Jack, Peterhouse

Easter 1893

President	Mr P. Green, St John's
Vice-President	Mr A.A. Jack, Peterhouse
Treasurer	*Mr O. Browning, King's
Librarian	Mr E.E. Sikes, St John's
Secretary	Mr C. Fisher, Trinity

Michaelmas 1893

President	Mr A.A. Jack, Peterhouse
Vice-President	Mr C. Fisher, Trinity
Treasurer	*Mr O. Browning, King's
Librarian	*Mr W.H. Young, Peterhouse
Secretary	Mr F.G. Thomas, Sidney Sussex

Lent 1894

President	Mr C. Fisher, Trinity
Vice-President	Mr F.G. Thomas, Sidney Sussex
Treasurer	*Mr O. Browning, King's
Librarian	*Mr W.H. Young, Peterhouse
Secretary	*Mr F.B. Malim, Trinity

Easter 1894

President	Mr F.G. Thomas, Sidney Sussex
Vice-President	*Mr F.B. Malim, Trinity
Treasurer	*Mr O. Browning, King's
Librarian	*Mr W.H. Young, Peterhouse
Secretary	Mr W. Boyd Carpenter, Selwyn

Michaelmas 1894

President	*Mr F.B. Malim, Trinity
Vice-President	Mr W. Boyd Carpenter, Selwyn
Treasurer	*Mr O. Browning, King's
Librarian	*Mr J.McT.E. McTaggart, Trinity
Secretary	Mr J. Tait Wardlaw, King's
	Mr J.P. Thompson, Trinity

Lent 1895

President	Mr J.P. Thompson, Trinity
Vice-President	*Mr M.S.D. Butler, Pembroke
Treasurer	*Mr O. Browning, King's
Librarian	*Mr J.McT.E. McTaggart, Trinity
Secretary	Mr D. Shearme, Trinity

Easter 1895

President	*Mr M.S.D. Butler, Pembroke
Vice-President	Mr L. Stuyvesant Chanler, Trinity
Treasurer	*Mr O. Browning, King's
Librarian	*Mr J.McT.E. McTaggart, Trinity
Secretary	Mr D. Shearme, Trinity

Michaelmas 1895

President	Mr L. Stuyvesant Chanler, Trinity
	Mr D. Shearme, Trinity
Vice-President	Mr D. Shearme, Trinity
	*Mr C.F.G. Masterman, Christ's
Treasurer	*Mr O. Browning, King's
Librarian	Mr StJ.B. Wynne-Wilson, St John's
Secretary	*Mr C.F.G. Masterman, Christ's
	Mr P.W. Wilson, Clare

Lent 1896

President	*Mr C.F.G. Masterman, Christ's
Vice-President	Mr P.W. Wilson, Clare
Treasurer	*Mr O. Browning, King's
Librarian	Mr StJ.B. Wynne-Wilson, St John's
Secretary	*Mr F.W. Lawrence, Trinity

Easter 1896

President	Mr P.W. Wilson, Clare
Vice-President	*Mr F.W. Lawrence, Trinity
Treasurer	*Mr O. Browning, King's
Librarian	Mr StJ.B. Wynne-Wilson, St John's
Secretary	Mr A.F. Butler, Pembroke

Michaelmas 1896

President	*Mr F.W. Lawrence, Trinity
Vice-President	Mr A.F. Butler, Pembroke
Treasurer	*Mr O. Browning, King's
Librarian	Mr J.F. Leaf, Peterhouse
Secretary	Mr C.R. Buxton, Trinity

Lent 1897

President	Mr A.F. Butler, Pembroke
Vice-President	Mr C.R. Buxton, Trinity
Treasurer	*Mr O. Browning, King's
Librarian	Mr J.F. Leaf, Peterhouse
Secretary	*Mr E.W. Barnes, Trinity

Easter 1897

President	Mr C.R. Buxton, Trinity
Vice-President	*Mr E.W. Barnes, Trinity
Treasurer	*Mr O. Browning, King's
Librarian	Mr J.F. Leaf, Peterhouse
Secretary	Mr T.F.R. McDonnell, St John's

Michaelmas 1897

President	Mr E.W. Barnes, Trinity
Vice-President	Mr T.F.R. McDonnell, St John's
Treasurer	*Mr O. Browning, King's
Librarian	Mr J.F. Leaf, Peterhouse
Secretary	Mr W. Craig Henderson, Trinity

Lent 1898

President	Mr W. Craig Henderson, Trinity
	Mr N.C. Home, Trin. Hall
Vice-President	Mr N.C. Home, Trin. Hall
	*Mr W. Finlay, Trinity
Treasurer	*Mr O. Browning, King's
Librarian	Mr J.F. Leaf, Peterhouse
Secretary	*Mr W. Finlay, Trinity
	Mr B.N. Langdon-Davies, Pembroke

Easter 1898

President	*Mr W. Finlay, Trinity
Vice-President	Mr B.N. Langdon-Davies, Pembroke
Treasurer	*Mr O. Browning, King's
Librarian	Mr J.F. Leaf, Peterhouse
Secretary	Mr T.F.R. McDonnell, St John's

Michaelmas 1898

President	Mr B.N. Langdon-Davies, Pembroke

Vice-President	Mr T.F.R. McDonnell, St John's
Treasurer	*Mr O. Browning, King's
Librarian	Mr A. Brand, Pembroke
Secretary	Mr J.R.P. Sclater, Emmanuel

Lent 1899

President	Mr T.F.R. McDonnell, St John's
Vice-President	Mr J.R.P. Sclater, Emmanuel
Treasurer	*Mr O. Browning, King's
Librarian	Mr A. Brand, Pembroke
Secretary	Mr C. E. Guiterman, Trinity

Easter 1899

President	Mr J.R.P. Sclater, Emmanuel
Vice-President	Mr C.E. Guiterman, Trinity
Treasurer	*Mr O. Browning, King's
Librarian	Mr A. Brand, Pembroke
Secretary	Mr E.W.G. Masterman, St John's

Michaelmas 1899

President	Mr C.E. Guiterman, Trinity
	Mr E.W.G. Masterman, St John's
Vice-President	Mr E.W.G. Masterman, St John's
	*Mr A.C. Pigou, King's
Treasurer	*Mr O. Browning, King's
Librarian	Mr W.E. Jordan, King's
Secretary	*Mr A.C. Pigou, King's
	Mr G.F.S. Bowles, Trinity

Lent 1900

President	*Mr A.C. Pigou, King's
Vice-President	Mr G.F.S. Bowles, Trinity
Treasurer	*Mr O. Browning, King's
Librarian	Mr W.E. Jordan, King's
Secretary	*Mr E.H. Young, Trinity

Easter 1900

President	Mr G.F.S. Bowles, Trinity
Vice-President	*Mr E.H. Young, Trinity
Treasurer	*Mr O. Browning, King's
Librarian	Mr W.E. Jordan, King's
Secretary	*Mr G.C. Rankin, Trinity

Michaelmas 1900

President	*Mr E.H. Young, Trinity
Vice-President	*Mr G.C. Rankin, Trinity
Treasurer	*Mr O. Browning, King's
Librarian	Mr E.W. Barnes, Trinity
Secretary	Mr H.S. Van Zijl, St John's

Lent 1901

President	*Mr G.C. Rankin, Trinity
Vice-President	Mr H.S. Van Zijl, St John's
Treasurer	*Mr O. Browning, King's
Librarian	Mr E.W. Barnes, Trinity
Secretary	Mr F.W. Armstrong, St John's

Easter 1901

President	Mr H.S. Van Zijl, St John's
Vice-President	Mr F.W. Armstrong, St John's
Treasurer	*Mr O. Browning, King's
Librarian	Mr E.W. Barnes, Trinity
Secretary	Mr D.H. Macgregor, Trinity

Michaelmas 1901

President	Mr F.W. Armstrong, St John's
Vice-President	Mr D.H. Macgregor, Trinity
Treasurer	*Mr O. Browning, King's
Librarian	Mr R.V. Laurence, Trinity
Secretary	Mr P.B. Haigh, St John's

Lent 1902

President	Mr D.H. Macgregor, Trinity
Vice-President	Mr P.B. Haigh, St John's
Treasurer	*Mr O. Browning, King's
Librarian	Mr R.V. Laurence, Trinity
	*Mr J.McT.E. McTaggart, Trinity
Steward[9]	Mr E.J. Wyatt-Davies, Trinity
Secretary	*Mr E.S. Montagu, Trinity

Easter 1902

President	Mr P.B. Haigh, St John's
Vice-President	*Mr E.S. Montagu, Trinity
Treasurer	*Mr O. Browning, King's
Librarian	*Mr J.McT.E. McTaggart, Trinity
Steward	Mr E.J. Wyatt-Davies, Trinity
Secretary	Mr J.G. Gordon, Trinity

Michaelmas 1902

President	*Mr E.S. Montagu, Trinity
Vice-President	Mr J.G. Gordon, Trinity
Treasurer	*Mr J.R. Tanner, St John's
Librarian	Mr J.H.A. Hart, St John's
Steward	Mr R.V. Laurence, Trinity
Secretary	Mr J. Strachan, Clare

Lent 1903

President	Mr J.G. Gordon, Trinity
Vice-President	Mr J. Strachan, Clare

[9] From this date, a Steward was appointed as an annual officer, the office being held by a resident Senior Member of the University.

Treasurer	*Mr J.R. Tanner, St John's
Librarian	Mr J.H.A. Hart, St John's
Steward	Mr R.V. Laurence, Trinity
Secretary	Mr J.C. Arnold, St John's

Easter 1903

President	Mr J. Strachan, Clare
Vice-President	Mr J.C. Arnold, St John's
Treasurer	*Mr J.R. Tanner, St John's
Librarian	Mr J.H.A. Hart, St John's
Steward	Mr R.V. Laurence, Trinity
Secretary	Mr F.E. Bray, Trinity

Michaelmas 1903

President	Mr J.C. Arnold, St John's
Vice-President	Mr F.E. Bray, Trinity
Treasurer	*Mr J.R. Tanner, St John's
Librarian	Mr J.H.A. Hart, St John's
Steward	Mr R.V. Laurence, Trinity
Secretary	Mr M.F.J. McDonnell, St John's

Lent 1904

President	Mr F.E. Bray, Trinity
Vice-President	Mr M.F.J. McDonnell, St John's
Treasurer	*Mr J.R. Tanner, St John's
Librarian	Mr J.H.A. Hart, St John's
Steward	Mr R.V. Laurence, Trinity
Secretary	*Mr J.T. Sheppard, King's

Easter 1904

President	Mr M.F.J. McDonnell, St John's
Vice-President	*Mr J.T. Sheppard, St John's
Treasurer	*Mr J.R. Tanner, St John's
Librarian	Mr J.H.A. Hart, St John's
Steward	Mr R.V. Laurence, Trinity
Secretary	*Mr H.G. Wood, Jesus

Michaelmas 1904

President	*Mr J.T. Sheppard, King's
Vice-President	*Mr H.G. Wood, Jesus
Treasurer	*Mr J.R. Tanner, St John's
Librarian	Mr J.H.A. Hart, St John's
Steward	Mr R.V. Laurence, Trinity
Secretary	*Mr J.M. Keynes, King's

Lent 1905

President	*Mr H.G. Wood, Jesus
	*Mr J.M. Keynes, King's
Vice-President	*Mr J.M. Keynes, King's
	*Mr J.K. Mozley, Pembroke
Treasurer	*Mr J.R. Tanner, St John's

Librarian	Mr J.H.A. Hart, St John's
Steward	Mr R.V. Laurence, Trinity
Secretary	*Mr J.K. Mozley, Pembroke
	Mr H.W. Harris, St John's

Easter 1905

President	*Mr J.K. Mozley, Pembroke
Vice-President	Mr H.W. Harris, St John's
Treasurer	*Mr J.R. Tanner, St John's
Librarian	Mr J.H.A. Hart, St John's
Steward	Mr R.V. Laurence, Trinity
Secretary	Mr C.R. Reddy, St John's

Michaelmas 1905

President	Mr H.W. Harris, St John's
Vice-President	Mr H.L. Forsbrooke, Clare
	Mr C.R. Reddy, St John's
Treasurer	*Mr J.R. Tanner, St John's
Librarian	Mr G.F. Rogers, Caius
Steward	Mr R.V. Laurence, Trinity
Secretary	Mr S.J.M. Sampson, Trinity
	Mr A.C.O. Morgan, Trinity

Lent 1906

President	Mr S.J.M. Sampson, Trinity
Vice-President	Mr A.C.O. Morgan, Trinity
Treasurer	*Mr J.R. Tanner, St John's
Librarian	Mr G.F. Rogers, Caius
Steward	Mr R.V. Laurence, Trinity
Secretary	Mr A.P. Hughes-Gibb, Trinity

Easter 1906

President	Mr A.C.O. Morgan, Trinity
Vice-President	Mr A.P. Hughes-Gibb, Trinity
Treasurer	*Mr J.R. Tanner, St John's
Librarian	Mr G.F. Rogers, Caius
Steward	Mr R.V. Laurence, Trinity
Secretary	Mr H.A. Hollond, Trinity

Michaelmas 1906

President	Mr A.P. Hughes-Gibb, Trinity
	Mr H.A. Hollond, Trinity
Vice-President	Mr H.A. Hollond, Trinity
	Mr E.G. Selwyn, King's
Treasurer	*Mr J.R. Tanner, St John's
Librarian	Mr G.F. Rogers, Caius
Steward	*Mr N.R. Campbell, Trinity
Secretary	Mr E.G. Selwyn, King's
	Mr F.D. Livingstone, Peterhouse

Lent 1907

President	Mr E.G. Selwyn, King's
Vice-President	Mr F.D. Livingstone, Peterhouse
Treasurer	*Mr J.R. Tanner, St John's
Librarian	Mr G.F. Rogers, Caius
Steward	*Mr N.R. Campbell, Trinity
Secretary	Mr O.F. Grazebrook, Caius

Easter 1907

President	Mr F.D. Livingstone, Peterhouse
Vice-President	Mr O.F. Grazebrook, Caius
Treasurer	*Mr J.R. Tanner, St John's
Librarian	Mr G.F. Rogers, Caius
Steward	*Mr N.R. Campbell, Trinity
Secretary	Mr R.M. Pattison Muir, Caius

Michaelmas 1907

President	Mr O.F. Grazebrook, Caius
Vice-President	Mr R.M. Pattison Muir, Caius
Treasurer	*Mr J.R. Tanner, St John's
Librarian	Mr G.F. Rogers, Caius
Steward	*Mr W. Spens, Corpus Christi
Secretary	Mr W.G. Elmslie, Pembroke

Lent 1908

President	Mr R.M. Pattison Muir, Caius
Vice-President	Mr W.G. Elmslie, Pembroke
Treasurer	*Mr J.R. Tanner, St John's
Librarian	Mr G.F. Rogers, Caius
Steward	*Mr W. Spens, Corpus Christi
Secretary	Mr C. Bethell, Trinity

Easter 1908

President	Mr W.G. Elmslie, Pembroke
Vice-President	Mr C. Bethell, Trinity
Treasurer	*Mr J.R. Tanner, St John's
Librarian	Mr G.F. Rogers, Caius
Steward	*Mr W. Spens, Corpus Christi
Secretary	Mr E. Evans, Trinity Hall

Michaelmas 1908

President	Mr C. Bethell, Trinity
Vice-President	Mr E. Evans, Trinity Hall
Treasurer	*Mr J.R. Tanner, St John's
Librarian	Mr G.F. Rogers, Caius
Steward	*Mr W. Spens, Corpus Christi
Secretary	*Mr A.D. McNair, Caius

Lent 1909

President	Mr E. Evans, Trinity Hall
Vice-President	*Mr A.D. McNair, Caius
Treasurer	*Mr J.R. Tanner, St John's
Librarian	Mr G.F. Rogers, Caius
Steward	*Mr W. Spens, Corpus Christi
Secretary	Mr A. Ramsay, Caius

Easter 1909

President	*Mr A.D. McNair, Caius
Vice-President	Mr A. Ramsay, Caius
Treasurer	*Mr J.R. Tanner, St John's
Librarian	Mr G.F. Rogers, Caius
Steward	*Mr W. Spens, Corpus Christi
Secretary	*Mr J.R.M. Butler, Trinity

Michaelmas 1909

President	Mr A. Ramsay, Caius
Vice-President	*Mr J.R.M. Butler, Trinity
Treasurer	*Mr J.R. Tanner, St John's
Librarian	*Mr H.G. Wood, Jesus
Steward	*Mr W. Spens, Corpus Christi
Secretary	*Mr G.G.G. Butler, Trinity

Lent 1910

President	*Mr J.R.M. Butler, Trinity
Vice-President	*Mr G.G.G. Butler, Trinity
Treasurer	*Mr J.R. Tanner, St John's
Librarian	*Mr H.G. Wood, Jesus
Steward	*Mr W. Spens, Corpus Christi
Secretary	*Mr W.N. Birkett, Emmanuel

Easter 1910

President	*Mr G.G.G. Butler, Trinity
Vice-President	*Mr W.N. Birkett, Emmanuel
Treasurer	*Mr J.R. Tanner, St John's
Librarian	*Mr H.G. Wood, Jesus
Steward	*Mr W. Spens, Corpus Christi
Secretary	Mr H.P.W. Burton, St John's

Michaelmas 1910

President	*Mr W.N. Birkett, Emmanuel
Vice-President	Mr H.P.W. Burton, St John's
Treasurer	*Mr J.R. Tanner, St John's
Librarian	*Mr Z.N. Brooke, Caius
Steward	Mr E. Bullough, Caius
Secretary	Mr J.H. Allen, Jesus

Lent 1911

President	Mr H.P.W. Burton, St John's
Vice-President	Mr J.H. Allen, Jesus
Treasurer	*Mr J.R. Tanner, St John's
Librarian	*Mr Z.N. Brooke, Caius
Steward	Mr E. Bullough, Caius
Secretary	*Mr D.H. Robertson, Trinity

Easter 1911

President	Mr J.H. Allen, Jesus
Vice-President	*Mr D.H. Robertson, Trinity
Treasurer	*Mr J.R. Tanner, St John's
Librarian	*Mr Z.N. Brooke, Caius
Steward	Mr E. Bullough, Caius
Secretary	Mr K.F. Callaghan, Caius

Michaelmas 1911

President	*Mr D.H. Robertson, Trinity
Vice-President	Mr K.F. Callaghan, Caius
Treasurer	*Mr J.R. Tanner, St John's
Librarian	*Mr C.A. Elliott, Jesus
Steward	Mr E. Bullough, Caius
Secretary	Mr P.J. Baker, King's

Lent 1912

President	Mr K.F. Callaghan, Caius
Vice-President	Mr P.J. Baker, King's
Treasurer	*Mr J.R. Tanner, St John's
Librarian	*Mr C.A. Elliott, Jesus
Steward	Mr E. Bullough, Caius
Secretary	*Mr H.D. Henderson, Emmanuel

Easter 1912

President	*Mr P. J. Baker, King's
Vice-President	*Mr H.D. Henderson, Emmanuel
Treasurer	*Mr J.R. Tanner, St John's
Librarian	*Mr C.A. Elliott, Jesus
Steward	Mr E. Bullough, Caius
Secretary	Mr H. Wright, Pembroke

Michaelmas 1912

President	*Mr H.D. Henderson, Emmanuel
Vice-President	Mr H. Wright, Pembroke
Treasurer	*Mr J.R. Tanner, St John's
Librarian	*Mr Z.N. Brooke, Caius
Steward	Mr E. Bullough, Caius
Secretary	Mr H. Grose-Hodge, Pembroke

Lent 1913

President	Mr H. Wright, Pembroke
Vice-President	Mr H. Grose-Hodge, Pembroke
Treasurer	*Mr J.R. Tanner, St John's
Librarian	*Mr Z.N. Brooke, Caius
Steward	Mr E. Bullough, Caius
Secretary	Mr E.P. Smith, Caius

Easter 1913

President	Mr H. Grose-Hodge, Pembroke
Vice-President	Mr E.P. Smith, Caius
Treasurer	*Mr J.R. Tanner, St John's
Librarian	*Mr Z.N. Brooke, Caius
Steward	Mr E. Bullough, Caius
Secretary	Mr D.G. Rouquette, Sidney Sussex

Michaelmas 1913

President	Mr E.P. Smith, Caius
Vice-President	Mr D.G. Rouquette, Sidney Sussex
Treasurer	*Mr J.R. Tanner, St John's
Librarian	*Mr Z.N. Brooke, Caius
Steward	Mr E. Bullough, Caius
Secretary	Mr G.K.M. Butler, Trinity

Lent 1914

President	Mr D.G. Rouquette, Sidney Sussex
Vice-President	Mr G.K.M. Butler, Trinity
Treasurer	*Mr J.R. Tanner, St John's
Librarian	*Mr Z.N. Brooke, Caius
Steward	Mr E. Bullough, Caius
Secretary	Mr J.H.B. Nihill, Emmanuel

Easter 1914

President	Mr G.K.M. Butler, Trinity
Vice-President	Mr J.H.B. Nihill, Emmanuel
Treasurer	*Mr J.R. Tanner, St John's
Librarian	*Mr Z.N. Brooke, Caius
Steward	Mr E. Bullough, Caius
Secretary	Mr H.D. Barnard, Jesus

Michaelmas 1914

President	Mr J.H.B. Nihill, Emmanuel
Vice-President	Mr H.D. Barnard, Jesus
Treasurer	*Mr J.R. Tanner, St John's
Librarian	*Mr Z.N. Brooke, Caius
Steward	Mr E. Bullough, Caius
Secretary	Mr W.L. McNair, Caius

Lent 1915

President	Mr H.D. Barnard, Jesus
Vice-President	Mr H.I. Lloyd, Emmanuel
Treasurer	*Mr J. R. Tanner, St John's
Librarian	*Mr Z.N. Brooke, Caius
Steward	Mr E. Bullough, Caius
Secretary	Mr P. Vos, Caius
	Mr O.H. Hoexter, Emmanuel

Easter 1915

President	Mr H.I. Lloyd, Emmanuel
Vice-President	Mr O.H. Hoexter, Emmanuel
Treasurer	*Mr J.R. Tanner, St John's
Librarian	*Mr Z.N. Brooke, Caius
Steward	Mr E. Bullough, Caius
Secretary	Mr L.A.Abraham, Peterhouse

Michaelmas 1915

President	Mr O.H. Hoexter, Emmanuel
	Mr D.E. Oliver, Trinity Hall

Vice-President	Mr D.E. Oliver, Trinity Hall
	Mr W.H. Ramsbottom, Emmanuel
Treasurer	*Mr J.R. Tanner, St John's
	*Mr J.McT.E. McTaggart, Trinity
Librarian	Mr S.C. Roberts, Pembroke
	Mr B.G. Brown, Trinity
Steward	Mr E. Bullough, Caius
Secretary	*Mr J.W. Morris, Trinity Hall

Lent 1916

President	Mr W.H. Ramsbottom, Emmanuel
Vice-President	Mr F.O.C. Potter, Trinity Hall
Treasurer	*Mr J.McT.E. McTaggart, Trinity
Librarian	Mr B.G. Brown, Trinity
Steward	Mr E. Bullough, Caius
Secretary	Mr L. Harrison, Emmanuel

Easter 1916

President	Mr F.O.C. Potter, Trinity Hall
Vice-President	Mr L. Harrison, Emmanuel
Treasurer	*Mr J.McT.E. McTaggart, Trinity
Librarian	Mr B.G. Brown, Trinity
Steward	Mr E. Bullough, Caius
Secretary	Mr G.J. Paull, Trinity

It was resolved at a Private Business Meeting held on Monday 8 May 1916 to hold no elections for terminal officers in the Easter Term nor subsequently for the duration of the War, and that the functions of the Standing Committee be performed by the *ex officio* members of the Committee.

Ex officio members who carried on the business of the Society until the resumption of elections:

Chairman	*Revd J.K. Mozley, B.D., Pembroke
Treasurer	*Mr J.McT.E. McTaggart, Litt.D., Trinity
Librarian	Mr B.G. Brown, M.A., Trinity
Steward	Mr E. Bullough, M.A., Gonville & Caius

Easter 1919

President	Mr W.L. McNair, Caius
Vice-President	*Mr J.W. Morris, Trinity Hall
Treasurer	*Mr J.McT.E. McTaggart, Trinity
Librarian	Mr B.G. Brown, Trinity
Steward	Mr E. Bullough, Caius
Secretary	Mr C.D.B. Ellis, King's

Michaelmas 1919

President	*Mr J.W. Morris, Trinity Hall
Vice-President	*Mr G.H. Shakespeare, Emmanuel
Treasurer	*Mr J.McT.E. McTaggart, Trinity
Librarian	Mr B.G. Brown, Trinity
Steward	Mr E. Bullough, Caius
Secretary	Mr D.M. Reid, Emmanuel

Lent 1920

President	*Mr G.H. Shakespeare, Emmanuel
Vice-President	Mr D.M. Reid, Emmanuel
Treasurer	*Mr J.McT.E. McTaggart, Trinity
Librarian	Mr B.G. Brown, Trinity
Steward	Mr E. Bullough, Caius
Secretary	Mr L.A. Abraham, Peterhouse

Easter 1920

President	Mr D.M. Reid, Emmanuel
Vice-President	Mr L.A. Abraham, Peterhouse
Treasurer	*Mr J.McT.E. McTaggart, Trinity
Librarian	Mr B.G. Brown, Trinity
Steward	Mr E. Bullough, Caius
Secretary	Mr E.H.F. Morris, Christ's

Michaelmas 1920

President	Mr L.A. Abraham, Peterhouse
Vice-President	Mr E.H.F. Morris, Christ's
Treasurer	*Mr A.D. McNair, Caius
Librarian	Mr B.G. Brown, Trinity
Steward	Mr S.C. Roberts, Pembroke
Secretary	Mr G.G. Sharp, Fitz. House

Lent 1921

President	Mr E.H.F. Morris, Christ's
Vice-President	Mr G.G. Sharp, Fitz. House
Treasurer	*Mr A.D. McNair, Caius
Librarian	Mr B.G. Brown, Trinity
Steward	Mr S.C. Roberts, Pembroke
Secretary	Mr G.W. Theobald, Emmanuel

Easter 1921

President	Mr G.G. Sharp, Fitz. House
Vice-President	Mr G.W. Theobald, Emmanuel
Treasurer	*Mr A.D. McNair, Caius
Librarian	Mr B.G. Brown, Trinity
Steward	Mr S.C. Roberts, Pembroke
Secretary	*Mr W.D. Johnston, Christ's

Michaelmas 1921

President	Mr G.W. Theobald, Emmanuel
Vice-President	*Mr W.D. Johnston, Christ's
Treasurer	*Mr A.D. McNair, Caius
Librarian	Mr B.G. Brown, Trinity
Steward	Mr S.C. Roberts, Pembroke
Secretary	Mr R.E. Watson, St Catharine's

Lent 1922

President	*Mr W.D. Johnston, Christ's
Vice-President	Mr R.E. Watson, St Catharine's
Treasurer	*Mr A.D. McNair, Caius
Librarian	Mr B.G. Brown, Trinity
Steward	Mr S.C. Roberts, Pembroke
Secretary	Mr I. Macpherson, Trinity

Easter 1922

President	Mr R.E. Watson, St Catharine's
Vice-President	Mr I Macpherson, Trinity
Treasurer	*Mr A.D. McNair, Caius
Librarian	Mr B.G. Brown, Trinity
Steward	Mr S.C. Roberts, Pembroke
Secretary	Mr G.G. Phillips, Trinity

Michaelmas 1922

President	Mr I. Macpherson, Trinity
Vice-President	Mr G.G. Phillips, Trinity
Treasurer	*Mr A.D. McNair, Caius
Librarian	Mr A.L. Attwater, Pembroke
Steward	Mr S.C. Roberts, Pembroke Mr A.T. Bartholomew, Peterhouse
Secretary	Mr R. Northam, Queens'

Lent 1923

President	Mr G.G. Phillips, Trinity
Vice-President	Mr R. Northam, Queens'
Treasurer	*Mr A.D. McNair, Caius
Librarian	Mr A.L. Attwater, Pembroke
Steward	Mr A.T. Bartholomew, Peterhouse
Secretary	Mr R.H.L. Slater, Jesus

Easter 1923

President	Mr R. Northam, Queens'
Vice-President	Mr R.H.L. Slater, Jesus
Treasurer	*Mr A.D. McNair, Caius
Librarian	Mr A.L. Attwater, Pembroke
Steward	Mr A.T. Bartholomew, Peterhouse
Secretary	Mr S.V.T. Adams, King's

Michaelmas 1923

President	Mr R.H.L. Slater, Jesus
Vice-President	Mr S.V.T. Adams, King's
Treasurer	Mr A.L. Attwater, Pembroke
Librarian	Mr H.S. Bennett, Emmanuel

Steward	Mr A.T. Bartholomew, Peterhouse
Secretary	*Mr R. A. Butler, Pembroke

Lent 1924

President	Mr S.V.T. Adams, King's
Vice-President	*Mr R.A. Butler, Pembroke
Treasurer	Mr A.L. Attwater, Pembroke
Librarian	Mr H.S. Bennett, Emmanuel
Steward	Mr A.T. Bartholomew, Peterhouse
Secretary	Mr A.P. Marshall, Caius

Easter 1924

President	*Mr R.A. Butler, Pembroke
Vice-President	Mr A.P. Marshall, Caius
Treasurer	Mr A.L. Attwater, Pembroke
Librarian	Mr H.S. Bennett, Emmanuel
Steward	Mr A.T. Bartholomew, Peterhouse
Secretary	Mr G.W. Lloyd, Trinity

Michaelmas 1924

President	Mr A.P. Marshall, Caius
Vice-President	Mr G.W. Lloyd, Trinity
Treasurer	Mr A.L. Attwater, Pembroke
Librarian	Mr H.S. Bennett, Emmanuel
Steward	Mr A.T. Bartholomew, Peterhouse
Secretary	Mr J.W.G. Sparrow, Trin. Hall

Lent 1925

President	Mr G.W. Lloyd, Trinity
Vice-President	Mr J.W.G. Sparrow, Trin. Hall
Treasurer	Mr A.L. Attwater, Pembroke
Librarian	Mr H.S. Bennett, Emmanuel
Steward	Mr A.T. Bartholomew, Peterhouse
Secretary	Mr D.R. Hardman, Christ's

Easter 1925

President	Mr J.W.G. Sparrow, Trin. Hall
Vice-President	Mr D.R. Hardman, Christ's
Treasurer	Mr A.L. Attwater, Pembroke
Librarian	Mr H.S. Bennett, Emmanuel
Steward	Mr A.T. Bartholomew, Peterhouse
Secretary	*Mr A.M. Ramsey, Magdalene

Michaelmas 1925

President	Mr D.R. Hardman, Christ's
Vice-President	*Mr A.M. Ramsey, Magdalene
Treasurer	Mr A.L. Attwater, Pembroke

Librarian	Mr H.S. Bennett, Emmanuel
Steward	Mr A.T. Bartholomew, Peterhouse
Secretary	Mr H.G.G. Herklots, Trin. Hall

Lent 1926

President	*Mr A.M. Ramsey, Magdalene
Vice-President	Mr H.G.G. Herklots, Trin. Hall
Treasurer	Mr A.L. Attwater, Pembroke
Librarian	Mr H.S. Bennett, Emmanuel
Steward	Mr A.T. Bartholomew, Peterhouse
Secretary	*Mr P.A. Devlin, Christ's

Easter 1926

President	Mr H.G.G. Herklots, Trin. Hall
Vice-President	*Mr P.A. Devlin, Christ's
Treasurer	Mr A.L. Attwater, Pembroke
Librarian	Mr H.S. Bennett, Emmanuel
Steward	Mr A.T. Bartholomew, Peterhouse
Secretary	Mr A.L. Hutchinson, Christ's

Michaelmas 1926

President	*Mr P.A. Devlin, Christ's
Vice-President	Mr A.L. Hutchinson, Christ's
Treasurer	Mr A.L. Attwater, Pembroke
Librarian	Mr H.S. Bennett, Emmanuel
Steward	Mr A.T. Bartholomew, Peterhouse
Secretary	Mr M.A.B. King-Hamilton, Trinity Hall

Lent 1927

President	Mr A.L. Hutchinson, Christ's
Vice-President	Mr M.A.B. King-Hamilton, Trinity Hall
Treasurer	Mr A.L. Attwater, Pembroke
Librarian	Mr H.S. Bennett, Emmanuel
Steward	Mr A.T. Bartholomew, Peterhouse
Secretary	*Mr J.S.B. Lloyd, Magdalene

Easter 1927

President	Mr M.A.B. King-Hamilton, Trinity Hall
Vice-President	*Mr J.S.B. Lloyd, Magdalene
Treasurer	Mr A.L. Attwater, Pembroke
Librarian	Mr H.S. Bennett, Emmanuel
Steward	Mr A.T. Bartholomew, Peterhouse
Secretary	Mr H.L. Elvin, Trinity Hall

Michaelmas 1927

President	*Mr J.S.B. Lloyd, Magdalene
Vice-President	Mr H L. Elvin, Trinity Hall
Treasurer	Mr A.L. Attwater, Pembroke
Librarian	Mr H.S. Bennett, Emmanuel
Steward	Mr A.T. Bartholomew, Peterhouse
Secretary	Mr R.E. Stevenson, St John's

Lent 1928

President	Mr H.L. Elvin, Trinity Hall
Vice-President	Mr R.E. Stevenson, St John's
Treasurer	Mr A.L. Attwater, Pembroke
Librarian	Mr H.S. Bennett, Emmanuel
Steward	Mr A.T. Bartholomew, Peterhouse
Secretary	*Mr G. Crowther, Clare

Easter 1928

President	Mr R.E. Stevenson, St John's
Vice-President	*Mr G. Crowther, Clare
Treasurer	Mr A.L. Attwater, Pembroke
Librarian	Mr H.S. Bennett, Emmanuel
Steward	Mr A.T. Bartholomew, Peterhouse
Secretary	Mr J.G. Leathem, St John's

Michaelmas 1928

President	*Mr G. Crowther, Clare
Vice-President	Mr J.G. Leathem, St John's
Treasurer	Mr A.L. Attwater, Pembroke
Librarian	Mr H.S. Bennett, Emmanuel
Steward	Mr A.T. Bartholomew, Peterhouse
Secretary	*Mr H.M. Foot, St John's

Lent 1929

President	Mr J.G. Leathem, St John's
Vice-President	*Mr H.M. Foot, St John's
Treasurer	Mr A.L. Attwater, Pembroke
Librarian	Mr H.S. Bennett, Emmanuel
Steward	Mr A.T. Bartholomew, Peterhouse
Secretary	Lord Pentland, Trinity

Easter 1929

President	*Mr H.M. Foot, St John's
Vice-President	Lord Pentland, Trinity
Treasurer	Mr A.L. Attwater, Pembroke
Librarian	Mr H.S. Bennett, Emmanuel
Steward	Mr A.T. Bartholomew, Peterhouse
Secretary	Mr K. Adam, St John's

Michaelmas 1929

President	Lord Pentland, Trinity
Vice-President	Mr K. Adam, St John's
Treasurer	Mr A.L. Attwater, Pembroke
Librarian	Mr H.S. Bennett, Emmanuel
Steward	Mr H.A. Webb, Trinity
Secretary	*Mr C.W. Jenks, Caius

Lent 1930

President	Mr K. Adam, St John's
Vice-President	*Mr C.W. Jenks, Caius
Treasurer	Mr A.L. Attwater, Pembroke
Librarian	Mr H.S. Bennett, Emmanuel
Steward	Mr H.A. Webb, Trinity
Secretary	Mr L.J. Gamlin, Fitz. House

Easter 1930

President	*Mr C.W. Jenks, Caius
Vice-President	Mr L.J. Gamlin, Fitz. House
Treasurer	Mr A.L. Attwater, Pembroke
Librarian	Mr H.S. Bennett, Emmanuel
Steward	Mr H.A. Webb, Trinity
Secretary	Mr J.D.F. Green, Peterhouse

Michaelmas 1930

President	Mr L.J. Gamlin, Fitz. House
Vice-President	Mr J.D.F. Green, Peterhouse
Treasurer	Mr A.L. Attwater, Pembroke
Librarian	Mr H.S. Bennett, Emmanuel
Steward	Mr H.A. Webb, Trinity
Secretary	Mr K.W. Britton, Clare

Lent 1931

President	Mr J.D.F. Green, Peterhouse
Vice-President	Mr K.W. Britton, Clare
Treasurer	Mr A.L. Attwater, Pembroke
Librarian	Mr H.S. Bennett, Emmanuel
Steward	Mr H.A. Webb, Trinity
Secretary	*Mr F.E. Jones, Caius

Easter 1931

President	Mr K.W. Britton, Clare
Vice-President	*Mr F.E. Jones, Caius
Treasurer	Mr A.L. Attwater, Pembroke
Librarian	Mr H.S. Bennett, Emmanuel
Steward	Mr H.A. Webb, Trinity
Secretary	Mr A.H. Snell, Jesus

Michaelmas 1931

President	*Mr F.E. Jones, Caius
Vice-President	Mr A.H. Snell, Jesus
Treasurer	Mr A.L. Attwater, Pembroke
Librarian	Mr H.S. Bennett, Emmanuel
Steward	Mr H.A. Webb, Trinity
Secretary	Mr A.E. Holdsworth, Caius

Lent 1932

President	Mr A.H. Snell, Jesus
Vice-President	Mr A.E. Holdsworth, Caius
Treasurer	Mr A.L. Attwater, Pembroke
Librarian	Mr H.S. Bennett, Emmanuel
Steward	Mr H.A. Webb, Trinity
Secretary	Mr S.S. Dhavan, Emmanuel

Easter 1932

President	Mr A.E. Holdsworth, Caius
Vice-President	Mr S.S. Dhavan, Emmanuel
Treasurer	Mr A.L. Attwater, Pembroke
Librarian	Mr H.S. Bennett, Emmanuel
Steward	Mr H.A. Webb, Trinity
Secretary	Mr T.R. Leathem

Michaelmas 1932

President	Mr S.S. Dhavan, Emmanuel
Vice-President	Mr T.R. Leathem, St John's
Treasurer	Mr A.L. Attwater, Pembroke
Librarian	Mr H.S. Bennett, Emmanuel
Steward	Mr H.A. Webb, Trinity
Secretary	Mr M.L. Barkway, Queens'

Lent 1933

President	Mr T.R. Leathem, St John's
Vice-President	Mr M.L. Barkway, Queens'
Treasurer	Mr A.L. Attwater, Pembroke
Librarian	Mr H.S. Bennett, Emmanuel
Steward	Mr H.A. Webb, Trinity
Secretary	Mr T.A.W. Blackwell, Magd.

Easter 1933

President	Mr M.L. Barkway, Queens'
Vice-President	Mr T.A.W. Blackwell, Magd.
Treasurer	Mr A.L. Attwater, Pembroke
Librarian	Mr H.S. Bennett, Emmanuel
Steward	Mr H.A. Webb, Trinity
Secretary	*Mr S.B.R. Cooke, Caius

Michaelmas 1933

President	Mr T.A.W. Blackwell, Magd.
Vice-President	*Mr S.B.R. Cooke, Caius
Treasurer	Mr A.L. Attwater, Pembroke
Librarian	Mr H.S. Bennett, Emmanuel
Steward	Mr H.A. Webb, Trinity
Secretary	Mr G. de Freitas, Clare

Lent 1934

President	*Mr S.B.R. Cooke, Caius
Vice-President	Mr G. de Freitas, Clare
Treasurer	Mr A.L. Attwater, Pembroke
Librarian	Mr H.S. Bennett, Emmanuel
Steward	Mr H.A. Webb, Trinity
Secretary	Mr E.H. Evans, Caius

Easter 1934

President	Mr G. de Freitas, Clare
Vice-President	Mr E.H. Evans, Caius
Treasurer	Mr A.L. Attwater, Pembroke
Librarian	Mr H.S. Bennett, Emmanuel
Steward	Mr H.A. Webb, Trinity
Secretary	Count D.M. Tolstoy-Miloslavsky, Trinity

Michaelmas 1934

President	Mr E.H. Evans, Caius
Vice-President	Count D.M. Tolstoy-Miloslavsky, Trinity
Treasurer	Mr A.L. Attwater, Pembroke
Librarian	Mr H.S. Bennett, Emmanuel
Steward	Mr H.A. Webb, Trinity
Secretary	*Mr C.J.M. Alport, Pembroke

Lent 1935

President	Count D.M. Tolstoy-Miloslavsky, Trinity
Vice-President	*Mr C.J.M. Alport, Pembroke
Treasurer	Mr A.L. Attwater, Pembroke
Librarian	Mr H.S. Bennett, Emmanuel
Steward	Mr H.A. Webb, Trinity
Secretary	Mr A.W.G. Kean, Queens'

Easter 1935

President	*Mr C.J.M. Alport, Pembroke
Vice-President	Mr A.W.G. Kean, Queens'
Treasurer	Mr A.L. Attwater, Pembroke
Librarian	Mr H.S. Bennett, Emmanuel
Steward	Mr H.A. Webb, Trinity
Secretary	Mr C. Fletcher-Cooke, Peterhouse

Michaelmas 1935

President	Mr A.W.G. Kean, Queens'
Vice-President	Mr C. Fletcher Cooke, Peterhouse
Acting Treasurer	Mr H.S. Bennett, Emmanuel
Librarian	Mr H.S. Bennett, Emmanuel
Steward	Mr F.R.F. Scott, Magdalene
Secretary	Mr J.A. Dobbs, Trinity Hall

Lent 1936

President	Mr C. Fletcher-Cooke, Peterhouse
Vice-President	Mr J.A. Dobbs, Trinity Hall
Acting Treasurer	Mr H.S. Bennett, Emmanuel
Librarian	Mr H.S. Bennett, Emmanuel
Steward	Mr F.R.F. Scott, Magdalene
Secretary	Mr R.L. Miall, St John's

Easter 1936

President	Mr J.A. Dobbs, Trinity Hall
Vice-President	Mr R.L. Miall, St John's
Acting Treasurer	Mr H.S. Bennett, Emmanuel
Librarian	Mr H.S. Bennett, Emmanuel
Steward	Mr F.R.F. Scott, Magdalene
Secretary	Mr G.B. Croasdell, Pembroke

Michaelmas 1936

President	Mr R.L. Miall, St John's
Vice-President	Mr G.B. Croasdell, Pembroke
Treasurer	Mr H.S. Bennett, Emmanuel
Librarian	Mr H.L. Elvin, Trinity Hall
Steward	Mr F.R.F. Scott, Magdalene
Secretary	Mr R.V. Gibson, Caius

Lent 1937

President	Mr G.B. Croasdell, Pembroke
Vice-President	Mr R.V. Gibson, Caius
Treasurer	Mr H.S. Bennett, Emmanuel
Librarian	Mr H.L. Elvin, Trinity Hall
Steward	Mr F.R.F. Scott, Magdalene
Secretary	Mr M.W. Straight, Trinity

Easter 1937

President	Mr R.V. Gibson, Caius
Vice-President	Mr M.W. Straight, Trinity
Treasurer	Mr H.S. Bennett, Emmanuel
Librarian	Mr H.L. Elvin, Trinity Hall
Steward	Mr F.R.F. Scott, Magdalene
Secretary	Mr F. Singleton, Emmanuel

Michaelmas 1937

President	Mr F. Singleton, Emmanuel
Vice-President	Mr J.M. Simonds, Magdalene
Treasurer	Mr H.S. Bennett, Emmanuel
Librarian	Mr H.L. Elvin, Trinity Hall
Steward	Mr F.R.F. Scott, Magdalene
Secretary	Mr P.R. Noakes, Queens'

Lent 1938

President	Mr J.M. Simonds, Magdalene
Vice-President	Mr P.R. Noakes, Queens'
Treasurer	Mr H.S. Bennett, Emmanuel
Librarian	Mr H.L. Elvin, Trinity Hall
Steward	Mr F.R.F. Scott, Magdalene
Secretary	Mr S.M. Kumaramangalam, King's

Easter 1938

President	Mr P.R. Noakes, Queens'
Vice-President	Mr S.M. Kumaramangalam, King's
Treasurer	Mr H.S. Bennett, Emmanuel
Librarian	Mr H.L. Elvin, Trinity Hall

Steward	Mr F.R.F. Scott, Magdalene
Secretary	Hon. P.T.T. Butler, Trinity

Michaelmas 1938

President	Mr S. M. Kumaramangalam, King's
Vice-President	Hon. P.T.T. Butler, Trinity
Treasurer	Mr D.R. Hardman, Christ's
Librarian	Mr H.L. Elvin, Trinity Hall
Steward	Mr E.M. Wilson, Trinity
Secretary	Mr P.B. Hague, Emmanuel

Lent 1939

President	Hon. P.T.T. Butler, Trinity
Vice-President	Mr P.B. Hague, Emmanuel
Treasurer	Mr D.R. Hardman, Christ's
Librarian	Mr H.L. Elvin, Trinity Hall
Steward	Mr E.M. Wilson, Trinity
Secretary	Mr P.G.B. Keuneman, Pembroke

Easter 1939

President	Mr P.B. Hague, Emmanuel
Vice-President	Mr P.G.B. Keuneman, Pembroke
Treasurer	Mr D.R. Hardman, Christ's
Librarian	Mr H.L. Elvin, Trinity Hall
Steward	Mr E.M. Wilson, Trinity
Secretary	Mr E.H. Ades, Trinity

Michaelmas 1939

President	Mr P.G.B. Keuneman, Pembroke
Vice-President	Mr E.H. Ades, Trinity
Treasurer	Mr D.R. Hardman, Christ's
Librarian	Mr H.L. Elvin, Trinity Hall
Steward	Mr E.M. Wilson, Trinity
Secretary	Mr R.E.M. Le Goy, Caius

The election of officers was suspended and a Committee of Management appointed.

CHAIRMEN OF DEBATES:

Michaelmas 1939	Mr R.R. Pittam, Pembroke
Lent 1940	Mr G.L. Stewart, Fitz. House
Easter 1940	Mr J.R.A. Bottomley, Trinity
Michaelmas 1940	*Debates suspended*
Lent 1941	*Mr J. Maynard Smith, Trinity
Easter 1941	*Mr R. Williams, Trinity

358

Michaelmas 1941 *Debates suspended*

Lent 1942 ⎫
              ⎬ Mr H.B. Dunkerley, King's
Easter 1942 ⎭

Michaelmas 1942 Mr G.A. Leven, Trinity

Lent 1943 Mr R.S. Taylor,
St Catharine's

Easter 1943 Mr N.D. Sandelson, Trinity

Michaelmas 1943 Mr R.R. Feilden, Corpus

Lent 1944 Mr J.S.B. Butler, King's

Easter 1944 Mr C. Salmon, Trinity Hall

The election of officers was resumed.

Michaelmas 1944
President	Mr P. Goldman, Pembroke
Vice-President	Mr S. Clement Davies, Trinity Hall
Treasurer	Mr D.R. Hardman, Christ's
Librarian	Mr S. Smith, St Catharine's
Steward	Mr F.R. Salter, Magdalene
Secretary	Mr D.J.W. Coward, Trinity

Lent 1945
President	Mr S. Clement Davies, Trinity Hall
Vice-President	Mr D.J.W. Coward, Trinity
Treasurer	Mr D.R. Hardman, Christ's
Librarian	Mr S. Smith, St Catharine's
Steward	Mr F.R. Salter, Magdalene
Secretary	Mr M.P. Frankel, Peterhouse

Easter 1945
President	Mr D.J.W. Coward, Trinity
Vice-President	Mr M.P. Frankel, Peterhouse
Treasurer	Mr D.R. Hardman, Christ's
Librarian	Mr S. Smith, St Catharine's
Steward	Mr F.R. Salter, Magdalene
Secretary	Mr G.J. Carter, Magdalene

Michaelmas 1945
President	Mr M.P. Frankel, Peterhouse
Vice-President	Mr G.J. Carter, Magdalene
Treasurer	Mr D.R. Hardman, Christ's
Librarian	Mr S. Smith, St Catharine's
Steward	Mr F.R. Salter, Magdalene
Secretary	Mr W.J.E. Coventon, Magdalene

Lent 1946
President	Mr G.J. Carter, Magdalene
Vice-President	Mr W.J.E. Coventon, Magd.
Treasurer	Mr D.R. Hardman, Christ's
Librarian	Mr S. Smith, St Catharine's
Steward	Mr F.R. Salter, Magdalene
Secretary	Mr G.F. Boston, Clare

Easter 1946
President	Mr W.J.E. Coventon, Magd.
Vice-President	Mr G.F. Boston, Clare
Treasurer	Mr D.R. Hardman, Christ's
Librarian	Mr S. Smith, St Catharine's
Steward	Mr F.R. Salter, Magdalene
Secretary	Mr W.H.L. Richmond, Trinity

Michaelmas 1946
President	Mr G.F. Boston, Clare
Vice-President	Mr W.H.L. Richmond, Trinity
Treasurer	Mr D.R. Hardman, Christ's
Librarian	Mr S. Smith, St Catharine's
Steward	Mr F. R. Salter, Magdalene
Secretary	Mr I.S. Lloyd, King's

Lent 1947
President	Mr W.H.L. Richmond, Trinity
Vice-President	Mr I.S. Lloyd, King's
Treasurer	*Mr N.G.L. Hammond, Clare
Librarian	Mr S. Smith, St Catharine's
Steward	Mr F.R. Salter, Magdalene
Secretary	*Mr R.C. Mackworth-Young, King's

Easter 1947
President	Mr I.S. Lloyd, King's
Vice-President	*Mr R.C. Mackworth-Young, King's
Treasurer	*Mr N.G.L. Hammond, Clare
Librarian	Mr R.F. Bennett, Magdalene
Steward	Mr F.R. Salter, Magdalene
Secretary	Mr H.J.C. Berkeley, Pembroke

Michaelmas 1947
President	*Mr R.C. Mackworth-Young, King's
Vice-President	Mr H.J.C. Berkeley, Pembroke
Treasurer	*Mr N.G.L. Hammond, Clare
Librarian	Mr R.F. Bennett, Magdalene
Steward	Mr F.R. Salter, Magdalene
Secretary	Mr D.E.C. Price, Trinity

Lent 1948
President	Mr H.J.C. Berkeley, Pembroke
Vice-President	Mr D.E.C. Price, Trinity
Treasurer	*Mr N.G.L. Hammond, Clare

Librarian   Mr R.F. Bennett, Magdalene
Steward   Mr F.R. Salter, Magdalene
Secretary   Mr T.C. Hewlett, Magdalene

Easter 1948
President   Mr D.E.C. Price, Trinity
Vice-President   Mr T.C. Hewlett, Magdalene
Treasurer   *Mr N.G.L. Hammond, Clare
Librarian   Mr R.F. Bennett, Magdalene
Steward   Mr F.R. Salter, Magdalene
Secretary   Mr G.W. Pattison, St John's

Michaelmas 1948
President   Mr T.C. Hewlett, Magdalene
Vice-President   Mr G.W. Pattison, St John's
Treasurer   *Mr N.G.L. Hammond, Clare
Librarian   Mr R.F. Bennett, Magdalene
Steward   Mr F.R. Salter, Magdalene
Secretary   Mr D.K. Freeth, Trinity Hall

Lent 1949
President   Mr G.W. Pattison, St John's
Vice-President   Mr D.K. Freeth, Trinity Hall
Treasurer   *Mr N.G.L. Hammond, Clare
Librarian   Mr R.F. Bennett, Magdalene
Steward   Mr F.R. Salter, Magdalene
Secretary   Mr P. Cradock, St John's

Easter 1949
President   Mr P.C.M. Curtis-Bennett,
                    Christ's
Vice-President   Mr P. Cradock, St John's
Treasurer   *Mr N.G.L. Hammond, Clare
Librarian   Mr R.F. Bennett, Magdalene
Steward   Mr F.R. Salter, Magdalene
Secretary   Mr N.A.F. St John-Stevas,
                    Fitzwilliam House

Michaelmas 1949
President   Mr D.K. Freeth, Trinity Hall
Vice-President   Mr N.A.F. St John-Stevas,
                    Fitzwilliam House
Treasurer   *Mr N.G.L. Hammond, Clare
Librarian   Mr R.F. Bennett, Magdalene
Steward   Mr F.R. Salter, Magdalene
Secretary   Mr D.C.-H. Hirst, Trinity

Lent 1950
President   Mr P. Cradock, St John's
Vice-President   Mr D.C.-H. Hirst, Trinity
Treasurer   *Mr N.G.L. Hammond, Clare
Librarian   Mr R.F. Bennett, Magdalene
Steward   *Dr G.E. Daniel, St John's
Secretary   Mr R.G. Waterhouse, St John's

Easter 1950
President   Mr N.A.F. St John-Stevas,
                    Fitzwilliam House
Vice-President   Mr R.G. Waterhouse, St John's
Treasurer   *Mr N.G.L. Hammond, Clare
Librarian   Mr R.F. Bennett, Magdalene
Steward   *Dr G.E. Daniel, St John's
Secretary   Mr J. Ashley, Gonville & Caius

Michaelmas 1950
President   Mr R.G. Waterhouse, St John's
Vice-President   Mr J. Ashley, Gonville & Caius
Treasurer   *Mr N.G.L. Hammond, Clare
Librarian   Mr R.F. Bennett, Magdalene
Steward   *Dr GE. Daniel, St John's
Secretary   Mr G. Mathur, Magdalene

Lent 1951
President   Mr J. Ashley, Caius[10]
                    Mr G. Mathur, Magdalene
Vice-President   Mr D.G. Macmillan, Clare
Treasurer   *Mr N.G.L. Hammond, Clare
Librarian   Mr R.F. Bennett, Magdalene
Steward   *Dr G.E. Daniel, St John's
Secretary   Mr F.J. Williams, Trinity

Easter 1951
President   Mr D.G. Macmillan, Clare
Vice-President   Mr F.J. Williams, Trinity
Treasurer   *Mr N.G.L. Hammond, Clare
Librarian   Mr R.F. Bennett, Magdalene
Steward   *Dr G.E. Daniel, St John's
Secretary   Mr G.E. Janner, Trinity Hall

Michaelmas 1951
President   Mr F.J. Williams, Trinity
Vice-President   Mr G.E. Janner, Trinity Hall
Treasurer   Mr K. Scott, St John's
Librarian   Mr R.F. Bennett, Magdalene
Steward   *Dr G.E. Daniel, St John's
Secretary   Mr D.R. Hurd, Trinity

Lent 1952
President   Mr G.E. Janner, Trinity Hall
Vice-President   Mr D.R. Hurd, Trinity
Treasurer   Mr K. Scott, St John's
Librarian   Mr R.F. Bennett, Magdalene
Steward   *Dr G.E. Daniel, St John's
Secretary   Mr A.H. Sampson, Selwyn

Easter 1952
President   Mr D.R. Hurd, Trinity
Vice-President   Mr A.H. Sampson, Selwyn

[10] Resigned, 28 February 1951, to participate in the US debating tour.

Treasurer	Mr K. Scott, St John's
Librarian	Mr R.F. Bennett, Magdalene
Steward	*Dr G.E. Daniel, St John's
Secretary	Mr P.J. Mansfield, Pembroke

Michaelmas 1952
President	Mr A.H. Sampson, Selwyn
Vice-President	Mr P.J. Mansfield, Pembroke
Treasurer	Mr K. Scott, St John's
Librarian	Mr E.K. Bennett, Caius
Steward	*Dr G.E. Daniel, St John's
Secretary	Mr M.L. Hydleman, Downing

Lent 1953
President	Mr P.J. Mansfield, Pembroke
Vice-President	Mr I.J. McIntyre, St John's
Treasurer	Mr K. Scott, St John's
Librarian	Mr E.K. Bennett, Caius
Steward	*Dr G.E. Daniel, St John's
Secretary	Mr H.S. Thomas, Queens'

Easter 1953
President	Mr I.J. McIntyre, St John's
Vice-President	Mr H.S. Thomas, Queens'
Treasurer	Mr K. Scott, St John's
Librarian	Mr E.K. Bennett, Caius
Steward	*Dr G.E. Daniel, St John's
Secretary	Mr D. Mirfin, Magdalene

Michaelmas 1953
President	Mr H.S. Thomas, Queens'
Vice-President	Mr D. Mirfin, Madgdalene
Treasurer	Mr K. Scott, St John's
Librarian	Mr E.K. Bennett, Caius
Steward	*Dr G.E. Daniel, St John's
Secretary	Mr N.O. Tomalin, Trinity Hall

Lent 1954
President	Mr D. Mirfin, Magdalene
Vice-President	Mr N.O. Tomalin, Trinity Hall
Treasurer	Mr K. Scott, St John's
Librarian	Mr E.K. Bennett, Caius
Steward	*Dr G.E. Daniel, St John's
Secretary	Mr J.G.D. Shaw, St John's

Easter 1954
President	Mr N.O. Tomalin, Trinity Hall
Vice-President	Mr J.G.D. Shaw, St John's
Treasurer	Mr K. Scott, St John's
Librarian	Mr E. K. Bennett, Caius
Steward	*Dr G.E. Daniel, St John's
Secretary	Mr R.G. Moore, Trinity

Michaelmas 1954
President	Mr J.G.D. Shaw, St John's
Vice-President	Mr T. Dalyell, King's

Treasurer	Mr K. Scott, St John's
Librarian	Mr E.K. Bennett, Caius
Steward	*Dr G.E. Daniel, St John's
Secretary	Mr J.D. Waite, Corpus Christi

Lent 1955
President	Mr R.G. Moore, Trinity
Vice-President	Mr J.D. Waite, Corpus Christi
Treasurer	Mr K. Scott, St John's
Librarian	Mr E.K. Bennett, Caius
Steward	*Dr G.E. Daniel, St John's
Secretary	Mr J.N. Crichton-Miller, Pembroke

Easter 1955
President	Mr J.D. Waite, Corpus Christi
Vice-President	Mr J.N. Crichton-Miller, Pembroke
Treasurer	Mr K. Scott, St John's
Librarian	Mr E.K. Bennett, Caius
Steward	*Dr G.E. Daniel, St John's
Secretary	Mr K.W.J. Post, St John's

Michaelmas 1955
President	Mr J.N. Crichton-Miller, Pembroke
Vice-President	Mr M.D. Rosenhead, St John's
Treasurer	Mr K. Scott, St John's
Librarian	Mr E.K. Bennett, Caius
Steward	*Dr G.E. Daniel, St John's
Secretary	Mr I. Harland, Peterhouse

Lent 1956
President	Mr M.D. Rosenhead, St John's
Vice-President	Mr T.J.T. Metcalf, Downing
Treasurer	Mr K. Scott, St John's
Librarian	Mr E.K. Bennett, Caius
Steward	Mr J.R.Bambrough, St John's
Secretary	Mr R.F. Peierls, Caius

Easter 1956
President	Mr R.F. Peierls, Caius
Vice-President	Mr K.W. J. Post, St John's
Treasurer	Mr K. Scott, St John's
Librarian	Mr E.K. Bennett, Caius
Steward	Mr J.R. Bambrough, St John's
Secretary	Mr G.F. Bilson, Downing

Michaelmas 1956
President	Mr K.W.J. Post, St John's
Vice-President	Mr N.H. Marshall, St John's
Treasurer	Mr K. Scott, St John's
Librarian	Mr E.K. Bennett, Caius
Steward	Mr J.R. Bambrough, St John's
Secretary	Mr D.R. Fairbairn, Caius

Lent 1957

President	Mr N.H. Marshall, St John's
Vice-President	Mr D.R. Fairbairn, Caius
Treasurer	Mr K. Scott, St John's
Librarian	Mr E.K. Bennett, Caius
Steward	Mr J.R. Bambrough, St John's
Secretary	Mr K.G. MacInnes, Trinity

Easter 1957

President	Mr D.R. Fairbairn, Caius
Vice-President	Mr K.G. MacInnes, Trinity
Treasurer	Mr K. Scott, St John's
Librarian	Mr E.K. Bennett, Caius
Steward	Mr J.R. Bambrough, St John's
Secretary	Mr C.T. Norman-Butler, Trinity

Michaelmas 1957

President	Mr K.G. MacInnes, Trinity
Vice-President	Mr C.T. Norman-Butler, Trinity
Treasurer	Mr K. Scott, St John's
Librarian	Mr E.K. Bennett, Caius
Steward	Mr J.R. Bambrough, St John's
Secretary	Mr A. Iftikhar, St John's

Lent 1958

President	Mr C.T. Norman-Butler, Trinity
Vice-President	Mr A. Iftikhar, St John's
Treasurer	Mr K. Scott, St John's
Librarian	Mr E.K. Bennett, Caius
Steward	Mr J.R. Bambrough, St John's
Secretary	Mr J.H. Cockcroft, St John's

Easter 1958

President	Mr T.L. Higgins, Caius
Vice-President	Mr J.H. Cockcroft, St John's
Treasurer	Mr K. Scott, St John's
Librarian	Mr E.K. Bennett, Caius
Steward	Mr J.R. Bambrough, St John's
Secretary	Mr J.R. Warren Evans, Trinity

Michaelmas 1958

President	Mr J.H. Cockcroft, St John's
Vice-President	Hon. J.P.F.St L. Grenfell, King's
Treasurer	Mr K. Scott, St John's
Librarian	Dr J.H. Elliott, Trinity
Steward	Mr J.R. Bambrough, St John's
Secretary	Mr J.W.F. Nott, Trinity

Lent 1959

President	Hon. J.P.F.St L. Grenfell, King's
Vice-President	Mr J.W.F. Nott, Trinity
Treasurer	Mr K. Scott, St John's
Librarian	Dr J.H. Elliott, Trinity
Steward	Mr J.R. Bambrough, St John's
Secretary	Mr B. Walsh, Gonville & Caius

Easter 1959

President	Mr J.W.F. Nott, Trinity
Vice-President	Mr B. Walsh, Gonville & Caius
Treasurer	Mr K. Scott, St John's
Librarian	Dr J.H. Elliott, Trinity
Steward	Mr J.R. Bambrough, St John's
Secretary	Mr C.S. Tugendhat, Caius

Michaelmas 1959

President	Mr B. Walsh, Gonville & Caius
Vice-President	Mr C.S. Tugendhat, Caius
Treasurer	Mr K. Scott, St John's
Librarian	Dr J.H. Elliott, Trinity
Steward	Mr J.R. Bambrough, St John's
Secretary	Mr L. Brittan, Trinity

Lent 1960

President	Mr C.S. Tugendhat, Caius
Vice-President	Mr L. Brittan, Trinity
Treasurer	Mr K. Scott, St John's
Librarian	Dr J.H. Elliott, Trinity
Steward	Mr J.R. Bambrough, St John's
Secretary	Mr L.A.C.F. Giovene di Girasole, St Catharine's

Easter 1960

President	Mr L.A.C.F. Giovene di Girasole, St Catharine's
Vice-President	Mr D.A. Saunders, Trinity
Treasurer	Mr K. Scott, St John's
Librarian	Dr J.H. Elliott, Trinity
Steward	Mr J.R. Bambrough, St John's
Secretary	Mr A. Firth, Trinity

Michaelmas 1960

President	Mr L. Brittan, Trinity
Vice-President	Mr A. Firth, Trinity
Treasurer	Mr K. Scott, St John's
Librarian	Dr J.H. Elliott, Trinity
Steward	Mr J.R. Bambrough, St John's
Secretary	Mr A.C. Renfrew, St John's

Lent 1961

President	Mr A. Firth, Trinity
Vice-President	Mr A.C. Renfrew, St John's
Treasurer	Mr K. Scott, St John's
Librarian	Dr J.H. Elliott, Trinity
Steward	Mr J.R. Bambrough, St John's
Secretary	Mr P.G. Hancock, Emmanuel

Easter 1961

President	Mr A.C. Renfrew, St John's
Vice-President	Mr P.G. Hancock, Emmanuel
Treasurer	Mr K. Scott, St John's
Librarian	Dr J.H. Elliott, Trinity
Steward	Mr J.R. Bambrough, St John's
Secretary	Mr B.H. Pollitt, King's

Michaelmas 1961

President	Mr P.G. Hancock, Emmanuel
Vice-President	Mr B.H. Pollitt, King's
Treasurer	Mr K. Scott, St John's
Librarian	Dr J.H. Elliott, Trinity
Steward	Dr R.T.H. Redpath, Trinity
Secretary	Mr B.S. Augenbraun, St John's

Lent 1962

President	Mr J.S. Gummer, Selwyn
Vice-President	Mr J. M. Dunn, King's[11]
	Mr S. Rocksborough Smith, St John's
Treasurer	Mr K. Scott, St John's
Librarian	Dr J.H. Elliott, Trinity
Steward	Dr R.T.H. Redpath, Trinity
Secretary	Mr M. Howard, Peterhouse

Easter 1962

President	Mr M. Howard, Peterhouse
Vice-President	Mr S. Rocksborough Smith, St John's
Treasurer	Mr K. Scott, St John's
Librarian	Dr J.H. Elliott, Trinity
Steward	Dr R.T.H. Redpath, Trinity
Secretary	Mr W.I.C. Binnie, Pembroke

Michaelmas 1962

President	Mr B.H. Pollitt, King's
Vice-President	Mr W.I.C. Binnie, Pembroke
Treasurer	Mr K. Scott, St John's
Librarian	Dr J.H. Elliott, Trinity
Steward	Dr R.T.H. Redpath, Trinity
Secretary	Mr M.F. Cantley, St John's

Lent 1963

President	Mr W.I.C. Binnie, Pembroke
Vice-President	Mr K.H. Clarke, Gonville & Caius
Treasurer	Mr K. Scott, St John's
Librarian	Dr J.H. Elliott, Trinity
Steward	Dr R.T.H. Redpath, Trinity
Secretary	Mr S. Rocksborough Smith, St John's

[11] Resigned, 13 March 1962

Easter 1963

President	Mr K.H. Clarke, Caius
Vice-President	Mr C.M. Mason, Magdalene
Treasurer	Mr K. Scott, St John's
Librarian	Dr J.H. Elliott, Trinity
Steward	Dr R.T.H. Redpath, Trinity
Secretary	Mr M.S. Aiyar, Trinity Hall

Michaelmas 1963

President	Mr O. Weaver, Trinity
Vice-President	Mr A.J. Watson, Jesus
Treasurer	Mr K. Scott, St John's
Librarian	Dr J.H. Elliott, Trinity
Steward	Dr R.T.H. Redpath, Trinity
Secretary	Mr N.S.H. Lamont, Fitz.House

Lent 1964

President	Mr N.S.H. Lamont, Fitz.House
Vice-President	Mr J.C.H. Davies, Emmanuel
Treasurer	Mr K. Scott, St John's
Librarian	Dr J.H. Elliott, Trinity
Steward	Dr R.T.H. Redpath, Trinity
Secretary	Mr W. Treharne Jones, Selwyn

Easter 1964

President	Mr C.E. Lysaght, Christ's
Vice-President	Mr W. Treharne Jones, Selwyn
Treasurer	Mr K. Scott, St John's
Librarian	Dr J.H. Elliott, Trinity
Steward	Dr R.T.H. Redpath, Trinity
Secretary	Mr P.S. Fullerton, Caius

Michaelmas 1964

President	Mr J.C.H. Davies, Emmanuel
Vice-President	Mr P.S. Fullerton, Caius
Treasurer	Mr K. Scott, St John's
Librarian	Dr J.H. Elliott, Trinity
Steward	Dr R.T.H. Redpath, Trinity
Secretary	Mr J.V. Cable, Fitz. House

Lent 1965

President	Mr P.S. Fullerton, Caius
Vice-President	Mr J.V. Cable, Fitz. House
Treasurer	Mr K. Scott, St John's
Librarian	Dr J.H. Elliott, Trinity
Steward	Dr R.T.H. Redpath, Trinity
Secretary	Mr J.E. Costello, Fitz. House

Easter 1965

President	Mr J.V. Cable, Fitz. House
Vice-President	Miss S.J. Matheson, Girton
Treasurer	Mr K. Scott, St John's
Librarian	Dr J.H. Elliott, Trinity
Steward	Dr R.T.H. Redpath, Trinity
Secretary	Mr J.M.J. Burford, Emmanuel

Michaelmas 1965
President | Mr J.M.J. Burford, Emmanuel
Vice-President | Mr R.A. Perlman, St Catharine's
Treasurer | Mr K. Scott, St John's
Librarian | Dr R.M. Griffiths, Selwyn
Steward | Dr R.T.H. Redpath, Trinity
Secretary | Mr M.A. de Navarro, Trinity

Lent 1966
President | Mr R.A. Perlman, St Catharine's
Vice-President | Mr A.J. Vinson, Caius
Treasurer | Mr K. Scott, St John's
Librarian | Dr R.M. Griffiths, Selwyn
Steward | Dr R.T.H. Redpath, Trinity
Secretary | Mr B.P. Crossley, Trinity

Easter 1966
President | Mr A.J. Vinson, Caius
Vice-President | Mr B.P. Crossley, Trinity
Treasurer | Mr K. Scott, St John's
Librarian | Dr R.M. Griffiths, Selwyn
Steward | Dr R.T.H. Redpath, Trinity
Secretary | Mr M. Horowitz, Pembroke

Michaelmas 1966
President | Mr B.P. Crossley, Trinity
Vice-President | Mr M. Horowitz, Pembroke
Treasurer | Mr K. Scott, St John's
Librarian | Mr R.C. Trebilcock, Pembroke
Steward | Dr R.T.H. Redpath, Trinity
Secretary | Mr N.P.R. Wall, Trinity

Lent 1967
President | Mr M. Horowitz, Pembroke
Vice-President | Mr N.P.R. Wall, Trinity
Treasurer | Mr K. Scott, St John's
Librarian | Mr R.C. Trebilcock, Pembroke
Steward | Dr R.T.H. Redpath, Trinity
Secretary | Miss A. Mallalieu, Newnham

Easter 1967
President | Mr N.P.R. Wall, Trinity
Vice-President | Miss A. Mallalieu, Newnham
Treasurer | Mr K. Scott, St John's
Librarian | Mr R.C. Trebilcock, Pembroke
Steward | Dr R.T.H. Redpath, Trinity
Secretary | Mr I. Martin, Emmanuel

Michaelmas 1967
President | Miss A. Mallalieu, Newnham
Vice-President | Mr I. Martin, Emmanuel
Treasurer | Mr K. Scott, St John's

Librarian | Mr R.C. Trebilcock, Pembroke
Steward | Dr R.T.H. Redpath, Trinity
Secretary | Mr G.W. Martin, Magdalene

Lent 1968
President | Mr I. Martin, Emmanuel
Vice-President | Mr G.W. Martin, Magdalene
Treasurer | Mr K. Scott, St John's
Librarian | Mr R.C. Trebilcock, Pembroke
Steward | Dr R.T.H. Redpath, Trinity
Secretary | Mr K.W. Jarrold, Sidney Sussex

Easter 1968
President | Mr G.W. Martin, Magdalene
Vice-President | Mr K.W. Jarrold, Sidney Sussex
Treasurer | Mr K. Scott, St John's
Librarian | Mr R. C. Trebilcock, Pembroke
Steward | Dr R.T.H. Redpath, Trinity
Secretary | Mr P.J. Tyson-Cain, Downing

Michaelmas 1968
President | Mr K.W. Jarrold, Sidney Sussex
Vice-President | Mr P.J. Tyson-Cain, Downing
Treasurer | Mr K. Scott, St John's
Librarian | Mr R.C. Trebilcock, Pembroke
Steward | Dr R.T.H. Redpath, Trinity
Secretary | Miss H.V. Middleweek, Newnham

Lent 1969
President | Mr P.J. Tyson-Cain, Downing
Vice-President | Miss H.V. Middleweek, Newnham
Treasurer | Mr K. Scott, St John's
Librarian | Mr R.C. Trebilcock, Pembroke
Steward | Dr R.T.H. Redpath, Trinity
Secretary | Mr H.R.D. Anderson, Trinity

Easter 1969
President | Miss H.V. Middleweek, Newnham
Vice-President | Mr H.R.D. Anderson, Trinity
Treasurer | Mr K. Scott, St John's
Librarian | Mr R.C. Trebilcock, Pembroke
Steward | Dr R.T.H. Redpath, Trinity
Secretary | Mr R.K. Evans, Trinity Hall

Michaelmas 1969
President | Mr H.R.D. Anderson, Trinity
Vice-President | Mr R.K. Evans, Trinity Hall
Treasurer | Mr R.C. Andrew, Sidney Sussex
Librarian | Mr R.C. Trebilcock, Pembroke
Steward | Dr R.T.H. Redpath, Trinity
Secretary | Mr R. Dhavan, Emmanuel

Lent 1970

President	Mr R.K. Evans, Trinity Hall
Vice-President	Mr R. Dhavan, Emmanuel
Treasurer	Mr R.C. Andrew, Sidney Sussex
Librarian	Mr R.C. Trebilcock, Pembroke
Steward	Dr R.T.H. Redpath, Trinity
Secretary	Mr N.F. Stadlen, Trinity

Easter 1970

President	Mr R. Dhavan, Emmanuel
Vice-President	Mr N.F. Stadlen, Trinity
Treasurer	Mr R.C. Andrew, Sidney Sussex
Librarian	Mr R.C. Trebilcock, Pembroke
Steward	Dr R.T.H. Redpath, Trinity
Secretary	Mr P.L. Heslop, Christ's

Michaelmas 1970

President	Mr N.F. Stadlen, Trinity
Vice-President	Mr P.L. Heslop, Christ's
Treasurer	Mr R.C. Andrew, Sidney Sussex
Librarian	Mr R.C. Trebilcock, Pembroke
Steward	Mr G.W. Martin, Magdalene
Secretary	Mr R.M. Jackson, Jesus

Lent 1971

President	Mr P.L. Heslop, Christ's
Vice-President	Mr R.M. Jackson, Jesus
Treasurer	Mr R.C. Andrew, Sidney Sussex
Librarian	Mr R.C. Trebilcock, Pembroke
Steward	Mr G.W. Martin, Magdalene
Secretary	Miss A.-A. Stassinopoulos, Girton

Easter 1971

President	Mr R.M. Jackson, Jesus
Vice-President	Miss A.-A. Stassinopoulos, Girton
Treasurer	Mr R.C. Andrew, Sidney Sussex
Librarian	Mr R.C. Trebilcock, Pembroke
Steward	Mr G.W. Martin, Magdalene
Secretary	Mr D.J. Powell, St Catharine's

Michaelmas 1971

President	Miss A.-A. Stassinopoulos, Girton
Vice-President	Mr D. J. Powell, St Catharine's
Treasurer	Mr R.C. Andrew, Sidney Sussex
Librarian	Mr R.C. Trebilcock, Pembroke
Steward	Mr G.W. Martin, Magdalene
Secretary	Mr N.R. Davidson, Trinity

Lent 1972

President	Mr D.J. Powell, St Catharine's
Vice-President	Mr N.R. Davidson, Trinity
Treasurer	Mr R.C. Andrew, Sidney Sussex
Librarian	Mr R.C. Trebilcock, Pembroke
Steward	Mr G.W. Martin, Magdalene
Secretary	Mr C.R. Smith, Pembroke

Easter 1972

President	Mr K.F. Carey, Downing
Vice-President	Mr C.R. Smith, Pembroke
Treasurer	Mr R.C. Andrew, Sidney Sussex
Librarian	Mr R.C. Trebilcock, Pembroke
Steward	*vacant*
Secretary	Mr C.J. du M. Kenyon, Emmanuel

Michaelmas 1972

President	Mr C.R. Smith, Pembroke
Vice-President	Mr C.J. du M. Kenyon, Emmanuel
Treasurer	Mr R.C. Andrew, Sidney Sussex
Librarian	Mr R.C. Trebilcock, Pembroke
Steward	Mr S.M. Schama, Christ's
Secretary	Mr P.J.L. Weil, Queens'

Lent 1973

President	Mr A.G. Oppenheimer, Trinity
Vice-President	Mr D.A. Grace, Magdalene
Treasurer	Mr R.C. Andrew, Sidney Sussex
Librarian	Mr R.C. Trebilcock, Pembroke
Steward	Mr S.M. Schama, Christ's
Secretary	Mr E.M. Goyder, Trinity

Easter 1973

President	Mr D.A. Grace, Magdalene
Vice-President	Mr E.M. Goyder, Trinity
Treasurer	Mr R.C. Andrew, Sidney Sussex
Librarian	Mr R.C. Trebilcock, Pembroke
Steward	Mr S.M. Schama, Christ's
Secretary	Mr H.H.J. Carter, Caius

Michaelmas 1973

President	Mr E.M. Goyder, Trinity
Vice-President	Mr H.H.J. Carter, Caius
Treasurer	Mr R.C. Andrew, Sidney Sussex
Librarian	Mr D.J. McKitterick, St John's
Steward	Mr S.M. Schama, Christ's
Secretary	Mrs L.C. Grace, Girton[12]
	Mr D.A. Tyler, Trinity Hall

Lent 1974

President	Mr H.H.J. Carter, Caius
Vice-President	Mr J.T. Harris, Trinity
Treasurer	Mr R.C. Andrew, Sidney Sussex
Librarian	Mr D.J. McKitterick, St John's
Steward	Mr S.M. Schama, Christ's
Secretary	Mr P.S. Weil, Jesus

[12] Resigned, 25 October 1973

Easter 1974

President	Mr J.T. Harris, Trinity
Vice-President	Mr P.S. Weil, Jesus
Treasurer	Mr R.C. Andrew, Sidney Sussex
Librarian	Mr D.J. McKitterick, St John's
Steward	Mr S.M. Schama, Christ's
Secretary	Mr D.M. Bean, Trinity Hall

Michaelmas 1974

President	Mr P.S. Weil, Jesus
Vice-President	Mr D.M. Bean, Trinity Hall
Treasurer	*Revd S. Booth-Clibborn, Christ's
Librarian	Mr D. J. McKitterick, St John's
Steward	Mr S. M. Schama, Christ's[13]
	Revd J. Owen, Trinity Hall
Secretary	Mr D. P. Condit, Trinity

Lent 1975

President	Mr D.M. Bean, Trinity Hall
Vice-President	Mr D.P. Condit, Trinity
Treasurer	*Revd S. Booth-Clibborn, Christ's
Librarian	Mr D.J. McKitterick, St John's
Steward	Revd J. Owen, Trinity Hall
Secretary	Mr P.L. Bazalgette, Fitzwilliam

Easter 1975

President	Mr D.P. Condit, Trinity
Vice-President	Mr P.L. Bazalgette, Fitzwilliam
Treasurer	*Revd S. Booth-Clibborn, Christ's
Librarian	Mr D.J. McKitterick, St John's
Steward	Revd J. Owen, Trinity Hall
Secretary	Mr C.J. Greenwood, Magd.

Michaelmas 1975

President	Mr P.L. Bazalgette, Fitzwilliam
Vice-President	Mr C.J. Greenwood, Magd.
Treasurer	*Revd S. Booth-Clibborn, Christ's
Librarian	Mr D.J. McKitterick, St John's
Steward	Revd J. Owen, Trinity Hall
Secretary	Mr D.W. Johnson, Selwyn

Lent 1976

President	Mr C.J. Greenwood, Magd.
Vice-President	Mr D.W. Johnson, Selwyn
Treasurer	*Revd S. Booth-Clibborn, Christ's
Librarian	Mr D.J. McKitterick, St John's
Steward	Revd J. Owen, Trinity Hall
Secretary	Miss S.C. Nathan, New Hall

[13] Resigned, October 1974

Easter 1976

President	Mr D.W. Johnson, Selwyn
Vice-President	Miss S.C. Nathan, New Hall
Treasurer	*Revd S. Booth-Clibborn, Christ's
Librarian	Mr D.J. McKitterick, St John's
Steward	Revd J. Owen, Trinity Hall
Secretary	Mr K.B. Thapar, Pembroke

Michaelmas 1976

President	Mr P.J. Fudakowski, Magd.
Vice-President	Mr K.B. Thapar, Pembroke
Treasurer	*Revd Canon S. Booth-Clibborn, Christ's
Librarian	Mr D.J. McKitterick, St John's
Steward	Revd J. Owen, Trinity Hall
Secretary	Mr A.T.A. Dallas, Emmanuel

Lent 1977

President	Mr K.B. Thapar, Pembroke
Vice-President	Mr A.T.A. Dallas, Emmanuel
Treasurer	*Revd Canon S. Booth-Clibborn, Christ's
Librarian	Mr D.J. McKitterick, St John's
Steward	Revd J. Owen, Trinity Hall
Secretary	Mr J.A. Turner, Caius

Easter 1977

President	Mr A.T.A. Dallas, Emmanuel
Vice-President	Mr J.A. Turner, Caius
Treasurer	*Revd Canon S. Booth-Clibborn, Christ's
Librarian	Mr D.J. McKitterick, St John's
Steward	Revd J. Owen, Trinity Hall
Secretary	Mr A.J.B. Mitchell, Jesus

Michaelmas 1977

President	Mr J.A. Turner, Caius
Vice-President	Mr A.J.B. Mitchell, Jesus
Treasurer	Mr D.L. Baxter, Clare
Librarian	Mr D.J. McKitterick, St John's
Steward	Revd J. Owen, Trinity Hall
Secretary	Mr M.J. Turvey, Magdalene

Lent 1978

President	Mr A.J.B. Mitchell, Jesus
Vice-President	Mr R.D. Harris, Selwyn
Treasurer	Mr D.L. Baxter, Clare
Librarian	Mr D.J. McKitterick, St John's
Steward	Revd J. Owen, Trinity Hall
Secretary	Mr D.J.M. Janner, Trinity Hall

Easter 1978

President	Mr R.D. Harris, Selwyn
Vice-President	Mr D.J.M. Janner, Trinity Hall
Treasurer	Mr D.L. Baxter, Clare
Librarian	Mr D.J. McKitterick, St John's
Steward	Revd J. Owen, Trinity Hall
Secretary	Mr E.J.I. Stourton, Trinity

Michaelmas 1978

President	Mr D.J.M. Janner, Trinity Hall
Vice-President	Mr E.J.I. Stourton, Trinity
Treasurer	Mr D.L. Baxter, Clare
Librarian	Mr D.J. McKitterick, St John's
Steward	Revd J. Owen, Trinity Hall
Secretary	Mr A.D.G. Sells, Christ's

Lent 1979

President	Mr E.J.I. Stourton, Trinity
Vice-President	Mr D.J.A. Casserley, Jesus
Treasurer	Mr D.L. Baxter, Clare
Librarian	Mr D.J. McKitterick, St John's
Steward	Revd J. Owen, Trinity Hall
Secretary	Mr M.J. Booth, Trinity

Easter 1979

President	Mr D.J.A. Casserley, Jesus
Vice-President	Mr M.J. Booth, Trinity
Treasurer	Mr D.L. Baxter, Clare
Librarian	Mr D.J. McKitterick, St John's
Steward	Revd J. Owen, Trinity Hall
Secretary	Mr M.A. Bishop, Downing

Michaelmas 1979

President	Mr M.J. Booth, Trinity
Vice-President	Mr M.A. Bishop, Downing
Treasurer	Mr D.L. Baxter, Clare
Librarian	Mr D.J. McKitterick, St John's
Steward	Revd J. Owen, Trinity Hall
Secretary	Miss M.J. Libby, Girton

Lent 1980

President	Mr M.A. Bishop, Downing
Vice-President	Miss M.J. Libby, Girton
Treasurer	Mr D.L. Baxter, Clare
Librarian	Mr C.J. Greenwood, Magd.
Steward	Revd J. Owen, Trinity Hall
Secretary	Mr C.H. Gallagher, Jesus

Easter 1980

President	Miss M.J. Libby, Girton
Vice-President	Mr C.H. Gallagher, Jesus
Treasurer	Mr D.L. Baxter, Clare
Librarian	Mr C.J. Greenwood, Magd.
Steward	Revd J. Owen, Trinity Hall
Secretary	Mr D.N. Senior, Jesus

Michaelmas 1980

President	Mr C.H. Gallagher, Jesus
Vice-President	Mr D.N. Senior, Jesus
Treasurer	Mr D.L. Baxter, Clare
Librarian	Mr C.J. Greenwood, Magd.
Steward	Revd J. Owen, Trinity Hall
Secretary	Miss J. Kirkbride, Girton

Lent 1981

President	Mr D.N. Senior, Jesus
Vice-President	Miss J. Kirkbride, Girton
Treasurer	Mr D.L. Baxter, Clare
Librarian	Mr C.J. Greenwood, Magd.
Steward	Revd J. Owen, Trinity Hall
Secretary	Mr G.W.C. Kavanagh, St John's

Easter 1981

President	Mr P.M. Sugarman, St John's
Vice-President	Mr G.W.C. Kavanagh, St John's
Treasurer	Mr D.L. Baxter, Clare
Librarian	Mr C.J. Greenwood, Magd.
Steward	Revd J. Owen, Trinity Hall
Secretary	Mr P.N.L. Harvey, St Catharine's

Michaelmas 1981

President	Mr G.W.C. Kavanagh, St John's
Vice-President	Mr P.N.L. Harvey, St Catharine's
Treasurer	Mr D.L. Baxter, Clare
Librarian	Mr C.J. Greenwood, Magd.
Steward	Revd J. Owen, Trinity Hall
Secretary	Mr S.R.M. Baynes, Magdalene

Lent 1982

President	Mr P.N.L. Harvey, St Catharine's
Vice-President	Mr S.R.M. Baynes, Magdalene
Treasurer	Mr D.L. Baxter, Clare
Librarian	Mr C.J. Greenwood, Magd.
Steward	Revd J. Owen, Trinity Hall
Secretary	Mr B.C. Jenkin, Corpus Christi

Easter 1982

President	Mr S.R.M. Baynes, Magdalene
Vice-President	Mr B.C. Jenkin, Corpus Christi
Treasurer	Mr D.L. Baxter, Clare
Librarian	Mr C.J. Greenwood, Magd.
Steward	Revd J. Owen, Trinity Hall
Secretary	Mr S.H. Milton, Caius

Michaelmas 1982

President	Mr B.C. Jenkin, Corpus Christi
Vice-President	Mr S.H. Milton, Caius
Treasurer	Mr D.L. Baxter, Clare
Librarian	Mr C.J. Greenwood, Magd.
Steward	Revd J. Owen, Trinity Hall
Secretary	Miss M. McDonagh, New Hall

Lent 1983

President	Mr S.H. Milton, Caius
Vice-President	Miss M. McDonagh, New Hall
Treasurer	Mr D.L. Baxter, Clare
Librarian	Mr C.J. Greenwood, Magd.
Steward	Revd J. Owen, Trinity Hall
Secretary	Mr J.A. Lloyd, Fitzwilliam

Easter 1983

President	Miss M. McDonagh, New Hall
Vice-President	Mr J.A. Lloyd, Fitzwilliam
Treasurer	Mr D.L. Baxter, Clare
Librarian	Mr C.J. Greenwood, Magd.
Steward	Revd J. Owen, Trinity Hall
Secretary	Mr G.B. Davies, St John's

Michaelmas 1983

President	Mr J.A. Lloyd, Fitzwilliam
Vice-President	Mr G.B. Davies, St John's
Treasurer	Mr D.L. Baxter, Clare
Librarian	Mr N.J. Hancock, King's
Steward	Revd J. Owen, Trinity Hall
Secretary	Mr A.J.H. Lownie, Magdalene

Lent 1984

President	Mr G.B. Davies, St John's
Vice-President	Mr A.J.H. Lownie, Magdalene
Treasurer	Mr D.L. Baxter, Clare
Librarian	Mr N.J. Hancock, King's
Steward	Revd J. Owen, Trinity Hall
Secretary	Miss L. Chapman Jury, St John's

Easter 1984

President	Mr A.J.H. Lownie, Magdalene
Vice-President	Miss L. Chapman Jury, St John's
Treasurer	Mr D.L. Baxter, Clare
Librarian	Mr N.J. Hancock, King's
Steward	Revd J. Owen, Trinity Hall
Secretary	Mr L.P. Anisfeld, Trinity

Michaelmas 1984

President	Miss L. Chapman Jury, St John's
Vice-President	Mr L.P. Anisfeld, Trinity
Treasurer	Mr P.J. Greenwood, *no college*

Librarian	Mr N.J. Hancock, King's
Steward	Revd J. Owen, Trinity Hall
Secretary	Miss A.K. Kane, Girton

Lent 1985

President	Mr L.P. Anisfeld, Trinity
Vice-President	Mr C.D. Blackwood, Caius
Treasurer	Mr P.J. Greenwood
Librarian	Mr N.J. Hancock, King's
Steward	Revd J. Owen, Trinity Hall
Secretary	Mr M. Magarian, Trinity

Easter 1985

President	Mr C.D. Blackwood, Caius
Vice-President	Mr D.N. Walbank, Queens'
Treasurer	Mr P.J. Greenwood
Librarian	Mr N.J. Hancock, King's
Steward	Revd J. Owen, Trinity Hall
Secretary	Mr T.H. Oliver, St John's

Michaelmas 1985

President	Mr D.N. Walbank, Queens'
Vice-President	Mr T.H. Oliver, St John's
Treasurer	Mr P.J. Greenwood
Librarian	Mr N.J. Hancock, King's
Steward	Revd J. Owen, Trinity Hall
Secretary	Mr C.D. Steele, Girton

Lent 1986

President	Mr T.H. Oliver, St John's
Vice-President	Mr C.D. Steele, Girton
Treasurer	Mr P.J. Greenwood
Librarian	Mr N.J. Hancock, King's
Steward	Revd J. Owen, Trinity Hall
Secretary	Mr S. Srivatsa, Pembroke

Easter 1986

President	Mr C.D. Steele, Girton
Vice-President	Mr C.G. Earles, Sidney Sussex
Treasurer	Mr P.J. Greenwood
Librarian	Mr N.J. Hancock, King's
Steward	Revd J. Owen, Trinity Hall
Secretary	Miss A.L. McLauchlan, Newnham

Michaelmas 1986

President	Mr C.G. Earles, Sidney Sussex
Vice-President	Mr M.P.N. Tod, St John's
Treasurer	Mr P.J. Greenwood
Librarian	Mr N.J. Hancock, King's
Steward	Revd Canon J. Owen, Trinity Hall
Secretary	Mr M.P. Lindsay, Magdalene

Lent 1987

President	Mr M.P.N. Tod, St John's
Vice-President	Mr M.P. Lindsay, Magdalene
Treasurer	Mrs J.M. Womack, New Hall
Librarian	Mr N.J. Hancock, King's
Steward	Revd Canon J. Owen, Trin. Hall
Secretary	Mr A.P. Ground, St John's

Easter 1987

President	Mr M.P. Lindsay, Magdalene
Vice-President	Mr B.D. Lander, Sidney Sussex
Treasurer	Mrs J.M. Womack, New Hall
Librarian	Mr N.J. Hancock, King's
Steward	Revd Canon J. Owen, Trin. Hall
Secretary	Mr S.J. Greenhalgh, Trinity

Michaelmas 1987

President	Mr A.P. Ground, St John's
Vice-President	Mr S.J. Greenhalgh, Trinity
Treasurer	Mrs J.M. Womack, New Hall
Librarian	Mr N.J. Hancock, King's
Steward	Revd Canon J. Owen, Trin. Hall
Secretary	Mr S.L. Glass, St Catharine's

Lent 1988

President	Mr S.J. Greenhalgh, Trinity
Vice-President	Mr C.M. Kelly, Trinity
Treasurer	Mrs J.M. Womack, New Hall
Librarian	Dr P. Ayris, Gonville & Caius
Steward	Revd Canon J. Owen, Trin. Hall
Secretary	Mr P.C.W. Pressdee, St John's

Easter 1988

President	Mr C.M. Kelly, Trinity
Vice-President	Mr K.F. Bilimoria, Sidney Sussex
Treasurer	Mrs J.M. Womack, New Hall
Librarian	Dr P. Ayris, Caius
Steward	Revd Canon J. Owen, Trin. Hall
Secretary	Mr A. Aithal, Trinity

Michaelmas 1988

President	Mr P.C.W. Pressdee, St John's
Vice-President	Mr A. Aithal, Trinity
Treasurer	Mrs J.M. Womack, New Hall
Librarian	Dr P. Ayris, Gonville & Caius
Steward	Revd Canon J. Owen, Trin. Hall
Secretary	Miss C.-A. Doerries, New Hall

Lent 1989

President	Mr A. Aithal, Trinity
Vice-President	Miss C.-A. Doerries, New Hall
Treasurer	Mrs J.M. Womack, New Hall
Librarian	Dr P. Ayris, Gonville & Caius
Steward	Revd Canon J. Owen, Trin. Hall
Secretary	Mr N.A. Pink, Pembroke

Easter 1989

President	Miss C.-A. Doerries, New Hall
Vice-President	Mr N.A. Pink, Pembroke
Treasurer	Mr N. Durkin, Corpus Christi
Librarian	Dr P. Ayris, Gonville & Caius
Steward	Revd Canon J. Owen, Trin. Hall
Secretary	Mr S.A. Bourne, Sidney Sussex

Michaelmas 1989

President	Mr N.A. Pink, Pembroke
Vice-President	Mr C.H.M. Robson, St John's
Treasurer	Mr N. Durkin, Corpus Christi
Librarian	Dr P. Ayris, Gonville & Caius
Steward	Revd Canon J. Owen, Trin. Hall
Secretary	Miss S.M. Daniel, Christ's

Lent 1990

President	Mr C.H.M. Robson, St John's
Vice-President	Miss S.M. Daniel, Christ's
Treasurer	Mr N. Durkin, Corpus Christi
Librarian	Dr P. Ayris, Gonville & Caius
Steward	Revd Canon J. Owen, Trin. Hall
Secretary	Mr M.F. Harris, Corpus Christi

Easter 1990

President	Mr D.C. Willink, Magdalene
Vice-President	Mr M.F. Harris, Corpus Christi
Treasurer	Mr N. Durkin, Corpus Christi
Librarian	Dr P. Ayris, Gonville & Caius
Steward	Revd Canon J. Owen, Trin. Hall
Secretary	Mr M.S. Scott-Fleming, Clare

Michaelmas 1990

President	Mr M.F. Harris, Corpus Christi
Vice-President	Mr M.S. Scott-Fleming, Clare
Treasurer	Mr N. Durkin, Corpus Christi
Librarian	Mr N.J. Hancock, King's
Steward	Revd Canon J. Owen, Trin. Hall
Secretary	Mr R.S. Mitter, King's

Lent 1991

President	Mr M.S. Scott-Fleming, Clare
Vice-President	Mr R.S. Mitter, King's
Treasurer	Mr N. Durkin, Corpus Christi
Librarian	Mr N.J. Hancock, King's
Steward	Revd Canon J. Owen, Trin. Hall
Secretary	Miss E.D. Johnson, Queens'

Easter 1991

President	Mr R.S. Mitter, King's
Vice-President	Miss E.D. Johnson, Queens'

Treasurer	Mr N. Durkin, Corpus Christi
Librarian	Revd N. Hancock, King's
Steward	Revd Canon J. Owen, Trin. Hall
Secretary	Mr R. Malhotra, St John's

Michaelmas 1991

President	Miss E.D. Johnson, Queens'
Vice-President	Mr S.P. J. Nixon, Trinity
Treasurer	Mr H. Price, Darwin
Librarian	Mr N. Rogers, Sidney Sussex
Steward	Revd Canon J. Owen, Trin. Hall
Secretary	Miss C.V. Balding, Newnham

Lent 1992

President	Mr S.P.J. Nixon, Trinity
Vice-President	Miss C.V. Balding, Newnham
Treasurer	Mr H. Price, Darwin
Librarian	Mr N. Rogers, Sidney Sussex
Steward	Revd Canon J. Owen, Trin. Hall
Secretary	Mr N.P. Allen, Emmanuel

Easter 1992

President	Miss C.V. Balding, Newnham
Vice-President	Mr N.P. Allen, Emmanuel
Treasurer	Mr H. Price, Darwin
Librarian	Mr N. Rogers, Sidney Sussex
Steward	Revd Canon J. Owen, Trin. Hall
Secretary	Mr B.M. Elkington, Trinity

Michaelmas 1992

President	Mr N.P. Allen, Emmanuel
Vice-President	Mr B.M. Elkington, Trinity
Treasurer	Mr H. Price, Darwin
Librarian	Mr N. Rogers, Sidney Sussex
Steward	Revd Canon J. Owen, Trin. Hall
Secretary	Mr G.L. Barwell, Trinity

Lent 1993

President	Mr B.M. Elkington, Trinity
Vice-President	Mr G.L. Barwell, Trinity
Treasurer	Mr H. Price, Darwin
Librarian	Mr N. Rogers, Sidney Sussex
Steward	Revd Canon J. Owen, Trin. Hall
Secretary	Miss L.C. Frazer, Newnham

Easter 1993

President	Mr G.L. Barwell, Trinity
Vice-President	Miss L.C. Frazer, Newnham
Treasurer	Mr H. Price, Darwin
Librarian	Mr N. Rogers, Sidney Sussex
Steward	Revd Canon J. Owen, Trin. Hall
Secretary	Mr S. Swaroop, Magdalene

Michaelmas 1993

President	Miss L.C. Frazer, Newnham
Vice-President	Mr S. Swaroop, Magdalene
Treasurer	Mr H. Price, Darwin
Librarian	Mr N. Rogers, Sidney Sussex
Steward	Revd Canon J. Owen, Trinity Hall[14]
	Mr A. Stockley, Christ's
Secretary	Mr C.M. Farmer, Magdalene

Lent 1994

President	Mr S. Swaroop, Magdalene
Vice-President	Mr C.M. Farmer, Magdalene
Treasurer	Mr H. Price, Darwin
Librarian	Mr N. Rogers, Sidney Sussex
Steward	Mr A. Stockley, Christ's
Secretary	Mr S.D. Kirk, Emmanuel

Easter 1994

President	Mr C.M. Farmer, Magdalene
Vice-President	Mr S.D. Kirk, Emmanuel
Treasurer	Mr H. Price, Darwin
Librarian	Mr N. Rogers, Sidney Sussex
Steward	*vacant*
Secretary	Miss R.C. Penn, Churchill

Michaelmas 1994

President	Mr S.D. Kirk, Emmanuel
Vice-President	Miss R.C. Penn, Churchill
Treasurer	Mr H. Price, Darwin
Librarian	Mr N. Rogers, Sidney Sussex
Steward	*vacant*
Secretary	Mr N.J. Boys Smith, Peterhouse

Lent 1995[15]

President	Miss R.C. Penn, Churchill
President-elect	Mr N.J. Boys Smith, Peterhouse
Secretary	Mr D.H. Branch, Magdalene
Senior Treasurer	Mr H. Price, Darwin
Senior Librarian	Mr N. Rogers, Sidney Sussex
Steward	*vacant*

Easter 1995

President	Mr N.J. Boys Smith, Peterhouse
Secretary	Mr D.E.S. Reed, Jesus
Librarian	Mr N. Chatrath, Jesus

[14] Died in office

[15] A new system of officers was introduced: the posts of Secretary and Vice-President were combined as an appointed, annual role; and Presidents were elected two terms in advance, serving the first as President-elect.

Treasurer	Mr C. Teo, Emmanuel
Senior Treasurer	Mr H. Price, Darwin
Senior Librarian	Mr N. Rogers, Sidney Sussex
Steward	Mr C.M. Farmer, Magdalene

Michaelmas 1995

President	Mr D.H. Branch, Magdalene
Secretary	Mr D.E.S. Reed, Jesus
Librarian	Mr A.R. Cannon, Magdalene
Treasurer	Mr A. Seely, Trinity
Senior Treasurer	Mr S. Brooker, Emmanuel
Senior Librarian	Mr N. Rogers, Sidney Sussex
Steward	Mr C.M. Farmer, Magdalene

Lent 1996

President	Mr N. Chatrath, Jesus
Secretary	Mr D.E.S. Reed, Jesus[16]
	Mr R.G.A. Anderson, Trinity
Librarian	Miss K. Dietzel, Caius
Treasurer	Miss I. Waddell, Newnham
Senior Treasurer	Mr S. Brooker, Emmanuel
Senior Librarian	Mr N. Rogers, Sidney Sussex
Steward	Mr C.M. Farmer, Magdalene

Easter 1996

President	Mr A.R. Cannon, Magdalene
Secretary	Mr A. Walton, Emmanuel
Librarian	Mr M.J. Howard, Anglia Polytechnic
Treasurer	Mr A.M.A. Leek, Emmanuel
Senior Treasurer	Mr S. Brooker, Emmanuel
Senior Librarian	Mr N. Rogers, Sidney Sussex
Steward	Mr C.M. Farmer, Magdalene

Michaelmas 1996

President	Miss I. Waddell, Newnham
Secretary	Mr A. Walton, Emmanuel
Librarian	Mr H.C.S. Pipe, Caius
Treasurer	Mr G. Pope, Magdalene
Senior Treasurer	Mr S. Brooker, Emmanuel
Senior Librarian	*vacant*
Steward	Mr C.M. Farmer, Magdalene

Lent 1997

President	Mr A.M.A. Leek, Emmanuel
Secretary	Mr A. Walton, Emmanuel
	Mr T. Braithwaite, Jesus
Librarian	Miss P.C.M. Enoizi, Cauis
Treasurer	Mr S.S. Thapa, Caius
Senior Treasurer	Mr S. Brooker, Emmanuel
Senior Librarian	*vacant*
Steward	Mr C.M. Farmer, Magdalene

Easter 1997

President	Mr J. Shapiro, Peterhouse
Secretary	Mr R. Walker, Trinity
Librarian	Miss C. Gill, Emmanuel
Treasurer	Miss S. Raine, Trinity
Senior Treasurer	Mr S. Brooker, Emmanuel
Senior Librarian	*vacant*
Steward	Mr C.M. Farmer, Magdalene

Michaelmas 1997

President	Mr G.J. Weetman, Christ's
Secretary	Mr R.M. Mackley, Christ's
Librarian	Mr J. Carpenter, Trinity
Treasurer	Miss S. Currie, Newnham
Senior Treasurer	Mr C.A.E.T. Stevenson, New Hall
Senior Librarian	*vacant*
Steward	Mr C.M. Farmer, Magdalene

Lent 1998

President	Miss S. Raine, Trinity
Secretary	Mr R.M. Mackley, Christ's
Librarian	Mr A.P.M. Slater, Corpus Christi
Treasurer	Mr S. Hodsdon, Magdalene
Senior Treasurer	Mr C.A.E.T. Stevenson, New Hall
Senior Librarian	Miss C.J.E. Guite, Christ's
Steward	Mr C.M. Farmer, Magdalene

Easter 1998

President	Miss R. Durkin, Corpus Christi
Secretary	Mr R.M. Mackley, Christ's
Senior Officer[17]	Mr O.J. Wellings, Pembroke
Treasurer	Miss M.Y. Shiu, St John's
Senior Treasurer	Mr C.A.E.T. Stevenson, New Hall
Senior Librarian	Miss C.J. E. Guite, Christ's
Steward	Mr C.M. Farmer, Magdalene

Michaelmas 1998

President	Mr A.P.M. Slater, Corpus Christi
Secretary	Mr P. Rutland, Girton
Senior Officer	Mr N.R. Dholakia, Trinity
Treasurer	Miss S. Gledhill, Christ's
Senior Treasurer	Mr C.A.E.T. Stevenson, New Hall
Senior Librarian	Miss C.J.E. Guite, Christ's
Steward	Mr C.M. Farmer, Magdalene

---

[16] Resigned, 17 January 1996

[17] The office of Junior Librarian was renamed Senior Officer.

Lent 1999

President	Mr O.J. Wellings, Pembroke
Secretary	Mr G.J.B. Marsh, Christ's
Senior Officer	Mr A.J.C. Deane, Trinity
Treasurer	Mr F.G.K. Bevis, Madgalene
Senior Treasurer	Mr C.A.E.T. Stevenson, New Hall
Senior Librarian	Miss C.J.E. Guite, Christ's
Steward	Mr C.M. Farmer, Magdalene

Easter 1999

President	Miss S. Gledhill, Christ's
Secretary	Mr G.J.B. Marsh, Christ's
Senior Officer	Miss V.P. Perkins, Pembroke
Treasurer	Mr G.E. Chambers, Trinity
Senior Treasurer	Mr C.A.E.T. Stevenson, New Hall
Senior Librarian	Miss C.J.E. Guite, Christ's
Steward	Mr C.M. Farmer, Magdalene

Michaelmas 1999

President	Mr F.G.K. Bevis, Magdalene
Secretary	Mr G.J.B. Marsh, Christ's
Senior Officer	Mr E. Higgenbottam, Caius
Treasurer	Miss A.L. Newton, Newnham
Senior Treasurer	Mr C.A.E.T. Stevenson, New Hall
Senior Librarian	Mrs P.A. Aske, Pembroke
Steward	Mr R.M. Mackley, Emmanuel

Lent 2000

President	Miss V.P. Perkins, Pembroke
Secretary	Mr C.R.N.J. Brasted, Magd.
Senior Officer	Mr P.J. Abbott, Magdalene
Treasurer	Miss L. Bevin, Newnham
Senior Treasurer	Mr C.A.E.T. Stevenson, New Hall
Senior Librarian	Mrs P.A. Aske, Pembroke
Steward	Mr R.M. Mackley, Emmanuel

Easter 2000

President	Miss A.L. Newton, Newnham
Secretary	Mr C.R.N.J. Brasted, Magd.[18]
	Miss K.S. Huish, St Catharine's
Senior Officer	Miss S. Smith, Magdalene
Treasurer	Miss K.S. Huish, St Catharine's
Senior Treasurer	Mr C.A.E.T. Stevenson, New Hall
Senior Librarian	Mrs P.A. Aske, Pembroke
Steward	Mr R.M. Mackley, Emmanuel

Michaelmas 2000

President	Mr P.J. Abbott, Magdalene
Secretary	Miss K.S. Huish, St Catharine's
Senior Officer	Mr A.M. Ribbans, Caius
Treasurer	Miss G. Warnett, Sidney Sussex
Senior Treasurer	Mr C.A.E.T. Stevenson, New Hall
Senior Librarian	Mrs P.A. Aske, Pembroke
Steward	Mr R.M. Mackley, Emmanuel

Lent 2001

President	Miss D. Newman, Fitzwilliam
Secretary	Miss H. Berriman, Newnham
Senior Officer	Mr J.M. Brier, Christ's
Treasurer	Mr W. Hooker, Magdalene
Senior Treasurer	Mr C.A.E.T. Stevenson, New Hall
Senior Librarian	Mrs P.A. Aske, Pembroke
Steward	Mr R.M. Mackley, Emmanuel

Easter 2001

President	Mr W.M. Tan, Trinity
Secretary	Miss H.R. Berriman, Newnham
Senior Officer	Mr J. Devanny, Jesus
Treasurer	Miss A.M. Crowther, New Hall
Senior Treasurer	Mr C.A.E.T. Stevenson, New Hall
Senior Librarian	Mrs P.A. Aske, Pembroke
Steward	Mr R.M. Mackley, Emmanuel

Michaelmas 2001

President	Mr J.M. Brier, Christ's
Secretary	Mr T.H. Jeffery, Trinity
Senior Officer	Mr E.A.H.R. Evans, Trin. Hall
Treasurer	Mr A.C. Lee, Trinity
Senior Treasurer	Mr C.A.E.T. Stevenson, New Hall
Senior Librarian	Mrs P.A. Aske, Pembroke
Steward	Mr R.M. Mackley, Emmanuel

Lent 2002

President	Mr J. Devanny, Jesus
Secretary	Mr T.H. Jeffery, Trinity
Senior Officer	Mr T.B. Kibasi, Trinity
Ents Officer	Mr A.T. Lewis, Caius
Senior Treasurer	Mr C.A.E.T. Stevenson, New Hall
Senior Librarian	Mrs P.A. Aske, Pembroke
Steward	Mr R.M. Mackley, Emmanuel

Easter 2002

President	Mr M.W.S. Lynas, Trinity
Secretary	Mr T.H. Jeffery, Trinity
Senior Officer	Mr R.T. Vettasseri, Trin. Hall

[18] Resigned, 11 May 2000

Ents Officer — Mr R.S.P. Mott, Christ's
Senior Treasurer — Mr C.A.E.T. Stevenson, New Hall
Senior Librarian — Mrs P.A. Aske, Pembroke
Steward — Mr R.M. Mackley, Emmanuel

Michaelmas 2002
President — Mr T.B. Kibasi, Trinity[19]
Mr T.H. Jeffery, Trinity
Secretary — Mr T.H. Jeffery, Trinity
Miss S.E. Przybylska, King's
Senior Officer — Mr S.W. Radford, Peterhouse
Ents Officer — Mr E.C. Cumming, Downing
Senior Treasurer — Mr C.A.E.T. Stevenson, New Hall
Senior Librarian — Mrs P.A. Aske, Pembroke
Steward — Mr R.M. Mackley, Emmanuel

Lent 2003
President — Mr S.K. Kabraji, Trinity
Secretary — Miss S.E. Przybylska, King's
Senior Officer — Mr W.E. Gallagher, Trin. Hall
Ents Officer — Mr S.A. Morgan, Trinity
Senior Treasurer — Mr C.A.E.T. Stevenson, New Hall
Senior Librarian — Mrs P.A. Aske, Pembroke
Steward — Mr R.M. Mackley, Emmanuel

Easter 2003
President — Mr E.C. Cumming, Downing
Secretary — Miss S.E. Przybylska, King's
Senior Officer — Mr S.G. Parkinson, Emmanuel
Ents Officer — Miss J.M. Kumeta, Trinity
Senior Treasurer — Mr C.A.E.T. Stevenson, New Hall
Senior Librarian — Mrs P.A. Aske, Pembroke
Steward — Mr R.M. Mackley, Emmanuel

Michaelmas 2003
President — Mr W.E. Gallagher, Trin. Hall
Secretary — Miss S.E. Przybylska, King's
Senior Officer — Mr P.R. Bagguley, Homerton
Ents Officer — Mr A. Mak, Peterhouse[20]
Senior Treasurer — Mr C.A.E T. Stevenson, New Hall
Senior Librarian — Ms J.E. Ball, Trinity
Steward — Mr T.N. Milner, Peterhouse

Lent 2004
President — Mr S.G. Parkinson, Emmanuel
Secretary — Miss S.E. Przybylska, King's

Senior Officer — Mr R. Friedman, Emmanuel
Ents Officer — Miss K.M. Goodwin, Newnham
Treasurer — Mr A.P. Wright, Peterhouse
Senior Treasurer — Mr C.A.E.T. Stevenson, New Hall
Senior Librarian — Ms J.E. Ball, Trinity
Steward — Mr T.N. Milner, Peterhouse

Easter 2004
President — Miss K.I.D.I. Steadman, New Hall
Secretary — Miss K.M. Goodwin, Newnham
Senior Officer — Mr A.E. Ross, Fitzwilliam
Ents Officer — Mr A.R. MacDowall, Fitzwilliam
Treasurer — Mr P.R. Bagguley, Homerton
Senior Treasurer — Mr C.A.E.T. Stevenson, New Hall
Senior Librarian — Ms J.E. Ball, Trinity
Steward — Mr T.N. Milner, Peterhouse

Michaelmas 2004
President — Mr R. Friedman, Emmanuel
Secretary — Miss K.M. Goodwin, Newnham
Senior Officer — Mr J.M. Khan, Trinity
Ents Officer — Mr T. Ford, Corpus Christi
Treasurer — Mr M. Ahmed, Trinity
Senior Treasurer — Mr C.A.E.T. Stevenson, New Hall
Senior Librarian — Mrs P.A. Aske, Pembroke
Steward — Mr T.N. Milner, Peterhouse

Lent 2005
President — Mr A.E. Ross, Fitzwilliam
Secretary — Miss K.M. Goodwin, Newnham
Senior Officer — Mr A.J. Swersky, Queens'
Ents Officer — Mr L. Fitzjohn-Sykes, Selwyn
Treasurer — Miss J.R. Scott, Pembroke
Senior Treasurer — Mr C.A.E.T. Stevenson, New Hall
Senior Librarian — Mrs P.A. Aske, Pembroke
Steward — Mr T.N. Milner, Peterhouse

Easter 2005
President — Mr J.M. Khan, Trinity
Secretary — Mr R.P. Sidey, Selwyn
Senior Officer — Miss S.J. Pobereskin, King's
Ents Officer — Mr E. Ho, Downing
Treasurer — Miss L.J. Walsh, Fitzwilliam
Senior Treasurer — Mr C.A.E.T. Stevenson, New Hall
Senior Librarian — Mrs P.A. Aske, Pembroke
Steward — Mr T.N. Milner, Peterhouse

---

[19] Resigned, 29 October 2002
[20] Resigned, 17 October 2003

Michaelmas 2005

President	Miss J.R. Scott, Pembroke
Secretary	Mr R.P. Sidey, Selwyn
Senior Officer	Miss A.R.C. Thompson, Trinity
Ents Officer	Miss Z.S. Khan, Trinity
Treasurer	Mr L.E. Pearce, King's
Senior Treasurer	Mr C.A.E.T. Stevenson, New Hall
Senior Librarian	Mrs P.A. Aske, Pembroke
Steward	Mr T.N. Milner, Peterhouse

Lent 2006

President	Miss S.J. Pobereskin, King's
Secretary	Mr R.P. Sidey, Selwyn
Senior Officer	Mr C.E.G. Kaye, Trinity
Ents Officer	Miss K.F. Harries, Jesus
Treasurer	Mr N.T. Hartman, Darwin
Senior Treasurer	Mr C.A.E.T. Stevenson, New Hall
Senior Librarian	Mrs P.A. Aske, Pembroke
Steward	Mr T.N. Milner, Peterhouse

Easter 2006

President	Miss A.R.C. Thompson, Trinity
Secretary	Mr N.T. Hartman, Darwin
Senior Officer	Mr M.A. Jacobson, St John's
Ents Officer	Mr T.E.C. Pedelty, Trin. Hall
Treasurer	Mr P.Z. Cui, Trinity
Senior Treasurer	Mr C.A.E.T. Stevenson, New Hall
Senior Librarian	Mrs P.A. Aske, Pembroke
Steward	Mr T.N. Milner, Peterhouse

Michaelmas 2006

President	Mr L.E. Pearce, King's
Secretary	Mr N.T. Hartman, Darwin
Senior Officer	Miss B. Stefanska, Pembroke
Ents Officer	Miss E.K. Narozanski-Efthimiopoulou, Emmanuel
Treasurer	Mr A. Al-Ansari, Homerton
Senior Treasurer	Mr C.A.E.T. Stevenson, New Hall
Senior Librarian	Mrs P.A. Aske, Pembroke
Steward	Mr T.N. Milner, Peterhouse

Lent 2007

President	Mr M.A. Jacobson, St John's
Secretary	Mr N.T. Hartman, Darwin
Senior Officer	Miss K.I. Agathos, Trinity
Ents Officer	Miss O. Anubi, Newnham
Treasurer	Mr E.C.M. Blain, Pembroke
Senior Treasurer	Mr C.A.E.T. Stevenson, New Hall
Senior Librarian	Mrs P.A. Aske, Pembroke
Steward	Mr T.N. Milner, Peterhouse

Easter 2007

President	Mr A. Al-Ansari, Homerton
Secretary	Mr J.P. Robinson, Christ's
Senior Officer	Miss S.C. Yasmin, Hughes Hall
Ents Officer	Mr W.P. Wearden, King's
Treasurer	Mr T.H. Brown, Girton
Senior Treasurer	Mr C.A.E.T. Stevenson, New Hall
Senior Librarian	Mrs P.A. Aske, Pembroke
Steward	Mr T.N. Milner, Peterhouse

Michaelmas 2007

President	Mr R.J.A. Foxcroft, Churchill
Secretary	Mr J.P. Robinson, Christ's
Senior Officer	Mr M.E.H. Jarvis, Corpus
Ents Officer	Miss A. Sartogo, Homerton
Treasurer	Mr E.D. Bishton, Fitzwilliam
Senior Treasurer	Mr C.A.E.T. Stevenson, New Hall[21]
Senior Librarian	Mrs P.A. Aske, Pembroke[21]
Steward	Mr T.N. Milner, Peterhouse[21]

Lent 2008

President	Mr W.P. Wearden, King's[22]
	Mr L. Wei, Churchill
Secretary	Mr J.P. Robinson, Christ's[23]
	Mr G.W.J. Robertson, Christ's
Senior Officer	Mr C.J. Miller, Homerton
Ents Officer	Miss E. Sipos, Homerton
Treasurer	Mr L. Wei, Churchill
	Mr B. Salehy, Selwyn
Senior Treasurer	*vacant*
Senior Librarian	*vacant*
Steward	*vacant*

Easter 2008

President	Mr E.D. Bishton, Fitzwilliam
Secretary	Mr J.G. Blanchard Lewis, Jesus
Senior Officer	Miss O.F. Potts, Corpus Christi
Ents Officer	Mr M.J. Stacey, Homerton
Treasurer	Mr W.L. Redfern, Caius
Senior Treasurer	*vacant*
Senior Librarian	Mrs P.A. Aske, Pembroke
Steward	*vacant*

Michaelmas 2008

President	Mr A. Bott, Sidney Sussex
Secretary	Mr J. G. Blanchard Lewis, Jesus
Senior Officer	Mr S. Ginet, King's[24]
	Mr H.J. Walton, Magdalene

[21] All resigned, 31 October 2007
[22] Resigned, 2 February 2008
[23] Resigned, 29 January 2008
[24] Resigned, 12 November 2008

Ents Officer	Miss R.M. La Prairie, St Catharine's
Treasurer	Mr W.P.R. Dean, Magdalene
Senior Treasurer	Mr M. Brown, Emmanuel[25]
Senior Librarian	Mrs P.A. Aske, Pembroke
Steward	Mr J.M.S. Pereira, Downing

Lent 2009

President	Miss O.F. Potts, Corpus Christi
Secretary	Mr J.G. Blanchard Lewis, Jesus
Senior Officer	Mr J. Domercq, King's
Ents Officer	Miss R. Shimell, Homerton
Treasurer	Mr T. Chigbo, St John's
Senior Librarian	Mrs P.A. Aske, Pembroke
Steward	Mr J.M.S. Pereira, Downing

Easter 2009

President	Mr L. Fear-Segal, Robinson
Vice-President[26]	Mr J.A. Sharpe, Fitzwilliam
Secretary	Mr G.H. Tully, Trinity Hall
Senior Officer	Miss M.Å.C. Odin Ekman, Murray Edwards
Ents Officer	Miss E.E. Coghill, Trinity
Treasurer	Mr J.A.H. Shaw, King's
Senior Librarian	Mrs P.A. Aske, Pembroke
Steward	Mr J.M.S. Pereira, Downing

[25] The office of Senior Treasurer was abolished in October 2008, the duties being taken on by an employed Bursar

[26] The offices of Vice-President and Secretary were split again

Appendix II:
Chief Clerks, 1831–

Chief Clerks

Name	From	To
W. Matthews	1831	March 1841
J. Smith	March 1841	May 1843
John Willimott	June 1843	October 1874
J.R. Cross	October 1874	February 1892
Sir John Wilson Taylor	March 1892	June 1897
G.E. Adams	June 1897	June 1903
Stanley S. Brown	June 1903	February 1943
Frederick W. Curzon	February 1943	June 1948
Sydney A. Elwood	June 1948	June 1967
Roland F. Thompson	July 1967	August 1976
Barry Thoday	September 1976	June 1995
Sandra Finding	January 1998	July 2002

Office Managers

Jackalyn Grainger	October 2002	June 2004
Kelly Collinwood	June 2004	—

Bursar

Col. William A. Bailey MBE	August 2008	—

APPENDIX III:
TRUSTEES, 1857–

Dates of appointment are given where known.

18 May 1857	Dr J.T. Abdy, Trinity Hall[1]
	Dr J.B. Lightfoot, Trinity[2]
	Prof. C.C. Babington, St John's[3]
1 June 1857	The Revd W.G. Clark, Trinity[4]
	The Revd L. Stephen, Trinity Hall
	The Revd H.A.J. Munro, Trinity[5]
	H.J. Roby, St John's
5 May 1879	Prof. H. Jackson, Trinity[6]
	Prof. C.S. Kenny, Downing[7]
	Sir J.E. Sandys, St John's[8]
	The Rt. Hon. Prof J. Stuart, Trinity[9]
4 June 1883	The Revd J.W. Cartmell, Christ's
18 May 1885	The Revd H. Latham, Trinity Hall[10]
	The Ven. W. Cunningham, Trinity[11]

---

[1] Regius Professor of Civil Law, 1854–73
[2] Lord Bishop of Durham, 1879–89
[3] Professor of Botany, 1861–95
[4] Public Orator, 1857–69; Vice-Master, Trinity College, 1869–73
[5] Professor of Latin, 1869–72
[6] Regius Professor of Greek, 1906–21; (President, Easter 1864)
[7] Downing Professor of Laws of England, 1907–19; (President, Lent 1874)
[8] Public Orator, 1876–1919
[9] Professor of Mechanism and Applied Mechanics, 1875–90; MP, Hoxton, 1885–1902
[10] Master, Trinity Hall, 1888–1902
[11] Archdeacon of Ely, 1907–19; (President, Easter 1872)

4 November 1895	R.T. Wright, Christ's[12]
28 April 1902	W. Chawner, Emmanuel[13]
29 May 1911	Dr J.R. Tanner, St John's[14]
30 November 1914	Dr J.McT.E. McTaggart, Trinity[15]
24 November 1919	J.N. Keynes, Pembroke[16]
	H. McLeod Innes, Trinity
6 November 1922	Sir G.G.G. Butler, Corpus Christi[17]
	Prof. A.C. Pigou, King's[18]
	Prof. H.A. Hollond, Trinity[19]
5 March 1923	S.C. Roberts, Pembroke[20]
4 May 1925	Sir A.D. McNair, Gonville & Caius[21]
25 November 1929	Sir J.T. Sheppard, King's[22]
3 November 1945	H.S. Bennett, Emmanuel[23]
24 November 1947	Prof. Sir D.H. Robertson, Trinity[24]
6 June 1951	N.G.L. Hammond, Clare[25]
1 November 1954	The Rt. Hon. Sir H.U. Willink, Magdalene[26]
	Prof. K.W. Wedderburn, Clare[27]
13 May 1963	The Rt. Hon. Sir F. Lee, Corpus Christi[28]
	J.R. Bambrough, St John's[29]
25 November 1963	Prof. Lord Kahn, King's[30]

[12] Secretary to the Syndics of the Press; (President, Lent 1869; Treasurer, 1873–6)

[13] Master, Emmanuel College, 1895–1911

[14] Tutor, St John's College, 1900–12; Editor, *Cambridge Medieval History*; (President, Easter 1883; Treasurer, 1902–15)

[15] Lecturer in Moral Sciences, Trinity College; (President, Michaelmas 1890; Librarian, 1984–5, 1902; Treasurer, 1915–20)

[16] University Registrary 1910–1925

[17] MP, Cambridge University, 1923–29; (President, Easter 1910)

[18] Professor of Political Economy, 1908–43; (President, Lent 1900)

[19] Vice-Master, Trinity College, 1951–4; (President, Michaelmas 1906)

[20] Vice-Chancellor, 1949–51 (Librarian, Michaelmas 1915; Steward, 1920–2)

[21] President, International Court of Justice, 1952–5; (President, Easter 1909; Treasurer, 1920–3)

[22] Provost, King's College, 1933–54; (President, Michaelmas 1904)

[23] Emeritus University Reader in English (Librarian, 1923–36; Treasurer, 1935–8)

[24] Professor of Political Economy, 1944–57; (President, Michaelmas 1911)

[25] Senior Tutor, Clare College, 1947–54; (Treasurer, 1947–51)

[26] Master, Magdalene College, 1948–66; Vice-Chancellor, 1953–5

[27] Sir Ernest Cassel Professor of Commercial Law, LSE

[28] Master, Corpus Christi College, 1962–71

[29] (Steward, 1956–61)

[30] Professor of Economics, 1951–72

4 May 1964	A.Ll. Armitage, Queens'[31]
20 February 1967	Dr G.E. Daniel, St John's[32]
11 May 1970	The Rt. Hon. Lord Butler of Saffron Walden, Trinity[33]
	D.G.T. Williams, Emmanuel[34]
28 April 1973	Dr P. O'Higgins, Christ's
22 April 1974	Prof. G.H. Jones, Trinity[35]
6 June 1975	R.C. Andrew, Sidney Sussex
15 February 1977	T.C. Gardner, Wolfson[36]
1 October 1984	D.L. Baxter, Clare[37]
1 May 1992	C.J. Greenwood, Magdalene[38]
20 May 1992	Sir D.C. Calcutt, Magdalene[39]
1 Nov 1992	The Revd Canon J. Owen, Trinity Hall[40]
28 April 1994	Prof. the Lord Renfrew of Kaimsthorn, Jesus[41]
1 February 1995	Mrs J.M. Womack, Trinity Hall[42]
14 March 1997	Sir J.D.I. Boyd, Churchill[43]
	P.L. Bazalgette, Fitzwilliam[44]
	N.W. Brown, *no college*
	G.W. Freeman, Girton[45]
22 June 2006	Sir R.B. Dearlove, Pembroke[46]
29 April 2008	N. Butler, Wolfson[47]
23 September 2008	A. Swarbrick, *no college*[48]
	Dr N.J. Yandell, Corpus Christi[49]

---

[31] President, Queens' College, 1958–70; Vice-Chancellor, 1965–7
[32] Disney Professor of Archaeology, 1974–81; (Steward, 1950–5)
[33] Master, Trinity College, 1964–77; (President, Easter 1924)
[34] Rouse Ball Professor of English Law, 1983–92; Vice-Chancellor, 1989–96
[35] Downing Professor of the Laws of England, 1975–98
[36] University Treasurer, 1969–84
[37] (Senior Treasurer, 1977–84)
[38] (President, Lent 1976; Librarian, 1980–3)
[39] Master, Magdalene College, 1986–94
[40] (Steward, 1974–93)
[41] Disney Professor of Archaeology, 1981–2004; Master, Jesus College, 1986–97 (President, Easter 1961)
[42] University Treasurer, 1993–2003; (Senior Treasurer, 1987-9)
[43] Ambassador to Japan, 1992–6; Master, Churchill College, 1996–2006
[44] (President, Michaelmas 1975)
[45] Conservative Parliamentary candidate for Mid Norfolk
[46] Chief of the Secret Intelligence Service (MI6), 1999–2004; Master, Pembroke College, 2004–
[47] Chairman, Cambridge Centre for Energy Studies; (ex-Treasurer)
[48] Senior partner at the Cambridge office of Deloitte, 1999–
[49] Bursar, Corpus Christi College

Appendix IV:

Honorary Members, 1886–

Mr Alfred Waterhouse (Lent 1886)
Dr Oliver Wendell Holmes (Easter 1886)
Earl Kitchener of Khartoum and Aspall (Michaelmas 1898)
The Hon. Col. Theodore Roosevelt (Easter 1910)
Field Marshall Earl Haig (Easter 1920)
Admiral of the Fleet Viscount Jellicoe (Easter 1920)
Rear Admiral William Sowden Sims, US Navy (Easter 1921)
His Imperial Majesty Haile Selassie I, Emperor of Ethiopia (Easter 1936)
Admiral the Viscount Mountbatten of Burma (Michaelmas 1946)
Admiral of the Fleet Viscount Cunningham of Hyndhope (Lent 1946)
Field Marshal Viscount Alexander of Tunis (Lent 1946)
Field Marshal Viscount Alanbrooke of Brookeborough (Lent 1946)
Marshal of the RAF Lord Tedder of Glenguin (Lent 1946)
Mr W.R. Elworthy, ex-auditor (Easter 1947)
Mr Frederick W. Curzon, ex-Chief Clerk (Easter 1948)
HRH the Duke of Edinburgh (Michaelmas 1952)
The Hon. Pandit Jawaharlal Nehru (Lent 1955)
Mr Sydney A. Elwood, Chief Clerk (Lent 1963)
Mr Hubert H. Humphrey (Lent 1965)
HRH Prince Franz Josef II of Lichtenstein (Lent 1968)
Mr Kenneth Scott, ex-Treasurer (Easter 1969)
Dr R.T.H. Redpath, ex-Steward (Easter 1970)
Mr Alistair Cooke (Michaelmas 1973)
The Rt. Hon. Lord Butler of Saffron Walden, ex-President (Easter 1974)
Mr R.C. Andrew, ex-Treasurer (Michaelmas 1974)
The Rt. Hon. Harold Macmillan (Michaelmas 1975)
Mr Roland F. Thompson, ex-Chief Clerk (Michaelmas 1976)

Mr J. R. Bambrough, ex-Steward and ex-Trustee (Michaelmas 1976)
The Revd Canon Stanley Booth-Clibborn, ex-Treasurer (Michaelmas 1978)
Sir Robin Day (Michaelmas 1980)
HM King Constantine II of the Hellenes (Michaelmas 1981)
Lady Butler of Saffron Walden (Easter 1982)
The Rt. Hon. George Thomas MP (Viscount Tonypandy) (Easter 1982)
The Rt. Hon. Lord Denning (Lent 1983)
HRH Prince Charles, the Prince of Wales (Lent 1983)
The Most Revd and Rt. Hon. Lord Runcie of Cuddesdon (Michaelmas 1983)
Mr D.L. Baxter, ex-Senior Treasurer (Easter 1984)
HRH the Princess Anne (Lent 1986)
The Rt. Hon. Lord Hailsham of St Marylebone (Michaelmas 1987)
HM King Hussein of Jordan (Michaelmas 1988)
Det. Sgt John Goose, Cambridgeshire Constabulary (Michaelmas 1989)
Helen Suzman (Michaelmas 1989)
Mr Imre Pozsgay (Easter 1990)
Mr Rajiv Gandhi (Easter 1990)
The Hon. Ronald Reagan (Easter 1990)
Mr Nicholas Durkin, ex-Senior Treasurer (Easter 1991)
Mr Trevor Gardner, ex-Chairman of Trustees (Michaelmas 1992)
Mr Terry Waite (Michaelmas 1992)
HH the 14th Dalai Lama (Easter 1993)
The Most Revd Archbishop Desmond Tutu (Michaelmas 1993)
Sir David Calcutt QC, ex-Chairman of Trustees (Easter 1994)
Lech Wałęsa (Easter 1996)
Prof. the Lord Renfrew of Kaimsthorn, ex-President; ex-Chairman of Trustees
    (Lent 1997)
F.W. de Klerk (Easter 1997)
Mr Roy E. Disney (Michaelmas 1997)
Sir John Boyd, Chairman of Trustees (Easter 1998)
Prof Stephen Hawking (Michaelmas 2001)
Dr Hans Blix (Lent 2004)
Jackalyn Grainger, ex-Office Manager (Michaelmas 2004)
HE Jaap de Hoop Scheffer (Lent 2005)
President Jalal Talabani of Iraq (Easter 2007)

NOTES

1815–1939: AN INTRODUCTION

1 Lord Teignmouth, *Reminiscences of Many Years*, vol. I (Edinburgh: David Douglas, 1878), p. 47.

2 'A Trinity-Man' (J.M.F. Wright), in *Alma Mater: or Seven Years at the University of Cambridge*, vol. I (London: Black, Young and Young, 1827), pp. 202–3; A. Bayne (ed.), *The Autobiographic Recollections of George Pryme* (Cambridge: Deighton, Bell & Co., 1870), p. 117. Both cited in G. Martin, *The Cambridge Union and Ireland, 1815–1914* (Edinburgh: Ann Barry, 2000), p. 99.

3 'A Statement Regarding the Union' (Cambridge: E. & J. Goode, 1817).

4 Martin, p. 99.

5 Letter from 'The first Secretary and third President of the Union' (i.e. the Hon. C.J. Shore, later Lord Teignmouth) to *The Times*, 7 November 1866.

6 See for example P. Searby, *A History of the University of Cambridge, vol. III: 1750–1890* (Cambridge: Cambridge University Press, 1997), p. 93.

7 Wright, p. 202.

8 Cradock suggests that Wood came into the debate himself, but Whewell's account of the evening in his letter to Rose (see note 9) indicates that though the 'V.C. [was] in the house', the deputation were 'ushered into a room' to see him. Wright's description also says that it was just the University Orator and Proctors who intruded (Wright, p. 204). The only source suggesting Wood interrupted the debate

himself is Lord Teignmouth (Teignmouth, p. 54) – but, as Martin points out, he had graduated and was not at the debate himself.

9   W. Whewell to H.J. Rose, 25 March 1817, papers of William Whewell (Trinity College, Cambridge), R.2.99 1.

10 'A Statement Regarding the Union'.

11 By the future Lord Chancellor, Henry Brougham (*Parliamentary Debates*, vol. 34, 28 April 1817, cols. 20–1).

12 P. Cradock, *Recollections of the Cambridge Union, 1815–1939* (Cambridge: Bowes & Bowes, 1953), p. 9.

13 Martin, p. 115.

14 Martin (p. 124) explains that this was probably more to do with an attempt to censure the Treasurer for inefficiency at the business meeting beforehand.

15 Martin, p. 11.

16 Letter from Manning in the *Pall Mall Gazette* (1866), reprinted in *The Cambridge Union Society: Inaugural Proceedings* (London and Cambridge: Macmillan & Co., 1866), p. 64.

17 J.S. Mill, *Autobiography* (London: 1873), pp. 76–7.

18 ibid., p. 77.

19 K. Britton, 'J. S. Mill and the Cambridge Union Society', *The Cambridge Review*, vol. LXXVII, no. 1868 (29 October 1955), p. 92.

20 J. Venn and J.A. Venn, *Alumni Cantabrigienses: a biographical list of all known students, graduates, and holders of office at the University of Cambridge, from the earliest times to 1900*, 10 vols. (Cambridge University Press, 1922–54). Cradock does not mention Smith O'Brien in the body of his book, only in the list of officers (Cradock, p. 171); Martin has him as President but is surprised that he never spoke in a Union debate (Martin, p. x), and records that his grandson, though referring to O'Brien when he participated in a debate in 1911, made no mention of his having been President (Martin, p. 223).

21 See Searby, p. 534.

22 Cradock, pp. 53–4.

23 H.W. Harris, *Life So Far* (London: Jonathan Cape, 1954), p. 65.

24 C. Hollis, *The Oxford Union* (London: Evans Brothers Ltd., 1965), p. 122.

25 *The Book of the Cambridge Review, 1879–1897* (Cambridge: Macmillan & Bowes, 1898), p. 178.

26 Martin, p. 6. Special preparations had been made to allow a non-member to speak once before, in Easter 1874 (p. 143).

27 Cradock, p. 70.

28 D. Dutton, *Austen Chamberlain: Gentleman in Politics* (Bolton: Ross Anderson Publications, 1985), p. 16.

29 W. Everett, *On the Cam: Lectures on the University of Cambridge in England* (London: S.O. Beeton, 1866), p. 106.

30 ibid., p. 108.

31 R. Skidelsky, *John Maynard Keynes, vol. I: Hopes Betrayed, 1883–1920* (London: Macmillan, 1983), p. 113.

32 *Granta*, 8 November 1902.

33 Skidelsky, pp. 114, 121.

34 R.F. Harrod, *The Life of John Maynard Keynes* (London: Macmillan & Co. Ltd., 1963), p. 98.

35 *Granta*, 16 March 1905, in Skidelsky, p. 129.

36 Harrod, p. 98.

37 Skidelsky, p. 114.

38 Harris, p. 62. The ex-President from Trinity was most likely F.E. Bray (Lent 1904), as Harris describes him as 'a KC and no longer living'.

39 From Birkett's entry – by another ex-President, Patrick Devlin – in the *Dictionary of National Biography* (revised edn., Oxford University Press, 2004).

40 In Cradock, p. 111.

41 T.E.B. Howarth, *Cambridge Between Two Wars* (London: Collins, 1978), p. 23.

42 W.J. Butler (Secretary, Easter 1838, later Dean of Lincoln) does not seem to have been any relation.

43 R.A. Butler, *The Art of the Possible: The Memoirs of Lord Butler KG, CH* (London: Hamish Hamilton, 1971), p. 16.

44 Cradock, p. 120.

45 In Howarth, p. 145.

46 F.E. Jones (Lord Elwyn-Jones), *In My Time: An Autobiography* (London: Weidenfeld & Nicolson, 1983), p. 27.

47 Papers of Sydney Elwood (unfinished memoirs of his years at the Cambridge Union, 1923–67; hereafter Elwood MSS), pp. 73, 76.

48 Vice-President's report, Lent 1939.

1939–45: The Second World War

1   Howarth, p. 24.
2   J.E. Costello, *Mask of Treachery* (London: Collins, 1988), pp. 122, 153.
3   M. Carter, *Anthony Blunt: His Lives* (London: Macmillan, 2001), pp. 105–6.
4   Carter, p. 109. Cornford's father, F.M. Cornford, was a Fellow of Trinity, professor of ancient philosophy, and the author of a famous pamphlet, *Microcosmographia Academica* (1908), which offered satirical advice to the young academic politician; his mother, Frances, was the granddaughter of Charles Darwin.
5   M. Straight, *After Long Silence* (London: Collins, 1983), pp. 68–9, 72.
6   Carter, p. 186.
7   Straight, p. 91.
8   Ewart recalls him attending a clandestine meeting of communist students in Blunt's rooms that term (Carter, p. 192).
9   Straight, p. 79; Carter, pp. 183–4.
10   Carter, p. 185.
11   Straight, p. 101.
12   ibid., p. 104.
13   ibid., p. 106.
14   Cradock, p. 147.
15   Carter, p. 197.
16   Costello, p. 274.
17   *Spectator*, 5 June 1936.
18   Costello, p. 253.
19   *The Times*, 20 March 1971.
20   Howarth, p. 217.
21   E. Hobsbawm, *Interesting Times: A Twentieth-Century Life* (London: Allen Lane, 2002), p. 112.
22   *Daily Mail*, 25 July 2002.
23   *Cambridge Daily News*, 22 February 1933.
24   Howarth, p. 224.
25   F.A. Reeve, *Cambridge* (London: B.T. Batsford, 1976), p. 164.
26   L.S. Amery, *My Political Life, Vol. III: The Unforgiving Years, 1929–40* (London: Hutchinson, 1955), p. 147. The vote was 377 to 88.
27   *Cambridge Daily News*, 9 March 1938.

28 Simonds to Straight, 1 June 1940, in Straight, p. 151.

29 Cradock, pp. 153–4.

30 *Cambridge Daily News*, 9 March 1938; *Cambridge Review*, 22 April 1938.

31 ibid., 26 April 1938.

32 ibid., 1 February 1939.

33 *The Times*, 18 February 1933.

34 M. Ceadel, 'The "King and Country" Debate, 1933: Student Politics, Pacifism and the Dictators', *The Historical Journal*, vol. 22, no. 2 (June 1979), pp. 397–422.

35 Hollis, p. 186.

36 *The Times*, 11 April 1933.

37 *Cambridge Daily News*, 26 April 1939.

38 Howarth, p. 238.

39 Amery, *My Political Life*, p. 313.

40 Elwood MSS, p. 89

41 ibid., p. 93.

42 Sir James Bottomley, interview with the author, 23 July 2005.

43 Senior proctor (E.E. Rich) to J.R.A. Bottomley, 3 June 1940.

44 Stanley S. Brown to senior proctor (C.T. Seltman), 16 October 1940.

45 Seltman to Brown, 17 October 1940.

46 F. Inglis, *Raymond Williams* (London: Routledge, 1995), p. 77.

47 Elwood MSS, p. 104.

48 Seltman to Brown, 18 February 1941.

49 Elwood MSS, p. 104.

50 In R. Hayman (ed.), *My Cambridge* (London: Robson Books Ltd., 1977), p. 62.

51 Elwood MSS, p. 107.

52 Stevenson to Hardman, 4 December 1941.

53 Interview with author, 23 July 2005.

54 *Cambridge Daily News*, 14 September 1945.

55 Elwood MSS, p. 109.

56 *Independent Press and Chronicle*, 31 July 1942.

57 Hobsbawm, p. 112.

58 *Spectator*, 19 October 1945.

59 *Sunday Times*, 9 December 1945.

60 J.S. Boys Smith, 'The Combination Room and "D" Day', *Eagle*, vol. LXII, no. 270, June 1968, pp. 218–22.

61 ibid., p. 221 and n.

62 One such article, by R.A. Butler in the *Sunday Times*, 11 August 1946, relied on 'some recent literature which was circulated with the appeal for funds to rebuild the Society's buildings'.

63 *The Times*, 22 December 1945; Elwood MSS, p. 112.

64 Vice-President's report, Michaelmas 1944.

65 *Cambridge Review*, 20 February 1943.

1945–50: POST-WAR REGENERATION

1 H.W. Harris, *Life So Far*, p. 60.

2 Lord Hooson of Montgomery, 'Clement Davies: An Underestimated Welshman and Politician', *Journal of Liberal Democrat History*, vol. 24, Autumn 1999, p. 7.

3 *Varsity*, 15 October 1949.

4 *Cambridge Daily News*, 20 November 1946.

5 Reeve, p. 166.

6 *Cambridge Daily News*, 25 January 1939.

7 *Varsity*, 18 October 1947.

8 *Cambridge Daily News*, 16 October 1946.

9 *Daily Mail*, 16 October 1946.

10 *Daily Mail*, 22 January 1947.

11 *Cambridge Daily News*, 15 March 1947.

12 *Varsity*, 18 October 1947.

13 *Economist*, 18 October 1947.

14 B. Pimlott, *Hugh Dalton* (London: Jonathan Cape, 1985), pp. 42, 58.

15 *Cambridge Daily News*, 4 June 1947.

16 *Varsity*, 14 February 1948.

17 ibid., 4 December 1948.

18 *Cambridge Review*, 28 October 1950.

19 Interview with the author, 23 May 2007.

20 *The Times*, 5 February 1958.

21 *Varsity*, 15 November 1947.

22 Barnes to Mackworth-Young, 13 November 1947.

23 H. Berkeley, *Crossing the Floor* (London: George Allen & Unwin Ltd., 1972), p. 129.

24 Elwood MSS, p. 111.
25 *Varsity*, 12 June 1948.
26 *Independent*, 19 October 2001.
27 ibid.; correspondence with the author, 20 April 2008.
28 *Varsity*, 20 November 1948.
29 *Irish Press*, 17 November 1948.
30 *Varsity*, 20 November 1948.
31 *Irish Press*, 17 November 1948.

1950–55: GOLDEN AUSTERITY
1 Reeve, p. 166.
2 ibid., p. 170.
3 Interview with the author, 23 May 2007.
4 *Varsity*, 29 November 1947.
5 D. Hurd, *Memoirs* (London: Abacus, 2004), p. 537.
6 G. Janner (Lord Janner of Braunstone), *To Life! The Memoirs of Greville Janner* (Stroud: Sutton Publishing Ltd., 2006), p. 55.
7 *Varsity*, 30 April 1949.
8 Correspondence with the author, 22 May 2005.
9 ibid.; Elwood MSS, p. 211.
10 Elwood MSS, p. 152.
11 ibid., p. 152; *Varsity*, 25 October 1947.
12 *Varsity*, 13 November 1948.
13 ibid., 15 October 1949.
14 ibid., 28 January 1950.
15 N. St John-Stevas, *The Two Cities* (London: Faber and Faber, 1984), p. 25.
16 Elwood MSS, p. 186.
17 ibid., p. 187.
18 ibid., p. 188.
19 St John-Stevas, p. 26.
20 *Varsity*, 22 April 1950.
21 D. Walter, *The Oxford Union: Playground of Power* (London: Macdonald & Co., 1984), p. 144.
22 'Howard E. Shuman', Oral History Interviews, Senate Historical Office (Washington, DC, 22 July 1987), p. 41.
23 ibid., p. 41.

24 ibid., p. 43.
25 ibid., p. 44.
26 Walter, p. 134.
27 Sir R. Day, *Grand Inquisitor* (London: Weidenfeld & Nicolson, 1989), p. 39.
28 Walter, p. 144.
29 Day, p. 39.
30 ibid., pp. 62, 70.
31 ibid., p. 39.
32 Walter, p. 132.
33 Day, pp. 39–40.
34 ibid., p. 40.
35 *Varsity*, 4 February 1950.
36 Hurd, p. 83.
37 *Independent*, 15 March 1998.
38 *The Times*, 7 March 1956.
39 *Sunday Times*, 10 March 1991.
40 Derick Mirfin to his mother, 28 April 1953. The party was also featured in the next edition of *Tatler*.
41 S.C. Roberts to R.G. Waterhouse, 5 July 1950.
42 Derick Mirfin to his mother, 13 November 1952.
43 ibid.
44 G. Shaw, *In the Long Run: Tales of a Yorkshire Life* (Co. Durham: The Memoir Club, 2001), p. 51.
45 By 'H.S.T.' (presumably Hugh Thomas), 17 January 1953.
46 *The Times*, 17 January 2006.
47 C. Renfrew, 'Daniel, Glyn Edmund (1914–1986)', rev., *Oxford Dictionary of National Biography* (Oxford University Press, 2004).
48 Hurd, p. 80.
49 *Varsity*, 19 November 1949.
50 Elwood MSS, p. 242.
51 *Varsity*, 11 February 1950; *Cambridge Review*, 2 December 1950.
52 G. Howe, *Conflict of Loyalty* (London: Macmillan, 1994), p. 19.
53 Hurd, p. 83.
54 *Cambridge Review*, 10 February 1951.
55 Janner, *To Life!*, p. 54.
56 Elwood MSS, p. 348.

57 ibid., p. 266.

1955–9: SCANDALS, SQUABBLES, AND SUEZ

1   M. Weatherall, *From Our Cambridge Correspondent: Cambridge student life 1945–95 as seen in the pages of* Varsity (Cambridge: Varsity Publications Ltd., 1995), p. 23.
2   Elwood MSS, p. 278.
3   Vice-President's report, Easter 1954.
4   *The Times*, 17 October 1956.
5   Elwood MSS, p. 285.
6   *Varsity*, 17 May 1953.
7   Lord Thomas of Swynnerton, interview with the author, 7 March 2008.
8   ibid.
9   *The Times*, 18 October 1973.
10 Derick Mirfin to his mother, 12 May 1954.
11 ibid.
12 Derick Mirfin to his mother, 1 June 1952.
13 *Independent*, 27 April 1991.
14 Dalyell, interview with the author, 3 November 2007; Shaw, p. 62.
15 Interview with the author, 3 November 2007.
16 Shaw, p. 62.
17 *The Times*, 26 July 1996.
18 Derick Mirfin to his mother, 13 February 1955.
19 Interview with the author, 3 November 2007.
20 correspondence with Derick Mirfin, 24 October 2005.
21 ibid.
22 *Independent*, 24 April 2000.
23 Foreword to Shaw, p. xi.
24 *Independent*, 24 April 2000.
25 *Guardian*, 17 April 2000.
26 Shaw, p. 51.
27 ibid., p. 61.
28 ibid., p. 59.
29 ibid., p. 62.
30 Sir J. Nott, *Here Today, Gone Tomorrow: Recollections of an Errant Politician* (London: Politico's, 2002), p. 69.
31 ibid., p. 71.

32 Vice-President's report, Michaelmas 1956.
33 T. Benn, *The Benn Diaries* (London: Arrow Books, 1996), p. 40.
34 Weatherall, p. 31.
35 Nott, p. 66.

RECOLLECTION: EASTER 1959 (Nott)
36 Entry for 2 November 1956, Benn, p. 40.

1960–67: THE 'CAMBRIDGE MAFIA'
1 Sir N. Fowler, *Ministers Decide: A Personal Memoir of the Thatcher Years* (London: Chapmans, 1991), p. 26.
2 ibid., p. 26.
3 ibid., p. 27.
4 ibid., pp. 28–9.
5 *Observer* magazine, 28 November 1993.
6 *House* magazine, 13 May 1991, quoted in P. Riddell, *Honest Opportunism: The Rise of the Career Politician* (London: Hamish Hamilton Ltd., 1993), p. 76.
7 Riddell, p. 55.
8 *Guardian*, 10 October 1988.
9 ibid.
10 Martin, p. 15.
11 *Guardian*, 10 October 1988.
12 *Sunday Times*, 3 March 1996.
13 Sir D. Frost, *An Autobiography, Part One: From Congregations to Audiences* (London: HarperCollins, 1993), p. 36.
14 Fowler, p. 30.
15 A. McSmith, *Kenneth Clarke: A Political Biography* (London: Verso, 1994), p. 14.
16 *Independent on Sunday*, 7 March 1993.
17 Riddell, p. 64.
18 Fowler, p. 32.
19 M. Crick, *In Search of Michael Howard* (London: Simon & Schuster, 2005), p. 60.
20 Fowler, p. 33.
21 Riddell, p. 74.

22 *Nottingham Evening Post*, 9 July 1970, in M. Balen, *Kenneth Clarke* (London: Fourth Estate, 1994), p. 78.
23 F. Graham, *Playing at Politics: An Ethnography of the Oxford Union* (Edinburgh: Dunedin Academic Press, 2005), p. 77.
24 Crick, p. 66.
25 Riddell, p. 65.
26 *Sunday Times*, 14 March 1993.
27 Fowler, p. 33.
28 D. Owen, *Time to Declare* (London: Michael Joseph, 1991), p. 44.
29 Peter Temple-Morris, in Crick, p. 63.
30 *Independent on Sunday*, 7 March 1993.
31 Fowler, p. 33.
32 *Independent on Sunday*, 7 March 1993.
33 ibid.
34 Crick, p. 59.
35 Fowler, p. 34.
36 McSmith, p. 12.
37 *Varsity Handbook* (Cambridge: Varsity Publications, 1960), pp. 73–4.
38 *Varsity Handbook* (Cambridge: Varsity Publications, 1961), p. 95.
39 *Varsity*, 20 May 1961.
40 *Independent on Sunday*, 7 March 1993.
41 Crick, p. 67; McSmith, pp. 17–18.
42 Fowler, p. 35.
43 Crick, p. 65.
44 BBC Radio 4, *Desert Island Discs*, 4 July 2004.
45 Crick, p. 68.
46 ibid., p. 68.
47 David Hacking, in Crick, p. 69.
48 Balen, p. 33; McSmith, p. 18.
49 *The Times*, 25 April 1960.
50 Balen, p. 34.
51 Crick, p. 71.
52 McSmith, p. 20.
53 Crick, pp. 72–3
54 *Varsity*, 18 November 1961.
55 Balen, p. 35.
56 *Varsity*, 25 November 1961.

57 Balen, p. 41.

58 *Varsity*, 2 December 1961.

59 *The Times*, 10 March 1961.

60 *Varsity*, 3 June 1961; McSmith, p. 20.

61 *The Times*, 5 December 1961.

62 *Varsity*, 20 January 1962.

63 cited in *Independent on Sunday*, 2 December 1990.

64 *Guardian*, 10 October 1988.

65 *Varsity*, 27 January 1962.

66 ibid., 10 March 1962.

67 Crick, p. 75.

68 *The Times*, 6 June 1962.

69 ibid., 5 June 1962.

70 ibid., 11 June 1962.

71 ibid., 12 February 1963.

72 ibid., 13 June 1962.

73 Balen, p. 44.

74 ibid., p. 45.

75 *The Times*, 26 February 1963; *Varsity*, 2 March 1963.

76 *The Times*, 15 November 1997.

77 *Varsity*, 1 June 1963.

78 *New Cambridge*, 8 November 1963.

79 Crick, p. 69.

80 *Guardian*, 10 October 1988; Weatherall, p. 27.

81 *Independent on Sunday*, 2 December 1990.

82 e.g. Riddell, p. 2.

83 *Independent on Sunday*, 2 December 1990.

84 *Varsity*, 13 June 1964.

85 M.J. Petty, *Cambridge in Pictures: 1888–1988* (Cambridge Newspapers Ltd., 1988), p. 26.

86 His Honour Judge Burford, interview with the author, 19 March 2008.

87 *The Times*, 20 January 1965.

RECOLLECTION: MICHAELMAS 1962 (Pollitt)

88 See for example Crick, p. 76.

89 *Varsity*, 5 May 1962.

90 *Varsity*, 21 October 1961.

91 C. James, *Falling Towards England* (London: Jonathan Cape Ltd., 1985), p. 189.

92 H. Pollitt, *Serving My Time* (London: Lawrence & Wishart, 1940), p. 250.

1912–63: THE BATTLE TO ADMIT WOMEN

1 C.N.L. Brooke, *A History of the University of Cambridge, vol. IV: 1870–1990* (Cambridge University Press, 1993), p. 324.

2 Martin, p. 59.

3 ibid., pp. 59–60.

4 ibid., pp. 62, 282–4 (Tables 9–10).

5 R. McWilliams-Tullberg, *Women at Cambridge: A Men's University – Though of a Mixed Type* (London: Victor Gollancz Ltd., 1975), pp. 175, 192.

6 Martin, p. 62.

7 Elwood MSS, p. 367.

8 Walter, p. 162.

9 Elwood MSS, p. 370.

10 *Cambridge Daily News*, 30 October 1935.

11 Elwood MSS, p. 373.

12 *Cambridge Daily News*, 21 November 1939.

13 *Cambridge Daily News*, 12 June 1946.

14 Elwood MSS, p. 337.

15 *Cambridge Daily News*, 12 June 1946.

16 *Varsity*, 31 January 1948.

17 ibid., 20 November 1948.

18 ibid., 5 February 1949.

19 Elwood MSS, pp. 377–8.

20 Interview with the author, 13 November 2008.

21 *The Times*, 21 February 1955.

22 ibid., 21 February 1955.

23 Weatherall, p. 62.

24 *Time* magazine, 7 March 1955.

25 Elwood MSS, p. 381.

26 *The Times*, 25 April 1955.

27 D. Hutchinson, P. Houghton, C. Postgate and A. Wilson (eds.), *New Hall Lives: The Silver Street Years, 1954–1964* (Cambridge: New Hall Society, 2005), pp. 22–3, 29.

28 *Sunday Times*, 9 February 1958.
29 Elwood MSS, p. 383.
30 *The Times*, 13 March 1961.
31 ibid., 13 March 1961.
32 Elwood MSS, p. 384.
33 *The Times*, 18 October 1961.
34 ibid., 19 October 1961.
35 Elwood MSS, p. 385.
36 Obituary by Richard Lambert, *Financial Times*, 11 January 2005.
37 Elwood MSS, p. 386.
38 *Guardian*, 17 June 1994.
39 ibid., 17 June 1994.
40 Elwood MSS, p. 387.
41 *Varsity*, 26 May 1962.
42 ibid., 26 May 1962.
43 *The Times*, 16 November 1962.
44 ibid., 9 February 1963.
45 *Cambridge News*, 13 February 1963.
46 The Hon. Mr Justice Binnie, correspondence with the author, 6 August 2008.
47 *The Times*, 7 March 1963; *Varsity*, 9 March 1963.
48 Balen, p. 45.
49 Elwood MSS, p. 391.
50 *The Times*, 5 November 1963.
51 Elwood MSS, p. 392.
52 His Honour Judge Burford, interview with the author, 19 March 2008.
53 Weatherall, p. 64.
54 Dr Vincent Cable MP, correspondence with the author, 10 November 2008.
55 Interview with author, 19 March 2008.
56 ibid.
57 ibid. (Now Susan Whitfield, she taught at St Paul's and became headmistress of the independent girls' Notting Hill and Ealing High School in 1991.)
58 *The Times*, 1 June 1967.
59 *Guardian*, 5 October 1999.
60 Walter, p. 172.

61 Crick, p. 123.
62 *Guardian*, 17 June 1994.

1967–75: AN 'OPEN UNION'?

1 Weatherall, p. 46.
2 ibid., p. 13.
3 ibid., p. 35.
4 The Rt. Hon. Charles Clarke MP, interview with the author, 24 October 2007.
5 Obituary in the *Guardian*, 24 July 2003.
6 Special Minute of the Senate of the University of Edinburgh, 29 May 2005.
7 *The Times*, 16 May 1969; 13–14 August 1970.
8 H. Anderson, J. Hipkin and M. Plaistow (eds.), *Education for the Seventies: Transcriptions of the Cambridge Union Teach-In* (London: Heinemann Educational Books Ltd., 1970), p. ix.
9 Biography at www.princeofwales.gov.uk
10 J. Dimbleby, *The Prince of Wales* (London: Little, Brown and Co., 1994), p. 513.
11 S. Heffer, *Like the Roman: The Life of Enoch Powell* (London: Weidenfeld & Nicolson, 1998), p. 488.
12 *Memoirs of the Tripos* (University of Cambridge, Faculty of Economics and Politics, n.d.), p. 11; Heffer, pp. 488–9.
13 *The Times*, 29–30 October 1969.
14 Weatherall, p. 47.
15 Walter, p. 193.
16 Weatherall, p. 52.
17 *The Times*, 9 March 1971.
18 *Spectator*, 20 November 1971.
19 By Michael White in the *Guardian*, 14 April 1986.
20 *The Times*, 29 November 1971.
21 M. Parris, *Chance Witness: An Outsider's Life in Politics* (London: Penguin, 2003), p. 118.
22 *Newsweek*, 15 October 2007.
23 *Observer*, 16 October 1994.
24 *The Times*, 29 November 1971.
25 *Sunday Times*, 15 August 2004.

26 Interview with the author, 24 October 2007.
27 ibid.
28 *Stop Press*, 21 January 1972.
29 ibid.
30 *Varsity*, 4 March 1972.
31 *Stop Press*, 21 January 1972.
32 *Varsity*, 15 January 1972.
33 The Rt. Hon. Charles Clarke MP, interview with the author, 24 October 2007.
34 *Varsity*, 26 February 1972.
35 ibid., 22 April 1972.
36 *The Times*, 7 April 1972.
37 *Varsity*, 4 March 1972.
38 F.H. Stubbings, *Bedders, Bulldogs and Bedells: A Cambridge Glossary* (Cambridge University Press, 2001), p. 31.
39 The Rt. Hon. Charles Clarke MP, interview with the author, 24 October 2007.
40 *The Times*, 12 April 1972.
41 *Varsity*, 22 April 1972.
42 *The Times*, 12 April 1972.
43 The Rt. Hon. Charles Clarke MP, interview with the author, 24 October 2007.
44 *Guardian*, 9 February 1999.
45 Barry Thoday, interview with the author, 19 June 2006.
46 *Varsity*, 29 April 1972.
47 ibid., 6 May 1972.
48 *Stop Press*, 10 November 1972.
49 *Cambridge University Reporter*, special no. 10, 30 January 1973.
50 *Stop Press*, 17 November 1972; 19 January 1973.
51 *Stop Press*, 2 March 1973; *Varsity*, 3 February 1973; *Stop Press*, 9 March 1973.
52 *Cambridge University Reporter*, special no. 10, 30 January 1973.
53 P. Pagnamenta (ed.), *The University of Cambridge: An 800th Anniversary Portrait* (London: Third Millennium Publishing Ltd., 2008), p. 191.
54 *Stop Press with Varsity*, 26 January 1974.
55 Interview with the author, 24 October 2007.
56 Interview with the author, 7 August 2008.

57 Correspondence with the author, 11 August 2008.

58 *Guardian*, 3 January 2002.

1975–90: 'THE PASSION FOR FREE EXPRESSION'

1   *CAM: Cambridge Alumni Magazine*, no. 48 (Easter Term 2006), p. 45.

2   *Observer*, 1 August 2004.

3   Barry Thoday, interview with the author, 19 June 2006.

4   *Observer*, 23 September 2007.

5   *CAM: Cambridge Alumni Magazine*, no. 53 (Lent Term 2008), p. 45.

6   Interview with the author, 29 January 2008.

7   *Guardian*, 6 August 1994.

8   Graham, p. 210.

9   The Revd Fr David Johnson, interview with the author, 8 November 2008.

10 ibid.

11 *Daily Telegraph*, 4 December 2004.

12 *The Times*, 7 July 1993.

13 R. Hewison, *Footlights! A Hundred Years of Cambridge Comedy* (London: Methuen, 1983), pp. 175–6.

14 Weatherall, p. 15.

15 *Independent*, 15 November 1992.

16 *Cambridge University Reporter*, 10 December 1980; *Stop Press with Varsity*, 17 January 1981.

17 BBC Radio 4, *Today*, 2 October 2000.

18 Standing committee minutes, 10 May 1980.

19 *Stop Press with Varsity*, 24 January 1981.

20 *The Times*, 7 November 1989.

21 *Guardian*, 15 March 1999.

22 *The Times*, 9 March 1987.

23 *Daily Telegraph*, 15 November 1984.

24 R. Deacon, *The Cambridge Apostles* (London: Robert Royce Ltd., 1985), p. 183.

25 *Stop Press with Varsity*, 6 October 1981.

26 ibid., 23 January and 8 May 1982.

27 C. Flynn, 'History of the World Debating Championships', at flynn.debating.net/worhist.htm

28 *The Times*, 4 October 1980.

29 'About the agency', www.andrewlownie.co.uk
30 *Independent*, 1 September 1995
31 Obituary (by Lownie) in the *Guardian*, 31 August 1995.
32 *The Times*, 23 October 1988.
33 Interview with the author, 19 June 2006.
34 ibid.
35 *Independent*, 18 May 1992, cited at www.grahamdavies.co.uk
36 Interview with the author, 25 November 2008.
37 ibid.; *The Times*, 6 December 1990.
38 *Independent*, 6 December 1990.
39 Hon. Ronald Reagan, Address to the Cambridge Union Society, 5 December 1990, in D.E. Felten (ed.), *A Shining City: the Legacy of Ronald Reagan* (New York: Simon & Schuster, 1998), p. 96.

BIBLIOGRAPHY

Unpublished Material
Elwood, S.A., unfinished memoirs of his years at the Cambridge Union, 1923–67 (by kind permission of P. Elwood and E. Newman)

Published Material
Amery, L.S., *My Political Life, Vol. III: The Unforgiving Years, 1929–40* (London: Hutchinson, 1955)

Anderson, H., Hipkin, J., and Plaistow, M. (eds.), *Education for the Seventies: Transcriptions of the Cambridge Union Teach-In* (London: Heinemann Educational Books Ltd., 1970)

Ashley, J., *Journey Into Silence* (London: The Bodley Head, 1973)

Ashley, J. (Lord Ashley of Stoke), *Acts of Defiance* (London: Penguin, 1994)

Balen, M., *Kenneth Clarke* (London: Fourth Estate, 1994)

Bayne, A. (ed.), *The Autobiographic Recollections of George Pryme* (Cambridge: Deighton, Bell & Co., 1870)

Benn, T., *The Benn Diaries* (London: Arrow Books, 1996)

Berkeley, H., *Crossing the Floor* (London: George Allen & Unwin Ltd., 1972)

Boyle, A., *Climate of Treason: Five Who Spied for Russia* (London: Hutchinson & Co., 1979)

Boys Smith, J.S., 'The Combination Room and "D" Day', *Eagle*, vol. LXII, no. 270, June 1968, pp. 218–22

Britton, K., 'J.S. Mill and the Cambridge Union Society', *Cambridge Review*, vol. LXXVII, no. 1868 (29 October 1955), pp. 92–5

Brooke, C.N.L., *A History of the University of Cambridge, vol. IV: 1870–1990* (Cambridge University Press, 1993)

Butler, M. (Lady Butler), *August and Rab: A Memoir* (London: Weidenfeld & Nicolson, 1987)

Butler, R.A. (Lord Butler of Saffron Walden), *The Art of the Possible: The Memoirs of Lord Butler KG CH* (London: Hamish Hamilton, 1971)

Cambridge Review, The, *The Book of The Cambridge Review, 1879–1897* (Cambridge: Macmillan & Bowes, 1898)

Cambridge Union Society, *Laws & Annual Reports*, 1846–1948/9 (Cambridge: Hugh Foister; Foister & Judd; Fabb & Tyler Ltd.; S.G. Marshall & Son, 1846–1949)

Cambridge Union Society, *The Cambridge Union Society: Inaugural Proceedings* (London and Cambridge: Macmillan and Co., 1866)

Carter, M., *Anthony Blunt: His Lives* (London: Macmillan, 2001)

Ceadel, M., 'The "King and Country" Debate, 1933: Student Politics, Pacifism and the Dictators', *The Historical Journal*, vol. 22, no. 2 (June 1979), pp. 397–422.

Costello, J., *Mask of Treachery* (London: Collins, 1988)

Cradock, P., *Recollections of the Cambridge Union, 1815–1939* (Cambridge: Bowes & Bowes, 1953)

Crick, M., *In Search of Michael Howard* (London: Simon & Schuster, 2005)

Daniel, G., *Some Small Harvest: The Memoirs of Glyn Daniel* (London: Thames & Hudson, 1986)

Day, Sir R., *Grand Inquisitor* (London: Weidenfeld & Nicolson, 1989)

Deacon, R., *The Cambridge Apostles* (London: Robert Royce Ltd., 1985)

Devlin, P., *Taken at the Flood* (Norfolk: Taverner, 1996)

Devlin, P., 'Birkett, (William) Norman, first Baron Birkett (1883–1962)', rev., *Oxford Dictionary of National Biography* (Oxford University Press, 2004)

Dimbleby, J., *The Prince of Wales* (London: Little, Brown and Company, 1994)

Dutton, D., *Austen Chamberlain: Gentleman in Politics* (Bolton: Ross Anderson Publications, 1985)

Everett, W., *On The Cam: Lectures on the University of Cambridge in England* (London: S.O. Beeton, 1866)

Felten, D.E. (ed.), *A Shining City: the Legacy of Ronald Reagan* (New York: Simon & Schuster, 1998)

Forward, T., and Johnson, D., *The Spiritual Quest of Francis Wagstaffe* (Leominster, Gracewing Ltd., 1994)

Fowler, L. and Fowler, H. (eds.), *Cambridge Commemorated: An Anthology of University Life* (Cambridge University Press, 1984)

Fowler, Sir N., *Ministers Decide: A Personal Memoir of the Thatcher Years* (London: Chapmans, 1991)

Frost, Sir D., *An Autobiography, Part One: From Congregations to Audiences* (London: Harper Collins, 1993)

Graham, F., *Playing at Politics: An Ethnography of the Oxford Union* (Edinburgh: Dunedin Academic Press, 2005)

Harrod, R.F., *The Life of John Maynard Keynes* (London: Macmillan & Co. Ltd., 1963)

Harris, H.W., *Life So Far* (London: Jonathan Cape, 1954)

Harris-Burland, J. B. and Wynne Wilson, St.J.B., 'The Oxford and Cambridge Union Societies', *Strand* magazine, vol. 7, 1894, pp. 500–512

Hayman, R. (ed.), *My Cambridge* (London: Robson Books Ltd., 1977)

Heffer, S., *Like the Roman: The Life of Enoch Powell* (London: Weidenfeld & Nicolson, 1998)

Hewison, R., *Footlights! A Hundred Years of Cambridge Comedy* (London: Methuen, 1983)

Hobsbawm, E., *Interesting Times: A Twentieth-Century Life* (London: Allen Lane, 2002)

Hollis, C., *The Oxford Union* (London: Evans Brothers Ltd., 1965)

Hooson of Montgomery, Lord, 'Clement Davies: An Underestimated Welshman and Politician', *Journal of Liberal Democrat History*, vol. 24, autumn 1999, pp. 3–13

Hough, R., *Mountbatten: Hero of Our Time* (London: Weidenfeld & Nicolson, 1980)

Howarth, T.E.B., *Cambridge Between Two Wars* (London: Collins, 1978)

Howard, A., *RAB: The Life of R.A. Butler* (London: Jonathan Cape, 1987)

Howe, G. (Lord Howe of Aberavon), *Conflict of Loyalty* (London: Macmillan, 1994)

Hurd, D. (Lord Hurd of Westwell), *Memoirs* (London: Abacus, 2004)

Hutchinson, D., Houghton, P., Postgate, C. and Wilson, A. (eds.), *New Hall Lives: The Silver Street Years, 1954–1964* (Cambridge: New Hall Society, 2005)

Inglis, F., *Raymond Williams* (London: Routledge, 1995)

James, C., *Falling Towards England* (London: Jonathan Cape Ltd., 1985)

Janner, G., *Janner's Complete Speechmaker* (London: Business Books, 1989)

Janner, G. (Lord Janner of Braunstone), *To Life! The Memoirs of Greville Janner* (Stroud: Sutton Publishing Ltd., 2006)

Jones, F.E. (Lord Elwyn-Jones), *In My Time: An Autobiography* (London: Weidenfeld & Nicolson, 1983)

King-Hamilton, A., *And Nothing But the Truth* (London: Weidenfeld & Nicolson, 1982)

Lloyd, I.S., and Richmond, W.H.L., 'The 1947 Cambridge Union Tour', *The Quarterly Journal of Speech*, vol. XXXIV, no. 1 (February 1948), pp. 46–9

Lysaght, C.E., 'The Cambridge Union: Some Irish Footnotes', *Irish Times*, 13 February 1965

Martin, G., *The Cambridge Union and Ireland, 1815–1914* (Edinburgh: Ann Barry, 2000)

McNair, W.L., Morris, J.W., Reid, D.M. and Shakespeare, G.H., *Demosthenes Demobilised: a record of Cambridge Union Society debates, February 1919 – June 1920* (Cambridge: W. Heffer and Sons Ltd., 1920).

McSmith, A., *Kenneth Clarke: A Political Biography* (London: Verso, 1994)

McWilliams-Tullberg, R., *Women at Cambridge: A Men's University – Though of a Mixed Type* (London: Victor Gollancz Ltd., 1975)

Mill, J.S., *Autobiography* (London: Longmans, Green, Reader, and Dyer, 1873)

Murphy, R., *Last Viceroy: The Life and Times of Rear-Admiral the Earl Mountbatten of Burma* (London: Jarrolds, 1948)

Nott, Sir J., *Here Today, Gone Tomorrow: Recollections of an Errant Politician* (London: Politico's, 2002)

Owen, D. (Lord Owen), *Time to Declare* (London: Michael Joseph, 1991)

Pagnamenta, P. (ed.), *The University of Cambridge: An 800th Anniversary Portrait* (London: Third Millennium Publishing Ltd., 2008)

Parris, M., *Chance Witness: An Outsider's Life in Politics* (London: Penguin, 2003)

Petty, M.J., *Cambridge in Pictures: 1888–1988* (Cambridge Newspapers Ltd., 1988)

Pimlott, B., *Hugh Dalton* (London: Jonathan Cape, 1985)

Pollitt, H., *Serving My Time* (London: Lawrence & Wishart, 1940)

Riddell, P., *Honest Opportunism: The Rise of the Career Politician* (London: Hamish Hamilton Ltd., 1993)

Reeve, F.A., *Cambridge* (London: B.T. Batsford Ltd., 1976)

Renfrew, C. (Lord Renfrew of Kaimsthorn), 'Daniel, Glyn Edmund (1914–1986)', rev., *Oxford Dictionary of National Biography* (Oxford University Press, 2004)

St John Stevas, N. (Lord St John of Fawsley), *The Two Cities* (London: Faber and Faber, 1984)

Searby, P., *A History of the University of Cambridge, vol. III: 1750–1890* (Cambridge University Press, 1997)

Shaw, Sir G., *In The Long Run: Tales of a Yorkshire Life* (Co. Durham: The Memoir Club, 2001)

Skidelsky, R., *John Maynard Keynes, vol. I: Hopes Betrayed, 1883–1920* (London: Macmillan, 1983)

Skipper, J.F., *A Short History of the Cambridge University Union* (Cambridge: Henry Wallis, 1878)

Smith, D., *Raymond Williams: A Warrior's Tale* (Cardigan: Parthian, 2008)

Sparrow, J.W.G., *'R.A.B.', Study of a Statesman: The career of Baron Butler of Saffron Walden, CH* (London: Odhams Books Ltd., 1965)

Straight, M., *After Long Silence* (London: Collins, 1983)

Stubbings, F.H., *Bedders, Bulldogs and Bedells: A Cambridge Glossary* (Cambridge University Press, 2001)

Teignmouth, Lord (C.J. Shore), *Reminiscences of Many Years*, vol. I (Edinburgh: David Douglas, 1878)

Thorpe, D.R., *Selwyn Lloyd* (London: Jonathan Cape, 1989)

'A Trinity-Man' (J.M.F. Wright), *Alma Mater: or Seven Years at the University of Cambridge*, vol. I (London: Black, Young, and Young, 1827)

United States Senate Historical Office, Oral History Interviews, 'Howard E. Shuman' (Washington, DC: 1987)

Venn, J. and Venn, J.A., *Alumni Cantabrigienses: a biographical list of all known students, graduates, and holders of office at the University of Cambridge, from the earliest times to 1900*, 10 vols. (Cambridge University Press, 1922–54)

Walter, D., *The Oxford Union: Playground of Power* (London: Macdonald & Co. Ltd., 1984)

Weatherall, M., *From Our Cambridge Correspondent: Cambridge Student Life 1945–95 as Seen in the Pages of* Varsity (Cambridge: Varsity Publications Ltd., 1995)

White, R.J., *Cambridge Life* (London: Eyre & Spottiswoode, 1960)

Ziegler, P., *Mountbatten: The Official Biography* (London: Collins, 1985)

INDEX